C000182215

ASK0039352

THE INVISIBLE MAN

THE INVISIBLE MAN

THE STORY OF
ROD TEMPERTON
THE 'THRILLER'
SONGWRITER

JED PITMAN

The
History
Press

First published 2017

The History Press
The Mill, Brimscombe Port
Stroud, Gloucestershire, GL5 2QG
www.thehistorypress.co.uk

© Jed Pitman, 2017

The right of Jed Pitman to be identified as the Author
of this work has been asserted in accordance with the
Copyright, Designs and Patents Act 1988.

All rights reserved. No part of this book may be reprinted
or reproduced or utilised in any form or by any electronic,
mechanical or other means, now known or hereafter invented,
including photocopying and recording, or in any information
storage or retrieval system, without the permission in writing
from the Publishers.

British Library Cataloguing in Publication Data.
A catalogue record for this book is available from the British Library.

ISBN 978 0 7509 8256 6

Typesetting and origination by The History Press
Printed and bound by TJ Intenational Ltd

CONTENTS

PROLOGUE

Growing up in the 1970s with two older brothers, Nick and Nigel, my family home was often filled with music, the sounds and beats emanating from each room of the house, songs by T-Rex, Sweet and other darlings of glam rock and then punk and heavy metal, The Sex Pistols, The Clash and Motörhead.

Then, in 1977, while travelling to Cornwall on holiday in a Hillman Imp driven by my mother, for the first time on the radio I heard a song called 'Boogie Nights' by a band named Heatwave. From the moment the sound hit my eardrums, I knew my life had altered. I had never taken in such a hook, such a groove, such melody and I was transfixed and then transformed.

On that holiday, I bought my first ever LP, *Too Hot to Handle*, the album including 'Boogie Nights'. Every song matched the one I had first listened to just a couple of weeks before and soon my brothers' choices at home were being drowned out by the songs of a man called Rod Temperton. I was 11 years old.

I knew nothing about the man, of course. On the back sleeve of the album cover was a photo of each member of the Heatwave band and I was confused as to how a man who looked more like an accountant could have penned such songs. He was the band's keyboard player too, and I immediately started to wish I had taken up music lessons at school.

The following year, I bought the follow-up Heatwave long player, *Central Heating*, and then in 1979, while all my friends at school were hooked into Blondie, The Cars and an emerging band called The Jam, I steadfastly stuck to what I liked, Heatwave. I would invite friends over and try to get them to understand what *I* understood – this was music like no other, complicated harmonies and arrangements, hooks that could catch a shark and choruses that would live in my head, keeping me awake at night.

I knew I had fallen for the groove and it was a love affair that lasts still.

Other songs grabbed my attention none more so than Funkadelic's 'One Nation Under a Groove' and then Michael Jackson's 'Don't Stop 'Til You Get Enough'. Again, on the strength of those singles, I saved up my pocket money, did a few bob-a-jobs and headed to the record store to purchase the LPs.

I remember to this day playing the opening track to the Jackson album *Off the Wall*. The long version of 'Don't Stop' had me, but up next was a song that almost blew my mind. As it played, I headed over to the record player and watched for a few minutes as the vinyl spun round on the turntable. Song two was titled 'Rock with You' and, to my ears, it had a hook that sounded like Heatwave. As the record spun, I could make out in brackets beneath the title of the song the songwriter's name – R. Temperton. Was this really the same man who had already grabbed me with the hits, 'Boogie Nights', 'Always and Forever', 'Too Hot to Handle' and 'The Groove Line'? How had that happened?

I took the record off the player to see if this Temperton had written any more tracks on the album. He had – the title track and, for me, the best cut on the LP, 'Burn this Disco Out'. They all had a similar kind of sound, a relentless rhythm that simply wouldn't let go. For weeks, I hardly played any other track from *Off the Wall*, just the three written by R. Temperton. I drove everyone around me quite mad and did some damage to the floorboards in my bedroom due to my appalling dancing.

By now, I had become an avid reader of the magazine *Blues & Soul* and in one edition there was an interview with this man, Temperton. I ignored the rest of what was within the pages and headed straight to the feature. I sat the rest of the day in shock. Yes, this man was the same who had written those extraordinary Heatwave hits and he had more on the way for a band called Rufus and Chaka Khan and the Brothers Johnson. But what stood out most of all was that he was from England, from Cleethorpes in Lincolnshire, not a million miles from where I was sitting.

By the end of the decade I had started to grow a decent music collection, every bit of money I had was spent in a black music store in

Nottingham. All the stuff I had and listened to on the radio was black music from America, yet here I was now reading that my real hero was white and from Cleethorpes. I would bore everybody at school with this newfound knowledge. Nobody cared, nor did anybody believe me when both 'Rock with You' and 'Off the Wall' became enormous hits for Michael Jackson. At school, people would sing those and I would tell one and all who had written them. The general refrain was 'bollocks' – impossible.

From there on, I bought albums based on writers and producers, rarely on artists. Anything to do with George Clinton, Bernard Edwards and Nile Rodgers or Rod Temperton would soon find their way onto my turntable.

Of course, by 1983 everybody at school, all their friends and all the members of their families, some of whom weren't even alive, had a copy of the Michael Jackson album *Thriller*, of which the subject of this book also penned the famous title track. Yet, as the years passed by there was rarely anything written about the man and what he had achieved and I just couldn't work out why. Did he really exist? Was it all a made-up story to hide the real identity of the man behind the hits that also included 'Stomp!' by the Brothers Johnson, 'Give Me the Night' by George Benson and 'Razzamatazz' by Quincy Jones?

By the late 1980s and moving into the early 1990s, Rod seemed to have disappeared completely, bar a couple of new tunes on Quincy's *Jook Joint* LP. I had moved onto other obsessions, until one day I entered the World Wide Web for the first time, on dial-up. After spending an age trying to work out what this thing was, I managed to find a search engine and the very first name I put into it was Rod Temperton. What had he been up to for all these years and, most of all, what songs that he had written had I missed out on?

Unbelievably, I could find nothing on him and it wasn't just because of my own technophobia. There was just nothing there at all. So, I formed a plan to find him and try to sell a documentary on him to the BBC. I can't have been the only person on the planet to have been so affected by his music over the years and so often I had argued with people that Jackson did not write 'Thriller' every time it came on the radio at Halloween, but that it had come from the pen of a man from Cleethorpes.

It took me several years to find Rod, but in 2005, thanks to Neil, a friend of mine who had just set up his own production company, I did.

Rod had hit the news online, a tiny article hidden in the music press with a story that he had just sold his back catalogue to London-based Chrysalis Records. Here was my chance. We arranged a meeting in a café in central London, in Pimlico. Apparently, Rod had a house somewhere nearby.

Neil and I arrived early, and then, after half an hour, I saw this figure walk in. It was the man I had seen on the back of that first Heatwave sleeve thirty years before. It was Rod Temperton. My heart rate went into overdrive. I spent the next four and half hours shifting nervously in my seat, sharing endless frothy coffees and Marlboro Red cigarettes (I had read that he was a chain-smoker, loving this particular brand, only to discover that he had recently given up the habit – until now, in any case).

He often looked uneasy, wary of my knowledge of him and my obsession with his work. 'You know more about me than I do,' he joked. We chatted through his whole career – 'I didn't write that many songs actually, but I was lucky and a lot of them were hits' – and then, seemingly under duress, he agreed on principle to let me make the documentary – 'I doubt very much that anyone will be interested, I'm really not that interesting', he told me, but I politely disagreed.

However, in the hours we had spent together, not one person in the café looked our way, not one person stopped and asked for an autograph. Yet, I thought, everyone supping their drinks and munching on their cakes would know a song written by this great man if it had suddenly been played in there. I'm glad no song was, because I could imagine an embarrassed Rod just getting up and leaving.

Neil and I said our goodbyes and headed to the pub, where for some time I stood silent in disbelief that I had met Rod Temperton, a man who, strangely, sounded a lot like the former Conservative leader, William Hague – well, at least to my ears.

I spent the next year working on what became *The Invisible Man – The Rod Temperton Story*. It won Neil and I a Sony Award, the proudest night of my life (I sat right behind another hero of mine, Mark Radcliffe). The documentary, made during the evenings after I had finished my day jobs as a TV producer and presenter in Bristol and a columnist for the *Daily Telegraph*, was a labour of love. In fact, there was no labour in it.

And then it was over and I moved onto other things, making other documentaries on the album *Thriller*, as well as one on Ian Dury and the Blockheads. Even while making these, the name Rod Temperton would crop up from time to time. Blockhead Chaz Jankel (who shared a song credit on a Quincy Jones album with 'Ai No Corrida') and I spent time in a Muswell Hill pub, drinking Guinness and talking about Rod's music as well as Chaz's own ability to come up with something quite brilliant.

I waited to hear some new songs from Rod, songs that rarely materialised. There was one, 'Family Reunion', performed by George Benson, and I had read online that Mica Paris was working with Rod at the start of this decade. The truth of the matter was, however, that he never really needed to work again, the one song 'Thriller' making him a small fortune every time 31 October arrived and the tune would be played on the radio and at parties all across the globe.

Then, on 5 October 2016, after arriving to start a new life in Mexico, my phone started to ring requesting interviews about Rod. His death had been announced. I appeared on radio stations in the UK, Ireland, the USA and Australia. His impact on the music industry was global.

You can still hear the BBC documentary on Rod on YouTube, but the one thing lacking was a book on the man and his music. I hope that this goes some way to filling that void and I would like to thank all the contributors who spent time with me, Neil Cowling and Mark Goodier, who also did some of the interviews from where many of the quotes in this book were sourced.

To complete this mission, I also needed some new interviews, from those who I had never had time to speak to during the making of the BBC documentary. I emailed many others who had worked with Rod Temperton over the years and each one came back to me quickly, enthused about this project and answering my requests for interviews with vigour, using phrases like, 'I would be honoured to be involved'.

Suddenly, I found myself on the phone speaking to the likes of Herbie Hancock (I was shaking while making the call), Bob James and Derek Bramble, former Heatwave player and producer of David Bowie's album, *Tonight*, released in the mid 1980s. In the email reply, Derek described Rod as a friend and a mentor and this is something that came across in everybody I spoke to. Rod Temperton not only provided the world with some of the best songs I have ever heard but did so by seemingly making friends with everybody he worked with. He gave the likes of Michael Jackson, George Benson, Patti Austin and the Brothers Johnson some of their biggest hits. Rod was a genius, a man who would write and arrange songs in his head, as you will discover. Yet, he remained incredibly humble and private, his death only being announced after his funeral.

This is the remarkable story of a man who changed the lives of so many and still will, every time one of his songs is played on the radio or in a shop or, in the case of AeroMexico, every time you land after a long-haul flight when, rather than the usual elevator music, passengers are treated to 'Rock with You'. The story is told largely through the words of Rod and the many talented musicians he worked with, all of whom loved their time spent with him.

I would like to thank everybody who agreed to take part, either directly for this project or for the previously broadcast BBC documentary. I hope you enjoy reading it as much as I did compiling it.

1

THE STAR OF A STORY

The future music business was to alter memorably after Les and Ida Temperton gave birth to a boy, named Rodney Lynn, on 9 October 1949. And the town that created this lad who was to become a musical genius, one who would write some of the world's most famous songs? Not Hollywood, not LA, not New York, not even London, but Cleethorpes on the Lincolnshire coastline.

It was not long before Rod was introduced to the thing that would make him his fortune, if not the fame that should have gone with it – privacy was something he sought for much of his life, in spite of his enormous success. As Rod himself remembered:

My father wasn't the kind of person who would read me a story before I went off to sleep so, even as a baby or when I was really young, one year old or something, he used to put a transistor radio into my crib, right on the pillow, and I would go to sleep listening to Radio Luxembourg. Remember that? 208 meters. And so I would listen all night long while I was sleeping to this, hearing tunes like 'Love and marriage goes together like a horse and carriage' by Doris Day and all this kind of stuff. And I think somehow that had an influence on me because my parents weren't really musical. I mean my father had a good musical ear and played a bit of accordion at Christmas. My mother was not musical at all. So I think that having music by my ears while I was sleeping played a big part of my getting to love music. Well, I can't think of anything else, anyway.

Rod's first school was Reynolds Street in Cleethorpes, and it was there he first began to show off his talents:

> When I was at junior school, we had a really good music teacher, a lady called Mary Boulders. She did a lot of choral things which I liked. So, she spoke to my parents about having singing lessons and I said that I wanted to do that. So, I worked with her for a while and she used to enter me into local singing competitions and I always came second, I don't know why.
>
> I really enjoyed that time. Mary was a really good teacher. I had started to play my first musical instrument, the drums. I used to skive off school occasionally and while dad was at work, I would get in the living room with my snare drum and my symbol, and play along to the test card on the TV. They put that up, with some girl, a doll and a chalk board because there were no TV programmes on until five o'clock. So I used to play along to the test card, which had all kinds of music which was played continuously.
>
> But then, when I was 11, I went to boarding school and I lost that side of it but still retained some of it. They used to want me to sing in the choir at boarding school. And we were very lucky to have a great music teacher there. You see, I never wanted to take lessons. I wanted to be out playing with the lads. So they didn't push me and neither did my parents, to do piano lessons or anything like that, but the piano teacher did used to give some additional lessons after school and then directly afterwards he would sit and take tea in one of the classrooms. And I used to always go and sit with him afterwards and just talk about music. He was desperate for me to take piano lessons but I said that I didn't want to do that.

The boarding school in question was De Aston in Market Rasen and the schoolteacher he talked about was Ted Gledhill, who remembers Rod well:

> It would have been in the early 1960s when I came across Rod for the very first time as a teenager. There would have been around 350 pupils at school in those days, all male. He was an average kind of boy but very keen on music. The school really excelled at sport particularly

athletics, rugby and cricket but we also had active drama and music clubs – chiefly classical. I think Rod came into prominence when, during the annual music competition we had, I introduced a pop section. This was unheard of at the time because pop music at a grammar school was not encouraged. Rod formed a group for the competition and he was the drummer in it. The band did very well and that seemed to give Rod an outlet for what had to be an innate talent.

He was a good drummer but we had no formal drumming lessons at the school but he also had elementary piano lessons from a visiting piano teacher.

Rod added:

Ted Gledhill was great because we only used to have one music lesson a week but he used to come in and sit and do things like play a record and then we would all have to talk about it which was really exciting for me. It wasn't just a question of 'Oh let's sing some hymns', or something. Instead, Ted used to come in with things like *West Side Story* and Dave Brubeck and stuff like that. And that made it a lot of fun. And you know, my interest in music just grew and grew. I started to form this band and that band but I never thought I was a good enough drummer to be in them.

Ted Gledhill:

I've heard that Rod has said that hearing *West Side Story* in one of my lessons had a major impact on him. It thrilled him to bits because he had never heard anything like that before. Little did we know at the time how it would influence him but it's a soundtrack that embodies melodies, rhythm and all sorts of harmonies, all things which Rod excelled at later on. I think, too, that the Beatles had a tremendous influence on Rod. They were the band that everybody talked about at school.

Life was moving along nicely for Rod in the early 1960s. Pop music was livening up, thanks to the Beatles, in his teenage years. The young man was happy at school. Ted Gledhill:

I think boarding life suited him. One of the great advantages of boarding school is that it teaches a bit of independence but also the need to work in a team. As the songwriter Rod became he mastered both of those things, writing songs alone but then working alongside stars like Quincy Jones and the engineers and musicians. I presume some of the early experiences he had at school helped him. It probably kept him the very modest man he became, too. He once sent me an LP of *E.T.* and on the cover you see there is a credit to Quincy Jones and to John Williams but you have to look in the small print inside where his name is relegated as a composer of a tune called 'Someone in the Dark' which was one of the tunes featured in the film. Rod also sent me a copy of Quincy's *Back on the Block* and once again it is Quincy who gets all the credit but you mustn't forget that Rod was the assistant producer, arranger and composer on that so you can see that a lot of his light has been hidden under a bushel. That's boarding school for you!

The one thing I do remember from those very early days was that he had a wonderful sense of harmony in addition to an innate sense of rhythm and I'm sure that helped him tremendously because things start from a base and you work upwards, something he was able to do by adding layer upon layer of melody and counterpoint. Believe me, none of what he did was easy.

As for Rod, he remembers the first time he ever attempted songwriting while at school:

> We were entered for a school music competition and there were six categories and one of them was original song. Well we won, purely for the fact that nobody else entered that category so there was three of us who wrote this song and … so that was kind of the beginning of writing I suppose.

By the time Rod left school in 1969, pop music had gathered a huge amount of momentum. Thanks to bands like the Beatles, the Rolling Stones, The Who, The Kinks and so on, many kids coming out of full-time education aspired to be in a group, trying to be the next big thing. Rod was no different from many others. Rod:

When I left school, I wanted to be in a local band and they had a drummer who was a friend of mine, who was really good. And they kind of said, 'Well, we want you to be in the band', and I said, 'Well, nobody can afford to have two drummers, so what am I going to do?'

And they said, 'Well, we've got an old Farfisa organ, why don't you play that?'

I said, 'Well, how do you play it? What do you do?' It was the instrument used by Richard Wright on Pink Floyd's early albums such as *The Piper at the Gates of Dawn* and *Ummugumma*.

I remember one guy turning around to me and saying, 'Well, three fingers make a chord'.

So I said, 'Oh okay'.

And while they would sit with the sheet music to 'Summertime' or whatever it was we were learning, I would listen to them and then just figure it all out. And it was the luckiest thing that ever happened to me because I think about eight months after that I was a professional playing an organ and arranging for a whole band. So, it was obviously meant to be.

The bands I started playing in in England were into progressive rock, bands like Yes and King Crimson, that kind of thing. It was all going OK with one of the bands I was in but I always felt a little lost if I'm honest. We would play only four songs in our session, each song lasting for about thirty minutes with fifteen key changes, time signatures, everything. Then the whole thing collapsed very quickly and I thought that was that.

Instead, Rod looked to be heading into the world of computers:

Yes, I had a proper job when I left school. Before then, during the summer holidays I had been a lifeguard at a holiday camp and I used to make great money doing that. I used to work all hours under the sun earning twenty-five pounds a week. When I started to work it was five pounds a week and I thought, 'Blimey, how am I going to make do off this?'

So, when I finished school, during the first summer holidays after leaving, I had to have an idea of what I was going to do but the problem was that I just didn't have a clue. I always remember my dad saying to me, 'Get a job in computers, that's the future'. He was a visionary it seems. So, we found a job in the paper for a company called Ross Group who did the frozen fish and everything. The job was in their head office for a trainee computer operator. So, I went to Grimsby and got the job. I worked there for a year in the office and then I got the chance to go professional as a musician. I just jumped at the opportunity. That's what I really wanted to do, to try it and see if I could do it.

It's funny how things stick to you in life. Years later, I remember when Michael Jackson toured England, and either the *Daily Mirror* or the *Sun*, I don't remember which one, wanted to do a story on him every day he was in the country. And so they called me in LA and asked me if I would do an interview. I said no, I don't really do interviews. So unbeknownst to me, they sent reporters up to my home town to find out whatever they could, and I think they found my aunty and she told them a few things and somebody sent me the story some weeks later after it had all been out and it was unbelievable. You know, bearing in mind what I said about working for Ross Group, they came up with what was a great headline. I opened the newspaper and there was a picture of me on one side and a picture of Michael Jackson on the other side and it said, 'Grimsby Fish Filleter Reels in Fortune for Wacko Jacko'. Brilliant. But sadly wrong – I never filleted fish.

2

TOO HOT TO HANDLE

At the start of the 1970s – perhaps the greatest decade in terms of popular music through prog rock, glam rock, punk and disco, to name just four life-altering genres – Rod Temperton was a young man who had shown some musical talent from an even younger age but appeared to be heading into the new world of computers instead, in the north of England. By the end of it, he had written a number of international hits, most notably for a man who was to become one of the biggest stars in the world, Michael Jackson.

Music was, of course, still running through him and he became part of several bands in Hull including one called Hammer. The whole area – Hull, Grimsby and Cleethorpes – was to remain very close to the heart of Rod. As Simon Blow, a friend of Rod's and former sports editor of the *Grimsby Telegraph*, says:

> The first time I met Rod was at a performance by Heatwave at The Dunes, a small venue in Mablethorpe. The band around that time also played live at the Nunsthorpe Tavern in Grimsby. Rod once turned up at the Fisherman's Pub in Sea View Street, Cleethorpes, to take in some live music.

Rod:

> Cleethorpes has always been quite in front in music. I remember going to my first pop festival at the Boating Lake when they had the

Animals and people like that, and that was before Woodstock. The Jazz Club in Grimsby always used to have groups before they were famous and I think Cleethorpes is always a groovy place compared to others.

A move to Germany in the early 1970s doesn't sound like the start of a great love affair with music but, as so often happens in life, Rod just happened to be in the right place at the right time. Rod:

I was broke, stony broke, and I thought to myself that I had to get a job somewhere so I answered any job advertisements that I could find in the *NME* or *Melody Maker*. When I got to Germany, I joined a dance band called Sundown Carousel with Bernd Springer – I was the only one of us who spoke any English – and he and I had to play six hours a night on stage and it was all simple pop music, even though most of the things I had never heard of in my life. I remember getting there at one o'clock in the afternoon and they said, 'Well you have to play tonight, you know … we just lost the organ player'.

So I said, 'Okay.'

So I remember just getting all this material and learning the first two or three notes, you know, how it started out and thinking to myself, well I'm just going to have to wing it because there's no way to learn that stuff in that amount of time, in a few hours. But because of the complexity of the music I had been playing before, the prog rock stuff with all the time signatures and so on, it was kind of quite easy, so I got along pretty good with it. I didn't much like the long shows we did – that was awful – but it was an experience and a good one at that. I did this for a couple of years purely to make some money and to be able to start to build a writing career because I already knew that that was what I wanted to do.

For most of us mere mortals doing such a thing would take bravery and a lot of skill but, typical of the man, Rod knew even back then that a career as a player was an unlikely one for him:

By the time I got to Germany, I'd kind of decided that I wasn't going to be a great musician, a great player. I was okay on the Hammond organ I suppose but you know, I always wanted to be great. I used to sit at home in my flat in Worms in Germany, a place about 40 miles outside of Frankfurt, and really try to learn these scales and you know, keep going like that. But, and it is really as simple as this, every time I used to sit down I was so bored doing scales that by the time I'd finished an octave my fingers had run off into some melody. And I basically remember to the day when I just got up one morning and I sat there and I was messing about on the keyboard and I said to myself, 'You ain't ever going to be a musician player. You can forget this.' But obviously I had some leaning towards writing melody. And I don't actually think I ever looked back from that point because then it became the main goal, to create music rather than play it. And even to the point of time I joined Heatwave I basically told them, I said, 'I'm happy to do this and you know, I'd love to write for the band, but if we make it I'm going to pack up playing because all I want to do is write.' It was that clear in my mind.

I think it was very lucky, very lucky. I mean, I think people spend their whole lives trying to find out who they are and what they want to do with their lives and I guess I was about 21 or something and it just dawned on me that that was the way to go. And I never looked back. Of course, I still needed to find a band to write songs for. And doing that was very fortunate, too.

Heatwave were an emerging covers band in the early 1970s, fronted by the enigmatic Johnnie Wilder Jnr:

We were a band that was attempting various styles of music, being that we were working in Europe and all. But mostly we played a variety of US American soul music as it was called back then – R&B stuff it would be called today – a lot of dance material. You know, up-tempo and mellow type songs. We were really an all-round entertaining group. We put an ad in a music paper called *Melody Maker*, trying to find a keyboard player. A man called Rod Temperton was one of those who answered the ad, simple as that really.

Rod Temperton:

It was just one of those things. I was looking for a band as the one I was with was driving me crazy and they were looking for a keyboard player. The funny thing was that I was living in a flat in a town called Worms and this band just happened to be in Mannheim just half an hour or so away from me. I had no idea. I sent my application to a box number and I had no idea where it was. I sent the letter — it went to London — and they sent it back to Germany where the guys were. There was no clue in the advert in the *Melody Maker* or anything like that. It just said, 'Soul Band Needs Keyboard Player'. The next thing that happened was that I had a visit from the main man of the band, Johnnie Wilder.

Johnnie Wilder:

Rod was the first British guy that I had ever met personally. He spoke kind of funny but he had a good sense of humour and he was a very friendly guy. He was working with a German band at the time and after I learned more about him upon meeting him, he told me that he had worked with a rock band in England and different types of groups. He had an impressive enough resume and so we hired him.

I was just looking for a keyboard player but Rod had other advantages, too. One, he spoke English, that helped, and then after meeting him and seeing him play I kind of determined he was good enough, a good enough player and an entertainer. And I just knew he would fit into the group.

Rod:

At the time I joined Heatwave they were a covers band. They used to play Stevie Wonder, Earth, Wind & Fire, early stuff by Parliament/ Funkadelic, James Brown, stuff like that. I think the reason they took me on was because, for, well, two reasons. One that I wanted to be a writer and two, I had a few contacts in England. They wanted a chance to get out of Germany. So, I joined them. I didn't know anything about black music or writing black music at the time I joined them. And they played me all the things that were hot in America at the time, the very early sounds of Kool and the Gang and Ohio Players and stuff like that. And I used to just sit and listen to all this stuff and try to analyse it a bit and I used to love the way they put the rhythm sections together, I mean, it was just amazing. I just didn't know anything about R&B or soul music so I just had to turn my hand to it quite quickly. And so I kind of figured out how to do that and then attempted to write something for the band in that musical style. I think 'Super Soul Sister' was actually the first song I wrote for them that we tried on stage and that was okay. But then 'Ain't No Half Steppin'' really worked as a stage performance. People used to love it in the clubs. And then I wrote a ballad called 'Always and Forever'. And 'Always and Forever' we got to play on the stage for maybe a year and a half before we ever made a demo for a record. By that time, you know, it had become a big song in our repertoire so, you know, things had started to work out.

Johnnie:

After getting to know him much better I would hear and become very interested in the original songs he had on these small little reel-to-reel tapes he had in his apartment. He had this nice big one-bedroom apartment and his tape machine and keyboard. That's what I remember about the room. And he would play the tapes of his original songs and I was very interested because we weren't doing a lot of originals then. We were doing a lot of covers, and when he played the originals I was really interested.

To me, one of those first songs I remember hearing was 'Always and Forever'. It was kind of a rock tune, a ballad rock tune. That was one of the first ones, because I was a bit of a balladeer and I liked the slow material that he had. Some of the early songs we tried playing we eventually made a demo of. I don't remember the names of the other songs that he had but I do recall that he had jazz pieces, rock pieces; he had a variety of songs. There was definitely something there, something very good indeed that made me prick up my ears.

Alan Kirk was a member of a band called Jimmy James and the Vagabonds. He first met Rod in 1974 on a Soul Extravaganza tour:

Heatwave were third on the bill and we were on second. They used to blow everybody off every single night, they were so good. Some of the rhythms they used were fantastic. Everybody just fell off their seats trying to emulate them. Rod was a very down-to-earth guy and a brilliant songwriter. He was unusual. He reminded me of Doctor Who, the Tom Baker one, with his long trench coat, scarf and everything. I remember he had odd eating habits. I ordered a meal on the Isle of Man ferry and Rod couldn't afford one. I couldn't eat and so Rod took the cabbage and the ice cream I had. He mixed it all together and ate it together. I remember, too, him having to carry all of the gear for the band down the gangplank, his old organ which he called Betsy. It was all worn away and, on stage, he would have it propped up with beermats. He later had Betsy stolen. We played on that tour in pavilions, working men's clubs, nightclubs, anywhere that paid a buck.

On stage, Rod always just had his head down over the keyboards, hoping that his organ didn't fall over because of all the beermats underneath, holding it up. He had his head down and just got into it, into his rhythms. He was a very rhythmical keyboard player, not so much a soloist but a guy who could play really hot rhythms. And the rest of the band just got on with it, falling in behind him. I don't think Rod was ever that comfortable on stage. He was just a normal guy.

Andrew Platts, also a member of the Vagabonds:

Rod always seemed to be absolutely skint, so much so that he couldn't afford the ferry from the Isle of Man back to the mainland. We had a mini bus, like a crew bus for our band, and we actually had to put Rod on the floor once and cover him in his big, grey coat, hide him and smuggle him back to the mainland so he could get home. He just didn't have the price of a ticket at that time.

Alan Kirk:

His songs had a very progressive rock feel initially. He was in rock bands to start with, like Hammer, which played in clubs all around

Hull, and then he sorted out this methodical approach to the usual standard soul things they were turning out at that time. A worked-out bass line, rhythmic bass line, catchy bass line, always a catchy title, and then build your track up from the bass line. That was his way of working, a good formula. It certainly worked well for him. He was very methodical, sitting there with a tracksuit on, stopwatch around his neck. No longer than twenty seconds for the intro, straight into the verse. If it gets a little bit boring then straight into the chorus, bridge and things.

Johnnie:

> With these songs in our repertoire what we needed next was to get signed to a label to try to put them out. They worked really well for us as a live band but we now needed a bigger outlet for them. After Rod joined the band we worked a lot in the European market like Germany and Italy, all the European countries on that side of the water and Rod was then very instrumental in introducing us to a British agent and a manager who we eventually got. We started working in England more after we got a manager there. We chopped the tunes that Rod had written on our first demo. There were quite a few rejections from what we considered major labels at the time. And then we ran into Dick Leahy at GTO.

Born in London in 1937, Dick Leahy first came to prominence in the music business in the late 1960s as A&R manager of Phillips Records who included Dusty Springfield on their roster. Dick then worked as managing director of Bell Records and they produced a string of UK hit singles from the likes of David Cassidy, Gary Glitter, Showaddywaddy and Barry Blue, the latter soon to be another vital cog in the Rod Temperton machine. During the latter part of the 1970s, Dick moved to GTO Records.
Rod remembers:

> The three demos we cut for Dick were 'Super Soul Sister', 'Always and Forever' and a song called 'Strictly Private Property' that was a real pop song and everybody hated it. Dick was amazing and must have realised that there was some talent in the band so he snapped

us up and off we went. GTO was a great little independent label to be with and they served us really well. I guess hooking up with Dick was the first moment that everything started to move in the right direction.

Johnnie:

We were performing one night and Dick would come out and see us and after a few visits from his whole crew at his office we started to talk some more. It became a marriage. We made the demo up in Hull. We used to live in Hull when we moved to England and we did the demo in one of his friend's studios. We then shopped the demos around when we went down to London. And we went to publishers and record companies down there. Dick had the most entrance. I mean, he would come out to see us play. Then on, when we came to London and play again, we were surprised by most of his staff, his office staff, coming down to hear us and then, after the third time, it was on, it was he and our manager having conversations from then on.

Alan Kirk:

I recall Heatwave doing some original demos at Fairview Studios in Hull. We were fascinated because we knew they were going to be a success, so a lot of my band went to the studio to watch them put the demos together. We knew that we were watching a hit band being discovered for real.

So, the deal was signed but it was hardly all plain sailing from that point. Heatwave, as well as performing night after night, now had a record to produce and time was against them. Rod:

Before we did original material Heatwave was a very popular band in the clubs and so we would play seven nights a week, all the time. We never had any nights off and we'd be on stage three or four hours a night, all over Europe. It was just a great experience to get your chops up. Young kids these days don't have the opportunity we had.

It's so hard for singers today. You know, the first time that anybody hears them it's on some demo. They don't get mic technique, they don't understand how to work the audience and so it's very difficult for them. It's a shame that the discothèques took over from the live music, you know.

It was very different for us. We used to play all the time and then I would write after the gigs were finished. There was a club in Zurich in Switzerland called the Blackout, right by the airport and we would have a residency there three or four times a year, playing there for two weeks at a time. We knew the manager very well. We would finish our set at two o'clock in the morning and at that time everybody would leave and they would lock me in the club. There was a little room downstairs with an upright piano and I'd write there until the cleaner came to unlock the door and let me out at seven in the morning, often just as the sun was rising. I'd go over to the airport to have a bit of breakfast, go and get some sleep in the hotel and be back at two in the afternoon for rehearsal. We rehearsed every day when we were in places like that and we'd do that from two until about six, go and eat and then come back and play the gig. I did ridiculous hours but, boy, as it turned out, it was it worth it.

3

BOOGIE NIGHTS

Heatwave was a band begun by Johnnie Wilder Jnr while he was based as an American serviceman in West Germany, a country he remained in after his release from duty. The band was an unusual one in that its members were made up of musicians from many different walks of life. Johnnie was from Dayton, Ohio, a state that also produced the Ohio Players, Bootsy Collins and Roger Troutman, amongst many others. His remarkable vocal range allowed Rod the opportunity to try all sorts of different sounds in his writing. Johnnie also called upon his brother, Keith, to share lead vocals with him. The rest of the group sounded as if they belonged to the United Nations: on bass was Mario Mantese from Spain, Czechoslovak Ernest 'Bilbo' Berger was the drummer, while the guitars were provided by Jamaican Eric Johns and Brit Roy Carter. Rod, as we know, provided the keyboards.

Rod:

Initially, it was difficult being in a black R&B band given the kind of character I was. Heatwave was all a big dancing thing and so I used to sit there kind of timidly at the back on the keyboards. It wasn't that I was nervous, just that dancing about wasn't really my thing. But, as time went on, it felt more natural so I went on.

Simon Blow, writing in the *Grimsby Telegraph*:

After joining him to watch a razzy show at the Sands Theatre in Skegness, in which he even ventured from behind the keyboards to dance the bump on stage with a female fan, we went back to Church Avenue for a late night chat and cuppa. Next morning, back in Humberston, we had a long talk about the past and the future, interrupted only when his mum, Ida, arrived to cut his hair before Rod rushed off for a Heatwave gig that night.

Hardly the stuff of legendary rock and roll, of throwing TVs out of hotel windows after destroying the mini-bar, but this was simply the way Rod was made. As you read on, you will discover that, even given his enormous success, he never really changed as a person. This story was typical. Rod:

At the start of Heatwave, we didn't have much money, that was for sure, and so everything went back into the band. And I always remember the first time we actually got some money from the record company to buy some new equipment. We got some and a new van. And we parked it outside the hotel and the next morning it had gone. I couldn't believe it. But the interesting thing is that I used to play a really old Hammond organ, called Betsy. It was falling to pieces and the London Police two days later said, 'Well, we found this organ sitting in the middle of the road'. So the thieves had pinched all this new gear and pushed the organ out of the back of the van saying, 'Well we don't want that', and gone off with all the new stuff.

But, at this point in his life, Rod's confidence was starting to grow thanks to his songwriting skills, something that was starting to impress a lot of people. Rod:

I am very one-track minded in that respect. You know, when I start work on a song everything gets locked out. They could be dropping bombs in the garden and I wouldn't even know because I tend to lock myself away, not hearing the phone or anything as it takes me a while to lower into the next phase of writing. The first week on a song, I just paced around the house or hotel room looking at the walls saying, 'How the hell do I do this?' I was searching for inspiration.

Once Heatwave started to record their first album in 1976 things suddenly began to really take off. GTO brought in Barry Blue to produce it.

Barry had had a number of hit singles in the UK including 'Dancin' (On a Saturday Night)', 'Do You Wanna Dance?', 'School Love', 'Miss Hit and Run' and 'Hot Shot'. He also wrote 'Sugar Me' for Lynsey de Paul and 'Kiss Me Kiss Your Baby' for Brotherhood of Man.

Barry Blue:

I'd heard about this band, Heatwave. They were playing in a small club in Victoria in London, which was no bigger than a postage stamp, it was absolutely minute, but it had hundreds of people trying to get in. And this band came on and they just ripped the place up. What first attracted me to the band though, was that the songs were so strong – they were just so unique, absolutely unique in the way they were structured. They didn't seem to be structured like any other kind of R&B or funk songs I'd ever heard at that time. They seemed to have different inner melodies than you would expect, different kinds of parts, all the parts were skilfully worked out, all the harmonies were worked out. It was really quite dynamic, it was really different.

Johnnie Wilder, who was the frontman of Heatwave, and his brother Keith were fabulous front people and so I naturally assumed that they were the songwriters, it was just a natural thing to assume. Rod was always in the background; he was always kind of the musical force, obviously the musical force behind Heatwave and so many acts after that. I had no idea he was the writer of the songs I was hearing when I saw them that first time. He was very self-effacing, you know, and it was only after two or three meetings talking about the songs and maybe cutting an album together with them that I actually found out it was the keyboard player, Rod Temperton, that wrote them.

I'd just come out of finishing five or six hits for myself and I was going into production. I was working for CBS Records at the time as a staff producer, so I had a number of acts that I was working on. And my first love was always funk music, always R&B or soul, I had every Stacks record, every Atlantic record. But I could never find an act over here in England that I really wanted to work with … until Heatwave, that is.

I was very friendly with a great record man called Dick Leahy, and he first said to me there was one act that kept cropping up, people saying they were really good and that I should check them out. So, that's what I did and they were just dynamite. I knew straight away that this band was going to rip it up; they were going to be huge. They were on a level with Earth, Wind & Fire with songs that could stand the test of time. So, we just did a really small deal, you know, to try out a few tracks to see how it would work on a small label called GTO, which eventually got sold to CBS. Then we did the album that became *Too Hot to Handle*.

Johnnie Wilder:

Rod was very rhythmical and his thing was chopping that piano, being very rhythmical and now, he just had a good feel for R&B music. I guess I learned later on, that he had listened to quite a little bit of music plus he had been playing for a number of years. I wasn't surprised that he could, you know, rock with the best of them.

I had a bit of experience with recording, but not with my own band and writers like Rod, but going there with original songs, you know, you didn't think about how huge it could be. The thing was just to get a record deal firstly, then going in the studio recording the band, the actual band.

Keith Wilder, co-lead singer of Heatwave, talking to BBC Radio 5 Live on the day Rod's death was announced:

Rod was a quiet person, spending a lot of time by himself except when he was with all of us on the road or staying in a hotel. He spent most of his time writing. He would come up with a melody and lyrics to a song and Johnnie and myself would come up with the melody of how we wanted to sing the song.

Barry Blue:

In the studio Rod was very intense. Lots of fun, but very intense. He knew exactly what he wanted and wouldn't take second best. He was a deep guy, just totally possessing the will to find exactly what he wanted, and he knew what he wanted, he knew how that record should come out and it was my job as the producer to make sure he got what he wanted. It was my job to get the band sounding how the band should sound and an integral part of the Heatwave sound was Rod Temperton's writing.

John Cameron began his career in music at Cambridge University where he was vice president of the Footlights. He was soon writing arrangements for Donovan and had a US No. 1 with 'Sunshine Superman'. John had two hits as a songwriter in the late 1960s with 'If I Ever Thought You'd Change Your Mind' for Cilla Black and 'Sweet Inspiration', a Top 10 record for Johnny Johnson and the Bandwagon. He then composed the score for the Ken Loach film, *Kes*, and for *A Touch of Class*, for which he was nominated for an Oscar. His jazz-funk band, CCS, had four UK hits including 'Whole Lotta Love', which was turned into the iconic theme music for *Top of the Pops*. He also worked as an arranger for Hot Chocolate including on the hits, 'You Sexy Thing' and 'Every One's a Winner'.

At the end of the 1970s, John was approached by Alain Boublil and Claude Michel Schonberg to arrange and conduct a concept album based on Victor Hugo's *Les Misérables*. It was later produced as a musical by Cameron Mackintosh, becoming one of the most popular musicals of all time. Every version of the show for almost thirty years had the mark of John's orchestral score. John also scored many TV shows and films. He is clearly a man who knows his stuff and Barry Blue brought him into the studio with Heatwave to work with the band on their *Too Hot to Handle* debut LP.

John Cameron:

I first met Rod in the recording studio with the rest of the band, Johnnie, Barry, the lot of them. It was simply one of those, 'Can you pitch up and talk about something?' I had no idea what was going on although Barry had given me a bit of a heads up. So, I walked into the studio and they were halfway through making their first album. They had the tracks down and most of the guide vocals and Rod sat me down and we would start playing the stuff.

Their amazing rhythm section immediately took me aback. There was a great feel going on and straight away I knew that I was glad to be a part of it. Then we started to talk about brass and strings, some really off-the-wall things like wanting 'Boogie Nights' to start with a harp for the first minute and a half. It was great. This was pretty much still pre-synthesiser times and so you had to try and make things work with traditional instruments such as two basses and a harpsichord or how about we use an oboe, bassoon and a harp. You had to kind of think outside of the box and so when Rod started to talk about the harp intro to 'Boogie Nights' and the different ideas he had for the brass and string writing I was immediately with him because he had such smart ideas.

Often I would meet with people and it would be a bit of a sticky meeting because I might not think the tracks were that good but I had children to feed and that so I would just go along with it but with Rod and Johnnie Wilder there was never a question, it was just, 'Yes, I like it, what do you want me to do?' And the great thing about Rod was that he knew exactly what he wanted so we could easily talk about the best way to achieve it, what kind of musicians to bring in and so on. I had a really nice string section at the time that had been on all the Hot Chocolate stuff and then went on to work with me on all my movie scores. In fact, the leader of the seconds went on to be the leader of the *Les Mis* orchestra for twenty years or more. It was quite a good team I had! Then, we had amazing brass players like Tony Fisher and Greg Bowen, Derek Watkins and Ron Ross. I kind of had a house band which was nice.

Taking all these guys into the studio to work with Heatwave was just a huge buzz. Rod knew exactly what he wanted, it was all mapped out. He would say, 'Here I would like some brass, and these are the kinds of lines I want for the strings', and he had obviously imagined the whole thing clearly in his head, knowing exactly what the final song would sound like.

I think this is why I enjoyed working with Rod so much because he had a kind of cinematic way of thinking about things. When I wrote a piece of movie music, I would actually write it with all the intersecting lines in my brain before I started and Rod was the same. There was a kindred spirit there.

What didn't compute with me was the way Rod looked and the way he talked. He was producing these incredible songs, with an amazing R&B rhythm and while the fact that he was white didn't surprise me – as I knew a lot of white guys who were very funky – it was his accent that shocked me. He had this Cleethorpes accent that didn't fit in with the stuff he was writing at all.

The album *Too Hot to Handle* was finally completed at the end of 1976 and GTO released the first single 'Super Soul Sister'. It was a flop as was the follow-up, 'Ain't No Half Steppin'' which surprised the writer. Rod Temperton:

'Ain't No Half Steppin'' was our biggest song on stage. It would always bring the house down along with 'Always and Forever'. But the first hardly got noticed on release. That, as I soon discovered, was just how the record industry works. I thought 'Ain't No Half Steppin'' was a strong song that might get us noticed by the buying public but hardly anyone got to hear it all.

Barry Blue:

Our first single, released in England was 'Super Soul Sister' and it kind of died, but it was good in the clubs. The groups loved it at the places where we performed. I mean, it was a good dance tune. The second single was 'Ain't No Half Steppin'' and it got moderate airplay even though it was a very commercial sounding tune. Dick Leahy and the crew there at GTO – you would never meet a harder working bunch of people to promote a record than those guys – continued to press on and I think the fact that the band were so good live really helped us a lot. Even though we weren't selling any records, we had a good following in the clubs. People wanted to come and see this band and Heatwave were talked about a lot. Anyone who saw them left knowing that they had seen something special.

Then in early 1977, GTO released 'Boogie Nights' as the third single and it really took off. We didn't have a clue what it would do but it just took off on its own. The fan base from the live performances had continued to grow and they were building up such a big following. When we put 'Boogie Nights' out with a harp at the front, it just blew everyone away, it was so unique. It was so different.

Rod:

> There weren't many English R&B bands that actually broke out of
> England. Heatwave was a hit in England first. 'Boogie Nights' came
> out in 1977, March time, but it wasn't a hit in the US until October
> or November. So it actually all came out of England. I mean the
> guys in the band, we all lived in Germany at the time because some
> of the band were originally in the US military and so, that's where
> we all met over in Germany. But we got the record deal in England
> and then our first hit. It came out and it was straight to the top of
> the charts.

Blow everyone away 'Boogie Nights' certainly did. It reached the top of
the charts in New Zealand, and No. 2 in both the UK and US Billboard
charts. It was a smash, selling more than 2 million copies in the US alone.
The song itself, before the incredible groove kicks in, starts with a harp
and a drum solo. Rod recalls why:

> I believe in happy accidents. I think a lot of things that you are creat-
> ing are for your own style of how you work, it's not thought about
> consciously at the time. It's just the way it goes down with the rules
> you have to play by. I mean when I wrote songs for Heatwave, quite
> often I had to look at the musicians in the band and see what their
> strengths were and what they liked to do, and that was the politics
> within a band of getting people to play your music. So you know,
> the drummer loved jazz, swing jazz and so the beginning of 'Boogie
> Nights' starts with this swing thing which I wrote particularly in
> there for him, to get him interested. Because often people say to me,
> 'Why is that beginning like that?' And I say, 'Well, you know, it was
> the drummer. Once he got to play his bit he was happy.' That is how
> styles are created.
>   When we did the first album, I wrote a lot of things that really
> needed to have horns in there, but we didn't have horns in the band
> so I thought, 'Well, we are making a record so there are no reasons
> why we can't use horns'. But others in the band wouldn't do it.
> They wouldn't agree to have any horn parts in the songs. So I had
> to quickly rewrite things for vocal arrangements and the rhythm

arrangements and that's why Heatwave became this band with a big vocal sound. That's how it all developed. It was just a happy accident although we brought in John Cameron and added horns as well.

Johnnie Wilder:

Rod was the kind of writer who had the ideas in his head before he would even bring me in to start working the vocals and he would have me try different ideas on the same melody or off the same melody and I guess you would say he wrote to my voice, because I was the only voice doing the songs.

Rod did all the vocal arrangements of his songs on those first albums and the rhythm arrangements, too. What I liked most about Rod when he first became part of Heatwave was that he was very instrumental in helping the group learn their parts of cover songs and then of course, when we did his songs, he would teach the different instrumentalists their parts and the same thing with the vocals. He had his basic melody and we worked around the basic melody that he gave us. Rod was good about letting the group members and myself improvise a little bit, not too much away from his melodies, because if you didn't feel the songs the way that he wrote them, it didn't come off good to him and thus, if they weren't done the way he felt it, then he wouldn't be happy with the results. We soon realised that Rod knew exactly what he wanted his songs to sound like.

Barry Blue:

Why has 'Boogie Nights' stood the test of time? Is it the songwriting? Is it the production? I'd like to think it was the production but I have to say that it is a combination of production and songwriting prowess. Rod's music has stood the test of time and he went on to write absolute classics, as we know. He's an unsung hero of mine; I just think he is so underrated. He's unknown really to the major population. 'Boogie Nights' was a unique piece of work, I mean unique in the way that the time structures change from verse to chorus, to outro/intro, putting a harp on the front that was unheard of. In fact, Epic Records, the company that released the album in the States, told us that we would have to take that goddamn harp off. What did they know, eh? Rod and I had an affinity because we loved unusual instruments on pop records. I still do. On my first record I had a bouzouki and I've had really odd instruments floating around the studio for years. I don't know whose idea the harp was – probably Rod's – but you know, that's the affinity I had with him as a producer, that we saw these little things that would prick your ears up and say, 'What the hell is that sound?'.

John Cameron:

When 'Boogie Nights' was put out in the States all the radio stations cut the harp off the front and, you know, it sold to twenty-seven people. When they put the harp back on the front it flew to the top of the charts. That just showed that Rod knew more than everybody else. He knew it would work. No one else could see that but, somehow, he did. It was remarkable. I used Sheila Bromberg to play it. There's a fact that not many people might know that Heatwave used the same harp player as the Beatles for their song 'She's Leaving Home' from *Sgt Pepper*.

The band had laid the track with them doing that kind of jazz thing – 'Boogie Nights, whoa-whoa-whoa' – with the drummer playing ten to ten on the ride cymbal, and Rod said, 'I want harp playing all the way through this'. I went, 'Erm, OK', and we did it. That's the way it was. If Rod said, 'Let's try this, let's do that', you didn't question it. It was only afterwards that people started getting theoretical about it. What that harp introduction did – and this is where Rod was just so, so clever, was act as a sucker punch. It kind of drew you in and then drew you in some more and then suddenly went WHALLOP with that downbeat on the words 'Boogie Nights'. Somehow, without that harp, it was just like, 'Oh, there's a nice funky rhythm section', but with the harp, you knew what was coming but you had to wait that bit longer and then. WHALLOP. It was great and a great bit of programming on Rod's part.

I knew the song was very special. Nobody had any idea that it would become the hit and the song it became, still being played everywhere even today in 2016. I wish I had money to bet when

Cameron Mackintosh asked me what I thought of *Les Mis* and I said, 'I think it will be one of the most successful musicals since *West Side Story*', but I didn't. When I recorded 'Sunshine Superman' with Donovan, I knew that was going to be a hit and I remember thinking that, if there was any justice in the world, then 'Boogie Nights' would be a hit, too. It was just that struggle with the harp intro!

Barry Blue:

I think these songs on the first album definitely were written over a period of ten years. This is how Rod used to write. He writes like no other person I have ever met and as much as he can he will spend three months, four months, five months, up to a year on one song. He would certainly have had ideas that would have been shifted around to fit the R&B sound of the band but those same ideas would have been hanging around within him for a while. So, you've got, you know, nine songs on that first album, which were probably written over a ten-year period, which is why they are so tight and so strong and have lasted so long. Rod knew exactly what he was doing. My personal favourite on *Too Hot to Handle* has to be 'Always and Forever' because I think that is a classic ballad, a classic love ballad.

Andrew Platts was a member of Jimmy James and the Vagabonds and remembers doing a gig with Heatwave at the Palace Lido in the Isle of Man, just as 'Boogie Nights' was rising up the charts:

Rod again was absolutely skint. He was pot less, even though 'Boogie Nights' had just charted. When he did get his first royalty cheque, rather than go out and buy the big car or whatever it was that he wanted, his mum apparently had some problem with her hip. And Rod spent his first royalty cheque on putting her into hospital and getting her sorted out and having her hip replaced. I think that says a lot about what kind of guy he was. He was a really sort of down-to-earth nice bloke. You wouldn't necessarily notice him. If the band was in the bar after a gig you might not even know he was in the band because he did not make a lot of noise about what he was doing. He would just sit there and get on with it.

Yet America nearly missed out on what was to become a classic, as Rod recalls:

'Boogie Nights' was just something I wrote for the band that worked yet funnily enough, on stage that was never the great number, I mean 'Ain't No Half Steppin'' and 'Always and Forever' were much bigger on stage than 'Boogie Nights', but this was something I quickly learned – that a song which comes across great on stage in front of people isn't necessarily the one that comes across the best on record. 'Boogie Nights' was a great record and, you know, it took us to where we needed to go, it was a vehicle for us, particularly in America. Obviously the band wanted to make it in the States so that was important to the guys in the band. But initially we were very lucky. I think that the head of Epic at the time actually really believed in the record, and I think, if I remember right, 'Boogie Nights' was released twice in America. It was released in May and it didn't get anywhere, but the head of the record company, which was very unusual, especially today, said, 'This is a hit', and he released it again in October. It went straight to the top. It was amazing really.

Of course, I am very thankful to radio all over the world for playing the music I wrote, but as I say, it's sometimes very difficult to think in that kind of commercial mode. To be honest with you, just to write a song is the major achievement of the day. When I start to work on something I have no idea where it's going to come out of and the big thrill to me is actually finishing something and saying, 'Wow, that sounds pretty good', because you know if we all knew how to do it, to write a hit song, we would all be billionaires, we'd be doing it every week, wouldn't we? I mean I haven't got a clue what makes one song a hit and another a flop and I normally get it wrong. I just go there and I concentrate and I think about it until something flows through the fingers, and I think the trick is knowing when you've got something because, you know, I sit and play and play for days sometimes and nothing happens. I just get frustrated but then suddenly, I hit some change or some melodic sequence and that sends a shiver up me and, you know, that's it and then I am back on track. But how you get to that point, it is very difficult to analyse.

I'm sure if people watched me work – because I always work alone at the house or in a hotel room somewhere – but if people actually watched me, they would think that I was a raving lunatic. They would sit there and say, 'Well, he's been sitting there for six hours, just humming and running his fingers about. What is this guy doing?' But, as I say, I don't know what I'm doing either but eventually it just happens. You know, something comes. It's clearly a gift I suppose. All I know is that I am a very lucky man. I don't know where the gift came from. I would like to think it was God-given and it's spiritual, but I don't know.

After the success of 'Boogie Nights' across the Atlantic, 'Always and Forever' was chosen as the follow-up single in the USA. In the UK, *Too Hot to Handle* and 'The Groove Line' from Heatwave's second LP, *Central Heating*, were released before 'Always and Forever' was put out as a double A-side with the Johnnie Wilder-penned 'Mind Blowing Decisions', also from *Central Heating*. It became the band's second Top 10 smash in the UK when it spent two weeks at No. 9 in December of 1978. In America, it peaked at No. 18 and was certified platinum by the RIAA (Recording Industry Association of America).

In the late 1970s and right through the 1980s, 'Always and Forever' became a popular slow dance song at high school proms, particularly in inner city areas. It is still today a song that is widely used at weddings in the USA and is a staple of R&B or slow mood radio stations. Yet, the history of the writing of the song shows it had a very different beginning. Rod:

It was purely an attempt to write a romantic ballad for the singer. I mean the singer, Johnnie, was really good and I knew what he liked to sing. So I thought I should try to write a ballad that would work for the band and for him in particular. He told me that he really wanted to sing a strong ballad, a big ballad. There is no kind of hidden meaning behind it all really. I'm sure lots of people want to think that but it was just a pretty song. And the other, the funny thing about it was, back when I was working in England in bands before, I used to write all the music and somebody else in the band would write the words. Because it never interested me to write the words.

So when I went to live in Germany, here I am first of all faced with a band who spoke not a word of English so if I was going to carry on writing, I had to write my own lyrics. And I absolutely hated it and always did. 'Always and Forever' was the first lyric I wrote that got recorded for Heatwave. And, you know, I remember sitting having no confidence about my lyrics, certainly not the confidence I have with the melodies or the rhythm section and so I tended to try to hide the words in the melody. So I think about words that absolutely sit perfectly on the phrase that I'm doing musically so I won't hear the words anymore, so they are lost in the melody. I kind of hoped that the words always seemed that they should have been there and that's what I was always searching to find. And I always had this thing where you know, I write the music, I write the melody, I do all the arrangements and it's not until the last second, you know basically until I know we're going to cut it tomorrow, that I'll say, 'I guess I've got to come up with a lyric'. So, then I'll have a go at it.

Barry Blue:

I used to go out and see Rod writing in a place called Worms in Germany and he had a small, a very small, flat and there was no room for his organ which I think was called Betsy, if I remember rightly. So, everything had to be done within the one room, and he had piles of washing and he had the TV on top of the organ. I just don't know how he actually ever got to write anything because it was a nightmare. He had trams running outside but he made it. He just absorbed himself in the music and came up with these amazing songs. I think Rod Temperton is one of the all-time great writers.

I'll tell you the thing that is unique to Rod, is that he writes from the bass line upwards, his bass lines are melodies, his bass lines are as strong as his chords, and then the feel that he puts around the bass with the drums and loops etc., it's all kind of a jigsaw which all seems to fit, but every part is written, there's nothing that's kind of, 'OK, we'll get a guitar player to work this out'. Everything that I've seen Rod work on has been completely written from start to finish and not improvised at all.

Alan Kirk of fellow seventies band Jimmy James and the Vagabonds, said, 'The "Always and Forever" track was written on a Wurlitzer piano at the side of a pile of smelly washing, early one morning. I'm sorry to disappoint all the romantics!'

Andrew Platts:

I loved 'Always and Forever'. It was around when I met my wife and we used to smooch to it even though I knew it was written in his scruffy old flat next to a pile of dirty washing. It was such an unglamorous circumstance to write such a glamorous tune. But, boy, could Rod write some harmonies. I loved Heatwave's harmonies. They could always sing them live. Not long after that, I lost contact with him but I do remember that we had a heated debate about bass players being made redundant because of the synthesiser. Rod was very passionate about his music.

Keith Wilder told BBC 5 Live, '"Always and Forever" was a great love song, a ballad. Rod had originally written up-tempo songs and then he brought us this and Johnnie put his vocal on it and magic was made.'

John Cameron:

'Always and Forever' just came to me as a nice song being sung by Johnnie that needed a bit of good old-fashioned Gordon Jenkins-type strings behind it, you know. That was one when everything was already all in place, a nice catchy, melodic piece with a good vocal that needed some strings, thank you very much.

Two huge hits were in the bag along with another in the UK, 'The Groove Line', which became one of the best-known songs of the disco era by a group partly borne out of Britain. It charted at No. 12 in the UK chart and No. 7 in the USA. It was another Rod Temperton song to be certified platinum by the RIAA, again with more than 2 million sales in America.

Many a writer would be happy with that success, but not Rod. As Simon Blow put it in the *Grimsby Telegraph*:

Even then, as the writing offers were landing on his doormat, Rod had a vision of the future, a broader canvas, and he reckoned he had the next twenty years of his life mapped out. What happened, it's safe to say, is not what he anticipated.

4

LAY IT ON ME

Heatwave's first LP, *Too Hot to Handle*, certainly made an impression on both sides of the Atlantic thanks to the success of the singles, 'Boogie Nights' and 'Always and Forever'. The album hit No. 46 in Britain and No. 11 in the US. Though it was recorded in 1976, to my ears it still sounds as fresh as anything today. Every song on it could have been a hit single. It is an album with absolutely no filler whatsoever, a remarkable achievement for a band who were just starting out in the recording business. It sounds like nothing else, it tried to be nothing else. It was simply the skill of Rod Temperton, a man who knew little of the genre he was writing, but a man who conjured up his own version of it, a version which was complex and filled with character. It was unique and still is to this day, the extraordinarily gifted band and singers perfectly matched to the songs they had been given.

The band were still working at a rate of knots, touring the country as well as preparing them for the follow-up LP that became *Central Heating*. As 'Boogie Nights' climbed the charts, Johnnie Wilder and Rod Temperton headed to BBC Radio Nottingham to continue to promote their first long player. DJ Jon Holmes remembers meeting them:

In the 1970s record reps used to visit the radio stations and BBC Radio Nottingham was no exception. We used to look forward to the likes of Virgin, Island, CBS, and EMI coming and distributing their wares, all the new albums. Then there was GTO Records, an unfashionable label who later gave us The Dooley's and the rep came to me and I always used to feel a bit sorry for him and he thrust his album in my hand, *Too Hot to Handle* by a group called Heatwave, and said to me, 'Give it a listen'.

I felt a bit sorry for him so I went home and gave it a listen as requested. The next morning I phoned him up immediately and I said, 'This is amazing! A great record. I'm going to make it Album of the Week.'

He was so delighted, he said, 'I'll bring the band in, you can meet them.'

So the next thing of course was to do a bit of research about the band and I noticed that Rod Temperton wrote all the tracks. I couldn't wait to meet the man because the songs were so power-ful. Imagine my surprise when this band turned up, here is Rod Temperton, he looked undernourished, and he was white, yet the music sounded so black American. In fact, he looked as though he worked behind the counter at a fish and chip shop in Humberside and certainly not the writer of such classic tracks as 'Boogie Nights' and 'Always and Forever'.

This is the interview in full and I include it here because it perfectly sums up the character of a man who was soon to hit the stratosphere with songs like 'Rock with You' and 'Off the Wall' for Michael Jackson. Little did anyone – not even Rod Temperton – know that at the time of this:

Jon Holmes: 'It was our Album of the Week last week. *Too Hot to Handle*, the group Heatwave, who are of course, currently in the BBC Top 30 with that beautiful and very popular single "Boogie Nights" … and I think it's going to be one of the singles when we look back at 1977, as one of the singles of that year. It certainly will as far as Nottingham audiences are concerned I can tell you. I'm very pleased to say that in the studio, I have with me two members from Heatwave. I think it's fair to say, the key members, Johnnie Wilder and Rod Temperton.'

Rod Temperton: 'Hello, it's nice to be here.'

Johnnie Wilder: 'Good Afternoon.'

Jon Holmes: 'Can I first of all say how much I appreciate the fact that you've made it because I know you hared down here from Liverpool. In fact I think you got back to bed, like last night about 4 o'clock in the morning?'

Rod Temperton: 'That's correct, yeah.'

Jon Holmes: 'So where have you slept, I mean have you managed to sleep at all?'

Johnnie Wilder: 'Well actually, in fact when we got back to the hotel we had some guests who came back. Chris from The Real Thing and all, they were down to see the gig and they came back to the hotel and we sat up and talked roughly until about 5 o'clock before I actually laid in to get up for 8 o'clock this morning.'

Jon Holmes: 'You look so fresh, I can't believe it.'

Johnnie Wilder: 'It's misleading, the look.'

Rod Temperton: 'On the outside.'

Jon Holmes: 'If you look at the backgrounds of the various members of the group, Johnnie, and you look how they came together, you've already planned a half an hour documentary haven't you, really?'

Johnnie Wilder: 'It helps in interviews. When we're out of conversation we can always talk about the people in the group. The nationalities are spread; it wasn't intentionally done, originally. The idea came about when I was in Europe looking for different members to take the place of original members who left the original Heatwave. The idea came that it would be a nice thing if we could have a totally international group, producing the same type of sound. Our key figure is our drummer who's from Czechoslovakia and I met him in Switzerland when my original drummer left me in Germany. And Mario is from Spain; I met him also when I was working in Switzerland. He's been living in Switzerland and then Eric, he's from Los Angeles via Jamaica but he was living in England. And I met Rod a long time ago through a music paper in England, but I was working in Switzerland. He was in Germany at the time … the letter came … came to us from England while I was in Switzerland, then we went to Germany and met him, and started a working relationship.'

Jon Holmes: 'Well that's obvious, yes. I think I follow that. What exotic country is Rod from then?'

Johnnie Wilder: 'Great, great place! Great place.'

Rod Temperton: 'Britain, the best. A fantastic resort area called Cleethorpes.'

Jon Holmes: 'Cleethorpes is very fine, it is fine. It is nice, it is nice. What about your brother, I suppose, Keith Wilder is your brother isn't he?'

Johnnie Wilder: 'Keith's been with me a year and two months now. My last … the trip before this last one when I went home … he was working out there, and we were getting into the recording side and I was adding a lot of voices onto the tracks and I decided that, well, if I'm going to try and reproduce the sound on stage that we have on our record, I need more voices. I've always wanted to work with my brother professionally. He was working with differ- ent bands in America, out in California. So when I got back at that time I said, "Whenever you are ready to come let's go", and he came to Switzerland.'

Jon Holmes: 'We've worked out the pedigree of the group, and we've realised your passports must be heavily stamped. So let's have some music. This was actually the flipside of the music and I think it's a jam. It really shows the other side of the group as well. You've got "Super Soul Sister", which is the sort of funk side, and then you've got lovely, beautiful vocals on "All You Do is Dial".'

[Track Plays]

Jon Holmes: '"All You Do is Dial", another track from *Too Hot to Handle*. Also the flipside to the current hit "Boogie Nights" … and in the studio we have Johnnie Wilder and Rod Temperton from Heatwave. You … I think we've really just hit the nail on the head with how diverse the music is but, has it always been like that because you've been on the road quite a long time. It used to be Johnnie Wilder's Chicago Heatwave, that's right, isn't it?'

Johnnie Wilder: 'Originally it started out as Heatwave. On our first tour to Britain it was more popular to identify as an American because it was an American group, so we stuck the name on the front of it. But we've resolved back to Heatwave now, but the sound is basically the same … I mean we've been in rhythm & blues, that's all I've ever played professionally because I best express myself through that. But, with the different nationalities coming in and out we've got experience, you know, from the other fellows like from the other types of music that's been added in and out.'

Jon Holmes: 'Yes, I've asked this for the obvious reason that we have Rod with us, Rod Temperton. He wrote every song on this album. So how much influence has the songwriting been on the overall sound of the band?'

Rod Temperton: 'Well, I mean when I first joined the band I wanted to learn to write American music and it was a good opportunity, so the funky stuff came through that. I studied the American scene and what was going on there. I started writing from that. Personally I like writing slow songs. I like melody. Strong on melody, so that's my own thing. So, the writing has become varied through that I think, but, you know, I like both sides of the market and I know I've got that. I'm working with a singer that can sing both sides of the market. So you know, that's great. It's just exactly what we wanted.'

Jon Holmes: 'It is remarkable because I'm sure when people hear Heatwave, I'm sure when the record first came out, "Boogie Nights", and it hit the airwaves, everybody thought first of all that it must be

American and it must be an American composition. They wouldn't have thought a young lad from Cleethorpes wrote them.'

Rod Temperton: 'Well there you go.'

Jon Holmes: 'I don't want to down Cleethorpes but, you know, people love to put things into boxes and they would have said that that was definitely American.'

Rod Temperton: 'Yeah well, I mean, I've always preferred American music and American writers in fact. So I guess that my influences come from over that side all the time. So I guess that's why it sounds American.'

Jon Holmes: 'You've played the area before haven't you Johnnie? Here in Nottinghamshire.'

Johnnie Wilder: 'Yes we have. We've also tried to make an interview on BBC Nottingham before … we were late for it.'

Jon Holmes: 'That's right.'

Johnnie Wilder: 'We had bad luck, but we made it today.'

Jon Holmes: 'Yeah and I am very grateful you did. I should imagine visually having seen you on *Top of the Pops*, there's a lot of physical energy goes in to the act when playing live.'

Johnnie Wilder: 'Oh well, when we sleep good at night we can strum up a bit extra leg.'

Jon Holmes: 'Let's hear another track from the album. I asked you if there was one particular one you wanted to hear and you said, "Lay It on Me".'

Johnnie Wilder: 'That's my particular favourite track on the album. Mainly because I did all the vocal work you see, and I like these types of harmonies that we did put in here … and this … I've learned to sing full set in about the last three years and it's coming along and this one I think I did pretty good on.'

[Track Plays]

Jon Holmes: '"Lay It on Me" from Heatwave. You said you've only just learned to sing full set so how do you learn to sing full set? I mean there's the standard joke with the pliers; I assume you don't use those?'

Johnnie Wilder: 'Oh, well, if you think of it in terms of people naturally singing, the voice tone that they talk in, my tone is a second tenor. Much lower than say the vocal lead on that song. Well, over the years I've always liked artists like Eddie Kendricks and the Delfonics and things like that that always sing in that voice range … and I just kept trying and trying and you naturally tune your voice into being able to get those ranges. Well, if you keep on going like that it goes higher and higher and higher. And I've done that over three years now.'

Jon Holmes: 'And you're working on breaking a crystal glass are you one day?'

Johnnie Wilder: 'Yes! Another one of those types.'

Jon Holmes: 'You've had a very big hit with "Boogie Nights" and I've already hinted how popular it has been in Nottingham. How much has it changed your lives really? I mean, do you have a different reaction now when you arrive on stage in a club?'

Johnnie Wilder: 'We've been playing audiences in Europe. This is actually the first time we're back to do any work since "Boogie Nights" has been released and last night was the first gig and it's not going to change. It can't change our lives but the audience response has been sort of unbelievable. We've done support on big concert tours but like now we are following a hit record as they say and the audience is coming out in massive numbers and the response is just totally different. But yeah, it doesn't change us. We are striving to make the show much better than what it was before, record or no record. So we'll keep on pushing like that and building a better stage image and making the sound more like the records that we are producing and just generally entertaining much better.'

Rod Temperton: 'What change?'

Jon Holmes: 'I admire the group for a start because you are in the Top 10 and you're still bothering to come to Radio Nottingham.'

Johnnie Wilder: 'Once people make the record, if the entertainers forget that people made that record go where it did then they lose the contact with … actually where their roots were. I mean they started from the stage say, most groups start from the stage entertaining. People started liking the act; they build up popularity without having a record. Well, we definitely, wholeheartedly respect the fact that people made the record and we give it all back to the people.'

Rod Temperton: 'Yeah, I think it's very important to remember this, I mean we're just starting now on a ten-week tour of England and you know, we've got to play for those people who made "Boogie Nights" a hit for us. Yeah, you've got to give them that back.'

Johnnie Wilder: 'Plus we love entertaining.'

And that, folks, was that. One of the few records left of a Rod Temperton interview on the radio, done live, no less. I think if you research interviews on some of the other biggest selling songwriters from the UK such as John Lennon, Paul McCartney, Ray Davies and Elton John, you might find a little bit more than answering questions with, 'What change?'

5

PACK YOUR GRIP, TAKING YOU ON A TRIP

Central Heating picked up where *Too Hot to Handle* left off, Rod this time writing all but two of the songs on the LP, leaving Johnnie Wilder to pen 'Happiness Togetherness' and 'Mind Blowing Decisions'. Johnnie Wilder:

> For me when it came to writing, I think I started or tried my hand at it at the end of the first album and Rod was very much a big influence on my wanting to write more, in composing the songs that I did, he was a big help for me in the structure of my songs.

Barry Blue:

> The big hit this time was 'The Groove Line', a thumping and infectious groove that gets in your head and won't let go, a continuation of 'Boogie Nights', really. I know Rod didn't enjoy writing the lyrics as much as he enjoyed the music side of things, but you know he layers the music with lyrics, and the music and the lyrics have to go together.
>
> The lyrics don't have to be the most wonderful set of lyrics in the world but if they sound right, that's what he went for. He would pick up on a kind of vernacular of the time; I mean, 'The Groove Line' was just kind of a thing. I think the first line was 'Pack your grip/We're gonna take you on a trip', something like that. And he had a great knack of finding what was the current kind of phrases to use, like 'Beat Your Booty' and 'Sho'nuff Must be Love', the way

he spelled it and everything lyrically had to be spelled the way it sounded, so, you know, when you looked at the title 'Sho'nuff Must be Love' was spelled in the kind of the way that it sounded, which was a bit odd, but that's the way he wanted to write it so that's the way it had to be done.

He added American language to the American music he was producing. Heatwave were I think the first multi-racial band to break America, without question, the best British export R&B band to break America. I don't think people realised that, how they set trends, because the first album should have had a picture of the band on the front in America, but it got changed of course. Over In England, there *was* a picture of the band on the album cover but in America there was just a kind of melted disc in the street because, you know, American society was like that. Anything multi-racial was never heard of in those days. Rod, of course, never wanted to be centre stage anyhow. He was a man always in the background. He was a backroom boy, a driving force, and the engine on these great records that we were hearing or have heard over the years.

Just as 'Boogie Nights' had the unlikely harp in it, with 'The Groove Line' we had a kind of honky-tonk piano in the middle of the groove. Who else would have done that on a pop record? It's just odd but, again, it worked for us. The song also started with some cymbals. We did it in the bathroom, reversing the cymbals, fazing them. It shouldn't have worked either but it did and I think that's what made it such a great tune and such a strong album.

Orchestral arranger, John Cameron:

Working on *Central Heating* was a wonderful experience. It wasn't like what you often got when the band does their bit and then goes home and then I come in with the orchestra. There seemed to be people around all of the time. I remember going into the studio when they were doing 'The Groove Line' and we were talking about the next bit of stuff we going to record and the producer Barry Blue saying, 'Do you fancy playing the piano solo in the middle?'

They weren't sure what they wanted and Rod was saying, 'Try this', and so I tried a few bits of barrelhouse piano on it and they ended up putting a flanger on it and everything else. It was just kind of part of what the band was doing at the time. It was all done pre-beat synthesiser and so special effects were part and parcel of things back then. That started back in the sixties when people would say, 'Do you know what Phil Spector did with that? He'd put it through this thousand-watt thingy amplifier and put a mic on the other side of the room and then feed it through a power station down the road, then record it in the café!'

There were so many stories about how such-and-such a noise was made. Now, of course, you buy a piece of software and kind of go, 'Ah, Phil Spector, 3A'!

As I said, it wasn't one of those things when they did their bit, went home and I went in with the producer afterwards, it was all quite hands-on and very buzzy, a great experience.

'The Groove Line' was used in the final episode of the show *Freaks and Geeks* as well as in the 2013 movie, *Anchorman 2: The Legend Continues*. It was also sampled by Public Enemy in their song 'Sophisticated Bitch' on their 1987 album, *Yo! Bum Rush the Show*.

The other two stellar tunes on *Central Heating* were 'Send Out for Sunshine', which surely would have been another hit had it been released as a single. It is a song that immediately brings a smile to your face and makes you feel that all is good in the world although, lyrically, it is about sending out for sunshine, as life is so difficult. The other really incredible track that was never intended for a single release was another Rod ballad, 'Star of a Story'. When I asked Rod which was the favourite song he ever wrote, he quickly named 'Star of a Story' as the one; as did Quincy Jones and George Benson who covered the tune on his *Give Me the Night* album along with another cover of 'Turn Out the Lamplight', which had been left off the *Too Hot to Handle* LP along with another killer cut, 'Slip Your Disc to This'.

Barry Blue:

This is because Temperton ... well I wouldn't say that he overwrites ... but he was never happy, never satisfied with the song so he was constantly honing it, constantly changing it until he was absolutely 100 per cent happy with it, whereas most modern writers, most writers that we know of, would probably get to the chorus and then repeat the chorus for an hour. Rod would take another chorus, say chorus B, and add that to the end of the chorus and go on something completely different, which we did on 'Boogie Nights', amongst others. The end of the songs often throw in yet more harmony and there might be a change of key, just adding an extra layer to a song which already had you grooving. Even the songs we had to leave off albums would have been gifts for other artists.

Johnnie:

When I compare Rod to writers of that generation and writers today, for me Rod is like a Stevie Wonder. You see, Stevie Wonder is the ultimate of writers and singers for Johnnie Wilder anyway. And Rod could write songs especially when it involved me as a singer. Rod could write songs on a power with Stevie Wonder.

Then I have my favourite vocalists like Nat King Cole and others. Rod could pen a song for artists like that as long as they could feel him, you know, feel his type of writing, but I just, you know, I could be a bit biased of course. I was used to Rod's chord progressions and vocal style harmonies especially in the backgrounds.

As far as lead vocalists go, you know, he and I worked well. He did a lot of lead vocals on songs that I've sung, almost the majority of them, and then, let me see if there was a particular song. I don't have a favourite, but I enjoy and I listen to, you know, in my nostalgic moments, listen to 'Star of a Story'. That was one of his best-written songs for sure and I think we had the perfect arrangements in that song and the challenges that he put forth to me as a vocalist in doing that song were big ones. It has so many things that are going on and is a tremendous piece of songwriting.

Rod admitted:

Everything in 'Star of a Story' was just right. It ended up exactly how I imagined it right from the start. It was a different type of song for me to write and I was certainly stretching myself. Johnnie excelled with the vocals, too.

Bruce Swedien, Quincy Jones' engineer and a man who would soon be teamed up with Rod, said of the song, '"Star of a Story" stands out. It's my favourite of Rod's songs and boy that is a tough list to choose from. It's a very deep song. Listen to the lyrics and get into it. There is a tremendous meaning there.'

Barry Blue:

My favourite tune of Rod's is actually one which is not well known. It's called 'Star of a Story' which was on the *Central Heating* album. It's a fabulous song with a great, truly great, melody. It's just a unique tune and it shouldn't really work because the bass line doesn't work with the vocal and the vocal doesn't quite work with the chords, but when you put it all together, it's got this edginess about it which is just unique, it makes the hairs on the back of your neck stand up. It's a wonderful piece of work and showed what else Rod was capable of. He had already proved himself to be a fantastic writer but this one was something else. It had everybody who was working on it really excited.

Johnnie Wilder:

'Star of a Story' made me stretch. I'll put it like this. There were lines in that song where the voice and the strings, the violins especially, we alternated licks and I guess the truest listener would be able to tell when it's a voice and when it's the strings, but I love doing things like that. I would counter the horn lines that were played and then, on certain parts I would counter the string lines and that was a good feed for me to do. It was a good challenge to be able to do that and then do counter lead vocals. It was just a magic song and is still. It's one of those songs I wanted to re-record maybe a cappella. I would want to give a stab in the a cappella style just to see how much I could do with the voice as we did with the instruments in the first place.

John Cameron:

'Star of a Story' was a really off-the-wall experience. Rod didn't want it to be the usual kind of strings playing away behind as we had done on 'Always and Forever'. Rod wanted all of the lines to cross in exits, very contrapuntal, which I loved because I never liked writing great big slabs of chords. I much preferred having contrapuntal lines and a lot of what Rod wanted to do with Heatwave was to have these crossing lines, the intersecting stuff between the strings and the brass and all of that kind of stuff. It all worked great for me and doing that song was a memorable experience. It doesn't surprise me one little bit that those who really know about music love 'Star of a Story'. It is different and very complex and very clever.

The recording of the *Central Heating* LP, as with much of the story of Heatwave, contained some tragedy. Bass player, Mario Mantese, on returning from a party at Elton John's house in London, was stabbed in the heart by his girlfriend. He was in a coma for months, waking up blind, mute and paralysed. His replacement in the band was teenager, Derek 'Dee' Bramble:

My family knew Roy Carter, the rhythm guitarist for Heatwave. He was a friend of my sisters. Roy would come over at Christmas and we would hang out and then one Christmas he came over and I started singing. That's how I had started, as a singer in local bands. But, I loved the bass and so I picked it up and I got pretty good, pretty fast.

Roy had been on the road with Heatwave and he was like, 'Show me what you can do'. So, I picked up the bass in front of him and started wailing on it and I think he liked it, I think he was a bit impressed because at the time I was 13 years of age.

Months passed, blah, blah, blah, and then Mario had his accident and the band needed a bass player. By then I was about 14 or 15 and I had call from Roy saying, 'How do fancy joining the band?' That was kind of the long and the short of it. I came in on the back end of *Central Heating* and then went on tour with the lads on that album. But the first time I was on a whole album was *Hot Property*.

My first meeting with Rod was in Johnnie Wilder's flat in London. Already, even though I was so young, I wanted to be a writer and meeting Rod was like looking at God or something like that. He walked in and I thought, 'God, he's just an ordinary looking bloke'. I had seen his picture on the records before but him walking in with his Marlboros and his funny walk, you know, he was just generally unassuming. I just thought that was magnificent. I thought, 'Who is this guy with all this mustard?' Yet he was just a lad from Cleethorpes. It was immediately inspiring.

By this time, 1979, Heatwave were well established as one of the smoothest and funkiest bands around and Rod's talents as a writer were being recognised on both sides of the Atlantic. It was soon time to start writing for Heatwave's third LP, but the heavy work load of playing, writing and touring was starting to take a toll on Rod as he approached his thirties:

I decided to leave the band when we were making enough money that I could afford to leave the band and to be quite honest it was not a career decision in the sense of I knew what I was going to do. I had no idea where I was going. I remember standing on the side of the stage in, I think it was Birmingham, watching the new organ player play for the first time to see if he could get through the whole evening and then as the night finished and the crowd applauded, I knew he was perfect for the band and so I kind of waved goodbye to everybody and got the train back to London … and at that time I thought, 'What am I going to do now?'

So, I went back to Germany and not being the kind of person who could sell himself very well, I have no idea how to do that, I just locked the door and started writing and I figured, 'Well, we've had two albums out and they've done some good business all over the place and we've had some hit singles', so I figured, 'Well, if I am any good, somebody will call me, I guess, you know at some point'.

And, anyway, although I was no longer part of the band, in the meantime I had to write a third album for Heatwave.

That was one of the problems that, you know, once the success had happened and you've been on the road all the time, you know you are in a hotel, you get up in the morning, you fly to the next place, you arrive there, then you have to go to an in-store promotion. You finish that about six o'clock, enough time for a snack, and then go to the soundcheck and get ready for the gig. You go to the gig, you go to bed, and then you get up and do the same the next day. So the idea of writing an album at that point was virtually impossible. So, I knew that I needed to write this third album and I just couldn't be on the road anymore, anyway. So I had that to do and I just thought, 'Well, I have no idea where the next job would be coming from or what would happen so I just sat there and I figured, well somebody will ring sooner or later or at least I hope they do'.

Johnnie Wilder:

When Rod first wanted to come off the road I thought to myself, 'Wow, if he goes off the road, that means we are looking for another keyboard player that could play like he did', but in the end that was easier than I thought it would be. I knew that Rod would never leave the band until he was happy and I was happy with a replacement and that's when we met Calvin Duke, who used to play with the Fatback Band. We were touring with them and we both just fell in love with him.

Calvin had a great sense of humour, he was exactly what we needed in terms of somebody who could replace Rod and then add something to the group as well. But as far as his [Rod's] writing, now, I had no reservations about him going on to write because I knew that the more and more we played on the road he wanted to have time where he could write, either for our next album or just because he loved to write all the time.

I didn't doubt for a second that he would do even better things with his writing, especially after we had started touring in America and he and I had the chance to meet Quincy Jones. Of course, he fell in love with the material that he had heard from Rod before he even met him. So, no, no doubts about his writing and plus, I had the assurance of a friend that he would still write a lot of material for Heatwave. By then we, I think, we had become pretty good friends. He assured us always that he would always write for Heatwave as long as Heatwave was a going concern. And he did that on every album. He had made a commitment to writing as much as we wanted for the next albums and we were very thankful for that.

And with the pressure of being in a band full time now released, write he certainly did – for Heatwave's third LP, *Hot Property*, an album which spawned more hits. 'Razzle Dazzle' in the UK and 'Eyeballin'' in the USA, were the first two tracks on another excellent and smart album, although neither were as big as the hits from the previous two albums. The LP peaked at No. 38 in America, but oddly did not touch the charts in Britain at all. This in spite of another major change, Barry Blue being replaced by Phil Ramone as the producer.

Ramone had an enormously successful CV, having worked with some of the biggest stars in music so it was quite a coup for Heatwave to have him behind the mixing desk. Johnnie Wilder:

Rod and I were looking for a producer for our third album, the *Hot Property* album and Dick Leahy – I can't say enough about him – was gracious enough to let us look for people who we thought would enhance the sound of Heatwave. We were the kind of group that wanted to do things that would be, you know, fresh, what we call fresh here, you know, new, not doing the same thing over and over all the time but we quickly learned that audiences don't want to jump away too far. You know, they don't like to hear stuff too new from what they have heard before out of a band, so, at that time, we were looking for people and Quincy was at the top of our list to produce a Heatwave album. Unfortunately, he was tied up or had other commitments at that time. Then, we got the chance to meet with Maurice White of Earth, Wind & Fire. We had considered him.

We had on our list Bob James, and we met with the producer of Hall & Oates, a fairly unknown guy at the time before he wrote hits for Earth, Wind & Fire and so many others, that being David Foster, and of course Phil Ramone, then other guys that we thought would be good for Heatwave and maybe good for them as well, a new marriage of American producers and our band. I want to take nothing away from Barry Blue though, because without Barry Blue, I don't know. A lot of things we learned in the studio was the through the influence of Barry. And you talk about a guy that had a sense of humour and really was skilful in production, Barry was it along with Jamie, the engineer we had at that time.

A lot of good experience we got from those guys but we just thought we would like to move into the American market with an American producer. So, that's how we met Quincy. When we first went to Los Angeles, we got the chance to visit with him at his home. And also, I don't know, working together like Rod and I did in a band as a vocalist sometimes, the vocal style could cause Rod to alter a bit of his song, just a little bit, because he was more flexible than I was. The more I think about it, he was a bit more flexible at different times according to the song. He was keen that Quincy would be a good man to work with us but in the end it wasn't to be.

Barry Blue:

I think, first of all, the sessions with Heatwave were very intense, I mean those projects were very, very long, you know, thirty-six-hour stands. After the second album, I needed a rest from them, I needed a rest, if you like, from going backwards and forward to the States and doing the tours with them as well. So with a month or so before work was due to start on *Hot Property* I left, although I did come back to work with them on their fifth and final album. In the intra period, Johnnie Wilder had his accident, which kind of put lot of things on hold anyway, so I had to move on to other projects.

The accident was another chapter in the somewhat bizarre and twisted story of Heatwave. On 24 February 1979 a van broadsided Johnnie's car, paralysing him from the neck down and hospitalising him for a year, although incredibly he was still able to add vocals to the third Heatwave long player while confined to a wheelchair. Even when interviewing him in late 2005, just a few months before his death at the age of 56, Johnnie had to take constant water breaks. He struggled to catch his breath. He, as ever, battled through my questions for which I am eternally grateful. He was a rock. He talked a lot of how it was his dream to one day work with his buddy Rod Temperton again. Alas, it was never to be.

So, with Quincy Jones finishing off *The Wiz* and unable to produce Heatwave, in the end it was Phil Ramone who took the reins for *Hot Property*, but Rod was very soon to team up with the legendary jazz man and producer to try to come up with some songs for an album for the former child sensation Michael Jackson, who now wanted to show off his chops as an adult performer.

6

OFF THE WALL

The year 1979 was a difficult one for Heatwave even though they had produced another fine album, *Hot Property*, on which Rod Temperton, no longer a full-time member of the band, had written nine of the ten songs. The opening tune, 'Razzle Dazzle', certainly impressed many, including former Jimmy James and the Vagabonds' member, Andrew Platt:

> For me, it was the rhythms that got me. Some of the more complex rhythms. Rod was a bit daring as a songwriter, he wasn't conventional. He would put something that was off-beat and a little bit perhaps odd-legged into a song, and that's particularly true of 'Razzle Dazzle' because there's a little brass line in the middle of 'Razzle Dazzle' and it completely crosses the 1, 2, 3, 4 straight beats at 120 beats a minute. And I imagine there are people moving from foot to foot wondering which one to get off on again on the dance floor because it's just something odd and something different.

Johnnie Wilder:

> *Hot Property*. Wow. I just regretted that we didn't knock it all out before my accident, but even, even the way they finished mixing it in the end, they just pulled stuff out that Rod wanted in his songs. I think they did a great job without me having the opportunity of knocking it out the way I would have done it had I been at my best. I don't think I performed as well on those songs as I did on the

follow-up LP, *Candles*. Rod wrote more great songs and, you know, with the proper strength and pushing it out, it would have done better. Rod had me in mind on all those songs, all of them, especially the ballads. I love doing up-tempo songs, because we were a group that entertained, had a lot of dance routines and that kind of thing, but I just loved singing Rod's extraordinary ballads.

Derek Bramble:

Rod was just touched by the gods. There are a lot of people who have the groove but Rod was touched by some other stuff. When I listen to some of his stuff today, at the back end of 2016, I am transformed and I am a middle-aged guy now. Yet, his songs make me feel like a little kid. That's the gift, you know. It's the wonderment of music-making what he left for us, if you know what I mean. And there ain't many people who could do that in the way that Rod has done it, writing songs that stick the way that his have. There are moments today when I am in the car and I hear a Rod Temperton record come on and all of a sudden my day is better, just a lot better. It's the gift that keeps on giving. It doesn't matter how old you get or how many times you hear any one song of his, every time you hear that one song it's just like, 'Oh my God, this is on another level'. The fact that Rod was my mentor and my champion just makes me feel so fortunate, so lucky that he took me under his wing and decided to focus on me as he did in the years that followed.

I always remember recording *Hot Property* with Rod. He gave me the bass parts and I played it the way he gave it to me. With me, because I was a cocky young kid from Mile End in East London, I would say to him, 'Well, how about a bit of this and how about a bit of that?' And he was, like, 'OK, show me what you've got', and I showed him and what he liked, he liked and what he didn't like, he didn't like. I think Rod and me got along so well because in some weird and wonderful way, he saw a little bit of himself in me. I'm not saying that I could hold a candle to Rod, I couldn't tie his shoelaces if you asked me, because he is THAT guy, but a person like that doesn't take you in and let you stay at his flat for months on end just because of your good looks, you know! We got on like a house on fire.

His songs were the lifeblood of Heatwave even though he was no longer a band member and so he was omnipresent throughout. There wasn't a track laid down without him. That was always the case with every song we did of his. They were such fun songs to play, tunes like 'Eyeballin'' and 'Razzle Dazzle' but not easy and 'Therm Warfare' was no joke either. He had me play the bass all over the place. These songs, like all of Rod's, had evolved arrangements that broached on every part of American music, from the 1940s right through to the 1980s. There's a bit of be-bop in the horns, there's James Brown guitar licks, the drums are great jazz and pop licks and stuff. Rod was an arranger of extraordinarily huge talent.

With Phil Ramone behind the producer's desk, the band, having recorded much of the groundwork in Wembley in North London, headed to New York to finish the songs off with overdubs and mixing, and it was while working in the studio there that Rod's life was about to change. On the other side of America, in Los Angeles, Quincy Jones was starting work on Michael Jackson's first adult LP. His engineer for the sessions was Bruce Swedien. Bruce had first come to recognition for his work on Frankie Valli & the Four Seasons' *Big Girls Don't Cry* in 1962 for which he won a Grammy nomination. He had also recorded and mixed for jazz legends such as Count Basie, Art Blakey, Duke Ellington and Dizzy Gillespie. He had been working for some while with Quincy Jones:

> Quincy asked me to check out the Heatwave albums that were such big successes in the late seventies. He said that Heatwave was Rod Temperton's band and that we were going to be working on Michael's new album with Rod, so Quincy said listen to his stuff. So I went out and got the Heatwave records and, Holy Cow!, I simply loved Rod's musical feeling, everything about it. Now, this was a really good band, Heatwave was a really good band, but the concept of Rod's arrangements, his tunes, his songs was exceedingly hip. I loved them from the off.

Steven Ivory was a journalist, specialising in articles about popular culture for magazines. He wrote on eurweb.com:

One afternoon in the late 1970s, while hanging out at the production office of Quincy Jones on the A&M Records lot – I was probably there at the invitation of buddy Ed Eckstine, then running Quincy's production company – out of the blue, Jones asked me how I felt about the songs of Rod Temperton. At the time, Temperton was the keyboardist and chief songwriter for Heatwave, the dynamic UK-based seven-man band that scored with songs singularly created by Temperton, such as 'Boogie Nights', 'Too Hot to Handle', 'Always and Forever' and 'The Groove Line'. Heatwave struck fear in the hearts of R&B headliners, anxious about following onstage a band with a repertoire of smouldering dance hits and soul ballads and a take-no-prisoners live act that included vocalists/brothers Johnnie and Keith Wilder performing acrobatics.

Quincy, already a legendary figure in jazz, TV theme and film soundtrack production, was looking to fortify his foray into commercial R&B/pop initiated by solo albums that weren't so jazzy – *Body Heat, Mellow Madness, Sounds ... and Stuff Like That* – and protégé act, the Brothers Johnson (*I'll Be Good To You, Get The Funk Out Ma Face, Strawberry Letter 23*).

Remarkably, Jones was asking lil' ol' me, a fledgling 23-year-old music journalist writing for *Soul Newspaper*, if I thought Temperton's songwriting style could transcend Heatwave and be hits for other artists. Jones's question suggested his interest in enlisting the songwriter's services for future productions.

I paused for a few seconds and said something along the lines of, 'Hmmm ... maybe, Q ... but I don't know', the I-don't-know part delivered in a lilt designed to convey thoughtful wariness. Me. Giving Quincy Jones musical advice.

What I didn't realise then was that even as Jones patronised me with this query, he was negotiating with Temperton to bring the songwriter – never crazy about life as a musician on the road – from the UK to Los Angeles to begin working with him on various projects.

Fact is, Quincy's musical instincts were never more on point than the day he listened to a Heatwave record and decided to seek out a relatively unknown British songwriter named Rod Temperton.

Rod would become the creamy centre of Quincy's late 1970s/early 1980s hit run. Yet, he was a mild-mannered, badass white boy, but one who possessed a ridiculous command of black pop. Initially, there were discussions about Heatwave signing with Mellow Management, the Quincy Jones Productions subsidiary that managed the Brothers Johnson. Instead, Jones cut to the chase and offered Temperton the opportunity to be part of his unofficial team of go-to songwriters.

Alan Kirk:

I remember Rod telling me that he got a phone call from Quincy Jones, just like that, inviting him over for tea. Rod said, 'Quincy liked the *Central Heating* album we did and has now invited me over to LA for tea. He asked if I had any songs for Michael Jackson. I told him that I've got fifty in my drawer!' I think it was all down to Rod's lucky scarf and trench coat. That's what did it really, you know!

Rod:

I went to New York to work on the third Heatwave album and then got a call from Quincy Jones, which was quite amazing really. I mean, one night we were in the studio working and the phone call came through, and I sat there and he said, 'Well, hi. I'm working on an album for Michael Jackson, a solo album, and an album for Rufus & Chaka Khan and I have heard your two Heatwave albums and I would love you to write something for them.'

I was really shocked. I used to listen to Quincy's records on a Saturday afternoon in Cleethorpes with my mates, you know, round in the back bedroom. And I was really flattered. But the problem was – and I'll tell you the way I always worked, how intense it was – we were in the studio all day and all night with Heatwave, and I was concentrating on this album, the one which became *Hot Property*. So I basically had to say no. I turned down Quincy! Fortunately for me, Quincy wouldn't take no for an answer and kept me on the phone for about two hours and finally he said, 'Look, just write one song for Michael and one for Rufus'.

So, I said, 'OK, I'll try. But the only chance I've got to do it is at the weekends, because we are in the studio everyday working on Heatwave.'

And so he said, 'OK, don't worry about it, I'll organise sessions on Saturday and Sunday so we can fit around you.'

So I said, 'Fine.' Then I got off the phone and, you know, I was excited on the one side but then I was thinking, 'How the hell am I going to do this?' Because I finish at two in the morning – I was staying in the Hilton Hotel in New York City where I had a little keyboard in the room, and I had to go back there then after finishing in the studio and start writing for these projects. And you know, because I had no chance to meet Michael Jackson or Rufus beforehand, I figured that I had to write more than one song for each, you know, write two or three ideas at least to give them some kind of choice, because if they were going to fly me out to Los Angeles it would be a bit embarrassing if they hated what I did for them. So I wrote three musical pieces to take to LA and a couple of days before, Quincy called me and he said, 'Well, what musicians do you need?'

So I said, 'Well, we are going to need two guitarists and drums and bass and keyboards.'

And he said, 'OK, don't worry about it. I'll have it set up for when you get here. We will have a car to pick you up at the airport at two o' clock on Saturday.'

So, I said, 'OK.' And that was that.

So I finished this date on Friday night with Heatwave, caught the plane, got to LA and went straight to the studio out of the airport and I'll never forget it because you know, I walked in the studio and Quincy came to meet me and we shook hands and everything and basically he waltzed me straight through to the main studio room where all these top-flight session players were sitting. And you know, he opened the door and he kind of pushes me through and said, 'Guys, this is Rod. Hit it!'

I always say that there is a defining moment in your life because, you know, at that point I could have easily frozen and nothing happen, but I just kind of bit the inside of my mouth and answered, 'OK'.

So I went over to the drummer and sat down with him and said, 'Now here are the patterns I want, and this is what I want you to do and everything and onwards', and we cut the three tracks over the Saturday afternoon and the Sunday afternoon. They had to put

X, Y and Z on the box because I didn't have any lyrics yet so no title for the songs and I said to Quincy, 'OK, which one of three do you want?'

And he said, 'I want all three.'

I replied, 'Oh no!'

I'd now got to fly back to New York and had five days to write all the lyrics to do the vocals the following weekend and I still had to work every day and night with Heatwave in the studio. So off I went back to New York and sat up again, and I must admit I was absolutely shattered by all of this.

Then, the next weekend arrived and I went back to LA, met Michael at lunchtime for the first time, sat with him and taught him all the background vocals so we could stack all that up and record it. He was amazing; whatever I sang he could sing it straight back to me. So he would do all that and then I would do a rough kind of melody with the lyric on the tape and he took it home to learn it. He had the paper and everything and he would sit up all night and learn the lyrics so that he could come in on the Sunday and perform it rather than be reading off a sheet, you know. And on that Sunday afternoon we cut the lead vocals for 'Rock with You', 'Off the Wall' and 'Burn this Disco Out', which were the three songs of mine on the album. And basically that was it.

I think 'Off the Wall' was the first as that was the song I intended to write, the one song I was supposed to write for the album. That was the one I was hoping they would pick because from what little I could guess from hearing Michael's records, having not had a chance to speak to him and see what it really was he wanted and where he was heading, I realised that he sang very rhythmical melodies very well. You know, better than his long line melodies. I knew he could get his mouth round really good and get some bite into it. So that was really defined and also I knew he was going to be good at doing harmony, so the chorus which is a big block of harmony, you know, I wrote that specifically for him to do and so that was really the song that I planned, that would be the one they would pick, and then the others, 'Rock with You' and 'Burn this Disco Out', were kind of done secondary, you know.

Barry Blue remembers that the idea of 'Rock with You' had surfaced during the sessions for Heatwave's *Central Heating* LP:

Rod was kind of dabbling with 'Rock with You' when we were working on the second album and I just thought then that there was something that was going to blow out really big for Rod, that he just needed to go to the next level and not be confined by one particular band, you know, which was Heatwave, and he went on to write, not prolifically in terms of what you would say would be a normal output for a songwriter, but everything he writes and everything that is released by Rod is of such a high standard.

Writers these days tend to write for a project and then they move on to another project and then, you know, they're working with half of dozen different artists all at once, whereas I know Rod was working on very few songs for very few different artists at any one time.

Derek 'Dee' Bramble:

A couple of the tracks that went off to be Michael's songs, Rod and Johnnie had considered them for Heatwave but they didn't make it. They weren't fully formed songs at that time, they were just ideas and Rod then just plucked them out for Michael and once Michael came into play, the rest is history. Different people bring a different energy to the music and now I couldn't think of anybody else doing 'Rock with You', to be honest.

Bruce Swedien recalls his first meeting with a songwriter he was to work alongside for a number of years:

Quincy's car pulls into the parking lot at the studio. Quincy and his driver were in the front seat and in the back seat was this exhausted looking dude in a wrinkled trench coat. His eyes were red-rimmed with fatigue and he was staring into space. A Marlboro cigarette with a 3-inch ash was dangling from his lower lip. Now that was my first impression of Rod Temperton.

Quincy Jones:

I met Rod in a very strange way. It wasn't strange, but it was unusual. I was in the middle of doing a million records and he came by the house. I was living over on Strong Canyon Inn and he came over with Johnnie from Heatwave and they wanted me to manage Heatwave. I said, 'I don't know, I'm not a manager, and I'm just doing this thing for the Brothers Johnson.'

I knew Rod's songs of course and, boy, I was impressed. On meeting him I was really surprised. Like everybody else in there, I thought he was a brother, you know. He was white and came from some place called Grimsby which I had never heard of. We later on met at his home in Worms in Germany. His nickname has been 'Worms' ever since then, so in the studio we used to have his nickname as Worms, Bruce was 'Svensk' because he is Swedish and we used to call Michael 'Smelly' because rather than cursing he would say something was 'smelly'. So we had Svensk, Smelly and Worms.

In the end, we couldn't work the management thing out but it got me more interested in Rod and, in the end, we worked on *Off the Wall* and I got to cut the songs in just the way they were presented by him. It really impressed me from the first time I heard them, because I don't miss much. I have been listening to music from all sorts since 1947 so you hear the good stuff, you know, right away.

We sat down and played the piano and talked about his work and so forth. I told the Brothers Johnson to listen to his stuff and Bruce, too. Pay attention to Heatwave, I told them. Because there is a guy behind this group that has really got it together. You could tell from the bass lines and all of it.

Rod was working in New York with Phil Ramone on both a Heatwave album and writing a couple of songs for Karen Carpenter's solo record. I remember I was getting ready to do Michael Jackson's album, the one that became *Off the Wall* and one with Rufus and Chaka which Rod also penned the title track called 'Masterjam'. I asked him to write songs for both projects. And he just dove in, you know. Rod loves challenges. Nothing scares him. He brought us these three incredible songs for Michael and two for Rufus.

I remember first hearing them and I just said, 'Hey, hey, hey, this guy has got his thing, he has got it together'.

He was so funky. I just got to know him, you know, and the more I got to know him the more I was in love with him, personally and musically. Rod writes what he is. He is the most principled man I have ever seen in my life, you know. I have never ever enjoyed working with anybody more. He covers my back, you know, no matter what happens and I will do anything for him, you know, he is a very special man, a very special man and we've got that same junky work ethic I think.

We used to smoke a hundred and sixty cigarettes a night; four packs each of Marlboro Reds. People ran from us, man, I am telling you, because we were like vampires, you know. Up all night, you know. All kind of miraculous things happened during those nights when we first met, listening to the material and writing material, just miraculous things, and you know I think it shows in the results because, well, we tore it up, man.

Rod has got a gift. I think he is one of the greats; I put him up there with the greats, you know, because he understands the melody. He wrote like two thousand common melodies on any given song and there is a selection function, he understands all of it, you know, and that's what it's about. You are dealing with the common part, common lines and one great thing about working with him is because with all of his records he was trying to make them of value, especially when they had vinyl.

You have to listen to the songs over and over again, because you can't hear it all at once, you know. There are some records you can hear transparent and everything is right there, you know, like today. But with Rod it was all there, there is a rhythm section, maybe one little lick behind it. You are listening to a lot of lines and a lot of information coming through there and you just can't fight it. You can just listen to the bass line alone, you can just roll with that, you know, or what is happening with the drums. I remember on the beginning of 'Rock with You' there is a bass drum lick that immediately brings the whole world home. That was John Robinson doing that and you know it is written and arranged by Rod. That's just typical of the things he brings to a song, you know. Rod's songs have a million hooks. The hooks are everywhere, and he puts them all over the records.

Doing those songs was a challenge for everyone but it was not really a stretch in the end. You have to be sincere in everything you do; you can't just churn it out and hope for the best. You have to put something down, something you really believe in and that's what I always tried to do and what Rod did, too. There are a lot of supportive elements I think, that help as well, and we had a great set of musicians who just took it all in.

Barry Blue:

Rod and Quincy. The perfect synergy, the absolutely perfect synergy. I think that the two were meant for each other. I think the stuff that Rod did with Quincy Jones expanded Quincy's repertoire, expanded his knowledge of music, which is really hard because Quincy Jones is an absolute genius, as we know. But I think the combination of him and Rod has gone on and will go on forever.

While Heatwave's third album was failing to turn too many heads in spite of it being another excellent example of Rod's skills as a songwriter, from the up-tempo 'Razzle Dazzle' through the mid-tempo, 'All Talked Out' to the ballads 'First Day of Snow' and 'That's the Way We'll Always Say Goodnight', Michael Jackson's *Off the Wall* went through the roof and started the singer's move towards superstardom. It sold in excess of 20 million units across the world and Rod now had his first No. 1. 'Rock with You', the second single from the album, hit the summit of the Billboard charts in the US at the start of 1980 while it made it to No. 15 in the UK. 'Off the Wall', the one song that Rod took to LA really hoping it to be recorded by Michael, was the third single to be released, making the Top 10 on both sides of the Atlantic.

Rod:

When I went to write the lyrics in the second week for the songs, I was still thinking that was the one they would end up picking and you know, it was just a phrase that I heard around New York a lot, 'Off the Wall'. I thought, 'That's kind of nice', so I decided to use that. And then of course, when they decided that was going to be the album title, then they came up with the concept of him with the slightly short trousers and the, you know, white socks and put him in a tuxedo, so it kind of fitted the groove, you know?

Most songs take me forever to write but 'Off the Wall' was specific, a moment in time. I only had a limited amount of time so I guess I maybe came up with the music in about four days and the lyric in maybe two, the following week.

I mean that was from scratch but that's not normal for me. I mean to be honest with you I don't even from day one think I ever wrote – or had come out – anything more than ten or twelve songs a year. Now I might write six hundred ideas but they never see the light of the day, as they never get past my own market research. People should look in my trash!

One of the things that kept coming up during the interviews for this book was how Rod worked in the studio, telling the musicians and vocalists exactly what he was after to get his vision fully onto the record. In order to work the vocalist, whoever that may have been for each project, Rod would sing to them and get them to repeat his version back to him. Many of the contributors to this project spoke about Rod's guide vocals. The tracks had been laid, words not necessarily written, but Rod would head to the microphone to lay down an experimental vocal track to give the singer the feel he was looking for, for any particular song. Although I have no idea where it came from, nor the legality of it being on YouTube, such an example of Rod's guide for the singers can be heard on that website for 'Rock with You'.

Derek 'Dee' Bramble:

Ha, ha, ha. Rod had a terrible voice. When he did his own demos, I mean, you really have to have some foresight to see past his voice because it was that bad! I would tease him about it all of the time but he would say to me as a joke, 'Well, yeah, look at my record sales this week, son'. Oh my God, I'm laughing just thinking about him singing! Yes, music and melody were definitely his real strengths and he would always come up with those parts first and that's what he taught me, put the ideas down but don't let the track be more important than the song and that's one thing that I took away from working with him.

In spite of his lack of ability to sing, Rod Temperton had made it. His songs for Rufus and Chaka Khan, 'Masterjam' and 'Live in Me' (my personal favourite of Rod's songs), did less well but he was now – if not a household name – a man highly appreciated in the music business. Johnnie Wilder:

> For me, it didn't matter who the artist was that Rod would write for. The only thing I think I said to him was, 'Well, those songs, hmm … they could have been Heatwave songs', but no, I thought it was a natural evolution for Rod. I never really told him myself back then, but I don't think the writing style changed as such. I think the influence of other producers and getting to work with different musicians, the calibre that he worked with in America, just further advanced his writing skills.

At the 'Off the Wall' and 'Masterjam' recording sessions for Michael Jackson and Rufus and Chaka Khan was a young photographer, Bobby Holland:

> I remember those photos like it was yesterday. At that time, I was doing a lot of editorial stuff for magazines and record companies, some of the major labels and some of the smaller independent labels that we had like A&M, Casablanca and Motown. I was working for a lot of different record companies and also producers and one of those producers was Quincy Jones, much to my gratitude. It was a time of great creative expression when the independent labels didn't have the boundaries that the major labels had.
>
> Quincy had a company called Quincy Jones Productions and his office was based on the lot of A&M Records which used to be the old Charlie Chaplin Photo Studio. Back then, Quincy was signed to A&M Records. His production company hired me to document in photographs the projects they were working on. One of those many projects was the ground-breaking *Off the Wall*. At the time it was being done, no one, with the exception of Michael, realised that this was going to be a world-changing event.

That was the first time I remember being in the studio with Rod Temperton. I just recall this guy who was always there, wearing his little sweaters, a thin guy smoking cigarettes and just into the mix. He was not a needy guy like so many of the musicians who needed a lot of attention and stuff. Rod was just kind of laid back and quiet but I could tell even then that he was a major confidante of Quincy's. Quincy gave him a lot of respect – as he does everybody – but Rod held something really special in him. Quincy was one of the people who realised this guy's genius from very early on.

We all came to realise it later on, of course, but Quincy must have been one of the first people who recognised his greatness and wanted to have him as part of his team for what he was doing at that time. Even though Quincy was doing work for major labels he was a kind of independent forward thinker, trying the break down a new barrier and bringing in Rod as a songwriter certainly did that. He ensured that while I was shooting my photographs, I was not intrusive in the studio, just blending in to capture quietly what was happening without disturbing the mix. When I look back on those days, man, I can't even believe I was there. I was a young guy, about 20, so it was a phenomenal experience.

I loved listening to Rod, too. I admit, I love British accents. I just love the sophistication of the way you guys sound. I guess we both speak English but listening to Americans you would never know it was English! On top of that, Rod was just a fascinating guy, a fascinating guy. He was a baaad mother. He was baaad. It was just who he was. *Off the Wall* broke the sound barrier. It may have taken a while for people to realise that the same man wrote that and other massive hits like 'Give Me the Night' for George Benson but they got there in the end. The best way to describe Rod was that he was like Superman. He was the guy in the suit until he put his cape on. When Rod wrote his songs, he had his cape on and we all found out that this ordinary looking guy was Superman.

How did a man from Cleethorpes learn to make a monster groove like that with black musicians? I just don't get it. It was incredible. He always started a song with a ten or fifteen second intro, that little interlude that told you that a Rod Temperton song was coming. I think, too, he was blessed by having a group like Heatwave that had such a vast international sound. As a band and a unit they were so, so talented and the band, the Wilder brothers and Rod really complemented each other. It was a blessing to all parties concerned.

On *Off the Wall*, Rod was just like another guy in the room, like another guitar player or drummer. He didn't stand out at all. He was just another hard-working part of the unit. Quincy Jones has a big, big personality. He's a ringmaster, making everybody feel special. That allowed Michael Jackson to be very laid back, too. Like Rod, Michael knew he was a bad mother and would only become the Michael Jackson everybody knew when it was time to get on that microphone and do what he'd do. When he wasn't doing that he was right in the corner, listening to the playbacks or chatting with the musicians. Then, every now and then, he would hear something and he would perk up, like, one of the musicians would play a little piece of something and he would say, 'What is that? Play me some more of that.' And things would just kind of kick on from that.

A lot of the photos I took were during the tracking sessions of *Off the Wall*. They were laying down the tracks for that album and the Rufus LP, *Masterjam*. That one brought Rufus and Chaka Khan back together because their career had kind of waned a bit and they needed a boost. Quincy had Rufus working again with Chaka Khan. She had been singing on some of Quincy's own projects like 'Stuff Like That' so when it was time for Rufus and Chaka to get back together to do *Masterjam*, Quincy produced and Rod wrote both the title track and 'Live in Me', both great songs.

Now, I love music and secretly I always wanted to be a musician but I can't play a note, have never taken any classes and can't sing a note either, but I do love music. Being a photographer and then a filmmaker, it afforded me the opportunity to be close to music and being involved in the creation of the process. So, at that time, hearing those Rod songs for the first time, being put together in the studio was just great. I mean, nobody could fathom back then that they would turn into what they turned into, which was a tremendous career for Rod, but the thing about it is that his songs are everlasting.

When I listen to them now – and I still listen to them all the time – I hear great stories. The music back then – not just the stuff Rod did – told great stories and people took a lot of pride in being a craftsman at what they were doing, whether you played guitar, whether you played drums, whether you were an engineer, people took real pride in what they were doing. It wasn't about computers, saying we'll just do this bit here and then fix it up later, it was about amazing skills in getting the idea of a song to come out just how it was first imagined, knowing what instrument to put in here and what instrument to put in there, to get it just so. Man, these guys worked hard at that. That was the pride that I had, too, because everybody in the room, including myself, had to know what the hell they were doing and Rod certainly knew what he was doing while still being so laid back, not boisterous or offensive at all. I think he had a secret plan all along. I think people who really know what they are doing have a quiet confidence. Rod was a quite, determined and passionate musician and I can't recall him doing anything that was really crazy!

In fact, back then, I used to smoke cigarettes and a couple of times, I would be standing outside in front of the studio and Rod would pull up in a cab, a taxi cab, straight from the airport. He'd have his little bag, his sweater wrapped over his shoulder, he'd have a cigarette in his mouth and a Coca-Cola. He drank a lot of Coca-Cola. I would be, like, 'Erm … OK. Here comes just another guy.' I don't want to sound derogatory but he didn't look like he was finding anything exciting, yet this was the man bringing in these incredible songs. Sure, we found out later how exciting he was going to be but when I first met him, he was just a quiet giant. He knew how bad he was and Quincy definitely knew how bad he was. As did Bruce Swedien.

Bruce is a very special guy and super talented. Quincy relied on him so much. He had worked with everybody and Bruce, I think, also knew how special Rod was. I'm sure the musicians knew as well that here was someone with a gift, the gift of songwriting, and the gift of knowing all aspects of how to put a song together. You know when you are in a room with bad people and those bad musicians recognised that Rod was the man.

Rod also understood that he was working with greatness, for sure. I think he was glad to be in the studio with this particular group of people. Everybody that Quincy surrounded himself with, they are the shit at what they do, and they know what the hell they are doing. Quincy didn't have any weak links around him when he was creating. There were no weak links anywhere. Otherwise, you wouldn't make it. Everybody around Quincy had to be strong at what they were doing and Rod was very strong at what he did.

Bobby was right. Some major talent played on the *Off the Wall* sessions including George Duke, a man who was soon to produce several big hits of the eighties, most notably 'Let's Hear it for the Boy' by Deniece Williams. Prior to *Off the Wall*, George had produced many of his own jazz and funk albums, had collaborated with the slightly nuts Frank Zappa, and was getting ready to record his own, outrageously brilliant, *A Brazilian Love Affair*, one of my personal favourites of this period, a period blessed with some life-enhancing music.

George Duke:

Quincy used to hire me for certain dates, Michael Jackson dates or whatever Quincy was working on. Quincy calls me 'Dukey'. He calls me and he says, 'Dukey, I want you to come and play on this session', so I'd go down.

And all of a sudden this name Rod Temperton started showing up. You know musicians started coming along and going, 'Quincy's working with Rod', and I said, 'Who is he?'

The guys would say, 'You know he's the guy who wrote this, wrote that', and I said, 'Oh man!'

And all I remember is I think I actually thought he was black. So I walked in the studio I can remember seeing this guy and I asked, 'That's Rod Temperton? Man, how did he get his finger on the trigger?'

Quincy has a knack for knowing who to put together, what elements to put together to make a hit and he saw something in Rod that was very special. There was no doubt about it. And it worked! The bottom line is the guy had a knack for a hook. That's the bottom line. I mean, you know he came up at a time when melody was very important. I'm not sure it's very important any more, seems like a lot of other things, you know, but he came up at a time when melodies and hooks that people could remember were very, very important. And he had his finger on the trigger for knowing what melody, what group of notes to put together that everybody could remember all over the world. It was uncanny. It's amazing to me how he managed to conjure up the melodies he conjured up, ones that everybody could remember. They just seemed to flow out of him as naturally as talking. And that was an amazing thing. That was a very strong gift from that guy.

When you heard one of his songs, you said, 'That's a hit'. It's crazy, it's crazy. He became part of a sound and, as far as I'm concerned, he directed it because that was his material. There was definitely a sound associated with Rod and to me it became indistinguishable between Rod and Quincy even though I know he worked with Heatwave and some other groups. But, for me, when I first became aware of Rod, it was the association between him and Quincy and it was like a marriage with him and Bruce Swedien and all of them in there. It was a marriage made in heaven.

Heatwave was a big group. They had the same thing that all of Quincy's things had. That group of songs that everybody could remember and wanted to sing and wanted to dance to. It wasn't music that hit you over the head or made you think too much. It was just music, you know, you could shake your head to it and groove, you knew it was music for everybody. And that's something that's kind of missing nowadays. You know, music that's kind of race-less, that has nothing to do with, 'Oh this is black music, this is white pop music, this is world music'. Rod's music was universal and that's why Quincy looked at it as well and why they worked so well together.

There was a sound. It was smooth. The melodies all made sense. I mean they were songs, songs that had a very strong groove. I used to ask myself, 'Where did this guy get these hooks from?' I mean, it was interesting to me. He could just sit down and write a song, an art that has been lost over time. That was something Rod exemplified and I think that's why it worked and why his music has lasted so long and always will do. People will always play his stuff. Because they were songs and they are going to last a lot longer than just a groove. You put the two together and you've got something special.

When I arrived for the *Off the Wall* sessions, I could see that there was something there, something special. And of course it was a great time for Michael because the melodies he was able to sing, they just reached everybody because he, too, had this raw talent that he could really bring it home live as well as on the record. And with that master of production behind him and the songs to go with it there was just no way that it couldn't be a marriage made in heaven.

And maybe on the final analysis when Rod didn't write any more songs for Michael a lot of it went away from him. Something happened there as well. All I am saying is, boy, they had a time. Phew, it was strong. Michael was the King of Pop and maybe Rod was the King of Pop Songs. All I know is that I wish he had written something for me!

Derek 'Dee' Bramble said:

Rod and Quincy was absolutely a marriage made in heaven. Quincy was the ringleader to a lot of great musical giants. People like George Duke, Greg Phillinganes, Louis Johnson, these guys were just incredible, the very best in the business.

We did one of Heatwave's LPs at Westlake Studios while Rod was doing *Thriller* in the studio down the hall. So, he brought some of the musicians to play on our stuff. It was amazing. John Robinson, the incredible drummer, played on some of the Heatwave tunes. I don't think Bilbo had flown in yet and so John played on a couple of tracks. I can't remember if we kept them but it was very much a cross-collaborative project. We had Mel Gaynor from Simple Minds on there, too.

Rod got to the point in his life when he could pick who he wanted to play on his songs, choosing the ones that he wanted for each particular track, whichever one he needed and these were the best musicians on the planet. Like Quincy, Rod became a ringleader. They were such a draw, such a lifeblood for all of the musicians in LA at that time, people like Michael Boddicker, Steve Lukather, Jeff Porcaro, Herbie Hancock, everybody played on those records and really wanted to.

In spite of his success with one US No. 1 and a US No. 2, as well as other Top 10 hits under his belt, Rod remained Rod – very grounded.

Barry Blue:

Rod had a great love of a pair of brown boots. He wore them for four years, pretty much on and off stage. I think we got nominated for a Grammy on the first Heatwave album, we didn't win it, but I think we got nominated for one, and the guy, as we went in the door, on the red carpet, the guy said, 'Don't smoke!' So, Rod had to throw his cigarette out. They went through a couple of speeches and Rod said, 'I've got to go out for a cigarette', so he went out for a cigarette with me and the butt that he was smoking earlier was on the floor so he picked it up, relit it and started smoking it again so, you know, he was not one to kind of deal with things in a normal way. In fact, he did everything in different way, a Rod way. Rod was a unique guy.

Andrew Platts:

What can you say? He was just Rod. He just went about his business, doing what he did. He had this unbelievable inner confidence to just be himself all of the time. The fact that he suddenly found himself in LA working with the cream of the crop didn't faze him one little bit. Why would it as he had everybody dancing to his tune? I heard he was no different to the man who I had first met when Heatwave were just starting out, a Northern guy who liked to smoke and blend in with us ordinary folk.

Bruce Swedien:

Oh man, Rod used to drive me nuts. Sessions would start and I would hide his Marlboros. And I suppose that wasn't very nice but it was an awful lot of fun. Finally he gave up smoking altogether, but Rod's smoking habit at the time was legendary. Always a Marlboro. He smoked lots of cigarettes. As a matter of fact he once said that his father had some theory about the fact that if you smoke Marlboros you wouldn't get colds! But anyways Rod always had a Marlboro with a long ash dripping on the equipment. It drove me nuts.

Johnnie Wilder:

Rod was quiet in one sense, crazy in another, but he was not one for fanfare especially about himself. Rod just enjoyed music and enjoyed writing and I think he enjoyed working with talented artists. He's just a good guy, you know? Even with his success, he never changed.

We were on the road to Italy once and all of our main drivers were very tired and I was always the backseat driver when I wasn't driving myself and one night I said, 'Rod, why don't you take the wheel for about a half an hour?' Number one, he'd never had a license but he says, 'Sure', in his usual British way. Rod got behind the wheel, pressed the gas and just let it go and he was halfway on the other side of the traffic and on the wrong side and he got to drive all of ten minutes. Anybody on the highway or the roads better move out the way if Rod is in charge of a car!

7

GIVE ME THE NIGHT

Off the Wall was an enormous hit around the globe, becoming the most successful album by a black artist at that time. Rod's involvement may not have been all that time consuming but his songs played a crucial role in the success of the LP. And he had enjoyed his brief time working with Michael Jackson, who he described as 'one of the most professional people I had worked with because he was right on it all of the time':

> We did those three tracks I was involved in, in that two weekend period, and I came back a third weekend to do some synthesiser bits on some of the stuff. And so by then I knew the album and I'd heard everything else that was going on and so I was back there at the end of it when it was mixed. And at the end, I remember Quincy and I walking out of the studio and really thinking we had something. You know this was a very electric, exciting record. We didn't know how big it would be or what it was going to be but we knew we had something and I was very excited when we came out of there. It was a very good feeling.

In the meantime, Rod had finished off *Hot Property* and completed his work on the Karen Carpenter solo project, one that was then shelved until finally being released in 1996, although both of Rod's compositions, 'Lovelines' and 'If We Try', were released to the public in 1989 on an LP of previously unreleased Carpenters' songs. Rod:

Karen was an amazing talent, I mean, she had a really beautiful tone to her voice. What happened was the producer, Phil Ramone, who produced the third Heatwave album and me became friends and he had a chance to produce a solo project for her. So he asked me to come and do some vocal arrangements and write a couple of things for it. So I was involved in it that way and that was back in New York. And she was really amazing to work with. It was only about a year after that she died. It was terribly sad, you know, very sad. While I was working with her, she was certainly a very thin lady and it was hard. Some of the album was hard to do. But, she was a sweetheart. It was really such a shame.

Barry Blue:

I remember talking to Rod at the time and he was disappointed that the songs he did for Karen didn't come out as well as he would have liked because of her illness. She died not long after he had finished working with her.

After his success with *Off the Wall*, Rod now became a very busy man at the start of the 1980s, his decision to become a full-time writer and arranger really paying off. He may have wondered if he was making the correct decision when he waved goodbye to Heatwave on stage in Birmingham one night but he was now in demand as a songwriter. In spite of his success with Michael Jackson, he was still committed to his former band and now had a fourth LP to do for Heatwave, while Quincy Jones wanted to have more songs from Rod for his next project which was to become *Light Up the Night* for the Brothers Johnson. Rod:

Again, I was very lucky. From the first day I worked with Quincy there was a meeting of minds even though I was from Cleethorpes and he's from Seattle. I'm not sure where that meeting of minds came from but it was there. From working in the studio within the first hour it was like we had known each other all of our lives, from being kids. It was very interesting to me. We had hardly had similar upbringings and we were very different personalities, but we just clicked. We were together for a long time after working on *Off the Wall* and I love him to death.

Quincy Jones:

I had no idea that we were going to work together, you know. And it was ironic because he came to meet me and that's another kind of a divinity I think, that you have no choice in who you meet in life. It all just happened, and it was just like we had an energy. It was amazing, and then I was fortunate enough to meet his parents who were characters themselves and Rod was their only son. I said to them, 'Thank God, the world couldn't handle ten of those, you know'.

He is so special. His mum and his wife, Kathy, were cute, they were so cute, and they have such personalities and are just so contrasting in almost everything. I was always very happy when they came by the house and Kathy showed us how to do shepherd's pie because I love shepherd's pie. We just got closer and closer and closer in life and in music and in working together, it just all blended into one thing, you know. We would be at his house, working on stuff and in the middle of it, here we are breaking down some cabinet that Rod is building. I may have been something of a carpenter in the studio but I know nothing about carpentry in the real world but here we were, putting up this cabinet together with Kathy laughing at us and making us shepherd's pie, you know.

We were always teasing each other about it, the first cooking attempts and all that stuff. I don't know, it was just so great, a joy.

Rod had a very visual concept of music, as do I. For me that started in art first. Something in cartoons and things like that when I was a kid and it is a very visual kind of situation when you think of putting songs and albums together. You get into watercolours primarily and secondarily watercolours and then you go to other elements, other sounds. That's what we did with *Off the Wall*. I don't know if Rod and I ever talked about it, but I think there's something else that I've always admired about him because he thinks visually, too, you know. He is so visual in all his songs, *Thriller* especially.

More of that later, but back to the start of the 1980s and up next was the Brothers Johnson album. They were already tied in with Quincy Jones who managed them and had produced the brothers, George and Louis, for their first three LPs, all of which had been big hits in the US, *Look*

Out For Number 1, Right on Time and *Blam!* All three had shown what an expert producer in the pop and funk field Quincy Jones had become after a hugely successful career in jazz and big band music but, after the international success of *Off the Wall*, the pressure was on the producer and his team to provide the goods again. Rod Temperton was again called in to contribute. Rod:

> Brothers Johnson were actually signed to Quincy and they were successful before I came in to the picture. They had done three albums together and they were getting ready to do their fourth album. And Quincy asked me to work with them. So I would go over to Louis' house and we would sit there and bash out some stuff, you know.
>
> I wrote two songs myself, the two ballads 'Treasure' and 'All About the Heaven', and then I wrote the chorus for 'Stomp!' and bits and bobs for a number of the other songs that ended up on the album. We wrote that together, 'Stomp!'. And the other songs were basically ideas they started out with and they didn't have a hook or they had bits missing. So, I kind of put it all together with them. And then we went and did the album. That was great fun, I mean Louis and George were good people, you know, great people.
>
> 'Stomp!' was a great one to be involved with. It was a great dance record and it worked very well for us. It was a good time for us. It just had a great sing-along chorus.

Yes, it did, and it peaked at No. 7 in the US, No. 6 in the UK and hit the top of the charts in New Zealand, somewhat bizarrely, a country that always really took to the Rod Temperton sound. Years later, a percussion group out of Brighton, England became a worldwide sensation, taking their name from this song. The original cast members were to play on a cover of the song many years later. Rod:

> To be honest I was working so much at this time that I didn't even know half the things that were going on. It was a very exciting time for me, as it was for Quincy. We used to go to his house for a meal at the weekends and we would be having a party on the Sunday afternoon and the two of us would jump in a taxi, as neither of us could drive a car, and go all the way down to Hollywood to be the

first people to get the copy of the *Billboard* magazine to see where we were in the charts that week and we'd be sitting in the back of the cab, the two of us, you know, reading this stuff and laughing at the craziness of it all. It was a great time.

In 1980, Quincy Jones was setting up his own label, Qwest, and the first album to come out on that label was by George Benson. George was an established jazz guitarist but was looking for a serious crossover record and by joining up with Quincy and his team he was about to get one in the form of *Give Me the Night*. Rod again provided the title track and four others, 'Turn On the Lamplight' and 'Star of a Story', both previously recorded by Heatwave, along with an instrumental, 'Off Broadway' (George had previously had a hit with a song titled 'On Broadway'), and another hit, 'Love X Love'. Read on and you will see that there was not too much love lost between the artist and the production team in spite of this album being another mammoth success story.

George Benson:

There was a question that Quincy Jones asked me when we got ready to work together. He said, 'George, do you want to make the world's greatest jazz record, or do you want to go for the throat?'

And I laughed and said, 'Quincy, go for the throat, man!'

And we both laughed like crazy and he said, 'Well, OK, I'm going to bring out my A team'. And he did.

I said, 'I want those awesome musicians you used on Michael Jackson's record.'

But he not only brought the musicians, he brought the writer. And Rod Temperton was definitely one of the giant members of that organisation that made those albums that Michael Jackson catapulted to the top of the charts. That was the team, and that was the one that Quincy brought with him for my recording, and I've got to thank him for doing that … and thank Rod for hanging in there with me and sticking in there even though I was, you know, not agreeable at first. We came up with a record that was a classic.

I met Rod Temperton at the studio with Quincy Jones. I had heard he was the mastermind behind some of Michael Jackson's hits on the first smash that he did, 'Rock with You' being one of them, and that I thought was a masterpiece of music, right on the money. Rod had all of the things a person looks for in a song, you know, a story, a good hook, both musical and lyric-wise and I just thought it was genius writing. I said, 'Man, I've got to meet this guy.' And they told me he had written some standards in the R&B field from way back. I didn't know the group that he had been with. I had heard their name but I didn't know exactly who they were. I found out a lot of those things later on.

I had heard about the group Heatwave but I could not put my finger on anything they had done. Then I found out later they had done a song, 'Boogie Nights', that I had heard a million times. So I said, 'You mean to tell me that Rod wrote that song?' I said, 'Man, he was a master a long time ago, before he was rediscovered by Quincy Jones.'

Having said that, Rod did not fit the bill. When I first met him, he did not fit what I had pictured in my mind until he started talking. I could then tell he ate, slept and drank music. He was a real music man. I had met a few people like that in my life, but he was one of those rare birds that come along and they have a clear vision and a sound in their head that is there, and they won't quit until it comes out and comes alive. Those are the best kind of people to work with in the music business.

Quincy Jones:

We wanted to do an album with the same sort of sexy songs. I respect George like no other guitar player in the world. We gave him something bigger than anything he had ever recorded. I know that he enjoyed making the record and we had a lot of fun out in the studio. George always used to tease Rod about why he didn't have three or four watches. Three watches? What are you going to do with three watches? I remember Rod and I went to Japan, I think, and we stopped in Hawaii and George invited us to dinner. Rod got six watches and he wore all six of them. It was kind of a joke there, but we had a good time.

George Benson:

I actually had to turn over the control of the songs to Rod Temperton, which I wasn't used to, because he wouldn't give up on anything. You know, he said, 'Well I know my melody, I want it to go like this.'

I said, 'OK.'

Now, that's pretty tough for an artist to do because, you know, on most of my hit records, it came from my own improvisation. I would take a melody and twist it a little bit. You know, like with 'On Broadway'. I messed with it and turned it into, you know, something else, and also with 'This Masquerade', I gave it a different twist, you know, to make it personal. But Rod didn't give me that kind of leeway. But after we heard songs back and recorded a few times, I said, 'Oh I like the direction this is going. It's got its own identity.'

But I was in the middle of it. He was making me the star. So I'm telling this incredible story, although I'm telling it in his way. He was speaking like a person who was in the audience who was listening to the song, and he was telling me how to communicate to that guy.

I think Quincy Jones appreciated that a lot about Rod because he knew what he wanted to do and he knew how to get it done. So he put him in charge and made him the musical director. I've been used to working with musical directors. I worked with some of the best, and Quincy Jones is the clean-up man. He knows exactly what to do to make this thing come alive. He knows what the musicians should be playing on this music; he will not overdo it, and yet will make a clear and an undisputed statement that is modern and musical. So I had the best team there was in the music business when we did *Give Me the Night*.

Rod was writing 'Love X Love' as we were recording it. It was originally an instrumental. And when I heard it back on the way home – I was playing the tape in the car – I said, 'Boy, this is an incredible song', and the next day I went back and Rod said, 'We are going to change something in the song'.

I said, 'Whaaat?'

And so he changed it, and it sounded even better. It was an instrumental still. Then the next day he says, 'We are going to put some lyrics on this'.

I said, 'Whaaat?'

And we started doing the lyrics and the song took on a different life completely. You know it was now a song that was universal. You didn't have to be a person who was into instrumentals and who got off on instrumentals and listening to melodies only. When you tell that clear and decisive story and you have a great melody and background and it feels good, sounds good, then you go along with it because you know you've got a winner. And the song was so differ-ent than everything else that was going on, on the radio at the time. There was a great thing that Quincy Jones did with Rod. He would tell him what he was looking for. I wanted a song that sounded like Teddy Pendergrass' 'Close the Door' and that's what I got. That's what Quincy was able to do with Rod who would always come up with a winner, being bigger than the song that he asked him to do. Rod had his hands on the pop world. He knew the common ear and that was his value and Quincy recognised it.

Quincy Jones:

Number one, having Rod around me was a comfort. It was amazing what was going on from the structure of a song to the mix. He just knew how to do it, he had it all, every bit of the song he knew what to do with.

How the title song, 'Give Me the Night', came about is not clear with each side giving a different version of events. Whichever is correct, the song itself was another international hit for Rod Temperton, reaching the Top 10 in a large number of countries while peaking at No. 4 in the USA and No. 7 in the UK. George Benson:

The most incredible thing that happened during that album was that, we were finished with the record and we thought we had something that was very decent … and I went over to hear some of the takes and Quincy said, 'George, we've got one more tune'.

I said, 'No.'

We had been working on it for three months, every day for three months, in the studio all day you know, and half of the night … and he said, 'We've got one more tune. We think it's a really great song and we think that this song belongs on this album.' And it was the title song, 'Give Me the Night'. It was so incredible, it rocked from bar one, you know!

I said, 'Now this is going to be easy.' All the musicians came in and they were all fired up because they liked the song and, again Rod made me stick to the melody. For me, it sounded kind of restricting because I used to improvise a lot more than this, you know.

But Quincy had another point of view. He used all the things that people know me for, as in the second hook in the song. There had to be a musical hook and I started doing my thing with the guitar and the vocal thing together, and some formulas that I had. Like at the beginning of 'Give Me the Night', there was a little hook, 'Bling, Bling', on the guitar, and there was a name that Quincy gave that, that I cannot remember now, but he gave it a name. He said, 'George, play that thing that you do', and he mentioned the name of it, and I said, 'Oh, I got you', and I did a little doodling with that and he picked one of them, and he put it at the front of all the bars. Then, Lee Ritenour and myself did the hook, which was Rod Temperton's counter melody. It was a great hook and I suggested that Lee and me did it together. I said to Rod, 'Don't worry; I'm going to play it in octaves. Lee's going to play one octave down, I'm going to play the octave above or vice versa.' So he let me get away with that, but it worked out fantastic and that was the right song and it deserved to be the title track. That tune rocketed to an incredible place in musical history. It had a great story. It was a party record and it had several hooks. The first one actually launched careers, the one I mentioned with the guitar, 'Bling, Bling', because it launched Luther Vandross' career. He wrote that song, 'Never Too Much', because he fell in love with that little hook.

You know, he and I became very good friends when he later explained how that inspired him to write his smash tune also.

Rod said, 'I don't remember it that way at all, but I don't know. Maybe. I was working on an Aretha Franklin song at the same time.'

Quincy:

When you hear a song like that what is there to think about? You've got to be kidding me, you know. What I love about Rod is that he did his homework so when you are in the studio you know exactly where you are. He sings the demo to get everything set up. Rod is the greatest songwriter in the world but he is not a singer and he knows it, too. We had a lot of fun with him and Bruce.

'Give Me the Night' was serious. It was a mix, a mixture of great musicianship and with Patti Austin's vocals. It was a very unique concept during that period.

That song was right in front, that's Herbie Hancock on that session and he played a big role in it. He wrote some lyrics as did George and the song caught right into the personalities of all. There were multiple personalities on that record. That's what makes a great record, you know, when you have a lot of room to let those multiple personalities really be heard and not have somebody else on some rigid or epic plan, if you know what I mean.

The LP won three Grammy Awards in 1981 and reached No. 3 in the Billboard charts. It also brought attention to Patti Austin's acrobatic vocals which were tested by Rod Temperton's arrangements. Patti said:

Rod would sing the part to me, I would sing it back and then we would keep stacking until we finished. That was it. With Rod and Quincy, it was always very silly, a lot of fun in the studio. There were about ten minutes of singing and about two hours of joking around. 'Give Me the Night' was a challenge, however, but that was always fun. It was always fun working with Rod because you knew that whatever he gave you was going to be really difficult and complicated and challenging and that was what I loved, that's where I live, baby!

Now, how unusual was this in pop and R&B music? Well, it was perhaps generally unusual but there were other groups that used very tight harmonies and very unique kinds of backgrounds. A lot of that was going on then, they didn't use the same kinds of backgrounds that Rod did, but they had their own way of interpreting very intricate kinds of backgrounds. I think the background vocals in those days were possibly the most complicated of the backgrounds that I've sung through the years through different musical styles. But I don't think that Rod was always specifically trying to be R&B or pop orientated in the backgrounds that he came up with. He was just coming up with the backgrounds that worked with the foreground. Rod was less about trying to be pop and/or R&B and more about trying to be musical whatever that meant to the music you were doing backgrounds on.

Contrary to popular belief, having worked with Rod does not let you know anything about what makes a typical Rod song because there is no such thing as a typical Rod song. I could sing you a bunch of Rod songs and you would see how untypical they are, they don't resemble each other in many ways, they are all very individual and I think it is probably because he usually, as far I can recall, although he told me he works both ways, sometimes he will do the lyric first and then the music, and sometimes the music and then the lyrics. So everything is kind of tailored, so it's very, very individual, not at all typical or atypical.

George Benson:

We had the great singer Patti Austin in the studio waiting in the wings for Rod to give her something to do. And every time he said, 'Patti, try this', she would come up with an expert delivery. She never got in my way and actually enhanced everything I was doing and so I was never worried about anything. With Quincy Jones producing it and Bruce Swedien engineering, forget about it. I asked Quincy, I said, 'Quincy, are you worried about this record?'

He said, 'Yes, I want to make multi-platinum records, man. I can't afford to miss.'

I said, 'How are you going to miss, man? You've got me as an artist. You're Quincy Jones, we've got Bruce Swedien and Rod Temperton. How are we going to miss?'

The great thing that Quincy Jones used to do was so funny to us. We would work on the song and we would have enough of it together where you could get the gist of the song, the rhythms were always fantastic because he had a great rhythm section. He would give the tape of that day's work to his manager and say, 'Now don't, whatever you do, don't take this down to Spats and play it tonight'. Which means, 'Take it down to Spats and play it and let me know what happened'. His manager would say, 'OK, I got you.'

And he would come back the next day and say, 'A smash!' Because he would play it unannounced. They would play it in a club, a packed house, packed with people ... and they were all dancing ... and he would stick that song in the middle of all of that and if it worked in that context, the chances were good that it was going to be a hit. With 'Give Me the Night', he came back in the next day with a great report. He said, 'Man, they loved it. And they kept asking, man who is that? What record is that?'

And that all came from Rod's songwriting. He was a very quiet man during the sessions because he was always thinking. But when he made statements they were significant ones, and then he let me do my thing. He was actually a Benson fan, I could tell he liked my work, you know.

He didn't let me take over because, after all, that was his job to do the writing and to give us material that had the opportunity to go to the top of the charts. And he fulfilled his part of the job incredibly well with songs that were so different. You know, they are still classics in their own right. In my shows they are definitely the songs that are most identifiable, 'Give Me the Night' and 'Love X Love'. But there are some other things on that album too, the instrumental 'Off Broadway' that he wrote, which I thought was fantastic. It just came off the top of his head. He said, 'George, I've got this thing here, man. Bom, beee, do, do, de, do, ba, da, da, da, daaa, da, do, daa, do, do, do.'

I said to myself, 'I don't know about this one, Rod.' But, as it came together, I began to hear a little rock ... and that's something I don't do a lot of. But this song had a nice rock feel to it. So I tried to keep it simple and let the melody shine, and it did. The melody stood out, which is typical of Rod's tunes. They have unforgettable melodies.

I would have liked Rod to produce an album on me, but at the time he was working very closely with Quincy. So we never got an opportunity to do that, but that would have been a great scenario to have him produce a record on us. I know it would have been something spectacular, but he made money so fast he just disappeared into the clouds somewhere, you know. I heard he bought an island somewhere. He was certainly rich enough! He deserved all of his success. People have only ever had good things to say about him. I've really not heard anything bad about Rod Temperton, ever.

In fact, the pair did end up working together on the LP *Songs and Stories*, released in 2009. As already mentioned, aside from the hits produced for this album by Rod, George did a cover version of 'Star of a Story', the song so loved by so many, including the writer himself. Original singer of the song, Johnnie Wilder:

> Because I love George Benson, especially as a guitarist, I think he did a wonderful job on that song. I don't compare the two. I think what Rod did originally was astonishing. I would like to see somebody else cover that song and see, just to hear what their rendition of it would be, but I think when Rod wrote songs initially, not too many people covered them the way we did. But that's not to say that their versions aren't good, but I just think there was a magic to the time when he first penned them, I mean, those original ideas that came out.
>
> George had his own interpretation. I think he did a good job.

George Benson:

> We put it back in our show and we were shocked at the response we got for that tune. It's another one of those tunes that he does, you know when he puts it together and it's memorable and you can do them anytime and get the same good feeling you had when you first heard them. To have a repertoire full of Rod Temperton songs is nothing short of a winner. He has given longevity to my career and I have to thank him a lot for that. If, in your lifetime, you are fortunate enough to work with a man like Rod Temperton, and there are not that many, it's going to be an experience that will last a lifetime and it will be something that you gladly would like to do again.

Quincy Jones did work again with George Benson a few later on Frank Sinatra's 'LA is My Lady':

We had every great musician in the world on that session, but George said I just had him on there because of his name. Give me a break, man, give me a break. It was Frank Sinatra, you know. I mean, that doesn't make sense to me. It really doesn't, you know. That is a misinterpretation and I hope one day that George and I, if he ever talks to me, will sit down and work it out. But I was shocked. I would never hire anybody just because of his or her name. I mean, it's insane; he's got to play first.

George is one of the greatest guitar players that ever lived. 'Give Me the Night' was bigger than anything he ever recorded and that's great, you know. He won four Grammys and that is why I could not understand what the problem was. It was like we had done something wrong. What I do know is that because neither Rod nor me drove a car we had to pimp a ride every now and then with George. We did have a lot of fun in the studio, though.

Rod Temperton, along with his team of producer, Quincy Jones, and engineer, Bruce Swedien, were now extremely hot property. The man from Cleethorpes was living a life beyond anyone's dream by now. While working with the jazz legend George Benson, he also spent a short time with the Queen of Soul, Aretha Franklin, writing the infectiously catchy, 'Living in the Streets'. Rod:

I was lucky enough to write something for Aretha. I was working with Quincy on the Benson album, when Arif Mardin was doing Aretha's album and he asked me to do something so I went and met with him and played him a couple of things and he chose this song and I went in … and I guess I cut the rhythm section, but I actually have to be honest and say, I wasn't there when Aretha sang it. She came in at some point and sang it, that was great, but you know, I was actually working elsewhere at the time.

It was an OK song. I mean, again, I wish I could have given it more attention. I usually only ever do one thing at once. And I think, when I can't give it my full attention something suffers, you know, in the writing, and I don't like to do that to people. But, you know, Arif was a good friend of Quincy's and he's a great producer and I just wanted to help him out, you know, so I had a go at it, but it was not one of my favourite pieces.

In the same year (1981), Rod also worked on another project away from Quincy and his super-talented team, providing three songs, largely instrumental pieces for jazz pianist, Bob James, the LP entitled *Sign of the Times*. It was a project the now prolific songwriter enjoyed as he didn't have to think long and hard about vocals and how to fit them into his songs, 'Hypnotique', 'The Steamin' Feeling' and 'Sign of the Times', a song famously sampled by Warren G and De La Soul.

Bob James was famous for writing the theme tune to the TV show *Taxi*. He had met Quincy Jones in the early 1960s and worked as an arranger and as a piano accompanist for jazz singer Sarah Vaughn. He was then hired to work as an arranger, producer and studio musician for Creed Taylor's CTI Records. Bob recorded three solo albums for CTI before founding his own label, Tappan Zee. *Sign of the Times* was Bob's fourteenth solo project. He takes up the story, speaking to me exclusively for this book:

> I met Rod through Quincy Jones who was my friend. Quincy had been telling me all about Rod and how he liked my music. At that time I was looking for ideas to take my music in different and new directions so I contacted Rod and we just started up a conversation. He was very interested in my interest in classical music and in my interest in crossing over, incorporating classical music into my jazz stuff. One thing led to another and before I knew it, he had agreed to help me out on that project and contributed original compositions and helped me out in a co-production role.
>
> Rod had a very, very unique way of working which was completely different from the way I had previously worked and that's one of the things I loved about him. In one respect, you could call it a kind of seat-in-the-pants approach as a composer/creator. He would work for his own passion and in his own style which was just different from everybody else. He didn't come in with conventional written up music arrangements; he didn't work that way at all. He had a way of notating things on regular paper with the names of the notes in the order that he wanted them. He did the choral arrangements and wrote really interesting harmonies but he did it in a Rod Temperton way and therefore, a unique way.
>
> I was aware of his success with Heatwave and Michael Jackson at this point and so I was flattered that he wanted to work with me.

I think there was a question of both of us working together and collaborating, of us not necessarily being a stereotype of what one would expect of each other. We were both white but here we were doing R&B based or R&B influenced music. I had never met anyone liked Rod before and it was really interesting getting to know him face to face and working with him in the studio. It didn't register with me at the time that that style would have been appropriate for working with Michael Jackson.

I think he had a lot of the stuff he wrote programmed in his head. I loved Rod as a person, he had a wonderful sense of humour and we hit it off immediately in that respect so a lot of the creative process was about us just agreeing and talking about other music and what we liked. Because he worked in such a different way than I was used to it was very inspiring, very fresh and made me want to do my best to live up to the fact that he wanted to work with me.

I was a very conventional arranger of music. I worked with orchestras. I didn't always come into the studio with my arrangements prepared in advance because I also very often recorded the rhythm section first, the basic jazz aspect of it and the production of the vocals and strings were added after the fact. But, when I would do that kind of production I was working from conventional notation. The thing I found most fascinating about Rod was how he achieved the results that he did and getting the music to come out of his head and on to tape – and yes, in that era it was tape. It was before the digital era.

What I remember was how his mind worked and how he layered things. The most specific thing regarding that was how he worked with vocals. We were very fortunate that we had all the best New York studio singers working with us like Patti Austin and Luther Vandross. I had been working with them before with them usually coming in with conventionally notated chord arrangements. But the way Rod worked was to sing it to them in his unique kind of Rod Temperton style. He had scribbled on a piece of paper the harmonies instead of having the usual music manuscript paper. He would just call out the notes – G, E-Flat, E, G – he would just call them out that way.

Uniquely, at least for me, was that he wanted to record a four-part harmony chord arrangement from the bottom up with the lowest harmony first all the way through. He would have all the singers sing that part and then layer it, then multi-tracking it, doubling or tripling the tracks. Then he would move up to the next harmony note and then to the next harmony note, having them sing the line all the way through. Then the last part he would put on would be the upper, melodic line that would finish the part off. He wanted the singers to be able to hear the harmony first and to have all the harmony parts sung in a melodic and unique kind of way so by the time they got to know what the harmony was they had already layered all these parts and adding melody to it gave it a finishing touch.

Everybody loved it; they were blown away by it and went, 'Wow!' Rod knew exactly what he wanted but it didn't get revealed to everyone in the studio until that very last part was put on. I just thought that was a great way of working because most artists at the time did it the opposite way, we would put the melody track on first and then add the harmony notes underneath. It was quite an experience to watch Rod at work.

He was aware that I was not an R&B singer, I was a piano player and most of my songs were instrumentals. So, he came up with some kind of jazzy vocal syllables which weren't really words. He did a wonderful African chant piece – 'lagadda, jagadda' – which he invented for 'The Steamin' Feeling'. I think in his head, he was hearing voices as an instrumental track. He was quite incredible, really.

Working with Rod was the closest I got to having a shot in the super pop world. There were other reasons why his songs for Michael Jackson sold in their millions and millions and millions while mine didn't, because of Michael's magic as well as Rod's. For me, it was just a great experience working with Rod. I got to see inside the pop world and I believe that for both of us, it was just fun, almost like an extra-curricular project. I just enjoyed the whole process of working with him and getting to know Rod as a person. I still thought of Rod for a long time after working with him as a man from a completely different musical world – at least from the environment I was in – and I respected it and was thrilled with it – no pun intended.

Rod:

> Oh, that was really good fun, working with Bob on *Sign of the Times*.
> We had once talked of him being Heatwave's producer. We got on
> great. I didn't have to write any lyrics, not many anyway. I mean,
> I wish I could always write instrumentals. 'Off Broadway' for George
> Benson was the first instrumental I had on a record, so yeah, that was
> a lot of fun. I mean, I went on to do other mostly instrumental pieces
> with Bob James who was great fun to work with.

Rod also wrote one song, 'Macumba', on James' follow-up album, *Hands
Down*. Bob James:

> It was not unusual at that time to have an extra track which didn't
> make an album and I think that was one which was left over from
> the *Sign of the Times* sessions. It's funny how you forget these things,
> isn't it? The great thing was that we kept in touch over the years, not
> as much as I would have liked though. Whenever I came to London
> he would come over and hear my band and say hello and I am very
> grateful for that.

In the meantime, there was some more chart success in the UK with
Heatwave. Their fourth LP, *Candles*, included six more Rod songs with
'Gangsters of the Groove' and 'Jitterbuggin'' both hitting the Top 40.
Johnnie Wilder co-produced this time:

> It had become a little different for Rod by this stage. He was play-
> ing less and less on the records himself and working with people
> like George Benson, Greg Phillinganes and also artists like George
> Duke, Herbie Hancock and Paulinho Da Costa, legends of music,
> really. These were masters, great players and Rod was now working
> with musicians of that calibre on a daily basis. I would guess that it was
> an experience like no other that would only give you a chance to do
> more as a writer and let musicians like that knock licks out of what you
> have in your head and just enhance them a little more. He still wrote
> some wonderful songs for us like 'Posin' 'Til Closin'' but after my
> accident I never performed as well as I could have or had done before.

After missing out on the orchestral arrangement for *Hot Property*, John Cameron also returned to work on *Candles*, the album this time being put together in Los Angeles:

> Yes, I was roped into doing the fourth Heatwave LP and it was great. By now, I was doing movie scores and so the call came out of the blue. We did it out in LA with Jerry Hey and his brass section which was really nice. He did half of it and I did the other half, including 'Gangsters of the Groove'. Rod was not about as much as he had been for *Too Hot to Handle* and *Central Heating*, however. In fact, I didn't see much of him at all. By that time, Quincy had kidnapped him so he just phoned in the numbers down the line, you know.
>
> On the first two albums he was in the studio all of the time but on the fourth one I don't remember seeing him nearly as much. I used to run into Rod from time to time at dos and studio parties, that kind of thing, and he always seemed to be talking about how many days he could stay in the UK. Somehow or other, he had been thrown into this tax exile thing and he was always planning when he could get back to England to see his mum.
>
> The nice thing was, out in LA doing *Candles*, I'd got to know a lot of the technicians and musicians and the film guys over in the States so I felt quite at home there. The funny thing was, when we were cutting the album, doing the strings and reeds, we had a couple of English guys on the session, Rob Everett, who had moved out to the States about a year and a half before and had acquired a real Valley accent, and the other was Vic Feldman, the percussionist, who had been in LA for forty-odd years but had not lost his Jewish East London accent. Rod was the same. Always very English and proud to be so.

The records just kept on coming, a relentless work ethic paying dividends by now. The year 1981 also saw the release of Patti Austin's solo effort, *Every Home Should Have One*, again produced by Quincy Jones. Rod penned the songs 'Do You Love Me?', 'Love Me to Death', 'The Genie' and the US No. 1 ballad 'Baby, Come to Me' with James Ingram. When first released in the spring of 1982, it had minor chart success before being used as the romantic theme song for Luke Spencer, a leading character on the ABC soap opera *General Hospital*. So, 'Baby, Come to Me' was re-released in the autumn and hit the top of the US charts.

Patti Austin:

Rod altered my career by writing me a No. 1 record. And then he didn't do it again! That's very depressing! Yes, I'm kidding, just kidding. Yes, he wrote that song and I had a little to do with it as did Quincy and James Ingram. Everything we did with Rod was a collaborative effort and I think one of the things that makes him a genius is that he was able to bring the best out in everybody, as did Quincy. When the two of them were working in the studio together, it makes for a damn good record. And 'Baby, Come to Me' was a damn good record.

I don't ever remember a time when Rod wasn't in my life. I feel as though Rod has been in my life since birth and I guess he has in spirit and then physically he came into my life. I cannot remember the first impression of him because, all kidding aside, I really don't remember not knowing Rod. He's always been in my life in some kind of way, musically. He had the kind of demeanour that's very kind of laid back and not in your face, so I really don't have a pro-found memory of Rod leaping out from behind a door and saying, 'Hey, how you doing?' That's not a Rod Temperton kind of vibe.

He helped do a great solo album for me. I love 'The Genie' because he wrote it for me and its particularly silly, the lyric is very goofy and it's about my sense of humour, so I absolutely love that song. And I love 'Somethin' Special', which nobody knows, but me and Quincy and Rod and a handful of other people. It is such a great song and people ask for it at my shows actually. 'Somethin' Special' is one of the gazillion Rod Temperton tunes I love.

That tune appeared on Quincy Jones' *The Dude* LP and, again, Rod played a huge part of that success, writing four more songs, 'The Dude', 'Razzamatazz', which also featured Patti Austin on vocals, 'Turn On the Action' and the aforementioned, 'Somethin' Special'.

John Cameron:

Once Rod had started to work with Patti Austin and had his suc-cess with Michael Jackson, you just knew that he had slotted into the machine so well. I have to take my hat off to him. He just went out there to LA and found his niche. I had been a fan of Quincy's stuff for a long time. *In the Heat of the Night* is still one of my favourite film scores. And I love what he did with *The Wiz*, which, of course, then led to Quincy making *Off the Wall* for Michael and bringing in Rod. As a movie composer, Quincy was someone I really looked up to and admired. It was a shock when I heard that Rod was working with him but a great one and he deserved everything he got in terms of his success. Rod probably needed to work with Quincy for him to go that extra mile. Had he stayed within the confines of the British funk scene, he would have been successful, for sure, he was too good of a writer not to be, but he really needed to go out to America and push himself that little bit further which, of course, he did.

Away from Quincy, Rod also went into the studio with Herbie Hancock who he was now used to working with on Quincy sessions. The two had worked especially closely together on George Benson's *Give Me the Night* and Quincy's *The Dude*. It was a project far removed from the jazz that made Herbie his name in the music business. Rod wrote all but two of the songs on the ill-fated LP and told me that the only ones he was really happy with were the two in which Herbie had much of the song done first, 'Gettin' to the Good Part' and 'Give it All Your Heart'. To my ears, this was always a really fun album to listen to with good up-tempo tunes, but missing the touch of Quincy Jones and Bruce Swedien behind the desk. Had they been involved in this project then it may have been a much larger success.

Herbie was already a legend in the music business, starting his career with Donald Byrd before joining the Miles Davis Quintet. His own compositions such as 'Cantaloupe Island', 'Watermelon Man', 'Maiden Voyage', 'Chameleon' and 'I Thought it was You' had been huge successes. From 1978 through to 1982 Herbie dabbled with the world of jazz-inflected disco and pop music, the last of these albums being the one he worked on with Rod, *Lite Me Up*, before he ventured into jazz hip hop with the enormously successful 'Rockit' and then the remarkable Oscar-winning *Round Midnight*.

Herbie Hancock was another to speak exclusively for this book:

I'd met Rod in conjunction with working with Quincy Jones as a session musician on *Off the Wall* for Michael Jackson. I had never heard of his group Heatwave, as I wasn't really into the music of that time. You have to remember that the Baby Boomers were born in 1945 and I was born in 1940 so by the time rock and roll came around I was already in my twenties. At that time in the mid 1970s, I had a kind of tunnel vision about jazz and classical music. That meant that I didn't follow the whole pop scene the way most people did. So, I didn't know about Rod's band and only heard about him when he did the songs for *Off the Wall* and Quincy brought me in to play on them. I knew instantly that they were classics. Those songs really launched the career of one of the most talented and gifted artists of many generations in Michael Jackson.

I hung out with Quincy and Rod during those sessions and I soon realised that Rod was a great guy, one who knew more about me than I knew about him. He knew a lot about my music even though I only really knew him through the music he wrote for *Off the Wall* at that time. I found out from Rod that he had a great respect for me and what I had done in my career and I loved what he had achieved for Michael. So, at some point, I asked him if he would produce my next record with me and I was expecting him in some gracious way to say no. But, instead, he said he would be delighted to and so, to be honest, I said, 'Yeaaaah!' I was thrilled. And then we soon started working on what became *Lite Me Up*.

Rod was such a sweetheart, so unassuming, just a regular guy. He never paraded anything in front of anybody, never talking about his accomplishments. He would never say, 'Look what I did', or anything like that. He just wasn't that kind of guy, you know. I met his wife at that time, too, and she was also such a sweetheart, a wonderful woman. They were a wonderful couple actually.

Making *Lite Me Up* was great fun. Rod was great; he was really great to work with. He never said no to anything that I asked, he made wonderful suggestions for the songs and he never demanded anything of me. He really tried to help me realise and clarify the vision that I had for that particular record. Rod walked that tightrope that I have often walked between the artistry that I developed through jazz and my early beginnings through classical music and the pop culture of that time.

Rod never just walked into the studio with nothing and started to put it together there. We worked on the album for several hours in the studio every day once we got started. He would go home and probably have a little sleep and then come back the next day, always on time, and have not just one but several melodies that were worked out with the chord structure and we would then both kind of shape it. Rod was the one who did the primary shaping for most of those tunes. If he had a suggestion, he would voice it. This was the case on all the stuff I did with him and Quincy. The reason they wanted me in the studio was because they wanted me. If they wanted someone other than me, they would have got someone other than me! They wanted to hear my take on whatever the suggestion would be for any particular tune. I obviously offered something they were looking for.

Rod Temperton:

There is something wonderful about having been able to create something from scratch, from ground up, and hear it played back once it is completed. That's where I get my smiles. People say to me, 'Isn't it great to hear your music on the radio or in the store?'

Frankly, by the time you hear it on the radio, you are sick to death of it. The big moment in music for me is when I finish it for the first time and say, 'Oh, that's what I wrote'. Then, you know, that's what it is and that's really a great time. When it comes completely through you, then it's a bigger deal.

There are some times you are just inspired by something, you know. I remember Herbie Hancock, we were going to write something together and we just sat down and played a few chords and then let me see if I could come out with some melody. He played this chord sequence and I was going, 'Wow!' and I got out a little cassette recorder and I was thinking, 'I don't even need this. Here's a melody and you are telling me what the melody is just by playing those chords.' So that was just as magical really as creating it, well, I mean, we were creating it from scratch the two of us, but when, you know, when you are brought in at a song which is really already on its path, you know, the sound of it, the whole thing is created. It's somebody else's creation and I don't want to step on their toes but, if I'm being asked to help, then I'm going to consult with them all the time and say, 'Is that the kind of thing you want? Is that the kind of thing you mean?' I can only presume that they feel the same way about their music as I do about mine. I'm just trying to be helpful, that's all.

Herbie Hancock:

I was very happy with the way things turned out on that record although it didn't do anything! It just didn't seem to resonate with anybody at the time which surprised me because these were Rod Temperton tunes, man! He had just made hit after hit after hit but these were ones that did nothing. But I wasn't disappointed in anything that he did on that record. He really tried to help me as best he could. And, as far as I remember, he was happy with what we did, too. The end point isn't to sell a record, the end point is when you finish the record and say, 'I want to put this out'.

The songs on that LP were different than anything else, I think. There was nothing going on in that basic direction at that time. A lot of it sounds kind of old fashioned now because it was made quite some time ago. But it was a product of that time, verging my main interests which were jazz and dance music, a disco-ish kind of thing which I did on a couple of records such as *Lite Me Up* and another called *Feets Don't Fail Me Now* that Rod wasn't involved with.

Back in England and Barry Blue returned as producer for Heatwave's fifth album in 1982, *Current*. Rod again penned five songs with only 'Lettin' it Loose' getting much airplay. But, with Quincy and Bruce by his side, the hits kept coming for other artists, and the next to taste the Temperton magic was disco diva Donna Summer, who had just left Casablanca Records after a string of huge hits such as 'Love to Love You Baby', 'I Feel Love', 'Last Dance', 'MacArthur Park', 'Heaven Knows', 'Hot Stuff', 'Bad Girls' and 'On the Radio', songs which gave her the title of the Queen of Disco. Quincy Jones said, 'We were coming through the disco period, you know, and I mean, when you have been around this, I have been in this business sixty years, you see all the changes. We had a tough job, though, with Donna.'

Rod:

I believe David Geffen approached Quincy. David had got Donna signed at that point and they approached Quincy to do an album and, you know, Quincy agreed and I got involved and came up with 'Love is in Control (Finger on the Trigger)' and 'Living in America' and there was another one, something about … oh, yes, 'Love is Just a Breath Away'.

Those last two songs were actually pieces of music that were written by David Foster and the musicians had written the piece and they didn't have lyrics and so they asked me to do the lyrics. I did the lyrics for 'Living in America' and 'Love is Just a Breath Away'. 'Finger on the Trigger' was my biggest involvement on the record. It was another smash, too. So, that was fun but I think at that time, I was actually working with Stephanie Mills as well, on 'Time of Your Life' and 'Hold on to Midnight'. I was doing that on my own. So I was kind of in and out with Quincy for that Donna Summer album.

Not everybody was happy with the final result, however. The singer herself told the *Los Angeles Times*, 'Sometimes, I felt it was a Quincy Jones album that I sang on'. It was reported at the time that Donna Summer found Quincy Jones to be rather boisterous and controlling. The album took six months to complete, as Donna was pregnant at the time. However, the pair worked well enough for 'Love is in Control' to earn Donna Summer a Grammy nomination for Best Female R&B Vocal Performance.

'Love is in Control (Finger on the Trigger)' was another massive international hit, making it to No. 10 in the US and No. 18 in the UK. Rod had struck gold again. Since 'Boogie Nights' had reached No. 2 on both sides of the Atlantic, Rod had penned two US No. 1s with 'Rock with You' and 'Baby, Come to Me' and five other Top 10 hits. In the UK, thirteen songs written by Rod had made it into the Top 20.

That would have been enough for most people, but it was just the hors d'oeuvre. The main course was about to be served as Rod and Quincy Jones prepared themselves for the next Michael Jackson album, the follow-up to the 20 million seller, *Off the Wall*. What they produced next was to change the history of music forever.

8

THRILLER

Thriller, by Michael Jackson, is the best-selling album of all time. It became the first LP to be certified 32 x platinum, with estimated sales worldwide at an incredible 70 million. In fact, it has sold so many copies that it would appear that no one really knows just how many people across the world have a copy on vinyl, CD or as a download. It still sells plenty right to this day.

The LP won a record-breaking eight Grammy Awards. Thanks to Jackson, it changed choreography and dancing and thanks to a single vision from Rod Temperton and the theatrical skills of the Conger, it helped change how music videos were made right up until this day. This chapter tells the story of how the album was made and why it became the monster it did. Rod wrote three songs of the nine on the long player, including the title track, but unlike *Off the Wall,* the previous Jackson album, Rod's influence was far more than just penning these three tracks. He was effectively Quincy Jones' right-hand man throughout the production and was involved from the concept through to the finished mix. Thus, in this chapter, I will look in more depth at how the record came about, and why its impact was so far-reaching. A number of these quotations come from interviews that myself and fellow producer, Neil Cowling, did for a follow-up to our Rod Temperton documentary for the BBC called *Thriller: Michael Jackson's Masterpiece,* produced by Fresh Air Production.

First, let's go back to the time between *Off the Wall* and *Thriller.* As we know, Quincy Jones and Rod Temperton had had a string of international hits and were now the go-to team if success on the pop charts was the aim, even if the work with Donna Summer had failed to fully reignite her stalling career. Jackson, meanwhile, had been struggling a little since *Off the Wall* had been such a massive success in its own right. He is quoted as saying:

> Even at home, I'm lonely. I sit in my room sometimes and cry. It's so hard to make friends … I sometimes walk around the neighbourhood at night, just hoping to find someone to talk to. But I just end up coming home.

In spite of comments like this, Jackson wanted to be the biggest star in show business. He said of *Off the Wall*, 'It was totally unfair that it didn't get Record of the Year and it can never happen again'. Bruce Swedien:

> At that time, young people were only interested in video games, and I remember this like it was yesterday, we all walked in to the studio ready to begin production on *Thriller*, Quincy first then Michael then me and Rod. Quincy turned to us and said, 'OK guys, we are here to get the kids out of the video arcades and back into the record stores'.

Quincy Jones:

> Nobody ever knows, when they start a project, whether it will do well or not. If they do, or they say they do, they are lying. I don't think you should think like that, just let God or somebody else decide that and just do the best you can, give up everything you've got and if you get a few goose bumps, you know, that's the spread.
>
> It was insane because I had met Steven Spielberg when he was doing *E. T.* at Universal Studio and we were just starting doing *Thriller* at Westlake Studios. We met up at a restaurant, and I used to go to his shooting sessions and he had smoke all over the place and we could barely breathe and everything else. 'You come over to our studios and you will see us doing the recording thing,' he said. 'Let's try to show each other what our world is like.' and we literally did that. He gave me a director's chair and I gave him a synthesiser.
>
> We became very close and he said he wanted me to do a song with Michael for the *E. T.* album, not a soundtrack LP but a narra-

tive really, because, you know, it is a two-hour film and he wanted to take the two-hour version of the visual experience of the biggest film probably in the history of cinema and bring it down to a forty-minute oral version, you know, that has a narration in it, that explains it to people, what the story is about, whether they have seen the film or not.

We had started on *Thriller*. We had recorded Paul McCartney and Michael with 'The Girl is Mine' before because I was in the middle of doing the Donna Summer album and Paul was in Tucson and Steven says, 'Oh I would love for you to do a song with Michael for the *E. T.* album'.

I replied, 'That's major art you know, but OK let's do a song first for it', and so I called up Alan and Marilyn Bergman who had written the music and lyrics for many celebrated films and TV shows and they wrote 'Someone in the Dark' with Rod, and Michael came in and sang it. Steven loved it. He said, 'Great. Why don't you guys do the whole album?'

I said, 'Steven, we've gotten into trouble because the first single record with Paul and Michael is out and they are now expecting Michael's album. We've got to deliver this record that maybe even will catch up with *Off the Wall*.'

Many times, I have worked at three studious simultaneously with all kind of things going on, but this was just too much, you know.

The president and CEO of CBS Records, who Jackson was signed to, was Walter Yetnikoff:

I remember, I think I was sort of disturbed by it. I think I was a little disturbed by the fact that Michael was sort of blowing his exclusivity by doing that, but it's pretty hard to argue with Steven Spielberg and Quincy Jones. I mean, I don't mind giving it a shot but yeah, together they sort of had a pool of talent as well as a pool of money. You are talking about the hottest movie producer/director at the time and you are talking about certainly one of the hottest music producers at the time. So, I don't recall how violent I got but it was an argument that these people had too much clout for me to win. Did they pay us much money? Shit, I should have asked for a million.

I asked for half a million and they paid it so quickly so I obviously undersold, I should have asked for a million!

I had signed the Jacksons as a group and Michael wasn't too happy with how they were doing since leaving Motown and so he came to see me. He was like an 18-year-old kid at the time. He got Quincy to produce *Off the Wall* and it was a huge success. It had a lot of smashes on it and then it became pretty apparent to everyone that we had a talent beyond the Jacksons, we had Michael as a solo artist, stepping out. Just a few years before I wasn't sure I wanted to sign the Jacksons because Michael was having a hit, singing about a dead rat which was called Ben. I was saying that I didn't know if I wanted to pay all this money to a guy that sings about dead rats. It was a good thing that I didn't listen to myself.

Rod Temperton:

The album that became *Thriller* was a much tougher record to make than *Off the Wall*. We had done a few albums in between the two Michael Jackson ones and we had a team, I mean Quincy and Bruce and myself. I was still living in Germany and Quincy called and said, 'OK, it's time to do Michael Jackson's next record, so start coming up with some ideas'.

So I wrote probably about thirty-five or forty ideas, Polaroids, for songs that I then would come over and sit with Quincy and we would talk about the ideas and how they would work, and we went through everything. Quincy picked five tunes, I think, and said, 'Let's go to Michael's house and record some demos'. There were no words or anything, I just had some ghost words, you know.

So we went over to Michael's house and then did the demos with Michael putting some voice on them, just to get the feel of how it all sounded. And from that we picked three of my songs to actually record, and that was along with everything else that Michael had done by himself. He'd got a demo for 'Billie Jean' and the song with Paul McCartney. They had already recorded that one before I got there.

And so we went in the studio in April of that year, 1982, and we started to make this record. And of course Michael was really positive, you know. He said, 'I wanna do a hundred million', and we responded, 'Michael, calm down a bit. We'll be happy if we just have another hit.' But Michael was very positive. He was convinced that this was going to be bigger and better than *Off the Wall*. So, the pressure was really starting to build up and then, I think also, the record company was getting quite pressurised, too, and so, you know, we went through this whole process over the next few months, putting our hearts and souls into the record.

Quincy Jones:

We knew that when you make a record you have a concept from everything else but you have to leave room for everybody. That's the secret of it because there are other kinds of producers – I won't get into names and so forth – who are giving but it is still very rigid. They've got a focal point and a focus on just the one concept.

But I liked what the musicians brought to the record. I liked what Greg Phillinganes brought to the record; I like what Louis Johnson brought to the record, same with John Robinson, Jerry Hey and Steve Lukather. We worked as a team. Give me a break; we had everyone on that record. It was like a team, like a family. If there is anything stronger or more inspirational and rewarding and fulfilling than creativity then it is collective creativity and we had a lot of experience at many different levels on those songs on *Thriller*. We had all of that heavy energy together and so, here we were with all this talent in the studio along with Bruce and Rod.

Guitarist, Steve Lukather:

I came up with some cool parts on the *Thriller* LP and Quincy actually gave me an arranging credit on the record. Quincy was very gracious with credits as far as things like that go. He took a like to me and I did a lot of his records for a while during that era.

We did *The Dude* which was a great record. As a matter of fact I sang the original vocal on 'Ai No Corrida', which was the opening track. And I didn't feel comfortable doing it. I said, 'Q, man, I really think you should get somebody else to do this', but because Quincy dug my voice on the Toto records, he said, 'I think Steve will be great for this one', but I ended up playing on the whole record and that was Record of the Year, the album of the year, then the next year it was *Toto IV* that was the album of the year and the year after that it was *Thriller*. So, I was on the album of the year three years in a row in one permutation or another.

I was working with Greg Phillinganes and we always had our hands on everything everywhere. We were kind of, like, looming in those days, like recording studios had three or four rooms, so there would be three or four different sessions with different cats playing in different rooms and oftentimes, you know, we would switch up. We were like, 'Oh, man, come over here and play on this', and then some bruiser would grab somebody from the other room and it would end up with all of us sitting in the courtyard somewhere shooting the shit, having a sandwich during the break and just playing basketball and just shooting the shit. We just played on anything we were asked to. It was great fun, being part of it.

Keyboard player, Greg Phillinganes:

I'm from Detroit and a dear friend of mine who is a drummer was asked to audition for Stevie Wonder in New York and the night before he left I went to his house and you know, we celebrated and I was there just to support him, I was very happy for him obviously, but he insisted that I play some things on a cassette. And I was quite taken by that, so I did and he took the cassette and some days later I got a call from him early in the morning saying that Stevie Wonder wanted to see me in New York that day. And so I go there and it was my first time in New York, so literally I said, 'New York, just like I pictured it, skyscrapers and everything!'

And I go there and I get settled and I go to the Hit Factory Studio and I'm sitting there waiting and all of a sudden the elevator door opens up and there he is … the man that I idolised, I had all his records, his posters on my wall and everything. I told my friends in high school that I was going to eventually play with him. I'd never met him. So there he is, and we meet and we talk and we play a little bit. It was one of the greatest thrills in my entire life. And the next day I met the rest of the band, Wonderlove, and that was more like the formal audition. Later that night on the way back to the studio in the car, Stevie asked me, he says, 'How does it feel to be a member of Wonderlove?' And I just froze you know, because I heard so many things about him, I heard he was a practical joker, so I asked him if he was serious, and he said, 'Of course I am'.

I said, 'Well, would you mind telling my mother?'

So we get back to the studio and I pick up the phone and I call my mom and the first voice she hears is Stevie's. And he says, 'Hi Mrs Phillinganes, this is Stevie Wonder and I just want you to know that I really like your son, I think he's talented. I would like to have him in my band and I promise I will take care of him', all that kind of stuff, you know. So he then gives me the phone and for the next ten minutes this is what you hear [screams]. Needless to say I was a little excited. So I went back home and got the rest of my stuff and that was it.

And from there, I started doing a lot of session work and a lot in LA with Quincy. Any session with Quincy Jones was fun because you know you're going to eat good food because you know Quincy likes to eat. And he likes to eat good food so whatever he had, we would have the same quality of a meal, so that was always fun.

We had a lot of laughs, and we had interesting characters. Rod Temperton, who wrote a lot of the songs, was a great guy who knew exactly what he was doing. We knew him well by now, having worked on many sessions with him. He and Quincy just knew each other so well that they almost gelled together yet they were totally different characters. Rod was unassuming but had a great sense of humour. And, boy, could he write a tune! Incredibly complex stuff for which he had every part mapped out in his head. And Rod smoked for all of us. Twice. I mean it was crazy man. He had a separate room, because it was just nuts.

Quincy called him 'Worms', because he used to have a place in Worms, Germany. I didn't even know there was a Worms, Germany, but there is because later on I went there to visit him and to do a bit of writing and he had a little, tiny apartment in Worms and he would smoke, smoke, smoke. So I'm with him dying while trying to write with him, and he only had a certain window of time that he could actually open the window in his apartment because he would make too much noise for the neighbours so we had like this 10-minute window that he could have the window, he cracked the window open … and I was in there pale green trying to hang on and breathe while he chuffed away. It was a challenge but it was great fun.

Michael was fun too, actually. It was great working with him during those times. He, the songs he wrote, with all the parts too, just like Rod, so when it came to my parts he would just dictate them to me and I would play them. Rod and Michael did it the same way. I think, actually, that Michael may have learned his way from working with Rod. Everything was very precise. All I needed to do was show up and play just what they wanted.

I've been around the block myself and to be able to acclimate with this many solid musicians with stellar backgrounds … we all come from the same ilk in that way, the session background, which was a wealth of knowledge for us; it was like its own university. I started out with Stevie Wonder and that was like going to Wonder University, too, you know, and then from there branching off in the sessions working with just about everyone I ever wanted to, we all came from that same era. And it's now an era that is long gone. It doesn't exist anymore, sadly enough because of the way now music gets produced with the advance of technology. It's a different scene today.

One day, during the sessions for *Thriller*, we had some down time. There was something wrong with the recording desk, and it was going to be a while and Michael was getting a little bored so he said to me, 'Let's go across the street, let's go shopping'. So, because the studio that we recorded at was on this street and right across from this studio is a huge shopping mall called the Beverly Center. So I said, 'Are you sure you want to?'

And he says, 'Yeah.'

So he put on a disguise, he put on a big afro wig and these funky jacked-up teeth and dark sunglasses, and we walked out of the studio, down Beverly, we walked down the street, and we crossed the street to the Beverly Center. And, as we are crossing, I'm thinking to myself, 'I'm crossing the street with Michael Jackson', and it's just the two of us, no security, nothing, just the two of us. And we walked into the

Beverly Center and we looked around and I'm not looking at him, I'm looking at the people, you know, checking them out and you get, like, various reactions.

And then we kept walking and we spent a good amount of time, but after leaving – and he bought a couple of things, I think he bought a watch or something like that – and the girl at the counter was like, 'Um, thank you'. She wasn't really sure, but as we walked away she finally realised who it was. We went into a gift-wrapping department, one of the major stores, and we were sitting there and while we were waiting he was laughing at other people watching and there was this one little kid with a really interesting shaped head, he had like a big hook head, and Michael would sit there and snigger like he was in high school. He just said, 'Look at that kid with the head!' He was cracking up and I was sitting right next to him going, 'Why are you laughing at the poor kid?'

And then we walked around some more and we finally started getting a little crowd then we left. No security, no big hassles, we just calmly walked out.

Rod Temperton:

Quincy was always the boss man, but he has got such an amazing amount of experience and knowledge in the business and so I always nodded to Quincy. But, you know, part of the way I work, writing-wise, is that before I can really sit down and write something, I want as many clues on the artist and the project as I can possibly get, so I can get inspiration for what to write. So, it was always good if I was involved in the album throughout because then I hear what everybody else is doing, what the album then needs, what it is missing. I get to know the artist, and so I understand where they are coming from and what they are all about, and where they want to head with it.

And all these things help me, so I work quite often on lots of various bits of the record, you know, and it has always been my philosophy that if I can help somebody else's song become great, then it will sell that many more records and even if I didn't have the hit on that album I guess I will still be doing alright. So I just tended to work across the board on all facets. And you know, the other thing to remember is that Quincy and I had become such close friends by this time and we trusted each other so much, we could always bounce off each other. It was great to be able to bounce things off each other.

I've always enjoyed doing vocal arrangements and rhythm track arrangements. Whatever. And so I worked on all parts of the *Thriller* LP really, not just on the songs that I wrote for it.

Part of the writing process for me is that I hear it. It's not just about the melody; I hear lines coming at me all the time. Hooks and bass lines, hooks and guitar parts. From a commercial point of view you have got four minutes on a single, so if you are going to get through all of this mess to get to people's ears, you have to have all kinds of things … you know, ear candy … to get going. And so I get very specific with all the parts. There always has to be areas where the musicians can move, but if there is a guitar line, say, in the verse of the song, that I really see is a hook, then that's written out as that, it's an absolute given. And then when they get to the chorus maybe they don't have the lead role, so their own style of playing can come through more. So, there is always a bit of give and take, but there are certain elements that I want to be hit on that song, that I think are absolutely necessary for that piece to make it work the way I want it to.

With the lead singer you are trying to bring out their expression. You know, it has got to be theirs. As far as the general public goes, 'Who is Rod Temperton?' It's Michael Jackson's piece so you want him to shine and be the star of it. So, you want to be able to write the kind of things he will be able to express musically. But there are always going to be certain melodies, certain parts of the melody that have to be absolutely on the nail or else the piece doesn't work whoever the singer is. I can't be terribly specific because you have to have give and take in a piece.

Bruce Swedien:

The sessions were very light-hearted but very serious about the music. Me, Quincy and Rod all take music very personally but there was a lot of good food, silliness and craziness with the music centre stage. It was serious but not deadly.

Michael had Bubbles, his chimpanzee, and Muscles which was a 20ft boa constrictor. Rod got on great with them both. I've got some great pictures of Rod with Muscles, but Quincy was terrified of Michael's snake. Bubbles was kind of like an adolescent juvenile delinquent. Bubbles was sort of a pain. Michael was the easiest guy in life to work with in the studio. Rod would tease him. Michael had a nickname, 'Smelly'. He didn't curse, and so when something was bad, Michael would say, 'Ooh, that's smelly'.

We would actually have a lot of fun in the studio and that comes out, I think, in the music. Quincy and Rod have both said to me that even the good food we had during those sessions is there in the music.

Derek 'Dee' Bramble:

I spoke to Rod a lot when he was first working with Michael as we were doing *Hot Property* with Heatwave at the same time, and as a young kid myself I was fascinated to hear about Michael. The two of them got on well and Quincy was the anchor for that, he knew what Rod was bringing to the party. There was a respect from Michael for Rod. It's not like Rod had turned up in LA off the banana boat after all. The Heatwave records were very well received and everybody respected us as a band and as a musical entity, but taking Rod on board and letting him do his thing was a stroke of genius from Quincy. Listen to the stuff he did with Rufus and Herbie Hancock. These are cats in their own right yet they sat down and let Rod, this boy from Cleethorpes, hand it to them. I mean, what does that say about Rod Temperton?

Steve Lukather:

Quincy and Rod had a magic touch, man, you've got to give it to them. I think Q is one of the best casting directors for his choice of songs. That's where his talent really lies. You know, he gets the right cats and he gets the right tunes and the right songwriters, you know, and he lets everybody do their thing and he is also gracious to send flowers to my ex-wife with a note saying, 'Thanks a lot. We are sorry we had to keep him late.' He always made sure he took care of the cats, man, you know, I have to say. And then he has always been very nice to me, man. I had some wonderful experiences in the studio where there would be Herbie Hancock, Patti Austin and some unbelievable players. I mean, I did a whole bunch of records right in a row with him and Rod and it was a great learning experience.

Not that Steve and Greg knew that the songs they were playing on would become timeless classics and sell an enormous, record-breaking amount of copies. Greg Phillinganes:

Lots of people have this idea that when musicians or artists go into a studio they automatically know what they are working on is going to be a hit or not. That's the biggest myth in the world. You can't think like that. You can't go on saying this is going to be a 25 million seller or else you won't get beyond the parking lot. It doesn't go like that. You go in and you try to make the best record that you can do.

It's not like we sat around going, 'Oh yeah, this is going to, you know, break all records', because you are wanking at that point. You would never get beyond the bathroom. Depending how good it feels. You can't do it that way. It's all a myth and so you don't approach it like that. If you are wise, you don't anyway. Quincy, Rod and Michael, of course, strived to have an album of the highest quality songs possible. And at the end we all felt good about that and we just hoped for the best, but there are so many intangible elements that go into that, you can't predict that you are going to have a hit. It doesn't work that way.

Bruce Swedien said, 'We had no idea that we were making the biggest album of all time. The songs do have a life of their own, all with a huge personality but nobody could have known that.'

Each song on *Thriller* is, of course, a killer. Time to take a look at how a few of them came out the way they did, starting with the duet with Paul McCartney, 'The Girl is Mine', the only song on the LP that did not fully involve Rod Temperton. Paul McCartney:

Michael just rang me one day. This was in a very hot period having just done *Off the Wall* and he was screaming around with his success and selling millions. I didn't think it was him at first, because he's got the high voice. I thought it was a fan. I said, 'Hello, who is this please?'

He said, 'It's Michael Jackson, don't you recognise me? You don't think it's me do you?'

I said, 'It really is you Michael, isn't it? What's up?'

He said, 'I'd like to come over.'

I said, 'Yeah, lovely, great, come over to England, great. What for?'

He said, 'I'd like to make some hits.'

So, he did. He just came over and we started working together. We wrote two songs together, 'Say, Say, Say' and 'The Man', and we recorded both of those and then we did one for *Thriller*. It really is different working with people with that level of talent because they are just so keen on making a great record themselves that they really do half of the work for you.

Steve Lukather:

Jeff Porcaro [the famed drummer] and I got a call to work with Quincy on the *Thriller* record. This is initially the duet with Paul McCartney, first time we met Paul, who is a wonderful, beautiful cat and one of my all-time heroes. We were like, 'Come on, Michael Jackson and Paul McCartney are going to do a duet together. Wow, man.'

Quincy sent over the cassette to Jeff and Jeff goes, 'Look, come on over, man. Let's just sit down and dig the tune, man, because you know, this is Paul and Michael, this is going to be incredible, man.'

So, I get over to Jeff's house and he's got the cassette and he puts it on and we're just going, 'This is going to be absolutely fantastic, man.'

And the song starts, and it goes, 'The doggone girl is mine', and if I could have had a camera on Jeff's face, man. We fell about but when we got to the gig to cut the song, it ended up being cool. It ended being very cool, but just the lyric … we were cracking up with the lyric … 'The doggone girl is mine'? This is the cat who wrote *Sgt Pepper* and shit like that, do you know what I mean?

But Paul didn't write this one. That's in his defence. It ended up being an incredible session. It was just unbelievable and Paul and Linda were just unbelievably gracious and they invited Jeff and I to come over and be a part of his movie, *Give My Regards to Broad Street*. And we just hung out jamming Beatles tunes with Paul live on the sound stage for two weeks, hanging out with George Martin.

After we did 'The Girl is Mine', Paul himself sent thank you letters to everybody on the gig. I still have mine framed up in my house, you know. We had a great time. You know, it was a great honour. But, anyway, believe me, Paul McCartney is one of the greatest geniuses ever, but like, you know when I make the joke about 'The doggone girl is mine', I mean, it was just a silly lyric and I certainly didn't think that it was going to be the lead-off single of the biggest selling album of all time.

Steve Lukather also played a large role in the song 'Beat It', another to be written by Jackson himself:

I pretty much did everything other than the guitar solo on that record. I mean, that's a funny story because what happened was my buddy Eddie Van Halen, they wanted him to do a solo on it, so what happened was Quincy called Eddie who kept hanging up on Quincy, saying, 'Who the fuck is this?' He had no time for it until his old man figured out who Quincy Jones was.

Eddie's a Dutch rock and roll giant. He was one of the best guitar players ever. They sent the original version that they had cut up to Eddie's house for him to do a solo but Eddie didn't want to play the solo where Quincy wanted him to play the solo, so they cut the tape. When you cut the tape it will not sync back up again. So, what happened was, on that slave reel was Michael Jackson's voice, Michael hitting two and four on a drum case and Eddie Van Halen's solo. No click track, nothing, and Quincy called me and Jeff to ask if we could try to put the rhythm section back together with this so that we don't have to record the thing again.

And so Jeff and I were at Sunset Sound and Jeff, being the groove master of all time, went out first and he managed after a couple of takes to figure it out and play the whole song, play the groove.

And then I did the bass part and Quincy was like, 'I want to rock and roll, I want to rock and roll', so I put a stack of Marshalls on the thing and quadrupled it. It was kind of like tongue in cheek really. We would laugh to each other and say, 'They think this is a rock and roll song?' And then we put it all together.

Quincy called and he goes, 'It's too much, man. It's too heavy. You've got to tone it down.'

So, at that point I was invited down to Westlake with Michael and Quincy and I did the parts again. I did the version you hear today and then Michael dictated the rhythm parts to me, like all the da-da-da-da. It was all Michael's stuff, you know. As Greg says, he knew exactly what he wanted.

At that point I never thought this was going to be a big single and I don't think Eddie even got paid for the day. To this day he still talks about that. He's like, 'These guys didn't pay my scale!'

But 'Beat It' gave Michael rock credibility in rock radio and that's what they were trying to do, to crossover. Yeah, I did it … Jeff and I made that record. Quincy wasn't even there when we did our parts until I got to the studio with Michael and Quincy where we were finishing the final touches, but we made it work.

It was a golden age. It was the last of the great session era. You don't even have to play good anymore, man. If you are creative you can just sloppily play a part and your computer can fix it and turn it into a hook.

Quincy Jones:

We needed a black version of a rock and roll thing with power and that's what we got. We had to have Steve Lukather in one room and I put him on 'Beat It', you know, with the two Gibson speakers and with six packs of beer and I was calling from next door and he said that the speakers were on fire because he was mixing 'Beat It' and there was just stuff going on everywhere. We had no choice but to work all hours and we would put up with the work right until the last morning when we were still putting all the bass lines and everything else on 'Beat It'.

I begged Michael to do a song like 'Beat It', you know, and it really worked out.

Steve Lukather and Jeff Porcaro were in the band Toto at the time, and it was from that camp that another song, 'Human Nature', materialised, as the band's sadly now deceased bass player, Mike Porcaro remembered:

My brother, Steve, left Toto after we had recorded *Toto IV*. I think there was probably some frustration as Steve was starting to develop himself as a songwriter and I don't think he felt like he was really getting a chance with the limited space on a record to get some of his things across with Toto. He managed to get a tune on here and there and he had been developing as a writer over the years, to the point where I think he became a wonderful songwriter, but I think that frustration was in the back of his mind, wanting to get into some other things, such as film scores, and to get back into his piano and playing more.

All these things kind of conspired to bring him to the point where he wanted to step aside. Within months of him leaving the band he gets this tune on the *Thriller* record and it was just, you know, huge for Michael, and Miles Davis cut it further down the road. But I was happy for him because it showed that he had arrived as a songwriter, and that was good for him, being that he was doing what he was doing and trying to carve this road for himself. It was a good early initial sign for him.

Steve Lukather:

Steve Porcaro was still with Toto when he started to write 'Human Nature' but he hadn't finished it. He had the hook and he would play it all the time and stuff like that. At that point we were going, 'Oh no, man, we want to be more rock and roll, more rock and roll', and so he kept that one in his trick bag and when Michael was cutting *Thriller*, we were all on that record, he whipped that one out and finished it and we were all going, 'Oh, fuck!'

I was thinking, 'Thank God, thank God he didn't give it to Toto.'

Mike Porcaro:

You know, that tune may not have been right for Toto at the time and also it may have been cut to perfection for Toto at the time and still not been a hit. I mean that it is so arbitrary and it is the right combination of elements and talent, and the voice singing it, and this and that, that can make a tune fly or not fly. So, who knows what would have happened with Toto and that song.

Quincy Jones:

David Paich of Toto used to come over my house when he was a boy as I knew his father, Marty. We worked on a couple of demos with the band. We didn't like the first one but after some silence on the tape, suddenly on came this tune and I couldn't believe it. It had everything and it meant that we had to drop another song, written by Michael Sembello, called 'Carousel'.

Rod Temperton said, '"Carousel" was a great song but, lyrically, it didn't seem to fit in with where the album was going at that time.'

A Temperton tune, 'Thriller' went through a whole host of changes before becoming the song that it became. This story is now the stuff of legend. Rod:

Originally when I did my demo I called it 'Starlight' and the whole point of the piece, having worked on *Off the Wall*, was that it had to have the rhythmical churn of 'Don't Stop 'Til You Get Enough', which was my favourite tune on that first Jackson album. And so I wanted to write a piece that had that kind of rhythm, you know, action going on, but I also knew of Michael's love of melodrama and movies and everything and so I wanted to get some drama on the top of the piece. So that is how the music of 'Thriller' came about. Then when I came to write the lyric – by that time I'd got everything done, you know, the whole structure, all the parts – and Quincy said to me, 'Well, you man-aged to come up with the title for the last album so see what you can do for this album'.

I said, 'Oh, great.'

So I went back to the hotel and I wrote two or three hundred titles for this song, for this one song that, you know, my demo was 'Starlight', that's all it was, a demo. I used to ring Quincy up, two o'clock in the morning, and we would talk about it. He didn't like the title 'Starlight' so I came up with the title 'Midnight Man' and he said, 'That's more of what I want, there's a bit of mystery, a bit more where we should be heading'.

So I said, 'OK, let me think about it.'

And so the next morning I woke up and I just said this word, and what was really strange about it, as I said to you earlier, all of my lyrics I write, I try to melt in to the melody so they just seem like they've always been there.

'Thriller' – and I know this is very hard to say now because everybody knows it – but it's one of the hardest words to sing. If you sing, 'Cos this is Thriller', you know you are getting your mouth around that and I realised it was horrible to sing. But something in my head just said, 'This is the title'. You could visualise it on the top of the Billboard charts. You could see the merchandising for this one word, how it jumped off the page at you. So, I knew I had to write it as 'Thriller' and I wrote all the words very quickly, and then went to the studio and we did it.

At the end of the song, I had always planned on there being some talking, or some rap. Probably, you know, hopefully from somebody in the film genre who everybody would recognise their voice. At the time there was a girl who used to present a horror series in America called *Elvira* and when we were in the studio, Quincy said, 'Well who shall we get to do this then?'

And I said, 'Well, how about Elvira? Everybody knows who she is.'

And Quincy said, 'Wait a minute. My wife, Peggy, knows Vincent Price. Maybe we can get him to do it.'

I nearly fell on the floor because I remember being 9 years old and trying to get into the back of cinemas when it was X certificate, *The Pit and the Pendulum*, stuff like that, *The Mask of the Red Death*, or *The Fall of the House of Usher*. So I knew exactly that Vincent Price would be perfect, I thought it was amazing, and I thought that it would be fabulous if we got him to do this.

So Quincy called his wife and she called Vincent, and he said, 'Yeah I would be happy to come and do it'.

So it was planned for the following week, and at that point we just thought we would have him say something, you know, just some words, any words from some of films because as soon as Vincent opens his mouth you knew it was Vincent Price.

So, it went, of course, right until the night before he was due to record something and I left the studio to go back to the hotel and I then get a call from Quincy. He said, 'You know, Vincent's never been on a record before. He might find it a little difficult. We have the session at two o'clock tomorrow afternoon. Perhaps you can write some words for him to say.'

So I said, 'Yeah, OK, no problem. I'll put something together.'

And off I went to bed, thinking that I would write something when I got up in the morning. I was awoken by the phone ringing at 8 a.m. and my publisher was downstairs. He had flown in from England for a meeting with me and I had totally forgotten about this.

And so I thought, 'Oh my goodness!'

We then had breakfast together and this meeting went on and on and on until about noon … and the session, remember, is at two.

Finally he left and you know, I just got the pen and paper out and Quincy rang and said, 'Have you got it, have you got something?'

I said, 'Yeah, I'm working on it. Don't worry about it, I will have something.'

So I then started to write this rap for 'Thriller' and, you know, fortunately because of the visual thing of 'Thriller', the words for the song had come easy and things were just falling out of me. I mean, it was just so easy to visualise Vincent saying this stuff. And so the words were just falling out of me and I got one verse done and then jumped in the cab and I headed off to the studio for the session. I was frantically writing in the back of the cab. And when I got to the studio I saw this limousine pull up out the front, at the front of the studio, and out stepped Vincent Price. And I said to the cab driver, 'Go round the back. Go round the back.' So we raced round the back and I jumped out, went through the back door, grabbed hold of the secretary and said, 'Photocopy this, quick'.

And then I raced into the studio and put the photocopy on the music stand, and Vincent walked in and sat down and, you know, he just hit it. Two takes. He was absolutely amazing and that was a great moment for me, I really enjoyed that.

And to cap it all off, two years later — and I hadn't seen Vincent again after he left the studio — I was watching the Johnny Carson *Late Show*, which was the big chat show in America like *Parky* in the UK. Vincent Price was on it, because by that time 'Thriller' was huge, and he was talking about his experiences and how he loved the three verses I had come up with, only two of which were used on the final record. It was a humbling moment for me, really.

Darkness falls across the land
The midnight hour is close at hand
Creatures crawl in search of blood
To terrorise y'all's neighbourhood
And who so-ever shall be found
Without the soul for getting down
Must stand and face the hounds of hell
And rot inside a corpse's shell

[Missing verse]
The demons squeal in sheer delight
It's you they spy, so plump so right
For though the groove is hard to beat
Yet still you stand with frozen feet
You try to run; you try to scream
But no more sun you'll ever see
For evil reaches from the crypt
To crush you with its icy grip

The foulest stench is in the air
The funk of forty thousand years
And grizzly ghouls from every tomb
Are closing in to seal your doom
And though you fight to stay alive
Your body starts to shiver
For no mere mortal can resist
The evil of the Thriller
Can you dig it?!

Bruce Swedien:

From concept, it is really incredible. Rod will have a melody and maybe a harmony. Then he'll start on the lyric and he himself will record a scratch vocal. Now Rod Temperton's scratch vocals do require a bit of imagination, but the scratch vocal that Rod records for a piece of music may just have words that don't mean anything and he will leave those words in there – the right sounds and every-thing – but he will have throwaway words that are there until the actual lyric shows up.

Starting lyrics with Rod's music have almost nothing to do with the way these songs end up. For instance, 'Thriller' started life as 'Starlight' and I still have that original demo. Da dad a Starlight de de de! And that's how that song came into our lives. It was 'Starlight' and then this incredible stroke of genius, 'Thriller' came to be. To me, the really interesting thing about the Vincent Price rap or the spoken part of 'Thriller' is that Rod Temperton wrote a brilliant Edgar Allen Poe type of spiel in the taxicab on the way to the session. Now, when the chips are down like that, that's when you find out what true genius is really about.

I remember Quincy showed up at Westlake Studios with this funny little smile on his face looking like the cat that had swallowed the canary. He said that Vincent Price is going to be here at two o'clock and Rod Temperton is writing the rap at this very moment on the way to the studio in a taxicab. He also said to me, 'I don't think Vincent Price has ever been on a record before.'

So, Rod came into the control room with a Marlboro cigarette in one hand, a bunch of crumpled up papers in the other hand and he said, 'Quick, he's here. Vincent Price is here, I just saw him come in.'

He said to me, 'Give these papers to the secretary right away to photocopy so that we can give them to Vincent.' So Vincent came in and off he went. It was incredible.

It's not unusual, as I look back at that time, to have four rolls of 24-track tape. That's ninety-six tracks of tape. That's a lot of tracks. But if you listen to the music on 'Thriller' there are counter-melodies and it's all kind of a puzzle. Rod and Quincy's music is kaleidoscopic. Every time you hear it, you hear something different. That's part of the intrigue and the interest. That's part of why that music can hold our interest for so long.

Quincy Jones said, 'Anyway, the challenge came and it was no stretch for Rod because he is such a good writer. He has it all and is such an amazing writer. What he came up with was beyond all of our expectations.'
John Cameron:

All the brilliant earlier stuff that Rod wrote was obviously just practice for 'Thriller'. I always said that my office was the second table from the back in any airport canteen and Rod was obviously the same. 'Thriller' is such a benchmark song. It's not just that it's really funky and really catchy but that it's so unusual, all those chord sequences and the kind of slidey rhythmic thing on it. It's just totally original.

Greg Phillinganes:

I really enjoyed working on the song 'Thriller', the title track for the album. The only thing I regret about that, though, is that I didn't go to Vincent Price's session. I knew he was going to do the voice-over but I didn't make it to the session. I definitely regret that. I heard he knew just what he was doing and was awesome.

Six months had been spent in the studio creating the LP and, to put it into Quincy's words, he, Bruce and Rod 'were fried, really fried, I mean, wasted'.
'The Girl is Mine', released in October 1982, reached No. 2 on the Billboard charts and peaked at No. 8 in the UK. CBS Records were now keen on having the album delivered in time for the Christmas market. Rod Temperton:

We went through this whole process and we had a break in the middle and threw a few songs out and replayed others, put some new things together, and finally it got round towards the end of the year, November time, and the record company was getting really worried. They wanted it out for Christmas. And so we went to mix it and we were working all the hours, and you know, I remember finishing 'Beat It' at seven o'clock in the morning. And they took the tapes over to make a disc.

We reconvened back at the studio at two o'clock in the afternoon to listen to it and we didn't like it. It just wasn't electric. And so we kind of pleaded with the record company to get two more weeks to remix the whole thing. And so we took two days off, went and just chilled out, you know, and then came back and remixed the whole album in two weeks and by that time, I think they had taken over every CD and record plant in the country and they had guys, bikers outside the studio, ready to take the stuff to private planes to get it to all the CD and record factories because, you know they wanted it in the shops by, I don't know, the tenth of December or something and we were now in late November. We had about ten days to turn this whole thing around.

And the funny thing is, I remember, we came out of the studio ... I said before, when we came out after *Off the Wall* we kind of felt we had something magical, but when we came out of *Thriller*, I don't think we knew what we had. We were really fried. And I remember catching the plane back to England – and this is how quick the turnaround was, I got back to England and had been there for only two days when I opened the *Melody Maker* and there was a review of the record and you know what the headline was?

'The Thrill has gone.'

And I thought, 'Oh my God, now what?'

We were kind of, you know, shaking at this point.

Bruce Swedien:

I told the guys, I said it isn't going to sound right. I think on the first roll round on *Thriller* we had twenty-eight minutes on one side of the album and that's just too long. It wouldn't be competitive. And so we were listening to the playback with the Columbia executives and I wasn't very pleased with the sound and I noticed Michael slip out of the room and then Quincy and Rod and then I went. And Michael was in the next studio and he was absolutely sobbing. He said the sound wasn't right. I felt like saying, 'I told you so'.

So, we stopped the production and took three days off. We were burned. Then we cut down and edited all of the songs, making it eighteen to twenty minutes on each side. By doing that, the sound improved dramatically, one of the reasons why the sound of that LP is unique.

Greg Phillinganes:

Well yeah, at the first, after the first series of mixes, they didn't think it was terrible, Quincy thought some key elements musically were missing. So after that, that's when they ended up with 'Beat It', 'Billie Jean', 'Human Nature' ... and I think one more, as a matter of fact. I was at Michael's house when he premiered the demos for 'Beat It' and 'Billie Jean'. I was there with Rod and Quincy and those demos were striking, they were awesome. I was actually working on an album, a solo album, at the time, we were trying to get songs together and one of the demos he played for us was called 'Behind the Mask' and I instantly took on to that one, so after the meeting I went to Michael and said, 'Listen, if that one doesn't make it, do you think I could have it?' He said, 'Yeah', and so that's how I ended up with that. Didn't do much for me, like it did in the end for Eric Clapton.

Walter Yetnikoff, president and CEO of CBS at that time, said, 'I don't remember the mix being drastically changed. I don't remember listening to a mix and saying I hated it. I don't recall that, at all, but it was a long time ago.'

Michael Jackson's biographer, J. Randy Taraborrelli, wrote in *Michael Jackson – The Magic and the Madness*:

Nobody believed Michael. It's interesting that when the *Thriller* album was complete, Quincy Jones and others who worked on the record thought it was a fine album, but they told Michael that he perhaps had expectations that were not realistic for the album's sales. Michael became very upset with them and he actually threatened to not allow the album to be released at all. He called Walter Yetnikoff, who at that time was the chairman of CBS Records and told him that 'Quincy Jones doesn't believe in this project the way that I wanted him to and no one seems to believe in this project the way that I feel they should believe in it. I think it can be the biggest record of all time and if you guys at CBS aren't going to get behind it the way I feel you should then don't release it all.'

And, ultimately, of course, it did come out and ultimately Michael Jackson's instincts were right – it was the biggest record of all time, but who could possibly have known that at the time, except of course for Michael Jackson.

Rod Temperton:

And then, of course, shortly after the release of the album, that same week was the Motown special celebrating twenty-five years of the label with Michael doing 'Billie Jean' and showing off his moon-walk for the first time. That was it. It was all over. You know, 'Billie Jean' was an absolute smash, and you know, one of the big successes of *Thriller*.

I think that was one of the few times that really all parties came together to make it happen. You know, not only the singer, the musicians, the engineers, the writers, the producer, but all the record company people, everybody was on track with it, you know. The whole process of merchandising the record and going forward was textbook, because the idea, the choice of singles, captured the R&B market straight away. 'Beat It' followed 'Billie Jean', it was all planned at that point.

'Beat It' came out with the rock side of things going on and they held my song 'Thriller' back until almost a year after the release of the record, the album, and of course then they did the big video for it and so here comes 'Thriller', and it kicked it all off again. And then a few months after that came the Grammys where Michael won a whole host of awards. And that kicked it off all over again. So it just kept turning over and turning over, and that's really why it was so big, I think.

An estimated TV audience of 47 million people watched the Motown special. Motown founder, Berry Gordy:

I said, 'If you do this thing and you do it right, because of the popularity of this show, you could go into orbit.' And, of course, no truer words were spoken because when he did that moonwalk, he didn't know how it was going to come out, I didn't know how it was going to come out, adrenalin was flowing, but he did it and it was incredible. And there can never be a better performance than that because he will never have that enthusiasm and that fear that you have the first time you do it. It's like an opening night. You never know how it's going to come out. He did go into orbit, never to return back to this earth again.

Music entrepreneur, Jonathan King:

The entire audience, mainly made up of hard bitten cynical old industry people like myself, were on our feet cheering. And I looked around behind me and I saw the executives watching him do the moonwalk to 'Billie Jean' and I saw every single jaw dropping, and in every single set of eyes there was the horror – they had realised how much less talent the people they had to work with on a daily basis had than Michael Jackson. Michael doing the moonwalk on stage live for the first time is probably the single greatest performance I've ever seen of anyone.

Lamont Dozier, famed songwriter and producer:

At first I got these chills. I'm a very spiritual person, and I'm not easily moved, and this thing that was happening in that room got a hold of me. And it was like I reared out of my seat because it was so prominent, I mean it was so perfect when he threw the hat out and it was so ... it was like magic. I said this man has been blessed. This man has got the calling. I'm looking at my wife and I'm saying, 'Do you feel this?' and she's saying, 'Yeah, what's going on?' And the whole audience, the whole crowd stood up on their feet, and they were cheering. I've never seen anything like it. It was in the room and it was amazing. There was some magic there that night.

Michael Jackson:

> I see dancing as the most wonderful thing of all time, because people communicated through bodily movement before anything. I mean dancing is really showing your emotions through bodily movement and I think it's a wonderful thing to just get out on the floor and just feel free and just do what you want to do and let it come out. And when I dance I really feel it. I just feel free and I do what I feel. It's instinct. It's God. It's escapism. It's getting away from everything and just moving your body and letting all the tension and pain out, and just having a good time.

Jeffrey Daniel, former member of Shalamar, who taught Michael Jackson the moonwalk:

> I was there watching him and when Michael did it, people who saw me and knew me looked over to me and said, 'Hey Jeffrey, Michael's got your dance'.
>
> I was like, 'You go, Michael!', and after his performance I went over and spoke with him and I said, 'Michael, that was great but I was surprised that it took you this long to do it.'
>
> And, he said, 'I just wanted it to be perfect.'
>
> That dance gave Michael another signature dance that just catapulted around the world. He was already a great performer but to add this onto it was just like icing on the cake.

Bob James:

> It was no surprise having worked with Rod that his next project after *Off the Wall* with Michael was going to be huge although it probably was a surprise to Rod himself that the *Thriller* album went completely through the roof. There was certainly no surprise about Rod's talent but the unpredictability of the music business is something that continues to intrigue me. You just never know what is going to break through.

Walter Yetnikoff:

My memory is somewhat overshadowed by the gigantic success that *Thriller* did both artistically and in popular culture. Michael said that he was always going to do something like this; he was going to have pop music and dance mingle. Other than disco it had not really been done before. You had stylised groups, The Temptations and people like that, but never really dance in the sense that Michael meant it. I think we were all overwhelmed by the success that *Thriller* generated, the whole thing.

I think it was innovative. It was very, very different. Michael Jackson's style was different and again, the video component of the thing, and you know, having the ghouls and the skeletons floating around, you know, it was something different for pop music. And the dance sequences were obviously superb. Many people have tried to copy that. Even today you have people copying that sort of syncopated dance thing.

I think we finally sort of stopped counting how many records we sold once we got to forty-odd million. It was selling a million either a week or a month at one point. I think it was a million a week, which is incredible. We could hardly manufacture enough. I mean look how many hits you had on the *Thriller* record. Seven of the nine songs, I think.

Video, as Walter pointed out, played a massive part in the success of *Thriller*, especially the title song of the album. MTV had just begun. The man behind that station was Bob Pittman:

I was a radio programmer before MTV and had worked my way out from Mississippi, originally as a disc jockey and then they actually let me programme a couple of radio stations and had some pretty good success in Pittsburgh. And then NBC hired me in Chicago and when I was 23 they sent me to New York to programme the flagship station of NBC radio which was WNBC and we had a nice go over there. Then, a cable company was being formed, a cable programming company. Warner Communications sold half of their cable company to American Express and they formed Warner

Amex Satellite Entertainment Company and they hired me as their chief programmer.

And I came over originally to do an all-movie service, pay TV service, called the Movie Channel. It was the first twenty-four-hour movie service, the first all-movie service and we had pretty good success with that. And after we had success with that, they were looking to do more channels.

I'd done a TV show on NBC called *Album Tracks* back in, probably 1978, and had hosted it and produced it. We were playing around with the video clips which were out at the time. There were a couple of music networks out, actually, one down in Atlanta, I think, called Video Concert Hall that was on the air. So, our channel ... the pitch was we were going to do to FM, what FM did to AM. We were going to add another dimension to it, we were going to play the video clips and, in the pitch, well, you know, originally, we pitched everybody and the board director said no. We got together, the CEO of American Express and the CEO of Communications, Steve Ross and Jim Robinson. And we got in the big pitch and at the end of the meeting they said, 'Let's go'. So, that was the beginning of MTV and that's how I wound up there.

It was the programmer who let the team create the MTV network and then later I became the CEO of MTV networks that included Nickelodeon and VH1 and took us on the international markets until 1987.

I had been a radio disc jockey since I was 15 years old, music was in my blood but probably radio was in my blood and I really enjoyed it, enjoyed the excitement of being right there in the middle of the culture and, as you know, when you are talking people in their teens and 20s and early 30s, music really defines who they are. To be in the thick of it was always energising and fun and it moved at such a rapid pace that it was always fun to try and keep up with it.

Initially, the simple policy we were looking for at MTV was 'Do they have a video?'

Our biggest problem was there weren't enough videos being made, there were only 250 videos in existence and were available for us to play, most of them were from the UK and, if you remember, people talked about the second British invasion, because the

Americans weren't doing videos. So, part of our plan was to evangelise videos to try to get more and more people to do videos. And our theory was 250 videos wouldn't make a channel but if we were successful, more people would make videos and if we weren't successful, it didn't matter that there were only 250, because we were going to be out of business anyway.

So, that was the big calculated risk of it and then over time, we sort of began to work with where music was going, and if you remember that time, it was a whole new music scene emerging, I don't know how you would call it, alternative music? Now they call it 80s music. We were really the showcase for it because the radio wasn't playing it. We clearly were looking to be something other than radio; it was a mutually advantageous thing for the artists and us. I think MTV later was very, very responsible for careers that might not have happened without it. One of the examples that comes to mind is Duran Duran. Then, I'm sure there are many others, which I don't know would have happened without MTV.

I felt very, sort of, satisfied because I had been saying for years that there was a visual component to many music artists. Music artists, a lot of them look pretty good, you know, even today, a few of us are ageing a little bit, you know, but the tours of the Rolling Stones, the tours of Bruce Springsteen, they called it rock and wrinkles, but they are certainly still successful and certainly the visual impact is still there. So, I think it was helpful all around. MTV helped many of the artists who otherwise might not have made it as big and I think those artists helped MTV, because the videos themselves never really sold. Michael Jackson, at the time of 'Thriller', helped both parties the most.

You think about rock stars, or big music stars and that era and you really didn't know what they looked like because most of their album covers were some abstract art pics, not pictures of them. If you went to the concert to see them in Madison Square Garden, the reality was for everybody except those people in the first couple of rows, it could have been me on stage, because everybody looked like an ant.

And one of the first reactions we got at MTV was artists telling us, 'I can't believe it but I was eating in the diner and somebody said, "I saw you on MTV"'.

We had this unintended consequence of making the music stars celebrities. Because before then, they were pretty much, with the exception of maybe a handful, unrecognisable and suddenly their faces were there, people knew what they looked like, they knew how they moved, they knew how they dressed and it had a big impact. The other big impact we had which is sort of a corollary to that is that New York and London clothing styles began to be pushed across middle America, because they had never really seen those, because most of TV really showed everybody dressed in middle American garb not in the more cutting-edge clothing.

We did have a standards department that reviewed all the videos and, surely enough, we almost played everything we could get our hands on. I mean, clearly, we didn't play country music, but even some stuff that was on the borderline there it might have made it on during the early days of MTV.

Yet, it wasn't long before Bob Pittman and MTV found themselves in the middle of a race row. Criticism was mounting that not enough of the artists featured were black, and that included Michael Jackson. Walter Yetnikoff was one of the loudest critics:

Bob Pittman was a minister's son. He was the hippie from Mississippi. I thought he did a very good job in starting MTV. We may have had disagreements, you know! Tina Turner might have been on MTV but basically, MTV held itself out as a rock or a pop visual station. It was not designed, you know, for black artists, Tina Turner, to the contrary, notwithstanding. I mean anytime you say something that is a generalisation there is going to be one or two things which are not part of that generalisation. I don't recall MTV reaching out to anything other than pop or rock. I do know that they didn't want to play 'Billie Jean' and 'Beat It'. If Pittman wants to deny that, he should go back to Mississippi!

Bob Pittman:

I had my first lesson in PR in that era. It was actually Rick James who started it. We had turned down one of his videos for a song called 'Super Freak' from the standards department, although, I guess, if we saw it today, it would probably look pretty tame by today's standards. It didn't make it on the air. He made the accusation that there were no black videos on MTV, which was not true, I mean Tina Turner was on the air, a number of black artists of that time were. It is probably fair to say that there were a lot of black artists who didn't have videos, just like there were white artists who didn't have videos and instead of sort of dealing with the issue, we said to everybody, 'No, that's not true'.

Carolyn Baker explained in the book, *I Want My MTV*:

It wasn't MTV that turned down 'Super Freak'. It was me. I turned it down. You know why? Because there were half-naked women in it, and it was a piece of crap. As a black woman, I did not want that representing my people as the first black video on MTV.

Bob Pittman:

It went on and on and on, so we actually decided we needed to do something pro-active and we went out specifically to black artists and said, 'Look, we need you to produce a video', and when you came down the songs off *Thriller*, Michael Jackson was one of the artists we targeted, actually. It's when I met Quincy Jones and we said, 'We need some videos from this album, we need them to keep coming'.

The record company paid for 'Billie Jean' and 'Beat It' but they wouldn't pay for 'Thriller' and the only way it was going to be made was if we paid for it. It would have been a terrible precedent for us to start paying for the production of videos. So, what we did was we paid for *The Making of Thriller* video and the money used from that was then used to make the actual video for 'Thriller', and so we technically didn't pay for the production of the video, but the money we gave was used for the production of the video and that's the way 'Thriller', the video, got made. We had a long history at that point with Michael Jackson and for a number of years he was, I guess, on MTV with whatever he was doing. By the way, MTV did air *The Making of Thriller* as well.

Walter Yetnikoff:

I played very hard. I threatened to pull all of our staff. Had I done that, I think Warner Brothers would have done the same thing and then there would not have been an MTV. Thanks to my intervention, Michael Jackson made MTV. MTV made a lot of artists and I would have to say that between the whole thing Michael Jackson, MTV and the whole thing made me! I mean, you know this was sort of a circular kind of thing. Were it not for Michael Jackson and 'Thriller', then I don't think I would have had the same kind of career that I did, you know, with it, because it enabled us to take a lot of chances, there was money flowing in all over the place. It established us as money makers within a corporate structure which really looked down on the record business and it enabled me and the other people in the record business to take chances and to engage in adventures which I don't think we would have been able to, without it.

Quincy Jones:

MTV and Michael wrote each other to glory and it is kind of ironic because at the beginning MTV wasn't playing black music, you know. I remember Rick James was trying to get 'Super Freak' on. It was a phenomenon, really, because MTV was a brand-new concept, and I remember Bob Pittman said one time, 'I think people want to see rock 'n' roll as much as they want to listen to it'.

What are you talking about? That was in the early 1980s.

It was amazing because it was just a pure brand-new concept. He wrote up a business plan that the board threw out and said, 'I won't throw 39 million on something like that', and Steve Ross pulled him around the corner and said, 'Here's 50, go do it'.

And they were right, but in a way Michael defined what a video was really all about, you know, during that time, and they both, MTV and Michael, they rode each other to some incredible heights. Everything was right on both sides.

Bob Pittman:

I knew Walter well during that era. There was actually a reporter for
Forbes doing some story once in his office and he said, 'Oh, tell me
about it, why don't we set this story straight on "Thriller"?' and Walter
quickly changed the subject. As you know, record company guys, the
best thing they can do is be a hero to their artist and I think Walter
probably did that. I read some of Walter's stuff in his book and heard
of some stories that are attributed to Walter. I think part of the story
came from Walter who made himself. MTV wanted to play this video
and he wanted to play Michael Jackson. I think he made it into a case
where he got it played, and Michael Jackson believed it, thus becoming
a hero with this artist, that he made us do something. That's not really
unusual in the music business, as many people as possible take credit for
anything that is done and so I think, Walter probably jumped on that.

Walter Yetnikoff:

Michael Jackson did rely on Quincy Jones and Rod Temperton, yet,
when it came time for the Grammys that year where they awarded
all the Grammys for *Thriller,* he almost didn't want Quincy to win.
Why? Because he wanted to take the position that he was the producer, which he was not. Quincy Jones was clearly the producer,
I watched him produce it. Quincy used to call him 'Smelly' at that
period of time. But he was also sort of a father figure to him, as was I.
We were children of a different mother, but I was sort of a father
figure. Michael was a very sensitive child and he once said to me,
'You know, you grew up in a relatively normal situation, you played
ball, you did this, but I did not. I was a star at 6. Think what that
means, that I was now in a world where I was a star and I was 6 years
old, and you know, a child.'

He had very few people to talk to. Diana Ross was a sort of a god-
mother of his. He did worship his mother not his father so much, but
the mother. But being a star at 6 can be, you know, sort of difficult.
He did not live a normal life. He said to me, 'Think about it, the only
time I knew and I felt good was when I would see them making a
record or going out on tour. This was my whole life.'

This is not a normal upbringing. So, he was sort of a very, almost delicate in some ways, not in all ways, you know, human being. But he was also a very good businessman. He was able to read contracts, he understood what they meant. He did buy all the publishing later on of, you know, the Beatles' stuff, the songs where people advised him that the price tag was too high and it turned out that it was worth much more, whoever owns them these days. He spent a lot of money. He would go off in a car and he would go downtown and buy up movie posters, this, that and the other thing, his ranch up in Santa Barbara was full of really expensive toys that people had given him. So, he spent a lot of money and he was very astute in the business sense. But he was very, very fragile. I think he was more comfortable at parties hanging out with a bunch of kids and watching cartoons. I'm not trying to relate that to any of the other stuff, just saying that he was very childlike and he didn't trust a whole lot of people. He was very insecure.

On *Thriller*, along with Rod Temperton and others, Michael wrote some very good songs. Artists don't have to be Superman physically or even emotionally in order to do some pretty good songs. I wonder what Beethoven was actually like. He wrote some pretty good songs, too. Many creative people are really, you know, in a way, not part of this world. Maybe that's what makes them creative. The same could be said of Michael Jackson and Rod Temperton.

Bob Pittman:

The 'Thriller' video was the perfect storm, you know. First you had Rod Temperton's fantastic song. It is a classic composition from a man who conjured up so many. It was musically superb. Then you had an artist who was visually superb and then finally you had this new vehicle for exposure called MTV. Without MTV people might have never known that dimension of Michael Jackson. And you also have to give credit to all the people who produced the video, which they also managed to capture the essence of the music visually and even dance. If you think about it, until MTV came along, dance was sort of out of the visual world for the general public and MTV brought it back in to the general world. So thank goodness for all of those choreographers and dancers who managed to bring it all together. It was the perfect storm of how to bring other confluents, of all of those things coming together at that moment in time and it made something truly extraordinary.

I think Michael opened the door for the high production value artist, I think he opened the door for the big concert hall performers, the people would put on the big shows, the people would have as much visual to contribute as their music and I think he ushered that in and, by the way, I think that influence is seen in every video that was produced thereafter. He became the new gold standard for how you do a video, but I think less influential with the experimental artist and again, there are several types, hip hop I think was the biggest that emerged after that. But, you know, it had been going on sort of underground even in that period of time if you go back to the club scene in New York.

The LP *Thriller*, I think that was one of the greatest gifts we at MTV were handed. You know, we were going through a PR debacle with the whole Rick James thing, where we suddenly got put in a position of not playing black artists and Michael Jackson allowed us to solve that in one second because he wasn't a second-tier artist, he was absolutely the most popular artist of that moment, so he got seen by a lot of people, noticed by a lot of people and if anybody had any concerns that we weren't playing black artists, that was put to rest immediately with that. So, it solved the PR problem. Two, he solved the problem we had been trying to do, which is to take the art form up a notch, a dramatic notch, not incremental but let's take a quantum leap and he made the quantum leap for us. And third, I think he was the model for how a performer, what kind of performer you should be in the post–MTV era, it wasn't just about a good song, it was about a good song, and a good performance and he was again the role model for that as well.

Thriller was wildly innovative, I think it was probably Michael Jackson at his best, Quincy Jones at his best, Rod Temperton and Bruce Swedien and all the contributors at their best. Again, the same group of people had been playing around together on a couple of albums and suddenly they hit this one and it just all clicked and they had in MTV a willing partner in taking that to the world and without MTV I don't think they could have ever exposed it the way it deserved to be exposed. So, I think for everybody, it was the perfect storm.

Yes, the history of music had changed forever. And to think the very start of it, the embryonic moment of that, was the moment a man from Cleethorpes in Lincolnshire, England woke up one day in his Los Angeles hotel room and decided to rename the demo he had written as 'Starlight' to 'Thriller'. Rod said that he could visualise the success, he could see the word on top of the Billboard charts but not even he could have fully imagined just what it would lead to.

Because of it, Rod was now the hottest songwriter on the planet but, in spite of that, he still had time for his old friends from Heatwave, especially the young bass player, Derek Bramble:

Rod always helped me out. Let me tell you a quick story by way of explanation. I was in Dayton, Ohio and at this point I was 18 or 19 years old. The glow had gone off Heatwave by this time, the shine had gone off everything after the *Candles* and *Current* LPs. Rod's no longer there and Johnnie is no longer there and we had all these new members coming in. It just felt like we had turned into a cabaret act overnight. We were supposed to be playing a gig at this place, Wright-Patterson Air Force Base and I'll never forget it. I called Rod and I said to him, 'Rod, you know I want to be a writer. I just can't do this anymore. All the guys are in their 30s or 40s and here I am at 18.'

I told Rod that I just didn't want my entire future to be tied to this, playing with Heatwave. As much as I was appreciative of the chance and the opportunity, I just knew that this wasn't where I wanted to be.

So, on the phone Rod asked, 'So, what do you want to do?'

I said, 'I don't know but I just don't want to do this anymore.'

So, him and his amazing wife Kathy got off the phone saying that they would call me back in 20 minutes. Two hours later, I get a call back from them and Rod said, 'Well, this is up to you, Dee, but there's a plane ticket waiting for you at Dayton airport. If you want to leave, leave now. We've paid for the ticket, you fly and come and stay with us.'

I actually flew home to London first and then I went and stayed with Rod and Kathy in Worms in Germany where he still had a place. And it was there that we wrote 'Spice of Life', 'Victim of Emotions', four or five songs, and that was where I kind of struck out on my own, so to speak, from underneath the Heatwave band umbrella, all down to Rod and Kathy. I wanted to be a writer and producer and Rod was definitely in my corner. For him to reach across and pull me out of that situation, just like that, was incredible. He provided the out which didn't go down well with the rest of the guys because I just upped and left, which was kind of fucked up, but sometimes you've got to either shit or get off the pot. It was one of those life decisions and it was a moment that I will be eternally grateful for, to be able to take a decision and run with it.

In spite of everything that was happening to him at that time and all of his success, Rod always remained very grounded. He was able to be really confident and know his shit.

9

SWEET FREEDOM

Rod Temperton was still basking in the glow of the extraordinary success of 'Thriller'. His decision to rename 'Starlight' and give it that title, changed MTV and how music videos were made. The album surely had to be the peak of what a writer, producer, engineer or artist could ever manage. Yet, more hits were on their way.

Next up was work on a James Ingram solo album, *It's Your Night*, one which included another smash in the form of 'Yah Mo B There', a duet with former Doobie Brother, Michael McDonald:

James and I were recording a track for his first solo album and Rod was on that session mostly as a writer, you know. Once he had felt that the song needed a little bit more of a bridge he came up with that in a day in the studio, kind of boning up the song into something a little more exciting. That was my first meeting with Rod and the first time of seeing him do what he did. I was already a big fan of his, especially of all the Heatwave stuff and then, of course, the songs he did with Michael Jackson on *Off the Wall*. It was just exciting to get a chance to work with him, you know, and he brought a lot to the table on that song, making it a better song.

Although Rod Temperton was a name you heard a lot of in the business, I was very surprised when we met because I had no idea he was British. I always assumed that Heatwave were an American act. I had no idea they were a band out of England and for some reason that was never much spoken of here in the States. I don't think many people really realised that they were a British act because they had such an American R&B sound. Rod Temperton's sound.

It was at the beginning of the 1980s when we did 'Yah Mo B There'. They had all just finished doing *Thriller*, I think, and so it was 1980s kind of music, you know, where, you know, there were kind of more computer-generated rhythm tracks and things like that. So there seemed to be such a fine line there, where things sounded very techno, and yet Rod still had that groove factor, you know, kind of a dance groove factor in all of his records.

There were only a few guys who seemed to do records that way, largely synthesiser, keyboard kind of techno sonically, but somehow seemingly always having the groove, the dance groove was always very obvious and that's what I liked about it. I liked the fact that Rod had a great feel R&B-wise, but without sounding kind of rigid and techno, which was the style of a lot of bands who recorded that way, but Rod seemed to stand out at the time.

His stuff with Heatwave was just a real kind of fresh approach to R&B that hadn't come along in a while at that time. It seems like every band that makes a mark like that, they kind of do something that just hasn't been done in a while, if you know what I mean. It always captures the public's imagination if it gets a chance to and Heatwave was one of those kinds of bands. It was more traditional in its approach to R&B but there was just some twist and some turn in the songs that made them, you know, a whole new take on the groove.

I loved 'Always and Forever' and I loved the singer's voice and when I found out that the same guy wrote that and some of the Michael Jackson stuff for *Off the Wall*, tracks with such a great groove and bass line – stuff that was the real hallmark of the Heatwave stuff – I always wanted to work with Rod.

'Yah Mo B There' peaked at No. 19 in the USA and went to No. 44 in the UK in the same year, before a remixed version jumped to No. 12 the following year. The song earned James Ingram and Michael McDonald a 1985 Grammy Award for Best R&B Performance by a Duo or Group with Vocal.

In the same year, Rod also penned two songs for The Manhattan Transfer. Both 'Spice of Life' and 'Mystery', the latter later brilliantly covered by Anita Baker on her hugely successful breakthrough *Rapture* LP, made the charts. 'Spice of Life', co-written with former Heatwave band member, Derek Bramble, hit No. 40 on the pop charts while 'Mystery' stalled just outside the Top 100. Again, somewhat oddly, without Quincy Jones producing these songs didn't have quite the same impact as those he was cutting with Q.

Derek 'Dee' Bramble:

Rod had helped me quit Heatwave when I was no longer happy with them and he let me stay with him and Kathy for months in Worms where, even though I was just starting out as a writer rather than player, we put some songs down together. Rod would teach me. I sat there and showed him my ideas which I had come up with in London and he would say, 'Try this or do this'.

We had a great time, watching movies and making music and eating a lot. Kathy was brilliant, always looking after us both; it was just such a great laugh. I've got some photos somewhere of Rod and me sat on his sofa, scratching our balls, you know. That's how real it was, do you know what I mean? For me, this was a very close and a very unique relationship. He would sit me down and show me melodies and give me ideas for my music, tell me about the highs and lows. He gave me his take on how music should be transcribed and be fed to the listener and that has stayed with me until this day.

After he passed, obviously I was completely devastated but the ideals that Rod had, I now more than ever want to keep them alive. I know that I will never be Rod Temperton because only he could do what he did, but to be able to keep his kind of magic of music-making alive is very much at the forefront of my musical thinking right now. People can say it's dated, people can say whatever they want, but I know that there's a good in it that's almost timeless if you can get it right, you know, and that's as much as I can do to keep my old friend's spirit alive in what I do, do you know what I mean?

It's amazing, thinking back on those days, because Rod was actually working on *Thriller* for Michael and 'Spice of Life' was a song we did for that. The original title was 'Can't Take Your Lies', which was just me and my youthful lyrical interpretation. Rod said, 'This is a really good idea, let's push this up, let's do this, let's do that.' You know, he was a beast in the studio, he just knew what to do and he turned shit into Shinola. My youth was in full view on my demos, some of which I found only the other day.

'Spice of Life' was in the game for a while and was talked about as being part of *Thriller* and that is something I am very proud of. When it didn't make it, I got a call from Rod and he was in the studio with Stevie Wonder and he was putting harmonica on the song. I said, 'What's that about?' And he said, 'Well, we're now doing it for Manhattan Transfer.' I was thrilled. It sounded great, it was grooving. And it became a hit. Thanks Rod.

'Victim of Emotion', credited to Derek Bramble and David Grant, was released as the B-side to Jaki Graham's 'Round and Round' in 1985.
    Derek:

'Victim of Emotion' was so long ago, I can't remember if it ended up on the first album I produced for Jaki or not. But Rod and me also did a song called 'Natural Motion' together for Nona Gaye.

Writing these songs was just an education for me. It was a priceless experience. We spent a lot of time together. He would sit there for hours and hours on end trying to make things right. He would not give up on anything. He would stay up all night. I was a young pup, supposedly full of energy but he would always outwork me. In the studio together, I would sit and look around at four o'clock in the morning and he would still be going after it with cigarette in hand. It was such a monstrous sight for a young kid. He just wouldn't stop until he had it, until he felt comfortable with a song. As a young kid, it was great to see that kind of work ethic because then I saw what it took to be good. You don't just wake up, grab a pencil and there it is, you have to work at it, work at it. And then work at it some more.

But away from the work, we had a great time together. Rod absolutely loved movies. Movies were his big thing. We would work together and then watch films on a big-screened TV well before they became relevant, you know, one of those projection TVs. Apart from the TV, he was very understated. He wasn't a guy into all the gear, you know.

Now, let's just back up a minute. Derek Bramble told us about how his and Rod's song, 'Spice of Life', came together to eventually become a hit for The Manhattan Transfer. At the same time, Dee was working some demos with Jaki Graham and then he got a phone call:

I was in my apartment and I got a call from my manager and he said, 'Listen, somebody's going to be calling you. I can't tell you who it is because I'm not allowed to but don't leave your house as they are going to call you within twenty minutes.'

I thought he was winding me up, but I did what I was told and waited for the phone to ring which it did. I was, like, 'Hello?'

The voice at the other end said, 'Do you know who this is?'

I said, 'Sorry, but no.'

He said, 'It's David Jones.'

I was, like, 'What do you want, mate?'

He said, 'Well, you know, I heard you are the new hot shit in town so do you fancy coming in and producing my album with me?'

Then he said, 'It's David Jones, but you probably know me better by my stage name, David Bowie.'

I fell off my bloody chair. My response to that was, 'I can't because I'm washing my hair', and he laughed his arse off. That was my really nice introduction to my relationship with David Bowie and I co-produced his *Tonight* album in 1984.

Anyway, that same night, I called Rod to tell him. He was flying into London from LA and we agreed to go out for dinner in town. He took me out for dinner and we just sat there looking at each other, laughing our arses off. Neither of us could believe it. He had by now had all that incredible success with Michael Jackson and now here I was working with Bowie. I was never a Bowie fan, really. My sisters were and I appreciated the stuff he had done with Nile Rodgers on *Let's Dance* and the Serious Moonlight Tour, so when I got the call, I was like, 'Holy Shit!' And that's exactly what Rod said, 'Holy Shit!' We were sitting there at dinner, looking at each other and giggling, Rod beaming from ear to ear.

I know that made him really proud, do you know what I mean? Rod had believed in me, he really did believe in me, and the fact that someone like Bowie would see the good in me and want to work with me made him so proud. And you know what, making Rod proud was what really made me proud, too. Rod was like a coach to me, a life coach, a music coach, just a very good bloke in my life. I've had a few of them and Rod was right up there. He cared about me, he cared about what I was doing and when I acted up he would tell me that I was being an arsehole and he would give it to me straight, no bullshit, you know.

So, while Dee went into the studio with Davie Bowie, Rod took his love of movies to another level. Given what we now know of Rod's interest in the world of film, it was perhaps no surprise that he moved into a different direction. Quincy Jones was, by now, taking a break from producing one hit pop record after another and started working as a producer and writing the score for a film called *The Color Purple* and, naturally, he was to call on the talents of his good friend and colleague, Rod, who was to prove equally as proficient at writing for the movies, because he was nominated for an Oscar in 1985 for the film.

Rod Temperton:

Actually the very, very first thing I did for the movies was a film called *Escape to Athena* with Roger Moore and Telly Savalas, a Lew Grade war movie that I was asked to write the then title song for. And I did it and it was called 'Keep Tomorrow for Me'. Now that was, you know, back in the early Heatwave days. Barry Blue worked with me on that one back in late '78, I think.

Then the next thing would be, I guess, *The Color Purple*. Quincy was producing the film with Steven Spielberg directing, and Quincy wrote the music, the score for the film, but he was under an incredible amount of pressure with producing the film as well and one thing and another and so I guess he'd always had it in his mind that I would write with him for the song that was needed to be performed in the movie.

So, I always knew that I was going to be working on that, and so, also because of the pressure Quincy was under, I got involved in some of the themes of the movie. There were a lot of themes in that film, and about three or four I wrote with Quincy and then we did the song. It was another pressure thing. Quincy and I wrote the music and the melody but we didn't have the lyrics. We were at Quincy's house at ten o'clock at night and the next day they were actually going to do this at Universal Studios. We didn't have anything. No words at all.

We finally got a verse, it got to about four in the morning and we finally got a verse that we really liked and we looked at each other and said, 'Blimey, we need to go down to the studio soon so we had better get some help here'. So, we said, 'Who can we call? It's four o'clock in the morning.'

So, Quincy said, 'Now, let's get Lionel Richie.' Just like that.

So we called Lionel Richie at 4 a.m. and Quincy said to him, 'Get your buns over here'.

So the next thing, Lionel arrives in his pyjamas, you know, gets out of his car and he comes in and we sit there and we ganged up on it and finished off the lyric. As with the stuff for Vincent Price, that was another really nice moment, ringing up someone like Lionel in the middle of night and then getting the job done.

Quincy then rang Alice Walker, the writer of *The Color Purple*, the Pulitzer Prize-winning book the film was based on. She is a really wonderful lady. Quincy said to her, 'We've got it. Me and Rod and Lionel have been up all night.' And he read her the lyric over the phone and she cried, you know, she said it was just perfect and she couldn't believe that it was three guys who had written it because it's all about comparing women and the sister thing.

Again, that whole experience was a lot of fun because I was on the set at the film every day because when they were shooting this scene in the juke joint in the club on the set, you never knew, because it was all going down live, you never knew if Steven Spielberg wanted to change something, you know, at any given moment, so you had to be there. So we would sit out there on the set and I used to sit with Alice in the morning. She would be so worried. She had never worked on a movie before and she was always worried about how it was going because it is all done in fragments, you know. For me it was just a lot of fun just being there. I was actually on the set when they sang the song which was called 'Miss Celie's Blues (Sister)' and they filmed it through all this smoke and everything. It was quite fascinating.

Quincy Jones:

Rod came in and helped with a melody here and a title and an attitude
and everything else, which was just true and that, you know. As one of
the producers, I was kind of driving that movie really. We got Steven
Spielberg in and he had never done a film like that before.

He had *Schindler's List*, he had *Always* and *Hook*, all later on. This
was my first time producing a film, at 51 years old, and we didn't have
a lot of time. We started on 5 June and we delivered really fast for a
picture of that size with a $15 million budget. Oprah Winfrey got
$35,000. That was when I first found Oprah and Whoopi Goldberg.

We did three weeks of interior shooting because Steven was
having a baby with Amy Irving. Two days after the baby was born,
we get on the plane and go to 80 degrees or 90 degrees heat in
North Carolina with mosquitoes everywhere. When we got back
we were really fried and everybody needed to take a little rest and
I said, 'Holy Moly, we haven't got a score', and we needed fifty-four
minutes of music, you know. Unbelievable. I had six weeks to score
the whole thing. Six weeks, OK?

And so we get into it and start doing this song. Suddenly, I had
some chords and me and Rod started to develop a melody that
sounded like it was from the right period. By this time, Rod and I are
fried, man, I mean really fried, I mean wasted, and so I woke Lionel
Richie up in the middle of the night and said, 'Lionel, get over here,
man, help me with the lyrics. We've got some business to do.'

So, Lionel gets there, you know, and he got straight into his
system. He said, 'I've got my eyes on you. You woke me in the dead
of night. I bet you are thinking that I don't know anything about
singing the blues!'

It was beautiful, man. There was Lionel, Rod and myself there.
We just had to almost go blank. We sat around and just mumbled
about it and prayed over it, you know.

Rod was young then and he just jumped right into that period
for the film. That's Rod Temperton. He never has any problems
providing his thing. He has an open mind and an open heart and
God gave him a gift.

The Color Purple was nominated for eleven Academy Awards but failed to win any of them. Rod was one of a dozen who helped score and write the film's music. Rod, Quincy and Lionel Richie were nominated for Best Original Song for 'Miss Celie's Blues (Sister)', but lost out to Lionel's own 'Say You, Say Me', from the movie *White Nights*.

The final really big hit of Rod Temperton's illustrious career came in the same year that he was nominated for that Oscar. Along with Bruce Swedien and Dick Rudolph, the man who more than a decade earlier had written the classic and hernia-inducing tune (if you try to sing it yourself) 'Lovin' You' for his wife Minnie Ripperton, along with many other well-known songs and soundtracks, Rod produced the music for the film *Running Scared*, starring Gregory Hines and Billy Crystal. From it, Klymaxx's 'Man Size Love', written by Rod, reached No. 15 on the US Billboard charts, 'Say You Really Want Me' by Kim Wilde made it to No. 44, 'Once in a Lifetime Groove' by New Edition got into the Top 10 of numerous dance charts and 'Sweet Freedom' for Michael McDonald, another tune to be written by Rod, rushed up to No. 7 on the Billboard charts.

Barry Blue:

I was asked to write the lyrics for 'Sweet Freedom' by Michael McDonald and then at the last minute Rod just put together these lyrics for 'Sweet Freedom' and said, 'Let's use that'. To which I kind of thought, 'Well, it's a shame! But you can't win them all, I suppose.'

Rod didn't make a big fuss out of writing lyrics like a lot of people do and he uses phrases that are very commonplace, very, you know, light, but they work for his songs. 'Sweet Freedom' is a perfect example, it's not an unusual line, it has been done before, it's not kind of unique, but it works!

Michael McDonald:

By the time I was back in the studio with Rod to record 'Sweet Freedom', he was hot property, at that point in time part of the pop R&B hierarchy, if you know what I mean. He was like the Babyface or LA Reid of his day. Rod was probably the first guy in that kind of movement that would eventually lead to the kind of big hip hop movement in the US, you know.

Rod still lived in a town called Worms in Germany and I remember thinking, 'Wow, that sounds like a really remote strange little town!' He told me that it had the largest number of clocks per capita in any city, you know, large like Big Ben–type clocks and they would all go off at the same time every day, you know, and I remember thinking, 'Well, that sounds like a pretty romantic place to live! If you are going to pick a spot in the world to live …'

But, he was living pretty much in England part of the time as well and in Europe and then in the US for the remainder of his year, you know. I think he largely came over to the US just to work and spent any time he had off back home in England or Germany.

Rod Temperton:

The funny thing for me is that, from being a child, my love of movies was just immense, you know. I used to go to the movies all of the time. When I first came to America, on a day off we would go to see five movies on a Saturday. I would look in the paper and see one that started at eleven in the morning so we could be out by one to get onto the next one. The cinemas were all in one area of town so we would go all the way through until two o'clock in the morning. That's how much I really loved movies.

Of course, once you start working on movies, it's a whole different story and so it kind of ruins the image a little bit and it's very difficult to look back at anything you have worked on movie-wise and not remember some dramatic story, no matter how dramatic the thing is. You always find something that happened on a certain day and how you were trying to figure out this or that, you know, so it does kind of take away a bit of the fantasy of the movie. But, it's fascinating work, you know.

I mean, after *The Color Purple*, I then went on to do a movie on my own, this film *Running Scared*, which was with Billy Crystal and Gregory Hines, kind of a Chicago cop movie, and for that I had to write, I don't know, I think about six songs and about forty-five minutes of orchestral score, you know, a full score for the movie, and it was real pressure because you get the film at the last minute and, you know, here it comes, the film is coming out on a certain date and you've got to be done and so we were up day and night again doing that one.

It was a lot of work for me, but I enjoyed it, I had a lot of fun, you know, and managed to get in another hit off it, with 'Sweet Freedom' with Michael McDonald. Actually, that's one of my favourites, 'Sweet Freedom'. It was a nice one to do. Obviously it was inspired by the scene in the movie that, you know, the director said to me, 'This is a song, this is where I want this song to go and it's the whole thing of these two cops going on vacation in the Florida Keys and, you know, running around with the girls and everything.' So, the whole idea for the song came out of that and then I asked Michael to do it and he agreed, which was great and so, it was just wonderful to do it, you know.

And then there were songs for some quite different people, you know. Fee Waybill sang the title song for the film and Ready For the World was another group, another big hit, I think. It was interesting to do all these different things and then the next day you do a car chase, you know, which is a six, six and a half minute car chase that went through the streets of Chicago on to the L tracks, you know, bouncing about with trains and things, and the director wanted music all the way through this. It's so difficult to get all that together and be thinking about 'Sweet Freedom' and the other songs and areas at the same time, knowing you've got to get it all done.

I mentioned about taking away the fantasy of the movies by working on one and I think, after *Running Scared*, I realised that although it's great to write tunes for a movie, you just don't feel the same way as you do when you have finished a record, you know, because, and let's be honest here, the first reason for the music in a movie is to service that movie, you know. It's not about your music really, and shouldn't be. I mean it's the director's vision and it's about the characters and the story and the music just backs it up.

It was a very good discipline. It was very clearly defined. But when you are used to writing songs and creating records, it's a very different process that inevitably had me going back to doing records because I just thought that that was more fun for me than the movies. But you know, I managed to do it and I was thankful for that.

Michael McDonald:

It was kind of funny because the kid that did the demo of 'Sweet Freedom' that I heard is a friend of mine, he lives in Nashville. I see him all the time and he's a record producer, he's produced quite a few hit records in the country genre. Anyway, he was the singer on the demo and when I first heard it, I thought it was a hit record, to my taste, for sure. I just gave it my best shot when I got into the studio. I remember thinking when I first heard the track, I went, 'Man, this track is a hit! All by itself. If I can just get from the beginning to the end in one piece, I'm home free!'

Then, when I heard the first mix-down I remember thinking, 'Wow!' It just sounded so good, you know, and it sounded so different to me, as a track it was something unusual. It was great fun doing it, great fun working with those guys. Dick was a really funny guy and working with Bruce Swedien, who is a genius in his own right ... wow.

But, I'll be honest with you, I was totally surprised at what a big hit it was, you know! And especially in England, you know, I didn't expect that. It was that song that really opened the door to us, my band coming over and playing in the UK all these years later. We still come over and play a lot, and even the Motown stuff that I did years later, probably a large part it came from the 'Sweet Freedom' single. In its own way it introduced us to the UK audience, you know?

Rod just had that ability.

For me, he was in the same league as Burt Bacharach or Donald Fagen and Walter Becker of Steely Dan, those kind of artists. They get away with a certain line of sophistication that I think pop music frowns upon, but they pull it off so well and it feels so natural that people respond to it and I think sometimes the industry doesn't give the average audience enough credit for what they are listening to, you know, what they would be able to find compatible, and so many times they think, 'Oh, odd time signatures or a too sophisticated chord progression here and there will be lost on pop audiences and people won't listen to it'. But I found many times with writers like Burt Bacharach or Rod Temperton or the Steely Dan guys that they will prove that that's a rule that isn't necessarily true, you know.

Artists like Rod only come along once in a blue moon. He was one of the best songwriters and one of the brightest. Looking back on it in time and with retrospect, the music that Heatwave did and all the stuff that Rod did with Quincy will probably remain some of the classic R&B of all time.

That's because he constructed everything in his songs. Working with Rod was very low-key and strictly business, you know what I mean. He was just a very serious kind of musician and knew exactly how he wanted things to be, even in terms of the vocals that he wanted from me. So, he was very low-key but very much kind of a hands-on producer in terms of making a record with someone. I owe him a lot.

'Sweet Freedom' won Rod Temperton another award in the music industry as the song picked up the gong for the Best Film Theme or Song, defeating the other two nominations, 'A Kind of Magic' by Queen and 'In Too Deep' from Genesis. Between *The Color Purple* and *Running Scared*, Rod added yet another string to his bow. Rod:

Oh yes, we did the *Oprah Winfrey Theme*, the theme for her TV show. We came up with that during a weekend while working on *The Color Purple*. Oprah obviously knew Quincy from *The Color Purple* and she asked him to write the theme for her TV show, so Quincy and I went up to Idaho or somewhere like that, I don't know, for the weekend and we wrote this theme for Oprah Winfrey which was pretty good. So that was another different type of thing that I was able to do and it was just a lot of fun.

The time was now set for Michael Jackson's follow-up to the record-breaking *Thriller*. It was a question that so many had asked at the time of the release of *Bad*, again produced by Quincy Jones – just why did the album not contain any Rod Temperton songs after the man from Cleethorpes had penned so many of his classics and had such a big hand during the whole *Thriller* process? Well, modestly, here now is the answer to that conundrum from Rod:

Quincy worked with Michael on another album after I'd stopped. Well, no, that's not strictly true. I worked on *Bad* a little bit. I didn't have any songs on *Bad* but I worked on arrangements and bits and bobs, but I think he did some more stuff after that and, to be honest, I was asked to write, I think, on at least a couple of the albums after that and, you know, I'm always honest with it. I said, 'If I come up with something, I'll let you know.'

But, at that point, I didn't really know where Michael was going. I didn't understand the albums he later made in quite the same way I had done in the past, especially on *Thriller*. I could have said to him, 'If I come up with something that I think is going to be great for you, I'll call you', because I know Michael would always listen, you know, that's one thing. He would always listen to a song I sent him. I think so, anyway, but I just couldn't get a handle on where I thought he thought he was going. Does that make sense? It was a case of him moving in a new direction.

And so I never really got inspired or came up with an idea, so what am I going to do? I'm not going to send him just a bunch of things because I don't work like that. And I always figured that if I don't do that, so that he's just getting some cast-offs or something, that when I knock on the door and say, 'Well, I really think I've got a tune for him', perhaps they will say, 'Hey, let's do it'.

So, we will see. Maybe we will work together again one day. I'll never say never. You never know, I might write something else for Michael Jackson at some point, but I've got to be feeling it and, you know, I don't really know what his plans are or anything about his career at the moment. So, you know, it's just that I'm not in the picture.

Siedah Garrett, who we will hear from in the next chapter, said that Rod was:

… there for every step of the *Bad* record. He was certainly there every time I was there doing vocals, and so I would assume that he was there throughout all of the track building and the choosing of the songs as well. Quincy's really smart and dependent on Rod and Rod's choices and tastes and comments and influence. It says everything about Rod Temperton that he would play down his role on such an iconic album.

10

GROOVE OF MIDNIGHT

As we approached the end of the 1980s, in terms of writing pop hits, Rod's light was dimming just a little bit – how could it not after such an incredible success rate – although he continued to work and pen some typically fine tunes.

He teamed up again with Dick Rudolph to produce the excellent and criminally ignored *Kiss of Life* by Siedah Garrett, a woman who was making a big name for herself in the music industry in the mid to late 1980s. She was heavily involved in Michael Jackson's *Bad* album, singing a duet with Jackson on the lead-off single, 'I Just Can't Stop Loving You'. She also co-wrote 'Man in the Mirror', regarded by many as the best song on that LP. In a 2013 interview with Luka Neskovic, Garrett said:

> All I wanted to do was give Michael something he would want to say to the world, and I knew it couldn't be another 'Oh baby, I love you' song. It had to be a little bit more than that. It needed to have some substance. He hadn't recorded anything like this to that point. I was just taking the risk that he might not get it, you know.
>
> First of all, I needed to send it through Quincy because if Quincy didn't like it there is no way that Michael would've ever heard it. It was a huge privilege for me when Quincy decided that the song was good enough to play for Michael.
>
> I got involved with Quincy Jones when he wanted to put together his own Manhattan Transfer type group, and I think there were 800 people that morning and I was one of the first because

I'd been told about it early on, and I think I went in at seven in the morning or something like that, even though the gig started at noon, so I was really far ahead in the line, I think I was third or something like that. So, it was a massive cattle-call over a two-week period and, you know, you sign in for what day you want to come back in for an audition and I was like, 'I'm ready to audition today'.

So I auditioned that day and the guy that was running the audition, Tom Bailer, sort of videotaped my audition and he told me later that he ended up judging a lot of other performances by my performance that day, which was quite an honour. And then, over a period of like nine or ten months, I would get these letters, saying, 'Congratulations, we are down to 250 from 2,000', you know, 'Congratulations, we are down to 100, you're still in the running'.

This was over nine months. Then it was down to fifty, then twenty-five and then five and then finally there were four of us or something like that. And, during that time, I started doing everybody's demos, including for Rod and Quincy for Patti Austin's album they did and for Michael Jackson's. Different things were coming in and I think they were doing Patti at the time, *Every Home Should Have One*. Quincy and Rod were in the studio recording with Patti and Rod and Quincy would go, 'Who's that singer, man?'

Someone would reply, 'Oh, that's Siedah Garrett.'

Rod, 'Again?'

Somebody again, 'Siedah Garrett.'

So, I just kept coming up, and then I met them both working on *Thriller*. They were both such fun. It was really a fun time.

The album produced by Rod for Siedah, *Kiss of Life*, included two songs left over from the *Thriller* sessions all those years before, 'Groove of Midnight' and 'Baby's Got it Bad', a version of Jackson's unreleased 'Got the Hots' with rewritten lyrics. Siedah Garrett:

My initial introduction to Mr Rod Temperton was kind of like crash and burn, you know. He either liked you, or he didn't straight away, there was no middle ground, nothing to sift through. Rod was very, very straightforward and exceedingly English. So, take that for whatever you want it to mean but ... we liked each other straight away, actually. It was good.

When we first met, I had no idea that he was white, OK? His name was Rod, you know, and he was in one of my favourite bands of all time, Heatwave, and he wrote 'Gangsters of the Groove' and he wrote 'Always and Forever' and he had just tons and tons of hits that I just loved dancing to. I just didn't know that the Rod Temperton in Heatwave was this guy from Worms, Germany. You know, he lived in England for most of his life. It was just crazy. So when I met him I was a little surprised, I have to say.

But he refused to assimilate, he remained steadfastly and stoically British throughout his entire career and life and that is what remains endearing about Rod. He doesn't like to blend in or fold in, he's very much his own man and he led his own career in his own way and he didn't bow down to anybody, he didn't give up publishing, he didn't do any of the things that traditionally artists make mistakes and do. Rod was very, very careful with the way he planned his career, which is why he was so successful.

I had first worked with him way before on *Off the Wall*. That was what Quincy was working on when I finally met the whole clan, Quincy Jones, Bruce Swedien, Rod Temperton, you know, and all the players, Nathan East, Greg Phillinganes, all of the cats. It was a really, really heavy time and Rod was right there in the mix, chain-smoking like the Dickens, oh my God!

I remember when we were recording my album, my first solo album with Rod Temperton. We were in the middle of recording vocals, and Rod had a bad tooth, and I guess this day it was just really, really bothering him and it must have been really painful because I'm in the booth doing vocals and he says something like, 'OK, one more take ... a little ... just like the last one, one more time.'

And I see him, I start singing and I see him turn to the engineer and ask for something and the engineer pulls up the 'just one minute' sign and he runs off and he comes back with a pair of flat nose pliers. And Rod Temperton has a cup of black coffee in one hand, a cigarette in the other and he's chain-smoking the cigarette and he puts the coffee down, not the cigarette mind you, puts the coffee down, grabs these pliers, takes a good hold of that tooth that was annoying him and just yanks it out of his mouth. Couple of swigs of coffee, cough on the cigarette and he says, 'All right, that was a good take, love! Moving on …' That is classic Rod Temperton. Need I say more?

When Rod was working on my record, he went through engineers like packs of cigarettes, I'm telling you, he wore them out around the clock, they would have shifts, but he would be in every shift. It was just great. Rod just thrives on the work, that's all that matters.

And when he was there, he was there 110 per cent and when he was not he would be visiting one of his homes in different parts of the world. Chilling, you know. He had a very, very balanced yin yang lifestyle. When he was working, he was working, not sleeping, maybe eating because that's part of the whole life thing. I think food is the thread that weaved throughout his entire life as when he was working he still ate and when he was playing or chilling in his homes or on vacation, he still ate well. I just loved that about him. Rod had the perfect life, I used to tell him that all the time, that I wanted to be him when I grow up.

Barry Blue:

Over the years, I still worked with Rod on two or three different projects, and Siedah Garrett's album was one we worked on together. I wrote the title track 'Kiss of Life'. We've written about, I would say, half a dozen songs over the forty years that we have known each other. I've mainly tended to write melody lines and lyrics and Rod's done the music. Mostly, though, it's just not been in the right place at the right time. We've done three or four projects that way.

You know, maybe in the future, we'll start working together more closely. So we never really lost touch even though he lived a lot in LA while I've maintained my roots in London. We saw see each other regularly, and came back together again after thirty years on a project with Emily Friendship, so, you know, it's gone full circle! I am delighted that he always stayed a good mate. I'm delighted for his incredible success and I think more people should recognise him for the talent he is.

The uniqueness about Rod is that he is just the same as he was before he was successful, he has not changed a bit, he's just a mate, he's just a good mate. I look upon him as a mate, he looks upon me as a mate, and I think everyone who comes into contact with him feels the same way. He's just a really, really nice guy as well as being possibly one of the top pop geniuses of our time!

Siedah Garrett:

What was amazing about working alongside Rod was that he had a vast understanding of how all the instrumentation works with all the other things that go along with the track, the sound-engineering and the vocals and how everything lays together. It was magic really to see him work. Rod just has melodies coming out of his ears. He has melodies in the instrumentation and melodies in the vocals and just melodies throughout and they all blend so flawlessly together. He was just an incredible musical talent, arranger and writer.

I think Rod's work stands for itself in the history of music.

He's just an incredible contributor to our creative culture, to our artistic culture and he has influenced things in ways we may never know because his songs even to this day are being sampled and re-sampled and used and reused in different ways and in different arenas and his work is still generating more creative expression. He was invisible, almost a shadow over the whole artistic business, especially the music business. But I'm speaking of the whole culture. He has just interwoven in so many ways that we don't even know. His songs are like the air we breathe, they are in us, all around us, but we don't even think about it, it's just there.

That's what Rod Temperton was to me and I think to the world.

Unless you are that kind of artist or that kind of person with that kind of feeling and passion for the work that you do, you will not understand what that is, you don't get it. I totally understand that and Rod was a perfectionist at it. He lived well, he works on what he wants to work on, he invested well, so he has different beautiful homes all over the world with designers coming in to fit different fabrics and he designed all his bedroom furniture in his new flat ... castle ... in England.

He just had an amazing creative energy that people don't even know about, you only know about the music, but Rod was an incredible designer and he studied architecture as well. You don't move things around in the bedroom because the bed is in the wall and everything is in the actual building that it's in because it was designed exactly that way. Rod doesn't like bits of furniture sticking out, I guess. I noticed this from all these plans he had and all the houses he's got. Everything is very succinct and tightly grouped and can be put away and brought back out and put away again.

So, I think the layering of his musical abilities and the layering of his architectural creative abilities makes him quite a deep creative person, just the layers of his creativity are very, very deep and people only know the surface part of Rod, if that. I'd known him for years before I found out that he'd studied architecture when he was showing me the plans that he built for the furniture in the house. This is so weird. I was like, 'Dude, I've known you for twenty years and I never knew that about you.' He was like, 'Yeah, you know now', then puff, puff.

Quincy and Rod and the whole recording experience has taught me how to record songs and the progress of building a song and how to develop a song's structure and for every bit of it I was just a sponge. I was just there soaking it all up and I don't know any other way to do it. That's why when I was with the Brand New Heavies I had quite an intense time. Their work ethic was just not what I was used to. It was different, really different.

The next project for Rod was a return to working with his good friend Barry Blue, who was producing an album for Wayne Hernandez, who later went on to work with Damon Albarn and Gorillaz. Rod co-wrote with Barry two songs on the LP, called 'Telepathic', 'Dancin' on the Edge' and a minor UK hit, 'Let Me Call You Angel'. Barry Blue:

'Let Me Call You Angel' was a really good song. We wrote the two songs together. I would write some of the melody and then Rod would come in and finish it and co-author the lyrics together. It was a case of 'I'll take it this far and then you take over'. He worked mostly on the groove and the groove was something he was very

good at, of course. In fact, he was the best at creating the groove
– ever.

Yet, he couldn't write music, not in the normal way. He had the
power to create something in his head. Not to put too fine a point
on it, you know a savant can look at a drawing and then draw it in
his head or he can look at a photograph and then replicate it in a
drawing, to make it look exactly the same, well that was a talent that
Rod had. He could imagine a song already finished in his head, every
single part of it. And, he could do that without ever knowing musically how you would get to what he had in his head. That's certainly
a talent that not many people have got. He was born with it.

Siedah Garrett next worked with Rod on Quincy Jones' follow-up to
The Dude, 1989's *Back on the Block*. It was a remarkable LP featuring
legendary musicians from across three generations including Miles Davis,
Sarah Vaughn, Dizzy Gillespie, Ray Charles, Ella Fitzgerald, Ice-T, Big
Daddy Kane, George Benson, Luther Vandross, Dionne Warwick, Chaka
Khan, Bobby McFerrin, Take 6, Barry White, Al Jarreau, Al B. Sure!, James
Ingram, El DeBarge and Joe Zawinul, the man who wrote the implausibly
good 'Birdland' for Weather Report. Rod Temperton, along with Jerry
Hey, Ian Prince and Quincy Jones, won the Grammy Award for Best
Instrumental Arrangement for 'Birdland' on the *Back on the Block* LP.

Siedah Garrett:

Quincy and Rod were like brothers. They would butt heads sometimes artistically but they were also like brothers in that they really
needed each other deep down, on a soulful level, not just for the
projects they worked on together. That was just an excuse for them
to hang out together and to be creative and fun. Neither of them can
drive but Rod was a race car fanatic and go to Monaco every year
to go to the races. He doesn't drive but he is a race car enthusiast.
I don't get it, I don't get it. He was such an anomaly, I'm telling you.

Herbie Hancock also recalls Rod's love of fast cars and Formula One:

Because of Rod I got into auto racing. Rod loved Formula One
and he used to go to a lot of the races around the world. In fact, he

actually invited me and my wife – and paid for everything – to go to Shanghai to see the first ever Formula One race they had there. He went to Monaco lots of times as he had a house down that way and was a member of some race club or other, you know, a club for people who are really into Formula One racing. He got tickets every year to see some of the events. He always thought I could go with him for the races in Europe as I spent so much time there but I was only able to go with him one time. He shared himself with everybody; he was that kind of person. He was a model citizen, a model citizen of the world.

Rod Temperton:

Back on the Block was an extraordinary experience. Sometimes, I had to pinch myself. Here I was, this man from Cleethorpes, in the studio with the likes of Ella Fitzgerald and Sarah Vaughn. You couldn't make it up. I couldn't wait to get into work for those sessions. Working on 'Birdland', a song I loved anyway, was just magical, a totally unforgettable experience. Certainly, when I started out in the music game, I could never have imagined it coming to this.

The studio was a great place to be and there I was telling Ella and Sarah what to do. It was weird but lives with me forever. It's not the kind of thing you are likely to forget is it? Just all the people involved in the making of that record, wow. Quincy pulled in just about everybody he had known over the years and came up with something only he could have done. It might have been the highlight of my time working with him because it was sometimes like a dream being involved with that record. Such is life, though, and I guess I was just really lucky.

Derek 'Dee' Bramble:

Rod never talked about working with those kind of legends. He was just incredibly understated. I mean, if you walked into a room and sat talking to Rod Temperton, you wouldn't even know it was him. He just wasn't that kind of guy, he wasn't flash, and he wasn't a look-at-me guy. He just lived his life the way that he wanted to. If you asked him a question about him, he would answer you. I bet there are loads of people who have sat next to the writer of 'Thriller' on a train in England and not even known it was him.

Rod wrote and arranged 'The Secret Garden' for the LP, along with Siedah, Quincy and El DeBarge. It reached No. 31 on the Billboard charts while the *Back on the Block* album was a huge success across the world, peaking at No. 26 in the UK and No. 9 in the States. It won seven Grammy Awards. Rod Temperton had finished the decade of the 1980s with another smash, just as he had started it. He had become one of the most successful, and certainly one of the most respected and influential songwriters and arrangers of the 1980s.

Next up, back in the UK in 1992, Rod worked alongside Mica Paris for the album *Whisper a Prayer*. Rod wrote and produced four songs for the LP, 'You Put a Move on My Heart', 'We Were Made for Love', 'Two in a Million' and 'Love Keeps Coming Back'. Each song contains that special Rod Temperton magic and the first of them was covered by Tamia on Quincy Jones' *Q's Jook Joint*, released in 1996. Alas, Mica Paris was unable to contribute to this book.

That brilliant Quincy Jones LP contained new, fresh and modern versions of 'Rock with You', done by Brandy and Heavy D, and 'Stomp!' with Luke Cresswell, Fiona Wilkes, Carl Smith, Fraser Morrison and Everett Bradley, the original cast member of *Stomp* as well as Mr X, Melle Mel, Coolio, Yo-Yo, Chaka Khan, Charlie Wilson, Shaquille O'Neal and Luniz.

There was an additional new song penned by Rod for the album called 'Slow Jams', a celebration of bump 'n' grind R&B and featuring Babyface, Portrait, Barry White and girl band SWV, who were replaced by Tamia for a remixed single version which peaked at No. 2 in New Zealand, No. 68 in the States, as well as making No. 19 on Billboard's Hot R&B Songs chart. The single version earned a nomination for the Best R&B Performance by a Duo or Group with Vocals at the Grammy Awards of 1997. Twenty years after his initial success with 'Boogie Nights', Rod Temperton was still producing gold. It should have been a hit across the globe. Rod:

I waited around for the phone to ring. I've never been one to plan too far ahead because I'm very one-track minded. Whatever I'm working on today, I want to actually finish it to see it through to its conclusion before then I attempt to take on anything else. The timing was just right to work with Mica on some songs for *Whisper a Prayer* and it got to mean I spent some time back in London.

I think one of the biggest things to do is to please yourself first. You have to love what you are creating. You know, I have attempted quite a few times in my life to write strictly what I thought was a commercial pop song, you know, and say, 'OK, I'm going to write this, this is good, this a hit, this is a commercial pop song'. Every single time anybody has heard it, they've just laughed and thrown it in the trash. I swear to God. And so the one thing I learned through that is to please yourself first, you've got to write something that you truly believe is great and, I mean, from my point of view, it's impossible for me to sell myself for anything. I just say, 'Well, have a listen and if you like it, you know, we'll do it'.

But I've never been able to stand in front of somebody and say, 'Oh, this is great and we should be doing this and it's going to be like this' if I don't love it first, because there's just no way I could get up there, I just can't do that and so, you know, from a young writer's point of view, I mean, obviously it's great to get the craft and to be able to attempt to write all kinds of things because you have to find yourself, you have to find who you are in writing and what you can do. But still, the first criteria is write something that you love first and once you feel those hairs standing up on the back of your hand, you can go to the world with it.

11

THE INVISIBLE MAN

When recording the interviews for the BBC documentary that make up part of this book, Rod Temperton was working again with Barry Blue and a young and talented artist called Emily Friendship. This was pretty much the last known work for Rod before his untimely death. This is the interview with Emily in full, and I hope it gives a real insight into the man himself and what it was like to work with him after all of his enormous success as a songwriter:

JED: Right, you are a very fortunate person to be with working with Rod at the moment, tell me about the experience thus far.

EMILY: It's very difficult to sum that up in words, and coming from a lyricist that's a pretty stupid thing to say, but it's been absolutely incredible, an amazing experience. He is a genius when it comes to music, he has given me some of the most incredible experiences and I haven't even worked with him for that long, but yeah … the way he sees his music is the way I think an artist sees a painting, you know, he hears the entire song before he's even put his fingers on the keyboard and it's incredible and he really has got the best out of me. He knows how to get the best out of people.

JED: How did this come about, you working with Rod?

EMILY: Well, I was introduced to Rod through my publisher, Barry Blue. He sent my CD to Rod and we actually live quite close to each other, so I went out there and met him and yeah, we had a great time, I played my demos and then he played his songs, and that was quite funny ... I mean, I didn't actually know who he was when I met him, I'm ashamed to say. But his catalogue was quite a lot more impressive than mine at that point!

JED: What did he play you then? To sell himself to you?

EMILY: Oh God, I can't remember now. He has this silver CD with like some of the best songs ever, do you know, I don't think 'Thriller' was on it, but 'Always and Forever' and lots of songs that I recognised were.

JED: And once you heard them, you thought, 'God, all of these were enormous songs?'

EMILY: Yeah, absolutely! It was nice to do it that way, I mean, he's nothing like you would imagine. He's the most humble successful person I've ever met, I mean, if I didn't know who he was before I had met him, if I hadn't known what he had done, I think that I would have expected something quite different, but he was so sweet, he's such a friend to me, he's such a good person, he's a lovely person and I'm amazed that he has achieved what he has achieved ... that he has done what he has done and remained the way he is.

JED: So, how does the process go now? How do you write a song with Rod?

EMILY: I have to say, I have always been quite free when it comes to writing lyrics and working with him was ... well, it put me in a position where I had to work really hard. The first song that I had to write lyrics for I think it near enough took a month, there was just sort of a matter of trying to see what he likes, what he kind of imagined for that song, because the other thing is that he sees the song as a whole, he doesn't just, you know, put a couple a bits together and let me run off and do what I want. He has an idea so, you know, it was just kind of getting to know each other and then we wrote three songs or at least recorded songs within the space of about four days. So, it was definitely the hardest writing session I've ever done, but I feel like I gained so much from him and he's taught me so much, lyrics aside. I never knew I could sing the way that I sing with him!

JED: Is he writing the song and then you're writing the lyrics, is this how it's working?

EMILY: Well, this all comes down to technical terms. He basically writes the music, he has the melody ideas which I am very grateful for. He then gives me the opportunity to write the lyrics, because he doesn't do that with people, you know, he does it himself. He's not particularly a big fan of his own lyrics, but he knows that the music almost speaks to him, so I'm basically reading his mind for us to come up with something that works, and when it does work, ah, it's the best feeling in the world.

JED: Was it amazing when you first met him? Most people go, 'How does some guy from Cleethorpes, a white guy from Cleethorpes, come up with this kind of a sound?'

EMILY: I met this Northern guy, you know, and he was just very, very friendly. For me, it went in reverse. I never was at that point where I was nervous to work with him. As you know I've worked with some great producers, but, you know, I never had that with him and we gradually kind of grew together so that we ended up doing great stuff together, masterpieces!

JED: Are the songs right up there with 'Rock with You', 'Off the Wall', 'Thriller' ... the list is endless ... 'Give Me the Night', all the Heatwave stuff. Is it the same kind of style of music?

EMILY: I'm very proud of what we've done, I mean, they are great songs to me. I'm very used to working with bits and then, you know, you try your best, but working with him, I mean, it's been totally different.

We've got songs, good songs; the songs that, you know, make you want to hear the good stuff, the old good stuff. And this is the good stuff, I'm telling you.

JED: So what is he like to work with, you say he's a genius. Is he bringing the best out of you as well, so you actually like to work with him?

EMILY: Well, I don't quite know how to answer that. It just goes so easy. We listen to some music and pick the favourites and I go away. I like to write by myself, as I'm not as good at writing lyrics when I'm under pressure, but you've got to do it. So, then we'll come together and, you know, we'll rehearse it a bit and then we are off and we have our little cigarette break and coffee. But it's very relaxed, and he's very patient! This is a huge thing for me! I mean, I don't have a problem with working fast enough; I've got more than one track out in a day. But he is very patient and it has allowed me to basically reach my full potential.

I just hope that I can continue working with Rod because he's the best thing I think that's happened to my music career personally and professionally.

JED: How does Rod write? Does he just sit at the piano and doodle away and then sort of goes, 'Oh, I've got it! There's a tune?'

EMILY: He doesn't do it in front of me! He does it by himself, he does the music by himself and it takes him a while, you know. Everybody works so differently and everybody produces different things, but you know, as far as Rod is concerned, he takes his time and he is very focused when he's working with me.

Nowadays, I'm in a studio with one guy one day and then another guy another day but Rod and I have, you know, this piece of time that we've just dedicated to each other. It's just the way he does it; it just brings out the absolute best.

I've also been working with Guy Chambers, the man most famous, I guess, for writing with Robbie Williams, and he's fantastic. I loved working with Guy, we had such a laugh, I mean he's just hilarious!

I had so much fun in that session. I grew up with classical music and I find it so important that, when you're writing songs, that one of you is very musical and Guy is just incredible. He is very musical, very talented … and very funny!

JED: Is the experience completely different to working with Rod?

EMILY: Very much so, you know. Both are very talented, but work in a very different way from each other, you know? But both have been incredible experiences.

JED: Do you find it incredible that you are working with someone of Rod's stature?

EMILY: I do find it amazing … like I said, I'm ashamed to say that I'm not one of the world's most clued up women on, you know, the old soul, the good stuff. I'm certainly learning a lot about it now, but I grew up with classical music, so I know a lot more about Prokofiev and Tchaikovsky than I do about Heatwave. It did start to strike me when I had meetings and people had asked me who I was writing with, and I would say, 'I'm working with a guy called Rod Temperton'. And everybody said to me, 'Whaaaat? You're working with Rod!? Not some guy called Rod Temperton?'
   He plays me stuff, we sit down and listen to music moments and I've heard a lot of his stuff. He's very talented, I mean, it's quite amazing to hear those things when you're halfway through working on something with him yourself. It's like, 'OK, you did this and this and this? And this and this!?'

JED: Does this make you listen to his songs differently now that you are working with him?

EMILY: Yeah, absolutely. It's quite funny. I'm really proud and I'm really grateful, I mean, I do find myself singing a lot, especially as I love soul, I love the old stuff, the old-school stuff is great and I do find myself saying, 'Well, that's Rod! This is Rod! This is also modern, this is Rod, too.'

When I first realised that he genuinely did write for Michael Jackson, I got out my *Thriller* album and I went through it and I was like, 'He wrote this! And he wrote this! Oh, gosh!'

And then I went back and I said to him, 'You're really good, you know!' It was a bit of a late reaction, I know.

I've always been a huge fan and I still am of Michael Jackson's, but *Bad* was the first time I had anything pop. I had this one album. Then, a few years after that I bought *Thriller* and obviously I loved it. Then, I kind of went backwards and I bought the *Off the Wall* album a couple of years ago, and, you know, it was great!

JED: Does Rod write different styles for different people? Have you helped him in bringing any sort of classical sound out on the way you're working with him at the moment?

EMILY: No, I wouldn't say that. We are basically working on good songs. He's an amazing musician. I don't have to say anything, you know, his stuff is already there, it's all complete. And that's why it amazes me that he can wake up in the morning with this song in his head and he can hear everything, the percussion, the piano and violin … everything. He hears it before he's even touched the keyboard.

He's a total genius and I just love him for the fact that he's so humble, you know, you just wouldn't know what he's achieved. There should be a parade for Rod in this country. He's been so successful and you know, it's a shame that not so many people really know and appreciate what he has done. It's about time that they did. But, I mean, he won't like it, not one bit. He is a very humble and very private man. If that's what he wants, then that's the way it should be. But I think that he's the greatest thing since sliced bread.

Alas, the project, along with another with Mica Paris, never saw the light of day (not yet anyway) as Barry Blue, speaking to me for the purpose of this book, explains:

Emily decided that she wanted to be an actress rather than a singer and so she moved to New York and so we were left with all of these tracks but with no artist to record them, which was bizarre. I still have the demos of about half an album. Luckily we only did that amount, if I'm honest with you. They are brilliant tracks but whether anyone will record them and put them out, I just don't know. They should come out because they are great songs. The music industry is very weird and they are probably now finding a whole load of Rod Temperton tracks that Rod wrote and looking to release them. But the songs he did with Emily are there. Whether people realise or remember that he was working with Emily and Rod was enthusiastic about working with her, I don't know.

What I do know is that after that, Rod then recorded an album with Mica Paris and this is where the music industry sucks, really. Mica is a really good singer and Rod spent a lot of time on the album with her, a year and a half or so in 2012, 2013, around that time. He called me up when he had finished and I heard some of the tracks and he said to me, 'You know what, I've just finished this album and no one is interested in it'. He couldn't get a deal on it. I was fuming on his behalf, that someone that talented, one of the best songwriters that the UK has ever produced, who had spent all that time labouring on an album, couldn't get a deal. I was really shocked and he called me to see if I could get some interest in it. I said to him, 'I'll get back to you and sort something out', but it never happened. That album should definitely come out now.

Typical of Rod, he never dwelled on it. He was never good at promoting himself, in spite of all of his success. He took everything in his stride, at face value. If he heard that someone didn't like one of his songs he wouldn't ask, 'Well, why don't you like it?' He would just say, 'OK, I'll write another one'. He was that kind of guy, you know. Throughout his career, no one knew how talented he was because he had no one championing him. He did all right financially so he didn't pursue it.

I think, after that with Mica, he thought, 'I'm not bothered any more', and so he just decided to take a rest and travelled a lot. He had a lot of property all over the world and I heard that he even owned his own island near Fiji. Seemed like a long way to go for a holiday, though! He was very content.

I am these days a director for the Performing Arts Society in King's Cross in London and Rod would still come in to see me.

He was very down to earth. He never drove so he didn't want a big car and he never had any interest in having a chauffeur or that kind of stuff. He would come on the train and we would go to a café for egg and chips for lunch. He didn't want for anything, he was just very content with his life. He did a deal with Warner's before he died. He was a very astute businessman as well as a great songwriter, was Rod. His income from his songs was gigantic, deservedly so.

Mica Paris' manager, Nick Stewart, confirmed that Rod had written some tracks and asked Mica to add her vocals to them, which she did, but the money required for the music to come out was more than anyone was willing to pay. Nick also said that he had hoped to resurrect the project and spoke to Rod shortly before his death, but no agreement was forth-coming. Nick told me:

Rod was a very private individual and really was not very keen to do any promotion of the album. He was the kind of man who loved the fact that he could walk down the King's Road in London without anyone knowing who he was.

Now, surely, is the time for someone to put these songs out as a tribute to the master songwriter. There must be lots of people who would love to hear what Rod was able to conjure up in the second decade of the twenty-first century. Every single fan of his would be thrilled, I'm sure, if both the songs written with Emily Friendship and those down with Mica Paris now hit the market.

Derek 'Dee' Bramble:

Rod just continued to live his life, you know. When you've written some of the biggest records historically it allows you to take your foot off the gas. He had houses in Switzerland, London, LA, Bali, I think, all over the joint, and he and Kathy loved travelling, going off to weird and wonderful places.

As with any situation, every dog has its day and once the 1990s came in with the likes of Teddy Riley and all of those blokes, the temperature changed and the music styles changed. Michael Jackson started working with Teddy and then with R-Kelly and others.

Artists are always looking to work with the new, hot thing and that's just the straight truth of the world, you know, 'OK, what have you done for me lately?'.

Fortunately, Rod's body of worked kept more artists afloat than the artists would give him credit. Not that they would say that they could have done it without him. If I had been with Michael and working with Teddy there is no way that I wouldn't have had a Rod song on my record, there's just no way. But people change, times change and people move on, that's just the nature of things, you know.

Rod, left to his own devices, could get into the ring with anyone and that's the truth of it. He was always in the studio working, doing something with somebody, helping them out and giving something back. That was his way.

So, we know that there are demos of songs Rod wrote with Emily Friendship, we know that there is a completed album of Rod's songs done with Mica Paris which have yet to surface and Dee also has some stuff of his and Rod's which he is now undecided about. Derek:

I was just going through a box last week in the middle of November 2016 and I found all of mine and Rod's demos with me and Rod in a room singing. There's a bunch of them but the truth of the matter is that I don't know if I would ever put them on the Internet because these are my treasures and my personal memories, I don't know though. I found them so we'll see how that goes. Just to have found them and know I still have them on old cassette tapes means a lot to me. Actually, I don't even have a working cassette machine but I'm in the process of re-winding them all and making sure that they are not all broken. At some point, I would like to get them digitised and I'm actually trying to categorise them right now.

Listening to them brought me a lot of sadness but reminded me of the great honour I had of having him be my Obi-Wan Kenobi, if you like. For me to be able to go on and prove his belief in me was right as I went on to do stuff without him was such an amazing thing to be able to do. Rod was the lightning rod to my career so to still be in the game a little bit and working hard and enjoying it is a great way for me to pay him back. And I will do it with good intent, with integrity and the way Rod would have done it. That's now the best thing I can do.

The last known song of Rod's to be recorded was in 2009, a song co-written with Catero Colbert called 'Family Reunion', a return to working with George Benson for his album *Songs and Stories*, the first time they had worked together since the worldwide success of *Give Me the Night* twenty-eight years earlier. Speaking on *The George Benson Sessions: The Making of Songs and Stories*, George said this:

We approached Rod Temperton who worked with me on the album *Give Me the Night*. He wrote 'Love X Love' and 'Give Me the Night' itself that were the biggest songs of that particular record. Then with this album, he wrote the song called 'Family Reunion'. It was a great idea. How can you take a song about family and make it interesting? Well, Rod found a way, that's the kind of guy he is. I was elated when I heard the song. He promised me that he'd written something that I might think would be great and he was right. When I heard it I couldn't wait to sink my teeth into it.

Marcus Miller was the co-producer on the project:

'Family Reunion' was probably one of the first songs when we all went, 'Oh, yeah'. The guy sang to his wife that family is important; we've got to make sure that we keep our family together. We've been kind of drifting apart so let's have a family reunion. You know, you haven't heard that sung in a song before. Being able to find something new to sing about in this day and age is incredible. I think that is the strongest point of that song.

Yes, even closing in on his sixties, Rod Temperton was still able to draw inspiration to write something innovative and something hugely respected by musicians who still wanted to work with him. Rod:

I still think music today has got an awful lot to offer. There is new ground being broken. It's just every time, through every era, it's done differently and you have to go along with the flow to see where it's all going to. As far as looking at a song, as it always used to be, it's more problematic, more difficult to write if you only have a thread of sound going. But, it's an interesting challenge.

ALL ABOUT THE HEAVEN

The announcement of Rod Temperton's death on 5 October 2016 shook the music world. Twitter was filled with RIPs from many who had worked with Rod and from lots who hadn't ever had that pleasure, but were just inspired by the songs that filled Rod's brain, such as Boy George, LL Cool J and Mark Ronson. The latter tweeted, 'So devastated to hear that Rod Temperton has passed away, a wonderful man and one of my favourite songwriters ever, thank you for the magic.'

LL Cool J, who sampled Rod's 'Lady in My Life' for his hit song 'Hey Lover', said, 'We have lost a true genius', while Boy George described Rod as 'a great British songwriter'. Chic guitarist and top producer Nile Rodgers posted a photo of himself, Rod and Quincy Jones, saying, 'Your genius gave us a funkier world' – now, coming from Nile, that is saying something. He touched the hearts of the very funkiest.

It was typical that the announcement of Rod's demise came after Rod's private funeral had already taken place. That wouldn't surprise anyone, as he remained invisible through much of his illustrious career, just as he always wanted. As these final quotes suggest, Rod Temperton was a man like no one else.

Bruce Swedien:

I've worked with other artists like Jennifer Lopez, and so on, and I would call Rod and ask him to write a song for this particular artist and if Rod doesn't feel like he can do a song for someone he absolutely won't do it. He is not the kind of composer who will compose something or do a song just to do it. It has to have real meaning. I guess that is why he is not more famous, although the fact that he isn't is kind of amazing still. I read something in an industry magazine a while back. They called Rod Temperton and me the invisible men. We are guys most people have never seen.

Barry Blue:

I was shocked when I heard he had died. I had spoken to him about six weeks before and we made arrangements to meet up after the holidays, around the beginning of October. I found out about his death like everyone else, from a news wire. I wasn't aware that he was terminally ill, I was aware that he wasn't well, he was always coughing. He must have worsened very quickly after he had spoken to a doctor. I tried to contact his wife, Kathy, but we kept missing each other. They were together for a very long time and then one day just decided to get married. Again, that was Rod's style. He probably said, 'Let's get married tomorrow', and then they just did it. He was never one for big pageants or big occasions, big celebrations. He was very low-key about everything which is why he was so endearing. He had met Kathy when she was the PA of the GTO record company boss, Dick Leahy. That was when they met back in the mid-1970s.

The fact that he stayed under the radar for so long is remarkable, given that his songs are everywhere. You can probably hear one of them on the radio every single day and not even know it was a song written by Rod. Yet, you should know them. I think it is more unusual than people realise, because as I said before, he has the structure of the song in his head, the arrangement of the song in his head and nothing can divert from that. Any flick note as we call them, like blue notes that go between the melody, has to have a lyric on it as well, so if it gives you a line that goes 'ba ba dee-bap, ba dee-bap, ba dee-bap', that would have to all be in lyric form as well, so it's not kind of half written, it's all written, every bit of it, everything is scored and written, which is unique because a lot of writers would tend to say, 'Well, you know, we'll just put an "I believe" in there or we'll just kind of put a guitar lick in there'. There was nothing like that with Rod. I can't remember him ever doing anything like that. The way he worked was unique. He must have been born to do it. And boy, did he do it well.

Ted Gledhill:

I had a Christmas card from Rod and Kathy every year. It was always an outrageous one, one which was a marked contrast to all other Christmas cards. He came back to De Aston School in the late 1980s at the height of his success and he also got in touch with me straight away when he lived in Switzerland and invited me over. Over in Switzerland I was privileged to see one of his recording studios, which he used personally in Carona overlooking Lake Lugano. And there, I was amazed to see all the gold discs all the way around the room. He was a very generous host and I was most impressed. Once again, he was self-effacing. You had to ask questions to find out just what his achievements had been. About the only thing he ever admitted to possessing to me was a wonderful sense of harmony.

George Benson:

I love people, and I accept their personalities no matter who they are. You don't have to be a lovey-dovey type person because the world is full of different personalities. You've got 8 billion personalities and they are not all the same! So, if you expect people to fall into your box, you're going to be sadly disappointed because people just don't do that. You know, for me it's a privilege to meet people. Even the ones who are not so pleasant because then you have a challenge. How can I make this person understand that I really care about him, you know?

Me and Rod didn't always see everything the same way during *Give Me the Night*, but for me, the more we came to that conclusion, knowing we just had different personalities, we started to gel, the more creative things became because they only happen between these two people. You know, when I was with Quincy Jones I think differently to when I'm with Bruce Swedien or with Rod Temperton or with the great keyboardist, Greg Phillinganes. I know

Gregory very well and when we get together we think about music from a whole different point of view, but we are very, very flexible. We're not afraid of anything, and Gregory Phillinganes, I knew him when he was a kid, he wasn't afraid.

He tried to play a very difficult jazz tune when he was a kid, and he succeeded … and then all of a sudden I find out he was in Hollywood making records with some of the superstars, and he was still a teenager! I had the same thing happen with Earl Klugh. He was a kid when I met him, he turned out to be a tremendous musician and so was Gregory Phillinganes. Quincy, like Miles Davis recognised, was a great musician from far-off. He hears potential and he hooks into those musicians, he brings them into the fold, and he puts them to work in an environment that allows them to be themselves and to shine. That's what he did with me. And Rod Temperton was the same. He had a huge role to play and with so much musical talent at his disposal, he was able to produce some unique pieces of work. He wrote the biggest hits of my career and he did that with very little fuss at all.

Johnnie Wilder:

After coming off the road with Heatwave, Rod was travelling quite a bit back and forth working with Quincy Jones at the time. Yes, Rod became your regular jetsetter back in the day flying on the Concorde quite a lot. That's when Concorde was flying between Europe and America and also, he was a jetsetter when we recorded. We always went back to the studios in London, England to record all of the rhythm tracks, and our favourite place for Rod to write was at the Blackout in Switzerland where Rod would have a little room where we would lock him up with a piano. He would stay there all night and get a little sleep in the afternoon so we could go and play at night in a club. Then, at the end of the gig we would lock him up again and he would start writing. So, he went from that kind of life to jet setting all over the world and yet few people knew who he was or what he was up to. He just kept himself to himself most of the time but his ear for what was going on around him must have been incredible. He must have just soaked things up like a sponge.

Patti Austin:

Roddy never went anywhere without his woolly sweater and he taught me that, to always carry a sweater with you, you never know when it's going to get cold! I told him once that he had to stop smoking ciggies and to stop not writing a hit every two weeks. He did slow down a little bit and I told him that he's got to pick up the energy on that a little bit more and write more hits. We want at least a hit a week from Rod! To sum him up, this is my message to you. I'm summing him up pretty much as a sweater-wearing, cigarette-smoking lout!

But, I don't mean that. He was a fabulous, amazing, cool, funny, sensitive and deeply disturbed man. No, not really. Just kidding, I'm just kidding. I have to kid around when I talk about Rod. Gosh, he wrote 'Always and Forever', 'Boogie Nights', 'Baby, Come to Me' and 'Thriller'. The list goes on and on and on and on. His legacy? Only time will tell.

Barry Blue:

Rod was very competitive with games, like Monopoly or Chess, and his mind was filled with a lot of information such as obscure capital cities, stuff that you or I just wouldn't know. He loved that. He did enjoy the trappings of success as Kathy did, too, but he would never ram that down your throat. He was never big-headed, never star-struck. I remember he talked to me once about going into the studio with Barbara Streisand and, after about ten minutes he was calling her Babs. He was just that kind of guy. There are lots of famous people in the music business who you would never be able to talk to one-to-one, like Stevie Wonder or Paul McCartney, but Rod was always able to communicate with everyone. He got on with everybody with ease no matter how big they were in the music industry.

Quincy Jones:

The fact that he stayed invisible was his choice. And I've talked to him about that because he doesn't like to get around that stuff, you know. He's not self-promoted at all and not even close to being like that, you know. We've never been into that. Rod, he was a pain in the butt, man. I can't even get him to take an answering service. I'm telling you, he's got five houses now and I said to him, 'For crying out loud, get an answering service. I've been calling you and I can't get hold of you.'

But if he's not there, you can forget about it, you know, forget about emails and all that. He's got a mobile phone, well his wife Kathy has a mobile phone, not Rod, you know. I mean, if he's not home, you are not going to get him, trust me. I've spent thirty years trying. You are never going to get him. I bet if I called him right now, if he was in town right now, if he's not home, the phone will not be answering. When he told me the other day he was sleeping in some place and I was ringing him about thirty times to get hold of him. But, by the time he got to the phone, I'd hung up, you know. Man, he's a tough man to find if he doesn't want to be. And no one ever going to stop him in the street because they don't have a clue who he is.

He enjoys being the invisible man. Oh yeah. He does, he does. He lives like that. He lives like that. He has a place in Canyon, in the United States, in all over the place, well, almost all the place, even his woman, Kathy, wanted one in Worms, not a romantic destination … as yet. He has a country house in the south of France, a beautiful place, and he lives right next door to Ringo Starr, you know.

He likes his privacy and he likes good food, always. He would join me and together we would eat. And that kind of alienated some, with the things we did together. Man, we had some times.

I wouldn't know where to begin in summing Rod up, as well as I know him. That's a hard task, man. He's so many things. Then, if you ask me what my favourite song of Rod's is, it's like someone is asking me which of my seven kids are my favourites? Impossible. They are all my favourites. They are. All of Rod's songs have a totally different thing to say. And he takes chances all the time, Rod writes because he loves to write and he doesn't care whether a song of his is going to be a hit or not, you know. He did a couple with me and a couple with other people but he just writes, he loves to write, you know. He writes everything, which I really admire.

Rod would also spot a talented kid and would try to get a record there within an hour. Rod would see what was in him and take him under his wing, you know. It was a remarkable thirty years working with Rod Temperton. Thirty years? Yeah, something like that. Maybe more. I don't remember.

I think he was about 19 when we first met. He and Kathy are my two favourite people on the planet and will always have the biggest apartment in my heart.

Derek 'Dee' Bramble:

I was around when Rod and Kathy met. I was in the GTO office and Kathy was working for Dick Leahy. I loved them as a couple, they were a fantastic couple. She was the consummate English rose and he was just this unique cat from Grimsby and they made such a wonderful, wonderful couple. I loved being around them. It was always a great laugh. You know, they took my then girlfriend and me to Milan. They invited me to their house in Switzerland and we drove to Milan, as their place was on the Swiss/Italian border and we went shopping. They took us shopping in Milan like it was nothing. For him and Kathy just to get up and do that, that was just such a wonderful and kind thing for them to do. Together, they were just that, really wonderful and kind people.

Bob James:

Rod Temperton was a wonderful friend with extreme talent and I learned a lot from him. I was inspired by him indirectly in all of the projects I did after working with him. I am very proud to call him a good friend and was very saddened by the news that he had passed away. He was directly creatively responsible for some of the best-selling music of all time. He had a wonderful ability to find hooks, music hooks, and more importantly, words. He used words in his songs that were very universal and very catchy and memorable – things like 'Give Me the Night' and other songs that immediately had a memorable, simple, catchy and irresistible hook about them.

Yet, he remained so private. I loved that aspect about him. He was not a show-off and I never heard him brag about his own work. He loved writing songs and being in the studio putting them together and he also loved his privacy. I share a lot of that myself and that may be one of the major reasons why we got along so well. We were good friends privately and didn't need to make a big deal out of that. All I ever saw from Rod was a total positive energy and humbleness and a passion for doing the kind of unique work that he did. I am honoured to be interviewed for this book and having an association with him.

Herbie Hancock:

There was only one Rod Temperton. There was no competition. He has his own place in the music industry. I consider him a great artist. There is no formula for the hits he wrote. He was a very private man and I don't know how he managed that, but he did. He was a genius and figured out ways to ensure his privacy, considering the technology of the day with no emails and cell phones back then. I feel that unfortunately, because we didn't hear much from Rod for several years, that he kind of slipped off the radar, more or less. That was astonishing given what he contributed to the music culture, not just of the pop world, but also of music in general. The fact that he had such a humanitarian spirit is also something I consider to be great about Rod. If anything, the most important component a person can have in his life is his influence on others and I bet you can't find anyone to say anything bad about Rod. He was not only an amazing talent but he was a person with a great heart. It was an honour and a pleasure to work with him.

Barry Blue:

All artists have the wilderness years when you take for granted the great songs that you have done. Now, look back at the songs Rod Temperton wrote. One guy wrote all of these songs. Nowadays, you get ten writers penning a song, or six writing a song. People no longer put together songs like they used to do, it's all manufactured. Rod will be put up there now he has gone with the likes of

Paul McCartney and Ray Davis as one the best songwriters to have hailed from the UK. Yet no one really knew him. When you trot some of his songs out, 'Rock with You', 'Off the Wall', 'Thriller', 'Yah Mo B There', wow, to do all of this stuff. Incredible. 'Boogie Nights' is a song I still listen to and it still sounds new today. They played it on *X-Factor* last night and it sounded as if it was as fresh as a daisy, you know.

John Cameron:

Rod was a lovely guy. And a great musician. It was an absolute pleasure to work with him in those early days of Heatwave. There are only a few people you meet throughout your career and say, 'Ah, that was great', but Rod was certainly one of them.

Derek Bramble:

Whether Rod would like to think it or believe it is another matter, but he was a public guy because of his huge success. It's right that his achievements are now being recognised. I don't know of many English writers who have had such a profound effect on American music. Obviously there are John Lennon and Paul McCartney but, to be honest, such people are very few and far between but Rod is on that list. Alas, I didn't speak to him for the last eighteen months. I live in California and he moved back to London. When I found out he was sick, nobody could get in touch with him. Nobody really knew anything which was just the way Rod lived his life, an extraordinary existence. Jesus, he had a funeral and nobody was told about it. That is Rod to a T.

His music will live on forever, though. There is now going to be an 8-year-old kid somewhere who will pick up and hear the album *Off the Wall* for the first time. They will listen to 'Rock with You' and they will become as infected as we all have been because what Rod has given us and given the world is something so unique but something so kind of present that it doesn't matter how old you get, when you hear that stuff that he wrote your life will be changed for the better forever. These days, kids still cotton onto Michael Jackson as if he is still alive, you know, and that's the legacy of Rod. He gave us the gift that keeps on giving.

Photographer Bobby Holland:

I am so pleased to be part of a book on Rod Temperton. He is a man who never really got the do, the recognition his talents deserved because his music is so everlasting. And the songs came from a guy who was just so laid back.

Journalist, Steven Ivory, writing on eurweb.com:

Rod had the rarefied ability to craft both monster grooves – the first three Heatwave albums were his early audio résumé – sexy ballads like 'Always and Forever', Michael Jackson's 'Lady in My Life' – and everything in between, Michael McDonald's 'Sweet Freedom', the James Ingram/Michael McDonald hit, 'Yah Mo B There'.

In the shadow of his own tremendous talent, Temperton's Clark Kent normalcy made him an enigma. Temperton will forever be remembered as composer for the Jones-produced Michael Jackson albums *Off the Wall* and *Thriller*. Between both albums, he contributed just six songs but those songs – particularly 'Off the Wall', 'Rock with You' and 'Thriller', the title track for the biggest selling record in the history of the planet – became integral to the Jackson legend. Likewise, they've forever cemented Temperton's place in pop music songwriting history.

Temperton's up-tempo tunes are personified by their funky, exuberant urgency: aggressive, insistent bass line, enticing melody, colourful chord structure, sleek vocal harmonies and nifty bridge sections that make returning to the main groove all the more relentless.

Rod believed in setting a song up with a great intro. His up-tempo numbers, more often than not, feature beginnings that resemble a clarion call for the listener to get ready to get down. Example: the jazzy, wondrous opening of 'Boogie Nights'; the drama-filled intros of Jackson's 'Burn this Disco Out' and one of Temperton's lesser-known grooves, Aretha Franklin's 'Living in the Streets'.

Lyrically, most Temperton dance tunes sing of rhythm as a deliriously euphoric state of being. There's a funky exigency about getting down to it. Ever present is the phrase, 'There isn't' – usually followed by no use, no reason, no time to waste.

In Temperton's funky world there is a jubilant rebellion going on in the streets (which always rhymes with beat and heat), where we are all connected by our love of The Dance.

And almost always tucked in amongst this lyrical reverence for the boogie is a subtle message of positive ambition; the urging of one to take a chance and live life – life being a 'one-way ride' – to its fullest. On the mid-tempo 'Rock with You', rhythm is even a metaphor for romance ('… And when the groove is dead and gone/you know that love survives, and we can rock forever.').

Temperton's musical craftsmanship was rivalled only by his creative discipline. He'd work incessantly on a song until it met his approval. In the beginning of his partnership with Jones, before he bought a home in Los Angeles, he'd spend hours sequestered in his Hollywood hotel room sitting at a keyboard with a cassette recorder, coffee and cigarettes sitting atop it (this was before you weren't allowed to smoke in a hotel room), writing non-stop.

Rod's ideas for his songs were usually complete. When Quincy produced Tamia singing the Temperton ballad 'You Put a Move on My Heart' for his 1995 album *Q's Jook Joint*, he used British singer Mica Paris's version of the song – produced by Temperton two years earlier – as his production blueprint, following what the instruments played on the original to having Tamia replicate Mica's lead vocal down to the ad-libs.

Temperton's songs made him a very rich man. He and his wife, Kathy, had homes in Beverly Hills, Switzerland, France, Fiji and the UK. If there were kids in the picture, Temperton never shared. He kept the lowest of profiles and did so few interviews in his career – even at the height of *Thriller's* success and in the wake of the 2009 death of Michael Jackson – that the casual fan of his work often assumed the creator of all those ferocious grooves and passion-filled ballads was a black man.

So private was Temperton that by the time the public was made aware of his passing, his funeral had already happened. We still don't know the exact date of his death. Because of his immense reticence of the spotlight, Temperton was nicknamed, 'The Invisible Man'.

When photographer Bobby Holland shot the rare 1978 photos – in a Hollywood recording studio while Quincy and Temperton worked on *Off the Wall* – he recalled the songwriter's quiet demeanour.

'He was just sitting there in the room, not saying anything, observing,' said Holland. 'If you didn't know who he was, you would have wondered what he was even doing there. Just an ordinary cat.' With an extraordinary talent.

Rod Temperton:

Both me and Quincy were real junkies for staying up all night and creating. We often did really long sessions and when you are down to the wire you just have to do it. Funnily enough, a few years ago, we did a concert in Rome called 'We Are the Future'. It was to help children in war-torn countries. And I got there on a Wednesday afternoon in Rome and the concert was on Sunday. We didn't get any sleep at all, you know, and we were absolutely shattered by Monday morning. I don't know what happened but we were up day and night and there was so much going on. But, we did it. That's what you have to do.

Do I have a favourite moment in my career? No, no, I don't really have a favourite moment, well not like that, not in picking up an award or anything like that. My favourite moment is when I finish a song, that is the moment I cherish. That's the biggest moment of all. You have no idea what that means because just yesterday that song didn't exist on this planet, today it does. How it got to exist, who knows? But it does, and you managed to do it one more time and that's the reward. Actual rewards are gravy, you know, that comes later on if you are lucky, but you're not doing it for that. You are doing it because you want to finish that piece one more time, and then you want to go around that block again.

Alas, Rod Temperton has gone around the block one final time. In a year when the music world also lost David Bowie, Prince and Maurice White, to name just a few, we know that heaven is now one funky place and I bet the angels are dancing.

13

PHOOL 4 THE FUNK

Rod Temperton may have passed on but his list of fabulous songs will last forever, of course, and modern artists are still finding inspiration from them. In a world where sampling and cover versions are often heard, the songs of Rod Temperton will still be used to launch careers.

It was fitting that, as I was just writing the final few words of this book, I stopped to download a new LP by Rickey Vincent called *Phool 4 the Funk*. It is largely a tribute to the glory days of P-Funk, another one of my musical obsessions, with mentions for James Brown, George Clinton and Bootsy Collins, while, to some down-to-earth funk in the background there are interviews with the great, late Bernie Worrell, another to lose his life in 2016; and another P-Funk keyboard king and songwriter of extraordinary talents, being partly responsible for two of the best songs ever recorded, 'One Nation Under a Groove' and '(Not Just) Knee Deep', Walter 'Junie' Morrison; plus a finishing solo by Fred Wesley. Then, from nowhere, there is a cover version of Heatwave's 'Put the Word Out', the opening track from the *Central Heating* album, made nearly forty years ago. Little was done to alter the original version and it sounded as funky as ever and shows where Rod Temperton, the white kid from Cleethorpes in Lincolnshire, is in the list of great funkateers. From Hull to Hollywood, Rod 'funked up' with the very best of them.

The man behind the LP is funk historian, Rickey Vincent, writer of the much-acclaimed book, *Funk: The Music, the People and the Rhythm of The One*. He is also a well-known radio host with his programme on KPFA, *The History of Funk*, which has been running for the past twenty years in the San Francisco Bay Area. So, there was no one better to speak to in order to finish off this book:

If you are a DJ you always want to showcase a special, forgotten glorious track and if you are a club DJ you try to squeeze it in the mix with known songs, with the hits. I had an opportunity to make an album of my own and I wanted to sneak in a forgotten masterpiece, a masterwork from the old days and 'Put the Word Out' had been in my head since 1978. It was the genius of it, the layers of rhythms, of vocals, there are two entire songs on each channel, left and right, and you get two different songs. There are so many things happening and from the outside in it's just something to dance to but when you deconstruct it, it is a multi-layered castle of spectacular musical architecture. That's how I always felt about that song. So, it was always in my head and I felt like it was time to showcase funk on my record. My record producer loved the slow, big dinosaur stomp of big bump slow funk, which I love too, but I also know that funk comes in other flavours, more upbeat flavours, so I wanted to make sure an upbeat funk track was featured.

Heatwave were a part of my teenage life, they were a part of my adolescence, so I wanted to give a tribute on my record to Rod Temperton and a treatment to another band from Dayton, Ohio in Heatwave, a tribute to the worldliness of funk in general. Picking a Heatwave song was not just a random accident. I wanted to celebrate a band that came together in Europe with a writer who came out of whatever music training he had and whatever affection he had for black party music. The connection became something greater than the sum of the parts and with Heatwave's performance standards and Rod Temperton's songwriting that was a perfect match. Anybody who bothered to read some of the Heatwave album credits understood that right away and anyone who saw them or even heard them understood that there was something extra there, there was something going on.

Back in the day, as a teenager I saw Heatwave and the Commodores at the Oakland Coliseum, the famous arena where George Clinton landed his Mothership and many other famous recordings took place, and Heatwave smoked it. They were so hot that I was packing up and ready to leave because I didn't need to see the Commodores after that. I had been smoked out by the guys, the way Johnnie Wilder did acrobatics on stage and brought that energy. Every Dayton funk band has an extra kinetic level of energy in their music because of the way they were raised to battle each other, bands like Lakeside, Zapp and Slave, and people like that, they would all battle each other and the Wilder brothers, Johnnie and Keith, came out of that. Having to perform overseas as much as they did, they knew what to do on stage. Heatwave had it all, the sugar and spice, the yin and yang of the arrangements of Rod Temperton and the kinetic energy of the band's performers. I knew they were something special way back then.

So, when it came to recording my album, I wanted to let artists know about how good Heatwave – and Rod Temperton – were. My version of 'Put the Word Out' features all these younger artists from the Bay Area. The vocalist is a guy called Ziek McCarter, who is in a band called Conbrio, and he asked me about the song frequently because I think he wants to put it in his act. I'll tell you the first thing he said when I sent him and the producer, a guy called Will Magid, the track, he said, 'That's too complicated, I'm scared of doing a song like that'. He was intimidated because there was so much happening in it, musically and sonically with that record. Like I said, this guy is at the top of the line in terms of the Bay Area entertainers and singers but the youngsters are not used to making songs that have that many moving parts, that are that complex, but are arranged to sound so easily accessible at the same time.

Rod's songs have a subtle sophistication that is difficult to match. A lot of those late 1970s, early 1980s artists mastered it, but nobody has sat around and celebrated just how much genius goes into a club track, a club hit. Nobody talks about that. You can find somebody who will talk about Ornette Coleman or Thelonious Monk or Herbie Hancock and the genius that goes into their work, but the depth of musical understanding and how subtle things work to make something sound great – and you don't even know what it is that makes it sound great, sometimes until its gone – has been ignored with funk music. Rod Temperton understood that and I started to learn that as a funk fan, too.

All the great bands of that era typically usually have a keyboardist, who adds an extra music sound far beyond the norm but you can't put your finger on what it is, I'm thinking here of Larry Dunn's piano in Earth, Wind & Fire, Ronald Bell arranging those Kool & the Gang songs and Clay Smith. The guitarists – people who do things for these artists that do these things that you just can't put your finger on what makes it a step above the rest.

Rod Temperton did that, too. He put these slammin' funk tunes together, incredible pieces of funk. When I listen to those first two Heatwave albums, *Too Hot to Handle* and *Central Heating*, and pick out the title tracks and 'Ain't No Half Steppin'' I'm just taken back to when I was a kid. I wanted the big bump but I wanted the big bump with some real vocal arrangements going on and that's what Heatwave did and that's what Rod Temperton did, he put all those vocals in there so a knucklehead like me could appreciate the wild stuff but also recognise the quality of the mid-range sound such as on 'Star of a Story'. At the time I really appreciated that stuff, but as I matured I began to love it and I understood that not every artist could arrange sounds and styles like he did. So, Heatwave were clearly one of my favourite bands and 'Put the Word Out' was one of my favourite songs.

I didn't even know this, until the CD came out of *Central Heating*, that 'Put the Word Out' was the first track. Most people assume that 'The Groove Line' would have been the first track because that was the first single from the album. That meant that they respected that song even though it was not released as a single. It was just their way of saying, in a very highly orchestrated way but in an intense, contagious and exciting way, that 'We're back! And we've come something more musical than "Boogie Nights" and more exciting and we're going to grab you and not let go.' It starts with that disco-fabulous drum intro.

Thanks to Rod, I have to now work on a new intro to my funk book because he has brought disco into my life now. Rod wrote songs that were musical, important and joyful, songs that connect a lot of the dots, great disco funk tunes. Someone must have told him at the time that what he was doing was going to be a cash cow, someone at Epic Records or wherever, right up the chain of command must have said, 'You better get with the disco thing going on'. 'The Groove Line' has a disco version, you know, an extended seven or eight-minute version, that's very famous in the States.

Central Heating is Heatwave's best album, there's no doubt about that. It's got disco and funk and slow jams. Wow, the slow dancing tunes on there, forget it. Whoa! I love that album and so choosing a song from it for my record was a way to educate younger musicians that I have been involved with that perform around the San Francisco Bay Area. Everybody in the Bay Area loves old-school funk but they have to have the right opportunity to study an old-school funk song enough.

You know if you are going to remake a song like 'Put the Word Out', you have to study it, you have to study everything about it, so that can only help the younger musicians musical portfolio. I think that you learn everything by studying music like that. I was so happy to do it and bring these young guys on board to help teach them about Rod Temperton so they would understand that, if you are going to remake one of his songs, you need to go back to your regular stuff and think about the kind of playpen, entry-level music you've been doing and then compare it to what Rod Temperton arranged.

You start with pop songs and then you go further in and look into what gives a song staying power, what gives a song something special, so I like to think that I have helped point this group of folks I've worked with in the Bay Area, ones who are pretty established out here, that they need to understand that there's another layer. Although they are making some good music, it's kind of – well, I don't want to put it down, but the older stuff has more soul, more layers and more going on. They know that and it was a purpose for me to open the door to that. These guys thought they knew all the hits by Heatwave. Go back to those albums you already have and listen to all the special goodies on those records.

Everything about me remaking one of his songs was a tribute to him, his arrangements and his brilliance. We took a long time going through every little hook and every little bridge and all the things that went on in 'Put the Word Out' and then after that it was just a labour of love, I loved every minute of it, of putting those pieces in to make it sound just like the original but with its own contemporary feel.

The saddest thing, of course, is that right around the time I was releasing the record, Rod died. I kept telling the guys while we were making it that Rod was going to hear it so don't quit, as hard as it is. I wanted to make sure that he heard it one day. I told them, 'Yes, it's taking a long time to piece this together but when Rod Temperton hears it, it will all be worth the hard work.' That's what I kept telling them but, you know, unfortunately he never got the chance to hear what we did with his song.

Instead, I did a tribute to Rod on my radio show on KPFA and debuted the song we did. After all the deaths in the funk world in 2016, I was getting kind of used to this, but it was an honour to dedicate a show to such a genius. I just wish I could have met him and handed the record to him but it now lives on as a tribute to his amazing skills as a writer and arranger. I appreciated his work and want it to embellish a new generation. Rod's music helped my high school years and made them more beautiful and that is something I have always respected about him. He could tap into our moods as teenagers.

Rod thought about music in multiple parts and not many can do that. Remember, he joined a fully formed funk band but took them to another level. Everything he wrote sounds like there were two guitar players, even though it was probably one playing multiple parts and laying the tracks down. He had a vision to make each song sound full but not cluttered, he put things in there to make his tunes sound open and free but not empty. That was the standard back then, and Rod knew how to do it as the solo creator that he was. He sat down and listened to all the contemporaries like Earth, Wind & Fire, the Ohio Players. the Bar-Kays and all the Parliament records and Stevie Wonder's work. I think everybody then was trying to be Stevie Wonder back then; they were trying to make albums as diverse yet accessible as his.

For the most part it was a triumphant period of music because there were so many great, great records and great, great artists all operating at the same time. You could take your pick from Heatwave or the Brothers Johnson or Confunkshun or Cameo because whether it was organic or not, they all took the high standards very seriously and Rod Temperton elevated the standards while he was there.

That's why Quincy Jones nabbed him. It was pretty obvious from a consumer point of view that, after those first two Heatwave albums, Rod was going to become the star he did. Working with Quincy was the obvious next step and it was a necessary and brilliant career move.

Rod Temperton registers as one of the masters of the funk movement. The thing is that when you talk about the masters you have great bands that have players in the bands that are masters and then you have the bands that simply tower over everyone. It's difficult for anyone to get out of the shadows of George Clinton, now and forever, because of what he did for funk both back then and what he is still doing today. Once you sort of pass that, then you have this pantheon of brilliant writers and performers and Rod Temperton stands up with all of them as one of the real masters of funk. It's funny because nobody has any misconceptions that he came from Dayton, Ohio. Everybody knew he came from Britain, and yet he handled it with a certain fluidity, a certain stylistic grace that fitted perfectly.

That didn't come as a surprise because most of us got started on the Average White Band, who came out of Scotland, and we understood that funk could come from anywhere. To do funk music you have to be original. You can't have eight songs on an album that copy someone else, you can have one or two that copy someone else but the rest have to be original and Rod Temperton was always original as were the Average White Band, Alan Gorrie and those guys. They were OK with borrowing a style but they came up with a lot of original work as well. They and Rod were the funk wave of the British invasion. They could refer to certain styles but they also put their stamp firmly on the funk. If they hadn't, they might as well have gone back and played hotel lobbies.

Rod Temperton got that, he got that right away; just listen to the opening of *Too Hot to Handle*, that tells you all you need to know. That said straight away, 'These are the standards we've set, this is the style and this is how we are going to put our stamp on the funk, something we can expand on and make our mark.' Rod did just that and brought it on right from the off.

Once he worked with Michael Jackson on *Off the Wall*, he grabbed everyone. A lot of us held that missing person in our minds asking who was this man that kept on writing this funk. In the States, we knew that the Heatwave cats were from Ohio, Kool and the Gang were from New York, we could figure where a lot of these guys were from, but there were then the random elements. We all knew that Rod came from another spot and he did his thing, was just himself and never wanted to be a big shot. But, of course, what he contributed to the funk was a big shot.

I am just so glad that this book about him is happening and I'm proud and tickled that I was asked to be part of it, part of a tribute from this little edge of the world. Doing 'Put the Word Out' hopefully will get Rod noticed a bit more, but in a quiet way. You know, he wrote one of the biggest songs of all time with 'Thriller' and it's kind of spins your head that the man who did that and was at the top of the charts all around the world can remain so anonymous.

ROD TEMPERTON DISCOGRAPHY – SONGS WRITTEN BY ROD

HEATWAVE

Too Hot to Handle (1976)
Too Hot to Handle
Boogie Nights
Ain't No Half Steppin'
Always and Forever
Super Soul Sister
All You Do is Dial
Lay It on Me
Sho'nuff Must be Luv
Beat Your Booty

Extra songs added on 2015 remastered reissue:

Turn Out the Lamplight
Slip Your Disc to This
Special Offer

Central Heating (1978)
Put the Word Out
Send Out for Sunshine
Central Heating
The Groove Line

The Star of a Story
Party Poops
Leavin' For a Dream

Extra tracks added on 2015 remastered reissue:

Wack that Axe
Escape to Athena
Keep Tomorrow for Me (with Barry Blue)

Hot Property (1979)

Razzle Dazzle
Eyeballin'
This Night We Fell
Raise a Blaze
First Day of Snow
One Night Tan
Therm Warfare
All Talked Out
That's the Way We'll Always Say Goodnight

Candles (1981)

Gangsters of the Groove
Jitterbuggin'
Party Suite
Posin' 'til Closin
Dreamin' You

Current (1982)

Lettin' it Loose
State to State
Look After Love
The Big Guns
Hold on to the One

JAVAROO

Out (1980)
Change It Up

MICHAEL JACKSON

Off the Wall (1979)
Rock with You
Off the Wall
Burn this Disco Out

Thriller (1982)
Baby be Mine
Thriller
Lady in My Life
Got the Hots (unreleased)

E.T. THE EXTRA-TERRESTRIAL (1982)

Someone in the Dark (opening version) (with Alan Bergman, Marilyn Bergman)
Someone in the Dark (closing version) (with Alan Bergman, Marilyn Bergman)

RUFUS AND CHAKA KHAN

Masterjam (1979)
Live in Me
Masterjam

BROTHERS JOHNSON

Light Up the Night (1980)
Stomp! (with Louis Johnson, George Johnson, Valerie Johnson)
Light Up the Night (with Louis Johnson, George Johnson)
You Make Me Wanna Wiggle (with Louis Johnson, George Johnson, Valerie Johnson)
Treasure
All About the Heaven
Closer to the One that You Love (with Louis Johnson, George Johnson)
Celebrations (with Louis Johnson, George Johnson)

GEORGE BENSON

Give Me the Night (1980)
Love X Love
Off Broadway
Give Me the Night
Star of a Story (X)
Turn Out the Lamplight

Songs and Stories (2009)
Family Reunion (with Catero Colbert)

ARETHA FRANKLIN

Love All the Hurt Away (1981)
Living in the Streets

QUINCY JONES

The Dude (1981)
The Dude (with Patti Austin)
Somethin' Special

Razzamatazz
Turn on the Action

Back on the Block (1989)
Back on the Block (with Quincy Jones, Siedah Garrett, Caiphus Semenya, Ice-T, Melle Mel, Kane, Kook Moe Dee)
The Secret Garden (Sweet Seduction Suite) (with Quincy Jones, Siedah Garrett, El DeBarge)

Q's Jook Joint (1995)
You Put a Move on My Heart (by Tamia)
Rock with You (by Brandy and Heavy D)
Stomp! (by original cast members of *Stomp*, Mr X, Melle Mel, Coolio, Yo-Yo, Chaka Khan, Charlie Wilson, Shaquille O'Neal and Luniz)
Slow Jams (by Babyface, Portrait, Barry White and SWV)

THE COLOR PURPLE (1985)

Miss Celie's Blues (with Quincy Jones, Lionel Richie)
I'm Here (with Chris Boardman, Quincy Jones)

OPRAH WINFREY

Oprah Winfrey Theme Tune (with Quincy Jones)

PATTI AUSTIN

Every Home Should Have One (1981)
Do You Love Me?
Love Me to Death
Baby, Come to Me
The Genie

Carry On (1991)
Givin' in to Love

BOB JAMES

Sign of the Times (1981)
Hypnotique
The Steamin' Feeling
Sign of the Times

Hands Down (1982)
Macumba (with Bob James)

HERBIE HANCOCK

Lite Me Up (1982)
Lite Me Up!
The Bomb (with Herbie Hancock)
Getting to the Good Part (with Herbie Hancock)
The Fun Tracks
Motor Mouth
Give it All Your Heart (with Herbie Hancock)

DONNA SUMMER

Donna Summer (1982)
Love is in Control (Finger on the Trigger) (with Quincy Jones, Merria Ross)
Livin' in America (with David Foster, Quincy Jones, Steve Lukather, Donna Summer)
Love is Just a Breath Away (with David Foster, Donna Summer)

JAMES INGRAM

It's Your Night (1983)
Yah Mo B There (with James Ingram, Quincy Jones, Michael McDonald)
One More Rhythm

THE MANHATTAN TRANSFER

Bodies and Souls (1983)
Mystery (with Derek Bramble)

STEPHANIE MILLS

Stephanie Mills (1985)
Time of Your Life
Hold on to Midnight

Something Real (1992)
Never Do Wrong (with Carol Duboc, Ron Spearman, Vassal Benford)

JEFFREY OSBORNE

Emotional (1986)
We Belong to Love

WAYNE HERNANDEZ

Telepathic (1987)
Dancin' on the Edge (with Barry Blue)
Let Me Call You Angel (with Barry Blue)

RUNNING SCARED SOUNDTRACK (1987)

(Produced by Rod Temperton, Dick Rudolph and Bruce Swedien)
Man Size Love (by Klymaxx)
Sweet Freedom (by Michael McDonald)
I Just Wanna be Loved (by Ready for the World)
Running Scared (by Fee Waybill)
El Chase (by The Rod Temperton Beat Wagon) (with Jim Flamberg, Larry Williams)
Never Too Late to Start (By The Rod Temperton Beat Wagon)

SIEDAH GARRETT

Kiss of Life (1988)
(Produced by Rod Temperton and Dick Rudolph)
Groove of Midnight
Baby's Got it Bad (With Siedah Garrett)
Nobody Does Me

MICA PARIS

Whisper a Prayer (1993)
You Put a Move on My Heart
We Were Made for Love
Two in a Million
Love Keeps Coming Back

KAREN CARPENTER

Karen Carpenter (1996 – recorded 1979/1980)
Lovelines
If We Try

LAAM

LAAM (2004)
Fais De Moi Ce Que Tu Veux
Love's in the House Tonight

THE CONTRIBUTORS

The author wants to give his enormous gratitude to all those who took part in this book and the BBC documentary that preceded it:

ROD TEMPERTON

The man this book is all about, a man who, before his death was announced in October 2016, wrote some of the most magical music ever. He is a legend. Nothing more, nothing less. The world is simply a better place for the songs he wrote. Thank you for all the joy you have given to so many people around the world.

QUINCY JONES

Quincy Jones is an extraordinary record producer, conductor, arranger, composer, musician, television producer, film producer, instrumentalist, magazine founder, entertainment company executive and studio genius. He's probably done some other stuff in his spare time, too. His career in music spans six decades and he has had seventy-nine Grammy Award nominations and winning twenty-eight, including a Grammy Legend Award. He helped make Michael Jackson the global superstar he became and is the man who took Rod's music to another level.

BRUCE SWEDIEN

A five-time Grammy Award winner as an audio engineer (and nominated many more times), he is regarded by many as the very best in the business. He is noted for pioneering the Acusonic Recording Process, and made Rod's already sensational music sound just right.

GEORGE BENSON

A famed guitar player who has received a star on the Hollywood Walk of Fame, he sang to me in his dressing room ahead of a concert in Palm Desert, California, two days after I married my wife, Kate, in Las Vegas. It was the greatest week of my life.

HERBIE HANCOCK

The pianist, keyboardist, bandleader, composer and actor who created one of the original hip hop songs with 'Rockit'. He has to be one of the most forward-thinking musicians ever to be put on this planet. He is still winning awards today, even though he is now well into his seventies and into his sixth decade as a musician. I still get goose bumps when I hear his outrageous solo on Alphonse Mouzon's 'By All Means', which makes me wish I had attended just one music lesson at school.

JOHNNIE WILDER JNR

The founder of Heatwave who, in spite of his disability, gave me a fantastic interview shortly before he very sadly passed away in 2006 at the age of 56. It was his voice that initially propelled Rod's songs and made them what they became.

MICHAEL MCDONALD

The man with arguably the best voice ever recorded. He sang with two of my other favourite artists, Steely Dan and the Doobie Brothers. He is still going strong into his sixties and keeping the sounds of Motown alive.

STEVE LUKATHER

Steve gave me one of the best – and funniest – interviews I have ever conducted while with his band, Toto, in London for a project on the group who, between them, have played on records that have sold more than a billion copies. It's a project that I would still love to see the light of day one day soon. If you have enjoyed this then, who knows, it may do so yet. He is one of the greatest guitarists ever to pick up the instrument.

GREG PHILLINGANES

He was with Steve as a member of Toto at the time of the interview. Another very humorous man who has played keyboards on almost every album I own. Donald Fagen even wrote him a song, 'Lazy Nina', to thank him for his work on *The Nightfly*. He began his career with Stevie Wonder and became Michael Jackson's and Lionel Richie's musical director. Now in his sixties, he still looks about 25.

BARRY BLUE

Barry is a prolific music producer who took on Heatwave for their first two albums and then their fifth. He remained a good friend of Rod Temperton's right through the latter's life and gave me so much important information for this book that I honestly don't think it could have been done without him. He recently wrote some music for *Breaking Bad* which impressed my kids no end.

GEORGE DUKE

A brilliant keyboard player and pioneer, producer and writer in so many genres, he sadly passed away in LA in 2013 aged 67 – and the world immediately became a less funky place.

PATTI AUSTIN

Patti was a crucial cog in the Rod Temperton story, thanks to her incredible vocal gymnastics. A hilarious woman who, pleasingly, answered every question with a humorous aside. She appeared in the Oscar-winning documentary film *20 Feet from Stardom* about the skills of the backing singer, yet, front of stage, had her own US No. 1, Rod Temperton-penned hit.

SIEDAH GARRETT

Siedah is a true talent and songwriter in her own right who shared some very fascinating stories on Rod, the man. I've still not been to the dentist since I read about Rod pulling out his own tooth. Ouch! She has been nominated for two Academy Awards for Best Original Song, and won the Grammy Award for Best Song Written for Visual Media at the fiftieth Grammy Awards for co-writing 'Love You I Do' for the film, *Dreamgirls*.

DEREK BRAMBLE

Derek was a young whippersnapper who joined Heatwave as a bass player and became a long-time good friend with Rod Temperton and his wife. He co-produced David Bowie's 1984 release, *Tonight,* and is now hoping to keep Rod's spirit alive cutting all new songs for a couple of different projects. 'I'm going balls-to-the-wall to get these songs finished,' he said, using typical and wonderful Dee phraseology.

JOHN CAMERON

An orchestral arranger, composer and musician who rose to fame thanks to his work on *Les Misérables*, something that made my mother fall off her chair when I told her I had interviewed him for this book. He worked closely with Donovan, Cilla Black and Hot Chocolate. His band, CCS, recorded a version of 'Whole Lotta Love' that was for years used as the theme music for the British show, *Top of the Pops*.

RICKEY VINCENT

Ricky is an author, historian and radio host based in the San Francisco Bay Area. He knows more about the funk than any man alive, although he denies this, and was the last person we know of to record a Rod Temperton song while the great man was still alive. With a voice as smooth as a summer lake at dawn, he made me jealous as he told me that he had recently spoken with Fred Wesley.

STEVEN IVORY

Steven Ivory is an American journalist who spent time with Quincy Jones during and around the *Off the Wall* sessions. His help with this book was immeasurable.

BOBBY HOLLAND

Bobby is a Grammy-nominated photographer and filmmaker. Interviewing him was a real pleasure. He was keen and very enthusiastic. He says this, on the mptvimages.com website:

> When I think about Michael Jackson the artist I'm reminded of just how totally focused he always was about anything he was doing. Having grown up in the school of Motown, Michael learned from the best using every angle to become a total entertainer. He would

always arrive early at the studio for every photo session, very quiet and reserved, and he was always totally prepared, aware and involved with all aspects of the photo session: the music, lighting, lens, sets and the total vibe. When it was time to step in front of the lens he could really turn it on too and show everyone why he was the King of Pop.

Bob Jones, who was director of publicity at Motown Records, gave the title the King of Pop to Michael Jackson. Jones was one of those no nonsense professionals who worked with Michael and his brothers as the Jackson Five for many years. He later would leave Motown to become head of media for Michael's new company MJJ Productions.

James Brown has always been known as the Hardest Working Man in Show Business. Michael studied James Brown's every move and has to be known as The Second Hardest Working Man in Show Business.

Bobby was behind the cover shoot for Stevie Wonder's *In Square Circle* LP.

ALAN KIRK

A member of 1970s band, Jimmy James and the Vagabonds, Alan was involved in the original version of 'Blame it on the Boogie' by Mick Jackson, which was then picked up by the Jacksons. Alan owns Hilltop Studios near Chesterfield. He nearly made the big time in 2007 with the festive song, 'You're My Christmas Baby'.

ANDREW PLATTS

Another member of Jimmy James and the Vagabonds which toured with Heatwave in the early days, Andrew is now managing editor of the entertainment paper, *Mercury Newspaper*, in Sheffield. He and Alan were also in the band Big Business.

TED GLEDHILL

Ted is the man who helped Rod in his younger days. He may not have known it at the time but he now has to go down in music history as a very important human being.

AFTERWORD

Oddly, and here's a little fact to finish. De Aston School is in Market Rasen in the county of Lincolnshire. Market Rasen, or at least in a farmhouse nearby, was also the birthplace of another legendary British songwriter who co-wrote Elton John's hits – Bernie Taupin. Now, who would have thought? So, if you were born in or around Market Rasen and love music – just think on …

ABOUT THE AUTHOR

The Invisible Man is the second book by Jed Pitman, who also ghost-wrote *Crazy! My Road to Redemption*, the story of former England cricketer, Chris Lewis, also published by The History Press.

Jed began life as a radio presenter before co-creating the nation's first ever newspaper fantasy football game for the *Daily Telegraph* in the early 1990s. He wrote columns in the paper under the names Alan Handsome and Geoffrey Trueman for sixteen years. He has worked as an impressionist with John Culshaw for the BBC, was Head of Sport at ITV West (HTV) for a decade, winning several industry awards, and has also produced a number of award-winning music documentaries for BBC Radio. He has spent the last few years producing online cricket highlights for the ECB. He has also proudly worked at both Asda and Argos.

He now lives in Mexico with his beyond patient wife, Kate, and their pet iguana, Trump (he lives on a Mexican wall). He dedicates this book to his three children, Phoebe Mallia (named after the Queen of Funk, Mallia Franklin), George Clinton (need I say more?) and Charlie Bruno (well, his ex-wife put her foot down and wouldn't allow Bootsy or Maceo), all fans of the work of Rod Temperton.

With an extra big hug and thanks to Neil Cowling.

(This book was written in Huatulco, Oaxaca, Mexico.)

INDEX

C000181493

BULLETPROOF
BODIES

Body-weight Exercise for
Injury Prevention and Rehabilitation

ROSS CLIFFORD & ASHLEY KALYM

lotus
publishing

Chichester, England

Copyright © 2018 by Ross Clifford & Ashley Kalym. All rights reserved. No portion of this book, except for brief review, may be reproduced, stored in a retrieval system, or transmitted in any form or by any means – electronic, mechanical, photocopying, recording, or otherwise – without the written permission of the publisher. For information, contact Lotus Publishing.

First published in 2018
Lotus Publishing
Apple Tree Cottage, Inlands Road, Nutbourne, Chichester, PO18 8RJ

Anatomical Drawings Amanda Williams
Photographs Fiona Hook
Text Design Medlar Publishing Solutions Pvt Ltd., India
Cover Design Chris Fulcher
Printed and Bound in India by Replika Press

British Library Cataloguing-in-Publication Data
A CIP record for this book is available from the British Library
ISBN 978 1 905367 89 4

Contents

Preface

There has never been a better time to be involved in body-weight exercise. Over the last few years, body-weight training has held a top five position in the list of top fitness trends. But unlike wearable technology, which currently sits in first place, body-weight training is not really a trend. It is not new, and it is definitely not a fad that will fade into obscurity in the years to come. Although bodyweight exercise has been around for thousands of years as a formal training method, it existed long before this when humans increased their survival chances with running, climbing, jumping and lifting activities. It almost seems instinctive to us to use the weight of our bodies as a form of resistance.

In today's world, body-weight training is no longer an exercise option but instead a thriving community of people who value their physical function over a purely aesthetic outcome. Myriad online facilities now exist to take you from the most fundamental of human body movements through to spectacular feats of strength and flexibility, such as the human flag. There are groups that exist, bestowing kudos on their global members who achieve the Holy Grail that is the muscle-up. High-quality calisthenics books are available to explain and illustrate a range of progressive techniques and routines to suit both the novice and the expert fitness fan.

The focus of body-weight exercise has long been the development of strength, but many of the exercises will also develop mobility around joints and flexibility of muscles. This is largely because the exercises do not isolate muscle groups and immobilise large parts of the body; instead, body-weight training uses most of the body at any time while focusing the load on specific body areas. Often this requires the support of the core or stabilising muscles. All of this can be done anywhere and with a minimal amount of equipment, making it accessible in terms of location, cost and time. What more could you want?

The nature of this book differs slightly from the focus of most other body-weight training manuals and online facilities. It is the result of a partnership between a chartered physiotherapist and a calisthenics expert who have long appreciated the use of body-weight exercise in developing physical resilience to the strains of modern living, and the potential for these exercises to rehabilitate injuries that have already occurred. Without a doubt, if you were to regularly complete the exercises herein, you would develop increased strength, which is the capacity to *generate* force or pressure. But strength can also mean the ability to *withstand* force or pressure. This is the focus of *Bulletproof Bodies* – we combine strength gains with the concept of physical resilience, which is the capacity to recover quickly from physical stress and to spring back from physical difficulty.

Our aim is to demonstrate and *educate* how the principles of body-weight exercise can be applied to the prevention and rehabilitation of injuries in the musculoskeletal system. No matter how hard you train and how clean you live, you must understand that some injuries are inevitable. We cannot control all events and all external forces, but we can ensure that we are physically robust enough to absorb as much of this force as possible before we reach breaking point. Once broken, however, we must then guide our bodies back to the best function possible. This book will help you in achieving both of these aims.

We hope that this book will give you a deeper understanding and appreciation of the incredible human musculoskeletal system, and that you will come to know your own body better. This is not an academic textbook for trainee health or sports professionals, but is intended as a 'need-to-know' guide to common structures in the body and the problems that can develop. Once we have established this in an accessible way, we offer you a wide range of targeted body-weight exercises to rehabilitate and make resistant specific body areas. At the end of the book, we combine these exercises in set routines as suggestions for developing whole-body physical resilience. All of these exercises are tried and tested by both authors and have been used by us for many years to develop strength and recover from injury.

One final word regarding the exercises: at first sight you may wonder if we have misunderstood the effects of the proposed exercises. The answer is 'no': we have 're-understood' the exercises. For example, you may be familiar with the pull-up as a classic means of increasing size and strength of the back muscles, especially the latissimus dorsi muscles. Take a minute to think through this well-known exercise – gripping the bar, the initial pull at the elbows, and the bend in the elbows required to bring yourself to the bar. You may now be thinking about the forearm 'pump' that you get with this exercise. Now ask yourself – is this just a back-muscle exercise? The answer again is 'no'. Like all body-weight exercise, it is not 'just' anything. We will hopefully help you to see the wider benefits of body-weight exercise and reinterpret the gains available to you with this most fashionable of exercise trends!

Train smart.
Ross Clifford & Ashley Kalym

Abbreviations

ACL   Anterior cruciate ligament
ITB   Iliotibial band
LCL   Lateral collateral ligament
MCL   Medial collateral ligament

PCL   Posterior cruciate ligament
PFPS   Patellofemoral pain syndrome
ROM   Range of motion

1

Musculoskeletal Injury

Musculoskeletal injuries or disorders can affect muscles, joints, tendons and ligaments in all parts of the body. These issues can happen at any time during the lifetime, in the active and inactive, and can seemingly occur for no known reason. There may be an obvious trauma or injury that is responsible for the disorder, but more likely than not the pain or dysfunction comes on without trauma. It may be sudden, in that you awoke with it, or it may be a slowly worsening niggle that will not go away.

If you currently have such a problem, you are not alone. Musculoskeletal injuries are widespread, with lower back pain being the most common condition, affecting nearly everyone at some point in his or her life. Estimates suggest that in developed countries 4–33% of the population at any given time will experience lower back pain. In some countries, musculoskeletal disorders make up around 40% of work-related illness, suggesting that you are more likely to develop a musculoskeletal problem through your daily routine rather than through any kind of sports injury. It is therefore very likely that at some point in your life, probably in the not-too-distant future, this book may be of great use to you.

In this first chapter we will briefly look at the soft-tissue repair process, differentiate chronic from acute musculoskeletal problems, and outline general types of chronic musculoskeletal disorders.

■ Soft-tissue Injury and Repair

If at any point a force is applied to the musculoskeletal structures that exceeds their ability to withstand that force, there will be disruption to the normal structure

and function of that tissue. This may be minor and give you nothing more than a dull ache for a day or two. If you are no stranger to exercise or physical work, you may recognise this as muscle soreness, where there has been minor damage to the muscle tissue. With adequate rest and nutrition (see Chapter 4), this ache will subside as the inflammatory process passes and the muscle fibres are repaired and perhaps even made thicker and stronger. All of this is a normal process and happens on a daily basis as our musculoskeletal systems respond to the dynamic ebb and flow of forces applied to our bodies.

This book will focus on musculoskeletal problems more troublesome than muscle soreness, and more specifically on problems that have arisen when internal or external forces applied to body tissues have exceeded their tolerance and led to injury. We will take a broad look at the process of repair that many musculoskeletal structures undergo when injured, and discuss the reasons why some injuries do not fully resolve in the expected timescales. These are referred to as *chronic injuries*, and this book will offer targeted body-weight exercises to rehabilitate and build resilience to these types of injury.

KEY POINT: *Soft tissue and bone breakdown and repair happens on a daily basis; it is a normal process that takes place in response to the forces acting on your body.*

Injury and Inflammation

The 'injury' may take many forms, from the obvious stretching trauma of an ankle sprain to the prolonged excessive loading of spinal ligaments and discs. Ultimately, a force has been applied that exceeds the strength of the musculoskeletal structure, causing it to deform or break.

Damage may occur to cells, muscle fibres, connective tissue fibres, bone tissue or blood vessels passing through the area. If the trauma is extreme, several of these structures may be disrupted. If blood vessels are damaged, you will develop swelling, which may appear as bruising. Damage to cells and fibres will trigger the inflammatory process; this can also result in swelling, but is usually more delayed and can take several hours or days to develop.

Inflammatory chemicals irritate your nerve endings to cause pain, reminding you that you have an injured body part that needs rest. These chemicals can open blood vessels and make them leaky, leaving the injured area swollen, red and warm. The common advice in these circumstances is **PRICE** – **P**rotect the injured area, **R**est from further aggravating movements, apply **I**ce, **C**ompress the area to limit inflammatory fluid, and **E**levate where possible to allow gravity to aid in the drainage of the swelling. A fuller explanation of this method is not the focus of this book, and so we recommend in such cases that you see a qualified health or medical professional for further advice.

> **KEY POINT:** *Inflammatory chemicals irritate your nerve endings to cause pain, reminding you that you have an injured body part that may need a period of relative rest.*

The Repair Process

Inflammation following injury can last from a few hours to several weeks, depending on the severity of the injury. The inflammatory process is essential in order to 'kick-start' the repair process that begins alongside the inflammatory phase. During this repair process, new material is laid down to replace or bridge the original damaged tissue. In bone, joint lining and skeletal muscle, the new tissue is the same as that lost: it is like-for-like. In connective tissue, however, such as tendons, ligaments and the fibres around muscles, the original tissue is replaced: the 'makeshift' material is commonly known as *scar tissue*. Scar tissue is made of collagen fibres, and this material is the structural foundation of much of the body. Eventually the scar tissue may come to resemble the tissue around it, but it will never be the same. This may lead to ongoing injuries such as a niggling hamstring strain or an ankle ligament sprain.

After a while, the newly laid collagen begins to mature; this may start at around three weeks after injury and last for many months. Links develop between the collagen fibres to strengthen the healing tissue, and the fibres begin to shrink. These last two stages indicate why sometimes the healing process is never fully resolved.

> **KEY POINT:** *When connective tissue, such as tendons, ligaments and the fibres around muscles, is damaged, the original tissue is replaced by scar tissue made of collagen.*

When Repair Fails

As the collagen fibres in the healing breach begin to shrink and form strong bonds between themselves, you may be left with an area of scar tissue that is not fit for purpose within an otherwise healthy muscle, ligament or tendon. The fibres of these surrounding tissues will be lined up along the direction of stress, meaning that they can glide and extend under stretch and be able to take up the 'pull'. When scar tissue is laid down, it is done so in a haphazard way, running in all directions. If the healing wound does

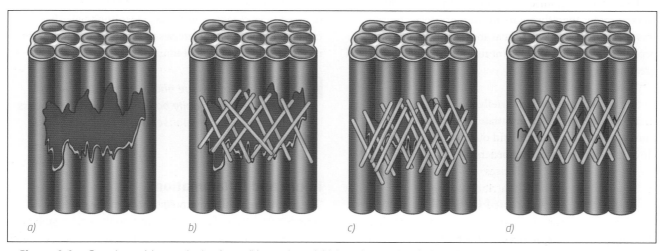

a)   b)   c)   d)

■ **Figure 1.1.** Scar tissue: (a) a tear in the tissue; (b) scar tissue laid down in a random fashion; (c) built-up tension around the area of repair, caused by too much time with lack of movement; (d) scar tissue better aligned to the natural tension in the tissue.

not undergo gradual loading and movement, the fibres are not 'remodelled' to align with surrounding fibres. The result is that you return to normal movement after a period of rest only to 'pull' the area again, creating more inflammation and more scar tissue. As the healing fibres shrink and strengthen, this also makes the area of injury less able to respond to stress and strain, leading to re-injury, inflammation and scar tissue formation. This cycle can become an ongoing process, as an excess amount of poorly constructed scar tissue is unable to replicate the original tissue. Such a cycle can form the basis of a chronic, ongoing or recurrent musculoskeletal disorder.

■ Differentiating Musculoskeletal Injury

When referring to an illness or injury, the term *chronic* by definition means to persist for long periods or to constantly recur. This is the basis of our discussion above when looking at scar tissue repair and the dangers of inadequate rehabilitation. Chronic injuries may also be referred to as *overuse injuries*, to distinguish them from injuries that come on quickly after obvious trauma, known as *acute injuries*.

Chronic overuse injuries are seen and experienced more often than acute traumatic injuries, and can easily arise from occupational, sporting or leisure activities. They tend not to be instantly disabling, and their onset is more gradual, with varying degrees of pain and dysfunction. The problem area may worsen with repeated exposure to the aggravating activity; this could be a gym or sporting movement, or more likely the result of sitting for long periods or repeating a manual task for work or leisure.

Chronic overuse injuries often result from a prolonged stress that exceeds the ability of the tissue to withstand that stress. This issue can occur in deconditioned and conditioned bodies, and can depend on the amount of stress, its duration and the nature of its application. Ultimately, we can look at three potential causes:

1. The tissue/body is poorly conditioned in relation to the demands of the task. In this book we focus on developing physical resilience in multiple body areas through functional exercises.
2. The environment has contributed to the injury. Look at the environment, such as desk set-up, driving position or any gym/sporting equipment, to see where changes can be made to ease stress to the body.
3. The activity creates excessive stress. When otherwise fit and healthy people develop lower back pain from sitting, they often want to know what is wrong with their spines. The answer is usually 'nothing'. The human spine is not built for sitting long hours in a position of spinal flexion (bending). Modify the activity.

■ Types of Chronic Musculoskeletal Injury

In Chapters 5 to 11 of this book we cover specific body areas and outline some commonly seen musculoskeletal problems affecting these regions. Many of the disorders discussed are chronic/overuse injuries or were once acute injuries but have failed to reach full repair. Such musculoskeletal disorders can affect muscles, joints, tendons and ligaments in all parts of the body. We will briefly outline here the types of problems that will be explored further in later chapters.

Muscle Strains

Muscle strains can occur throughout the body, but are most common in long muscles that cross two joints; this is because there are multiple demands on the muscle to move or control more than one joint at any one time. Such injuries are often seen in the hamstrings and the calf muscle, both of which are heavily loaded muscles and play an essential role in slowing movement and absorbing force. In the relevant chapters we provide specific exercises to target the function of these muscles in order to create resilience to everyday loads. Strains to both the hamstrings and the calf can become chronic when the scar tissue is not properly rehabilitated. Again, recommended targeted exercises to complete the rehabilitation process will be given.

Tendon Problems

Tendon problems were once considered to be an inflammatory problem, but as you explore the body chapters in this book, you will see that we attribute them more to degeneration of the tendons. This notion is based on current thinking and research in this area, and we offer targeted exercises to help rehabilitate 'tendinopathies' or to develop resilience to developing tendon disorders. Common problematic tendons include those at the shoulder (Chapter 5), the elbow (Chapter 6), the knee (Chapter 9) and the ankle (Chapter 10).

Ligament Problems

Ligament sprains can become chronic if not fully rehabilitated. The scar tissue within the healing ligament may be of poor quality if you have not developed a gradual load through the ligament. When stress is suddenly applied, even with normal activities, you may find that the area swells and becomes painful. Such a problem is commonly seen in the ankle after an 'inversion' sprain. There may even be some instability in the area following ligament injury, and so it is essential that the muscles can react adequately and provide additional support to the joint. We offer targeted exercises to develop resilience and rehabilitation for ligament stability injuries to the shoulder (Chapter 5), the knee (Chapter 9) and the ankle (Chapter 10).

Joint-specific Problems

Finally, it is worth considering joint-related problems. Especially, but not exclusively, in weight-bearing joints, osteoarthritis can develop; this is a relatively common disease in older joints but it is not just an affliction of the elderly. Age may be one factor in joint osteoarthritis, but there are many other contributing factors, such as genetics, obesity and prior injury. Nutrition and hydration may also play a part (Chapter 4). Many people hold the notion that osteoarthritis is a condition that will just get worse, or that movement will aggravate it. Neither of these ideas is necessarily true, and we offer targeted exercise as an evidence-supported form of managing pain and dysfunction from osteoarthritis.

All of the disorders discussed in this chapter can be managed in part with movement and exercise, which is the basis of this book. In the next chapter we will explain why body-weight exercise is a suitable means of developing resilience to injury, as well as a basis for rehabilitating chronic injuries. We hope that you will achieve as much freedom from pain and dysfunction as we have by applying these principles to your lives.

2

Advantages of Body-weight Exercise

At this point it is perhaps worth examining why body-weight exercise is so good for injury prevention and rehabilitation, and why traditional methods are not as effective as they could be. A key reason for the latter is that traditional methods of injury prevention and rehabilitation rely on isolating the targeted body part. Ideally, in order to protect against injury, the body area in question should develop strength through a functional range of motion (ROM). The movements should also focus on supporting and stabilising muscles, and not just on the 'big-gun' movement muscles.

■ Fundamental Movement

Traditional physical therapies rely on isolated movements, corrective exercise and other practices that do not always maximise rehabilitation by developing multiple body areas in a functional way. The goal of rehabilitation should be simple: to make the body as strong, mobile and injury free as possible. If this goal is achieved, the potential for injury will be reduced, and the rehabilitation of an existing injury will be much quicker.

Take the example of someone who has an injury that prevents them from squatting properly or performing lower body movements. The traditional route would be to introduce some stretching to aid flexibility, build strength using some exercise machines, and perhaps incorporate some movements to encourage the correct firing of the muscles in question. These approaches are all fine in theory but do not address the root problem and client aim of being able to squat.

Consider an approach that involves a variety of methods to achieve the aim, but with the fundamental movement at the heart of the programme. In the example above, this would involve squatting-based movements as early as possible, with different progressions built in. Developing the squat through a squatting-based activity would take care of the strength, mobility, flexibility and muscle firing patterns together in a single coordinated method.

■ Minimal Equipment

Physical therapies, personal training and gym environments can sometimes focus on expensive or complex equipment for the prevention and rehabilitation of injury. This may require ongoing access to such equipment or specialist knowledge in order to achieve your rehabilitation or training goals. In this book we present an alternative option, where most of the movements can be performed either without any equipment, or with equipment that is relatively cheap and readily available. This means that the exercises and methods outlined in this book can be performed in most places, from the home to a hotel room, and are not limited to times of access to specialist apparatus or knowledge. You will see, however, that throughout this book we do advise you seek specialist health or medical attention whenever you are not able to easily identify the cause of your pain or dysfunction. We acknowledge that in these instances there is no substitute for an expert face-to-face opinion.

■ Natural Movement

Another advantage of using body-weight exercise for the prevention and rehabilitation of injury is that the movements used are based on naturally occurring movements. Moving the joints of the elbow, knee, hip and shoulder through a large range while under load is common in children, but in many cases the ability is lost as we get older. Replicating this movement during exercise in adult life is a logical way to restore functional movement at the joints. Squatting, lunging, pushing, pulling, twisting and stretching are all naturally occurring movements that are used to advantage in body-weight exercise. In many weighted exercises the goal is to move external weights in ever more elaborate ways, none of which truly replicate the natural human movements that all of us engaged in regularly as children.

■ Variation

Body-weight exercises can be good for maintaining motivation and interest in exercise in general, owing to the large number of possible exercises that are available. Movements can be joint specific, such as a wrist support, or involve lots of large muscle groups, such as the jump squat. The important thing is that it is very difficult to become bored when you have such a vast number of possible movements to perform in each workout. There are also many different ways of performing body-weight movements, including singly, in circuits, for a period of time, for a number of repetitions, in a progression towards a specific movement, and so on. This means that, even if the same exercises are used, there are many ways to perform those particular exercises. For example, if we take an exercise like the pull-up, there are easily 20 or more different variations that can be performed. Of course, not all of these will be suitable for injury prevention, and some may be beyond your current ability, but the important fact is that a wide range of possibilities and variety is available.

■ Progression and Regression

Another great feature of body-weight exercise is that the movements can be made more difficult or less difficult without the need for adding new equipment. Making an exercise easier is known as *regression*, and is a very useful concept when injured or after a period of detraining. It can also be useful for those who have never exercised but are keen to make a start. If we take the push-up as an example, this can be made easier in many ways, for example by altering the angle of the body, by dropping to the knees instead of balancing on the toes, and even by reducing the ROM. Conversely, increasing the difficulty of an exercise is known as *progression*. If again we take the push-up as our example, we could increase the ROM, slow down the movement or place the feet on a raised platform, all of which will make the movement more difficult.

3

Getting Started

Before starting any exercise routine, whether preventative, rehabilitative, for gains in strength or for aesthetic purposes, it is always recommended to seek the advice of a suitably qualified health or medical professional. You may be carrying an injury that you are unable to associate with those described in this book, or it may be in an 'acute' stage that requires some initial management before beginning a body-weight exercise programme. While the majority of exercises in this book are safe and appropriate, even for the out-of-condition individual, some can be riskier than others if not performed correctly or in the presence of an undiagnosed injury. Visiting a health professional can ensure that you are starting on the right path to rehabilitation. This book will then help to supplement and progress your physical resilience with functional multi-muscle and multi-joint exercises.

■ Basic Physical Requirements

Our endeavour in writing this book was to make it usable by a large proportion of the population, including those who are injured or who are returning to exercise and seeking to protect themselves from injury. Accordingly, there are no real physical requirements or base level of fitness required to start on this journey. For some exercises, a certain level of strength and ability will be beneficial, but this level will reveal itself when you move through the exercises within the book. In such cases we provide guidance on how to modify the exercise to suit different levels of ability.

When starting any exercise programme, many people are concerned that they may not have adequate physical ability to perform it. To address this apprehension, we have included a wide range of exercises and movements that can be performed by almost anyone, anywhere and with minimal equipment. We present a range of exercises, often with variations, to target a range of abilities. It is impossible for us to take into account the ability of every individual reader, and so it will be up to you to explore and test your physical limits. We recommend starting with the easiest exercises and moving on to the more difficult ones once you have mastered the basics. This way, you will determine your baseline and develop a strong foundation to build upon naturally. Throughout this book, we will remind you that you should not overlook the 'easy' or 'basic' exercises; if you do, it will be at the expense of realising later that there are weaknesses in your base strength and resilience to injury.

The physical requirements for the exercises in this book differ from chapter to chapter. *Strength* refers to the ability of muscles to exert force. The stronger your muscles, the more force you can apply, and the more successful you will be with movements that require strength, such as the pull-up. *Mobility* is simply the ability of your body to move into certain positions without being hindered. For example, the deep squat position is a real test of mobility in the lower body, since most people have the strength but not the mobility to fully assume the position. *Flexibility* refers to the ability of the muscles to allow the joints to move into extreme positions. Touching one's toes is an example of flexibility. As we outlined in the introduction to this book, *resilience* can be thought of as the ability to withstand or respond to the forces applied to the body. We therefore focus on how you can develop strength and mobility to improve your physical resilience.

■ Making Enough Time

The amount of time you can devote to a regime of injury prevention and rehabilitation will depend on your own personal circumstances in terms of not only how much physical time you have available but also the nature of your injury or injuries. You must also consider the timescale required for you to regain function, whether this be an occupational or sporting demand, or a goal to reduce pain.

We all have 24 hours every day at our disposal; however, with regard to exercise and physical training, the challenge is finding the time within your hectic day to complete your training programme. There is no magic answer to this universal problem, but we do offer one piece of advice – work out your priorities. For example, many of us watch some television every day, and this is time that can also be used to exercise. Ask yourself whether you would rather continue with lower back pain or that niggling hamstring, or be up to date with the latest TV drama. The option of training and protecting against injury must always be weighed against the time and effort costs of training. If rehabilitating your sore shoulder is more important to you than watching the latest episode of your favourite television programme, then you will likely find time to do it. The fact that many of these exercises can be done daily in your living room for 10 minutes means that you can probably have the best of both worlds!

How much time to devote to injury prevention and rehabilitation will depend on personal circumstances. A niggling ankle injury may only require a few minutes of attention each day, whereas a long-standing lower back problem caused by years of physical neglect or overuse will take more time to rehabilitate and recover. We recommend that you proceed slowly and build your training from the ground up. If you are already quite active and have a regular physical routine, it will be easy for you to add some of our suggested exercises to your programme to protect against or rehabilitate injury. Time spent doing this will not be wasted.

■ Equipment

An effective and solid injury prevention and rehabilitation routine does not require huge amounts of expensive equipment. Nearly all of the exercises we present in this book can be performed without the use of equipment, which makes them accessible and practical for most people. Occasionally there are some exercises that require additional equipment; however, we have kept these to a minimum and ensured that such equipment is either commonly found in most gyms or inexpensive and readily available. The following sections outline the equipment that you might need to perform some of the movements in this book.

Pull-up Bar

A pull-up bar is an essential piece of body-weight exercise apparatus that allows you to manipulate the effect of gravity as the resistance. Exercises benefitting from this piece of equipment include the scapula pull-up, triceps dip and false-grip hang, to name a few. Pull-up bars can be found in almost any good gym, and they can also be purchased for home use. The criteria that you should look for in this apparatus are: 1) a bar thickness that is comfortable to hold (too thick and it will be difficult to hold onto; too thin and the hands will pinch); 2) a suitable height from the ground, enabling easy and safe access; and 3) a sturdy point of attachment, ensuring your safety.

If you do not have a pull-up bar in your gym, or if you train from home, there are other options available. Pull-up bars for home use are now quite popular, with choices for many different situations. One option is to use a pull-up bar that secures to the doorframe, requiring no screws or bolts of any kind. If this is too temporary, it is possible to fix a pull-up bar to a wall or ceiling (but these obviously require a location that allows this, such as a basement or garage). Another option is a stand-alone unit that has a base and frame that support the bar; these types often come with dip bars as part of the structure, and so they can be a good investment (and are often cheaper than even a six-month gym membership). Alternatively, look for suitable fixed objects that can be found in many parks, which would also allow you to train outdoors.

Foam Roller

Foam rollers are essential for the process known as *foam rolling*, or the technique known as *myofascial release*. They come in many different types, ranging from very soft, suited to beginners, to much harder, suitable for those who are more experienced. Foam rollers are also available with a variety of features: some have raised bumps and patterns on them, which are designed to apply a little more pressure than if the roller was smooth. Most gyms these days will have foam rollers, of various types. If the gym you frequent does not have them, or if you train from home, they can be purchased at low cost, either on the Internet or in good sports shops.

Exercise Mat

An exercise mat is recommended, especially for some of the exercises that put pressure on the hands and wrists. They are also useful for performing many of the movements that require you to place your knees on the ground. There are many different types of exercise mat: some are thin and more of a yoga-type mat, while others are thick and more suited to exercise classes. Nearly every gym will have these; if not, they can be found at low cost on the Internet or in good sports shops.

Abdominal Wheel

The abdominal wheel is used for only one exercise in this book, namely the kneeling roll-out. This movement is one of the most demanding core exercises that exists, and can contribute significantly to spinal strength and resilience. The kneeling roll-out is a more advanced exercise, and so you may want to try this when you have mastered many of the other exercises suggested. Abdominal wheels normally consist of a bar with a wheel in the centre. The wheel size will differ depending on the model that is available to

you, and the bar will have space for both hands to grip. In our experience, abdominal wheels are not found in every gym, but many do have them. If you find that your local gym does not have abdominal wheels, they can be purchased at low cost on the Internet or in good sports shops. They have no serviceable parts, are very simple and sturdy in construction, and will remain usable for many years.

Dip Bars

Dip bars are used for exercises such as the scapula dip. They can be found in most modern gyms, and have a main feature of parallel bars approximately two feet apart, at about shoulder height from the ground. In gyms they can normally be found as part of a larger frame, usually paired with a pull-up bar.

If you are not a member of a gym, or if you wish to train from home, dip bars can be purchased relatively cheaply. They are different from pull-up bars in that they will need to be fixed to a wall somehow, and will need to be sturdy enough to support your weight safely. Another alternative is to use the backs of two chairs, or other solid objects that will be strong enough and stable enough to support your weight. If you have the space and the funds, the larger pull-up bar frames usually have dip bars attached as well, killing two birds with one stone. Alternatively, check out your local park for suitable equipment.

Exercise Ball

Exercise or gym balls, sometimes called *Swiss balls*, are very common in most gyms (and homes!) around the world. They have become more popular in recent years because of the surge of core training and exercising on unstable surfaces. The gym ball is suggested in this book for a knee exercise, but it can also be used for many other movements that are not discussed in this book. The balls can be purchased at low cost in sports shops or on the Internet, and are a good investment.

Exercise Step

For some of the exercises, it is useful to have a step or platform that can be used to make the movement easier. For example, the push-up type exercises can be made easier if the hands are raised relative to the feet, as the lower body is supporting more body weight. Most gyms will have steps of varying heights, or otherwise have graduated blocks that can be used to modify the height of the step as needed.

If you do not belong to a gym, you can purchase exercise steps and platforms on the Internet or in good sports shops for home use. In addition, you can also use objects around the home, such as stairs, steps or even the edges of sofas. Be creative, but always safe.

Barbell

A piece of equipment needed for the shoulder dislocate exercise and some other movements is the barbell. It should preferably be light and strong, and suitable for small weights. Steer clear of the Olympic-style barbell, as the bar alone weighs 20kg (44lb) and is therefore not very useful for the vast majority of readers.

The ideal barbell to use would be the same as the one used in group exercise classes. These are usually much shorter and lighter than full-size Olympic barbells, and accommodate small weights easily, making them perfect for the exercises we advocate in this book. You may even find that a wooden dowel, such as a broom handle, is sufficient and provides a low-cost and accessible alternative.

Elastic Therapy Band

The elastic therapy band can be very useful when it comes to body-weight exercise. In this book we use it for some of the shoulder movements, such as the shoulder dislocate alternative. Elastic therapy bands for exercise come in many different strengths and thicknesses, with some being very easy to stretch and others providing more resistance. Most gyms will have bands of varying strengths. If you are not a member of a gym, or if you train at home, elastic therapy bands can be found at low cost on the Internet or in good sports shops.

Gymnastic Rings

Gymnastic rings are perhaps the most specialised piece of equipment that can be used in this book. We do not suggest many exercises requiring this apparatus; however, if you like body-weight exercise, gymnastic rings are generally a useful thing to have. They are seldom seen in most commercial gyms, but the benefits of using them are undisputed. Gymnasts are widely regarded as being some of the strongest athletes (kg for kg) on earth, and so anything that can be taken from their training methodology and used in injury prevention and rehabilitation is well worth it.

As gymnastic rings are not commonly available in gyms, you will probably have to purchase some. They are actually quite cheap if you buy the nylon versions (rather than the official wooden rings), and they will last a lifetime if properly looked after. Rings come with straps that can be used to attach them to a pull-up bar or other fastenings. It is a good idea to make sure that this secure point is sufficiently high, preferably above head height. This way, you will be able to lower the rings to floor level or waist level and have plenty of space above to move. This is especially true with exercises such as the German hang (Chapter 5, Goal Exercise 5.14), where you need to be suspended in the air while close to the ground.

4

The Role of Nutrition and Recovery

A significant part of injury prevention and rehabilitation is knowing when to rest. Contrary to what many people believe, the body does not get stronger and more resilient during training sessions or workouts. The body repairs itself when it gets the chance, and this occurs when you engage in rest. The meaning of rest here is not necessarily a day on which you do absolutely nothing, but a day on which you perform no excessive or repeated physical activity. This 'rest' day will give the body a chance to recuperate and repair the damage done to it in the training sessions you have performed.

In this chapter we are going to look at various factors regarding nutrition, rest and recovery that are important to consider for injury resilience and rehabilitation.

■ Nutrition

There is an old saying along the lines of 'you cannot out-train a bad diet'. This suggests that all of the physical activity in the world will struggle to outweigh the effects of a poor or inadequate diet. For this reason, we cannot ignore the importance of this subject when developing a book on physical training. Your time is precious and we want you to maximise the gains from your hard work and efforts.

In addition to rest and good-quality sleep, nutrition is a key factor in recovering from workouts, staying injury free and rehabilitating existing injuries. There are two factors that must be considered when talking about nutrition: the first is the type or quality of nutrient, and the second is quantity. It may be obvious that meat, fish, eggs, vegetables, fruit and other natural foods are the types that you should eat. Natural, unprocessed foods present the body with easy-to-

access nutrients in a form that our digestive systems have evolved to deal with.

It is a little trickier, however, to quantify the amount or volume of food that should be consumed to recover and grow following workouts, and to reduce the onset of chronic musculoskeletal injury. On the one hand, you must eat enough food so as to not deprive the body of the nutrients that it needs, but not so much that unwanted weight gain becomes an issue. Thankfully, it is very difficult to eat so much natural food that non-lean weight gain results. Even the largest and strongest humans on the planet (athletes who compete in professional strongman competitions) have to force themselves to eat huge quantities of food to get as big as they are. Natural food is rarely high in calories, and so mountains of vegetables will still only contain a similar calorie content to a very small portion of junk food. Junk food tends to be 'dense' in calories, and so to eat enough of it to fill you up means consuming a large amount of energy. And do not even get us started on washing it down with a fizzy or juice drink. Such foods and drinks are often high in sugars and/or saturated fats. It is now accepted that a calorie is not just a calorie: the source of that unit of energy is important to understand, as some chemicals are processed much more easily than others, while some go straight to storage (usually as fat).

The quantity of food that you need will vary depending on a number of factors, including age, height, weight, muscle mass, training history and genetics. We can only offer general guidelines here, since every reader will differ with respect to the factors listed above. The first guideline is to eat at least three meals a day, ideally spaced out equally. You do not want to get into the habit of missing meals or of eating a small amount at one sitting and then a large amount at another.

The second guideline is to ensure that a protein source is present in every meal. Protein is the nutrient that has the highest satiety rating of any nutrient, keeping you feeling fuller for longer. Protein also provides the building blocks of muscle and connective tissues, such as tendons and ligaments; these are all structures stressed and strained by physical training and daily postures and movements. Developing lean mass in the form of muscle will raise your resting metabolism, meaning that even at rest you will have energy-hungry cells that require feeding; this will contribute to keeping your weight under control. It also means that you must keep feeding the beast in order to maintain that newly gained muscle mass. Having well-developed muscles and connective tissues will also contribute to your physical resilience by protecting joints and absorbing external and internal forces.

The third guideline is to make sure that you drink enough water during the day. Chronic dehydration can be misinterpreted by the brain as hunger, driving the desire to take on unneeded calories instead of essential fluids. Muscle, connective tissue and joints require an adequate water composition to ensure normal physiological functioning and resistance to daily trauma.

Avoid junk and processed food wherever possible for the reasons discussed above. As a simple clarification, junk and processed food is anything that is far from the natural source food. This includes all of the usual culprits, such as fast food, sugary snacks, drinks that are a luminous colour, and anything else with an unnatural appearance. You can also add to this list processed sugar and flour, and any other product that has been highly refined or processed.

Basic Nutrition for Growth and Repair

While the advice so far in this chapter has been general enough to improve health for the vast majority of people, there are some specific nutrients that will help with injury prevention and rehabilitation.

Protein

You are made of protein. From the enzymes that regulate your cell activity, to the structural muscle and connective tissue fibres, protein is essential for repairing and replacing such things on a daily basis. As the entire premise of this book revolves around building resilience and strength in the body to reduce the incidence and severity of injury, and to rehabilitate existing injuries, it makes sense that protein is perhaps number one on the list of important nutrients.

The protein that you consume in your diet, whether it is from animal or plant sources, is made up of building blocks called *amino acids*. Once digested, the amino acid 'blocks' are reorganised to build new structures within your body. This process could be the repair of the ligament collagen fibres that you damaged during an ankle sprain; it could also mean an increase in muscle mass to support and power occupational or sporting activities. With regard to building muscle mass, or at least ensuring adequate muscle repair, the general daily recommendation is to take in two grams of dietary protein for every kilogram of body weight.

Calcium

Strong bones are essential for maintaining skeletal strength and for protecting against bony injury, such as a stress fracture. Calcium is needed for strong bones, as it is one of the key minerals that impregnates and hardens the protein framework of your skeleton. This particular nutrient is often linked solely to a dairy-based diet, but there are in fact many dietary sources of calcium. Lots of people, not necessarily just those who are lactose intolerant, are moving towards a dairy-free diet. By learning about other sources of calcium, you need never be short on this essential mineral nutrient, whatever your preference. Sources of calcium include:

- Milk
- Kale
- Sardines
- Yogurt
- Broccoli
- Watercress
- Cheese
- Bok Choy

Vitamin D

Vitamin D is a nutrient that is tied inextricably to calcium, in that the body needs vitamin D to be able to process calcium for bone health. In other words, you can drink all of the milk in the world, but if you do not ingest adequate vitamin D, your body will not be able to utilise all of the calcium.

Vitamin D can be found in a range of foods, and a balanced diet should provide sufficient amounts. The body will also synthesise vitamin D with exposure to sunlight, but the vitamin is more readily available from sunshine, with the consensus being around 20 minutes of direct sunshine a day. This does not mean exposure to harmful UV rays, and so sunscreen should still be used. Exercising outdoors for 20 minutes a day with a bulletproof-body routine will contribute immensely to physical health and resilience.

Vitamin C

Most of us have heard the old adage that vitamin C is good for keeping colds away, but the evidence for this is lacking. What most people are not aware of is that vitamin C is also very good for injury prevention and rehabilitation. There are a number of reasons for this:

1. It helps in the building of collagen, which is vital for repairing connective tissues, such as ligaments and tendons, and the general support structures of the body.
2. It increases the amount of iron absorbed from food, useful in haemoglobin production for improved oxygen-carrying capacity.
3. It is a known antioxidant, protecting the body's cells from harmful free-radical activity.

There are a lot of foods that contain vitamin C – here are a few suggestions:

- Broccoli
- Papaya
- Bell peppers
- Brussels sprouts
- Strawberries
- Pineapple
- Oranges
- Kiwi fruit
- Cauliflower
- Grapefruit
- Tomatoes

How much vitamin C to include in your diet is up for debate: the normal recommended daily allowance is 90mg for men and 75mg for women. Some studies have suggested that increasing this amount to 400mg can be more optimal for health. One scientific study recommended taking 1,000–2,000mg of vitamin C every day for a short time (five days) following injury. Vitamin C is water soluble, however, and cannot be stored in the body; it is therefore likely that excessive amounts will be lost without any benefit.

Before you run off to the shops to buy hundreds of vitamin C pills, we offer a word of caution. Massively increasing vitamin C intake can result in some side effects, including nausea, abdominal cramps, headaches, fatigue and even kidney stones.

The Importance of Carbohydrate

Carbohydrate has had some bad press recently regarding health and weight loss. The media can have a tendency to advocate 'throwing the baby out with the bath water'; with respect to diet, this means excluding even beneficial carbohydrate. Carbohydrate is an important nutrient that contributes to health and athletic performance. What we really need to be aware of is the *source* of the carbohydrates being taken into the body.

We can understand this a little more easily if we think of starchy and non-starchy carbohydrates. *Non-starchy carbohydrates* are those that still provide the energy that our bodies need, but do not have the high calorie content or the blood-sugar raising properties that starchy carbohydrates do. Leafy vegetables, carrots, cauliflower, green beans, sweet corn and sweet potatoes are some examples of non-starchy vegetables. Try to include as many of these foods as possible in your diet. A typical meal, for example, might be grilled chicken breast, peas, broccoli, carrots and brown rice. This will contain protein from the chicken, fat from the chicken, and non-starchy carbohydrates from the vegetables. Everything the body needs will be present in this type of meal, and as long as you try to stick to this type of eating plan, you will find that your health, weight-loss, fitness and injury-prevention goals will be achieved.

In contrast, *starchy carbohydrates* are those that are found, for example, in bread, pasta, potatoes and rice. They are normally stodgy and moderate to high in calorie content, and can contribute to weight gain if eaten to excess. If we expand this to include processed foods, such as cakes, donuts, ice cream and chocolate, you can see how eating these might contribute to weight gain and to an increase in body fat percentage. It makes sense from a health perspective to limit the intake of these types of food as much as possible. Eating rice and potatoes is fine, but try to go for brown rice, and limit potatoes to a sensible minimum.

The real culprit is processed and refined carbohydrate. As the name suggests, these are not naturally occurring states of carbohydrate; they are, however, derived from natural foods, and this is where the confusion can arise. You may often see products being badged as 'no added sugar', or 'contains natural sugars'. Sugar is a natural substance, found in abundance throughout many natural foods. It is the way in which this sugar is delivered to the body, however, that requires attention. Some sugars after being processed are difficult for the body to handle, and so either are converted to storage (weight gain!), or add to the workload of the liver (where toxins are processed!).

Across the developed world, we are now seeing an increase in metabolic syndromes, obesity and non-alcoholic liver disease. Further discussion on this topic is beyond the scope of this book, but there are plenty of other information sources out there from which you can learn more. A final word on this matter – make your body work for its calories. If they come easily, and in large amounts, then common sense might suggest this is not what our systems have evolved to process.

Hydration

The statistic that says that the human body is composed of 60% water indicates that this often-overlooked nutrient is essential, and that this is one fact worth taking seriously. Chronic dehydration is thought to affect a significant percentage of the population; the situation is made worse by the modern diet, as many people substitute other drinks for water. Relying on coffee, tea, soft drinks and possibly alcohol as a source of hydration is an unwise decision. Both coffee and tea contain caffeine, which is a known diuretic, and this will cause you to lose water by urinating more. Soft drinks contain water, but they also contain a concoction of other chemicals that you may not want in your body, including copious amounts of refined and processed sugar. In addition to being 'empty' calories that cannot really help to repair your body, sugar will make losing weight (if this is one of your goals) much more difficult. There really is no point in moving one step forwards if your regular soft drink intake is moving you two steps backwards.

Many people face the problem of not knowing how much water to drink in a given time period. To help you out in this regard, we have included a simple table to show you how much water you should aim to drink in a 24-hour period (Table 4.1). Note that the water intake will vary, depending on a number of factors, including climate, fitness, body size and the amount of exercise performed.

Alcohol Consumption

Alcohol consumption is a debatable issue in terms of its effect on health, with several reports suggesting that moderate intake, such as a glass of red wine, can actually be beneficial. If this is the case, the benefits are unlikely to be entirely derived from the alcohol, but rather from the properties of the grapes that make up the wine.

If you are injured or rehabilitating an injury, or perhaps seeking to stay injury free, the best course of action would be to drink as little alcohol as possible. Processing alcohol requires time and effort, and incurs a cost to your body in terms of energy and nutrition that cannot be used for

■ **Table 4.1.** Recommended water intake (24-hour period).

Your weight (kg)	Your weight (lb)	Water intake in litres
45.5	100	1.5
50	110	1.7
54.5	120	1.8
59	130	2
64	140	2.1
68	150	2.3
73	160	2.4
77	170	2.6
82	180	2.7
86	190	2.9
91	200	3
95.5	210	3.2
100	220	3.3
104.5	230	3.5
109	240	3.6
113.5	250	3.8
118	260	3.9
122.5	270	4.1
127	280	4.2
132	290	4.4
136.5	300	4.5

growth and repair to build a stronger and more resilient body. If you have an acute injury, be aware that alcohol acts as a vasodilator (causes dilation of the walls of blood vessels), and may cause further swelling in the injured area; this may in turn increase the time to heal.

■ Rest and Recovery

Sleep

Sufficient good-quality sleep is a fundamental aspect of injury prevention and rehabilitation. Getting enough sleep is vital in order for the body to repair itself properly, but a lack of it is unfortunately rife in today's modern culture; reasons for this may include worrying about work, family, money or health. Sleep deprivation may reduce your ability to cope with these factors during your waking hours and so lead to a vicious circle. Talk through your problems before you try to sleep, or even write down your problems before bed in an attempt to offload your mind.

In addition to the normal worries of life causing below-par sleep quality and quantity, poor 'sleep hygiene' is now well recognised as a modern-day affliction. Sleep hygiene refers to daily habits that can be modified to enable better sleep. Going to bed at a sensible time and not staying up to watch television can improve the quality of sleep immensely. Go to bed when you start feeling tired, rather than fighting the urge and distracting yourself with other activities, such as watching TV or sitting at a computer.

Avoid using display-screen technology, such as your phone or tablet, before going to sleep. It is common in the modern world for many people to check their phones or electronic devices before they go to bed, or even to peruse them while in bed. Reading in bed is increasingly being carried out using electronic devices, much to the detriment of getting to sleep successfully. There are now filters and specific modes on many devices that reduce the blue light that is known to impact on brain function. If you have to use your electronic device in bed, it is a good idea to turn the filter feature on, or better still leave your phone in another room. Your social media notifications will not go anywhere, and will be waiting for you in the morning.

Ensuring that you are in bed before midnight is often regarded as sound sleeping advice; this is especially true if you have to get up early. The notion of eight hours of solid sleep has recently been questioned, with some scientists suggesting that the body naturally wakes after three to four hours, before later needing a further block of three to four hours. Just do not eat biscuits during the break!

The power nap has also gained popularity in recent years, and science is beginning to support this practice. The body seems to have a natural dip in the mid-afternoon that supports a power nap. There are also recommendations to consume caffeine before the power nap to improve post-nap alertness.

Quality sleep regulates normal hormone control, including growth and stress hormones, as well as the hormones involved in blood-sugar control. The effects of improving your sleep may therefore have an impact on many areas of your life, including psychological wellbeing, weight control and physical resilience to injury.

Reducing Stress

Reducing stress is another important aspect of injury prevention. Stress, in whatever forms it takes, can have profound detrimental effects on the body. Psychological stress is difficult to avoid in the modern world; worries about money, work, the pressures of family and the uncertainty of the future can all be very real. Unless measures are taken to deal with the thoughts associated with these perceived problems, the stress that results can

soon spiral out of control. This stress can manifest itself in the form of physical problems, from raised blood pressure to increased muscle tension. Chapter 5 of this book examines how stress can show itself in shoulder and neck posture, later leading to dysfunction. You may be familiar with the sensation of increased shoulder/neck muscle tension causing aches and pains.

A discussion of the ways of dealing with daily issues and life in general is not within the scope of this book, but there are a few things that you can do to help combat the rise of stress and its impact on the body. First, make sure that you remain active, both physically and mentally; a strong body and mind will make coping with stressful situations much easier. Second, ensure that your sleep and nutrition are optimal, as described earlier. Eating well will give you more energy, a better physical composition and better health in general, all of which will help deal with stress; they may even resolve some of the health and weight issues that caused the stress in the first place.

How you spend your rest days is also very important. If you have a perceived stressful job and life, then find positive ways to use this stress response, such as exercise or an active hobby. Rest and relax during the days that you are away from work. Be with people whose company you enjoy, and surround yourself with positive distractions.

Ways of Sitting

Many desk-based jobs require sitting down for long periods of time; this can contribute towards many of the physical problems explored throughout this book. Tight or weak muscles may eventually manifest themselves in chronic injury and pain that niggle away at you during day-to-day activities. Two of the most common consequences of sitting for long periods are shortened hamstrings and spinal problems, especially in the area of the lumbar spine.

If your job requires you to sit at a desk, there are things you can do to make this less of a problem: getting up and stretching the hamstrings, hips and spine every hour is good practice. Look through the relevant chapters of this book and add some simple mobility exercises to your working day (if space and company policy allow). You might also try working at a standing desk, as this may negate the constant stress of a sitting posture. If your place of work has an ergonomic assessment facility, we recommend that you use it. If it does not, ask yourself if your work set-up or postures feel right to you. If they don't feel right, they probably aren't, and so play around with them.

At home you may also find that you spend a lot of time sitting; this may be for a number of reasons, including watching television, reading, eating an evening meal or even spending time with family or friends. There are some adjustments that can be made here, though, with perhaps the best solution being to sit on the floor with the legs stretched out in front. Even a cross-legged position on the floor will provide a welcome stretch to the hips and lower back. These positions might be uncomfortable at first (especially if your hamstrings and lower back are tight); however, soon enough your hamstrings will lengthen and become more flexible, and the positions will become much more comfortable. Sitting like this will not require any special equipment, and the normal activities you perform at home can still be enjoyed with little or no impact. Even better, try doing some of these activities without sitting at all; for example, spend time catching up with family by going for a walk with them, or read while standing up.

Forward Head Posture

A physical ailment that has appeared in recent years is the forward head posture: in this condition the head and neck jut forwards, leading to muscle imbalances in the neck and shoulders. A common cause of this problem is the use of mobile phones and other electronic screen devices, whereby the head is constantly looking down and fixed in a restricted field of vision for extended periods. The long-term consequences of this are not yet clear, as such electronic screen devices have not been around long enough for firm conclusions to be drawn.

The weight of the head is approximately 5–6kg (11–13lb). If the head and the shoulders move forwards, out of ideal alignment, the activation of the neck extensor muscles will increase dramatically. For every 2.5cm (1") of forward head posture, the weight of the head on the spine can increase by approximately 4.5kg (10lb); this may lead to increased neck muscle tension and excessive strain on the underlying joints of the neck.

To combat forward head posture, the best course of action is to limit the use of mobiles and other electronic devices as much as possible; at the very least, one should try to use them in a way that will not contribute towards the problem. Ask yourself whether or not using a device like this is contributing towards your day. If checking social media is not impacting your life in a positive way, and is adding to the development of a forward head posture, then put the device down and start moving.

Chapter 11 of this book covers some simple and effective exercises to supplement this advice and reduce that forward head posture.

Overtraining

In the context of injury prevention and rehabilitation, the concept of overtraining is worth considering. In its simplest definition, *overtraining* refers to the act of training with too much intensity and too often, with inadequate rest between training sessions, leading to reduced training gains; in other words, more becomes less. This type of training causes many physical and psychological problems, but the main one that we will consider here is the impact of a lack of adequate recovery. If you train too often at a high intensity, the physical trauma that is done to the body will not be repaired before the next training session. If the sessions keep on coming at the same intensity and frequency, the body will slowly deteriorate until a point where injuries become inevitable and overall physical performance decreases. Such relentless stress on the body will reduce the resilience of bone, muscle and connective tissues (such as ligaments and tendons) to further stress. You may also experience mental fatigue and adverse effects on your immune and hormonal systems.

To deal with the issue of overtraining, it is best to keep a training log and note down when you feel tired or worn out, or when you start to get niggling injures. If you are an endurance sport athlete, try training with a heart rate monitor and log your efforts. These methods can be very effective for identifying the onset of overtraining and knowing when to take a step back. Sometimes, less is more!

5

The Shoulder

Introduction to the Shoulder

You may know the shoulder as a single joint that is capable of an amazing range of movements and functions. In reality, it is best considered as a *complex*. This term is not used because it is a complicated joint, but rather to highlight the fact that there is an orchestra of components all working together to bring about movement and stability of the shoulder region. The shoulder has allowed humans to interact with, and manipulate, the external world. From washing your hair to fastening a bra, the shoulder is called upon to move through a range not seen in any other joint; in sport and exercise these demands increase significantly.

Humans display an emotional connection with the shoulder joint. Notice how the shoulders can rise upwards towards the ears during times of stress, with an uncomfortable tension building up in the surrounding muscles. The shoulder complex can also reflect our mood – the slumped shoulders when we are feeling low or the shoulders pulled back with pride. When painful, the shoulder has an ability that no other joint seems to have to the same degree; it can immobilise itself. Picture the fallen Tour de France rider cradling their immobilised arm after a collarbone (clavicle) injury. It is not unusual to see a patient with a frozen shoulder reaching across their body to grip their painful upper arm and fix it against their body. In this way it can be totally relieved of its functional duties.

By acknowledging the shoulder complex for what it is – a collection of moving and stabilising parts – you will better appreciate the overview of anatomy that follows. This will lead you on to discover how and why some of these structures become dysfunctional, causing pain and restriction of movement.

Functional Anatomy of the Shoulder

Passive Structures

The term *passive structures* will be used in its very broadest sense throughout this book to refer to any structure in the musculoskeletal system that cannot move itself. That is, its resting state can only be changed by something acting upon it, whether this is gravity, somebody moving it on a person's behalf, or a muscle and tendon pulling against it.

The passive, or inert, structures are those that give the fundamental shape and inherent stability to the joint; examples are bones, cartilage, ligaments, capsules and bursae. The relationship of these structures can be seen in Figure 5.1.

The obvious bones of the shoulder complex are the scapula, humerus and clavicle. We should also include the posterior chest wall created by the ribs, and the upper breast bone (sternum).

KEY POINT: *The joint between the clavicle and sternum (sternoclavicular joint) is the only true joint connecting the arm to the rest of the body! It is a small joint with a tremendous responsibility.*

The sternoclavicular joint does not act alone in providing attachment and transmitting forces between the body and the arm. When performing body-weight exercise, or any form of physical loading, there is a special relationship between the scapula and ribcage that creates a powerful bridge for the passage of power. It is not considered a true articulation, yet this 'false' joint is key to the proper functioning, positioning and stability of the shoulder joint.

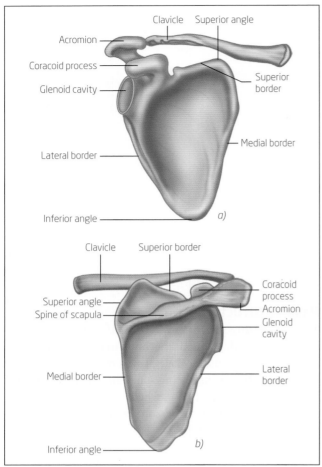

■ **Figure 5.1.** Bones of the shoulder complex: (a) anterior view; (b) posterior view.

Dysfunction of this relationship can lead to multiple pain problems around the shoulder complex and can cause some of the problems explored below. As you will discover later in this chapter, body-weight exercises are ideally suited to addressing many of the problems arising from poor scapulothoracic movement control.

The shoulder complex is reinforced by ligaments and a joint capsule. These structures stabilise the moving parts of the shoulder, limit excessive or unwanted movements and provide positional feedback to your brain. The *subdeltoid bursa* seen in Figure 5.2 is so named because of its location beneath the deltoid muscle of the shoulder.

The subdeltoid bursa is also referred to as the *subacromial bursa* because it partially sits under the bony shelf of the scapula, known as the *acromion*. It is here that this fluid-filled sack becomes dysfunctional and a potential source of shoulder pain (see 'Subacromial Pain Syndrome' below).

Active Structures

In their simplest form, *active (contracting) structures* will be regarded here as those capable of generating movement. Muscles do this by contracting (shortening) in response to electrical impulses generated either consciously or subconsciously. As they contract, they pull on their tendons, which in turn exert a force on bone to cause movement at a joint. Because muscles can only pull and not push, they cannot return a joint to its original position where gravity or other forces are neutralised. You will therefore see muscles arranged in opposing pairs; perhaps the most famous of these duos crosses both the shoulder and the elbow – the biceps and triceps – as shown in Figure 5.3.

If you are asked to think of other muscles at the shoulder, your first thought might be the deltoid muscle. While this muscle is absolutely essential in generating force at the shoulder to power the arm from the side or to press it above the head, it actually has a very minor role in rehabilitating the shoulder.

KEY POINT: *For bulletproof shoulders, focus on developing the muscles and tendons of the rotator cuff, and the muscles that control the scapula.*

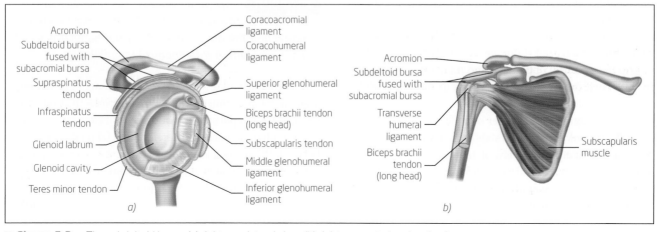

■ **Figure 5.2.** The subdeltoid bursa: (a) right arm, lateral view; (b) right arm, anterior view (cut).

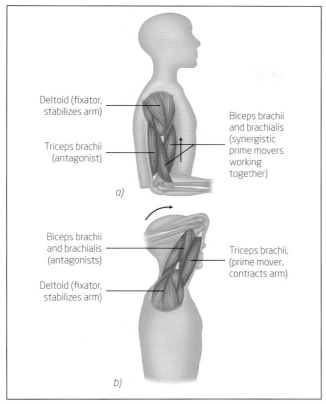

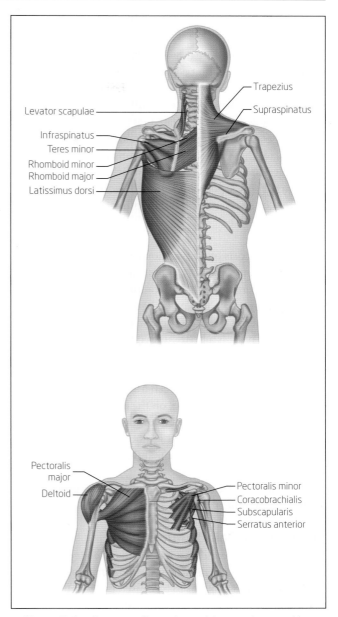

■ **Figure 5.3.** Group action of muscles: (a) flexing the arm at the elbow; (b) extending the arm at the elbow.

The *rotator cuff* is a dynamic compressive support that maintains the head of the upper arm bone (humerus) in the socket provided by the scapula. It plays a very important role in shoulder joint function. In addition to being dynamic stabilisers, the muscles and tendons of the rotator cuff contribute to proper movement at the true shoulder (glenohumeral) joint. The rotator cuff is made up of:

- Supraspinatus
- Infraspinatus
- Subscapularis
- Teres minor

All four of these short muscles originate from the scapula and insert on the head of the humerus. If the position of these bones relative to one another is altered through poor posture or muscle imbalance, the function of the cuff muscles will be compromised.

We must, however, consider all the muscles acting on the scapula if we truly wish to rehabilitate or make resilient the shoulder complex. These muscles include the trapezius, rhomboids, levator scapulae, latissimus dorsi, teres major, deltoid, pectoralis major, pectoralis minor, serratus

■ **Figure 5.4.** Rotator cuff muscles and the muscles attaching the upper limb to the trunk.

anterior, coracobrachialis, biceps brachii and triceps brachii. Isolating these muscles and their functions would be difficult and possibly counterproductive. Functional loading will therefore recruit these muscles as and when required to perform the movement properly. This is the basis of body-weight exercise as a rehabilitation/physical resilience method.

KEY POINT: *The body recruits groups of muscles to perform a particular function rather than individual muscles.*

■ Common Shoulder Dysfunction

The wide variety of pure movements normally available at the glenohumeral joint combine to create an extensive circular movement, known as *circumduction*. This can be fully appreciated when you 'windmill' your arms. The large degree of movement is facilitated by the scapula as it travels over the posterior ribcage. To fully maximise shoulder function, we therefore also need to consider the position of the ribcage, as this is the 'stage' on which the shoulder joint performs. If this is poorly positioned because of posture or trauma, then stress is placed on other structures to compensate.

During a diagnosis of dysfunction at the shoulder, you may hear nonspecific terms such as *impingement syndrome* or *frozen shoulder*. Paradoxically, the better our understanding of pathology has become, the looser and more nondescript the diagnoses have been in recent years. This actually reflects a better understanding of shoulder problems – tissue dysfunctions often coexist! It is very difficult to pinpoint the cause of shoulder pain to a single structure, and there has not been a scan invented that can detect pain. Dysfunction, on the other hand, can be obvious to a well-trained health or medical professional. The shoulder is a fairly honest joint that often reveals its secrets through patterns of pain and movement.

Some of the key features of common shoulder problems will be explored next.

Subacromial Pain Syndrome

You may hear this condition described as *impingement syndrome*, *rotator cuff disease* or even *rotator cuff tendinopathy*. It is thought to be caused by an entrapment of the soft tissues in the space below the bony shelf of the acromion, hence the term *subacromial* (Figure 5.5).

This rotator cuff dysfunction may in turn lead to reduced control of the head of the humerus bone and contribute further to the subacromial impingement.

In clinical practice and in the research literature, the term *subacromial pain syndrome* is becoming more common. This is partly because it is difficult to observe impingement on scans like ultrasound, but also because we cannot be sure of a single structure being the cause of pain. The 'impingement' may involve not just the rotator cuff tendons but also the long head of the biceps muscle and the bursa. Thickening of the bursa, the rotator cuff tendons and the shoulder ligaments can further reduce the available space for movement. Add in poor shoulder posture and you have a recipe for pain. According to some research, subacromial impingement syndrome is the most common diagnosis for shoulder pain.

Before we leave the overview of this pathology, it is worth considering the concept of tendinopathy of the rotator cuff tendons. It has often been regarded as an 'overuse' tendon disorder, but this has been brought into question more recently. Some evidence suggests that degenerative tendon change is due to many factors, one of which could be a form of underuse; that means not used sufficiently in the context in which the injury may have occurred. This again suggests that loading the tendon in a controlled way with body-weight exercises may make the tendon more robust and restore pain-free function.

Very often, small tears may be found in the rotator cuff tendons; however, these are often treated effectively with nothing more than physiotherapy/loading exercise and modified shoulder movements. The tears may respond well to steroid injections, but this is considered to potentially weaken the tendon further and possibly increase the risk of further tears or rupture. If you are unsure, seek advice from your qualified medical or health professional.

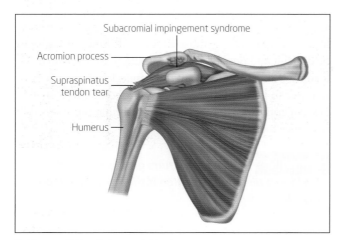

Subacromial impingement syndrome

Acromion process

Supraspinatus tendon tear

Humerus

■ **Figure 5.5.** Subacromial impingement.

KEY EXERCISE 5.1: SCAPULA DIP

Primary Target Area: Muscles around the scapulae
Sets: 3
Reps: 10
Rest: 30–45 seconds

This is an exercise for activating the scapula muscles; it uses the same starting position as a triceps dip, but has no movement from the elbows. The scapula dip is a useful exercise for those who are not used to supporting the

entirety of their own body weight. You will need access to a dip bar as described in the equipment chapter, or other similar set-up. If you have a kitchen worktop that meets in an internal corner, you may find this a suitable surface for this exercise.

1. To perform the scapula dip, grab the dip bar with both hands facing inwards. Push yourself up until your elbows are straight.
2. From here, draw your shoulder blades downwards, away from your ears, without bending your elbows. Keep going until you cannot rise any further. This is the starting position.
3. Lower yourself down without bending your elbows. It should feel like your ears are dropping to meet your shoulders.
4. Push back up again until you reach the starting position. This counts as one repetition.

Teaching Points

The scapula dip is tough not primarily because of the strength required, but because many people struggle to keep their elbows straight when performing the movement. Try to isolate the shoulders as much as possible, and think about keeping the elbows straight to avoid excessive

muscular strain here. Watching yourself in a mirror or getting a training partner to help is a good idea.

Rotator Cuff Injury

Much of the discussion on this topic has already been covered in the previous account of subacromial pain syndrome. In many cases, traumatic tears to the rotator cuff tendons will be small or only penetrate part way through the thickness of the tendon. Movement-based rehabilitation, with or without steroid injection, is often tried in the first instance. This is where your body-weight rehabilitation programme can provide good functional recovery. However, where there has been more severe trauma, or perhaps your tendons are not what they were 60 years ago, you may want to get a thorough assessment from a qualified and experienced health or medical professional. If they do suspect a large tear or rupture of the rotator cuff tendons, you may be referred for a scan of the shoulder. Even in these cases, surgery may not be the best option, and you may be advised to initially try movement-based interventions. You may choose to slowly introduce body-weight exercises into your routine as pain and function allow.

KEY EXERCISE 5.2: FROG STANCE

Target Area: Muscles around the scapulae
Sets: 3
Duration: Hold for 10–20 seconds, once in position
Rest: 30–45 seconds

The frog stance, also called the *elephant stand* or *crane*, is a static strength position used mainly in yoga and gymnastics. It is valued for its ability to build strength in the upper body, especially the shoulder complex, forearms and hands. The frog stance has an element of balance to it; therefore, when performing it, make sure that the surrounding area is free of objects. We recommend using an exercise mat to protect against any falls.

1. To perform the frog stance, crouch down and place your hands on the floor, shoulder-width apart. Splay your fingers wide to aid in control and balance.
2. Place your knees on the outsides of your elbows, allowing the arms to take some of your body weight.
3. Lean forwards, moving more and more weight onto the arms. Allow the elbows to bend if they want to. Hold at this point if you feel you are not able to take any more weight through the arms. As you get stronger over the weeks, you can progress the exercise as described in steps 4–5.
4. Keep leaning forwards, moving onto the tips of the toes. Once you get into this position, you will feel as though the upper body is supporting most of your body weight. From here, try to raise your feet into the air slightly so that only your hands are in contact with the ground.
5. Hold this position for as long as possible, using the muscles in the hands and forearms to control your balance. Keep your shoulder blades down, away from your ears!

Teaching Points

The frog stance is not overly difficult strengthwise, but the main issue for many people is wrist flexibility and the balance aspect of the movement. See the exercises in Chapter 7 to improve your wrist strength.

To improve your balance, there is no substitute for practice. Accordingly, make this exercise a regular part of your physical routine, and you will soon see rapid progress.

Stiff, or 'Frozen', Shoulder

The term *frozen shoulder* is commonly used in public parlance to describe a stiff and painful shoulder of any origin. Clinically, the term has been criticised, as it does not describe the exact condition. The current trend is to call it a *contracted shoulder*, and this in part suggests that the capsule around the true shoulder joint has become tight or shrunken. This condition reduces movement in the same way that a very tight and shrunken jumper would limit your arm movements.

Frozen shoulders are generally regarded as being of two types, depending on whether the condition happened for no apparent reason (primary), or whether there was a recent history of trauma or immobilisation of the shoulder (secondary). Crudely speaking, the condition is considered to go through a freezing stage, a frozen stage and a thawing stage. The first stage is characterised by increasing pain and stiffness, and this can really begin to disturb your sleep and daily function. The middle stage involves a levelling-off of symptoms, and you coming to terms with the restriction. The final phase sees the shoulder become progressively more mobile and less painful. The literature varies in its views about recovery rates, but most frozen shoulders will recover almost all function in one to three years.

It is recommended to exercise caution with any sort of physical rehabilitation for this condition. In the early stages, exercise is less likely to work and could cause a flare-up of your pain. The body-weight routines proposed here are better suited to the latter stages of the condition, but should only be performed if the joint can move into the required positions. As the frozen shoulder progresses through the different stages, so too can your body-weight exercises.

KEY EXERCISE 5.3: CHEST STRETCH

Target Area: Shoulders, chest
Sets: 3
Duration: Hold for 15 seconds
Rest: 10 seconds

The pectoral muscles of the chest can have a large impact on the flexibility of the shoulders, especially in bringing the arms over the head and in moving the arms back horizontally. The muscles can pull the shoulder into a rounded position. Being able to move the shoulders without hindrance is therefore important in order to maintain optimal function and stay injury free.

1. To perform the chest stretch, place one palm against a solid object, such as a wall or doorframe. Make sure that your hand is at the same level as your shoulders.
2. Keeping your elbow straight, turn your body in the opposite direction so that your chest opens.
3. Keep turning until you feel the stretch in your chest. Hold this position for the required time, change arms and repeat.

Teaching Points

As with most stretching, there comes a point when the level of your flexibility is sufficient to allow functional body movements. This process may take longer if you are recovering from a shoulder problem, such as the stiff shoulder, or if you have long-standing muscle shortening. From this point on, your stretching will take on a different purpose: for warming up and maintaining your level of flexibility. How long it takes will depend on many things, including your age, training background and initial flexibility.

Acromioclavicular Joint Dysfunction

The *acromioclavicular joint* is a small joint between the outer edge of the collarbone and the acromion part of the shoulder blade; it can be a source of discomfort and dysfunction. Problems may be precipitated by a trauma, such as falling onto an outstretched hand, or by a direct blow to the shoulder. In these cases, the injury can be classified in three degrees, with grade 1 being a mild sprain and grade 3 being disruption and dislocation of the joint. Grade 3 injuries are much less common, while grades 1 and 2 could benefit from some stability-focused

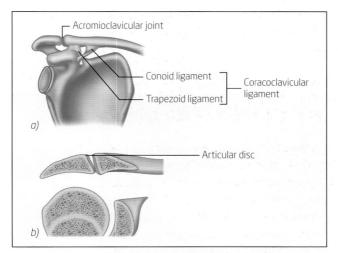

■ **Figure 5.6.** Acromioclavicular joint: (a) anterior view; (b) coronal view.

body-weight exercises that target scapula and shoulder positioning and control.

In later life, the acromioclavicular joint may be affected by degenerative osteoarthritis. This can be the case particularly where there has been a history of heavy use or trauma in the affected shoulder. Here, the joint space has narrowed and the mechanics of the joint are not what they once were. Degenerative changes around the joint may even impact on the subacromial space, and so contribute to pain that is subacromial in origin (see above). Mobilising the joint through loaded body-weight exercise may be of benefit in this situation, but if you are unsure then seek initial advice from a suitably qualified and experienced health or medical professional.

> **KEY EXERCISE 5.4: BAND SHOULDER DISLOCATE**
>
> **Primary Target Area:** Shoulders, chest
> **Sets:** 3
> **Reps:** 10
> **Rest:** 20 seconds

The band shoulder dislocate is the first of three variations of a shoulder mobility exercise. The words *shoulder dislocate* can conjure up a painful image, but it is nowhere near as excruciating as it sounds. It is a great exercise for increasing mobility in the shoulder joint.

For this band version, you will need an elastic therapy band to use as the resistance. This method allows the distance between the hands to be narrow or wide depending on the flexibility of the shoulders. Any elastic band suited for exercise will work, and they can be found in gyms quite readily; they can also be purchased cheaply in sports shops and on the Internet.

1. To perform the band shoulder dislocate, grab an elastic band with both hands and hold it in front of your pelvis. Both elbows should be straight and your grip loose but strong.
2. How wide your hands are will dictate how tough the exercise will be: the wider your hands, the easier the movement, and the narrower your hands, the more difficult. The band will stretch if you need it to.
3. Start to raise the band up and over your head, keeping your elbows straight and your arms wide. As the band goes over your head, you will most likely feel tightness in the shoulders and need to widen the hands in order to reduce the pressure.

4. Keep going until the band reaches your lower back. At no point should you bend the elbows.
5. Reverse the movement until you reach the starting position. This counts as one repetition.

Teaching Points

Using the band for this first stage is very useful, as it allows you to widen your hands during the difficult parts and narrow them when it becomes easy. As you find the exercise becoming easier, you can start with your hands in a narrower position; this way, there will be more resistance when stretching the band as you move through the difficult phase of the movement.

Summary

Once you or your health/medical professional have come to a reasoned diagnosis, you can then start to plan your rehabilitation in the light of the expected timescale for recovery. The good news is that, given the nonspecific definitions of pathology at the shoulder, you need not concern yourself with specific isolated rehabilitation. Keep it functional, feasible, free from pain and, where possible, fun! The following section will guide you through some suggested body-weight exercises that can both prevent injury and promote recovery from injury of the shoulder complex.

■ Body-weight Exercises for Shoulder Injury Prevention and Rehabilitation

Now that you have an idea of the anatomy of the shoulder and some of the more common injuries that affect the area, it is time to look at body-weight exercises which will help to both prevent injury and rehabilitate existing injuries.

In general, the exercises are listed here in order of difficulty, with the easiest appearing first. Exercises that are similar, such as the scapula pull-up and the one-armed scapula pull-up, demonstrate how you can progress.

With regard to the difficulty of an exercise, we are talking about the strength and mobility required to perform it. Keep this in mind when trying to address your own rehabilitation or injury prevention goals.

EXERCISE 5.5: SHOULDER STRETCH

Target Area: Shoulders, chest, back
Sets: 3
Duration: Hold for 15 seconds
Rest: 10 seconds

One excellent test of shoulder flexibility is the ability to raise the arms up over the head without any hindrance. This may be a limitation when recovering from a stiff shoulder, but may also be a predisposing factor for developing subacromial pain syndrome. This exercise is great for developing shoulder flexibility.

1. To perform the shoulder stretch, kneel down and place your palms flat against the floor in front of you.
2. Push your hips backwards and move your chest towards the ground. Keep pushing the shoulders and chest down to the ground to increase the stretch. Hold this for the required time and then rest.

Teaching Points

If you find that you can touch the ground with your chest, you can place your hands on a raised platform of some sort, such as a step or exercise box. This will allow you to stretch the shoulders further.

The rotator cuff musculature is a potential site of injury, as described previously. Stretching these muscles is challenging but very rewarding. This exercise will also stretch a stiff (frozen) shoulder, but go easy! You will need a bar for this stretch, the best option being either an exercise class barbell or a broom handle.

1. To stretch your rotator cuff, grasp a bar with one hand curled around, with the bar pressing against the outside of your upper arm.
2. With your free arm grab the bar towards the bottom, and pull it up towards the ceiling. You should feel a stretch deep in the shoulder. Hold this for 10 seconds, change arms and repeat.

Teaching Points

This stretch can feel strange at first, especially if your posture might have caused muscle imbalances in the rotator cuff. It is quite easy to push too hard with the working arm, and so take it slowly and build up to increasing the stretch.

EXERCISE 5.6: ROTATOR CUFF STRETCH

Primary Target Area: Rotator cuff muscles
Sets: 3
Duration: Hold for 10 seconds
Rest: 10 seconds

EXERCISE 5.7: SCAPULA FOAM ROLL

Primary Target Area: Muscles around the scapulae
Sets: 3
Duration: 10 seconds
Rest: 30–45 seconds

The scapula foam roll is an effective exercise for the shoulders and targets the muscles around the scapulae. It works the same as any other foam-rolling exercise by mobilising the soft tissues and allowing you to maintain pressure on the sore and knotted tissues. As mentioned in the equipment chapter, the hardness of the foam roller will dictate how painful the process will be. A softer material is best to start with; you can then graduate to a harder material as the body area becomes more resilient.

1. To foam roll the muscles around the scapulae, lie down with your upper back on the foam roller. Plant your feet and raise your hips into the air.
2. Hug yourself by wrapping your arms around yourself to stretch your back muscles. This makes them more accessible and easier to target.
3. Roll backwards and forwards slowly on the roller over the muscles of the scapulae for 10 seconds, and then rest.

Teaching Points

This version of the dead hang differs slightly from standard versions in that the aim here is to engage the shoulders and position the scapulae correctly. This is vital for developing this exercise into the scapula pull-up, which requires 'pulling' with the scapulae to improve their function and develop injury resistance. Concentrate on not bending the elbows; this will help in activating the correct muscles at the shoulder.

EXERCISE 5.8: DEAD HANG

Target Area: Shoulders, chest, back
Sets: 3
Duration: Hold for 20 seconds
Rest: 30–45 seconds

As the name suggests, this exercise involves hanging from a pull-up bar to activate the rotator cuff, and to stretch those muscles around the chest and back which pull on the shoulder. The dead hang puts a lot of demand on the hands, wrists, forearms and elbows, and so is a great overall conditioning exercise. Here, we are using it to target the shoulder where the distracting force at the joint develops the supportive function of the rotator cuff. The way the shoulders are positioned in this exercise is key to achieving maximum gains.

1. To perform the dead hang, grab a pull-up bar with both hands in an overhand grip position. Tuck your thumbs under the bar.
2. Now hang with straight arms, keeping the rest of your body relaxed. From here, pull your shoulders down so that they move away from your ears. Do not bend your elbows.
3. Hold this position for the required amount of time, and then rest.

EXERCISE 5.9: SCAPULA PULL-UP

Target Area: Muscles around the scapulae
Sets: 3
Reps: 10
Rest: 30–45 seconds

The scapula pull-up builds on the dead hang (Exercise 5.8), and when used correctly can effectively develop the supporting muscles of the shoulder. There are a number of stages to this exercise, allowing it to be adapted to a wide range of abilities. We will start with the normal version.

1. To perform the scapula pull-up, grab a pull-up bar with an overhand grip, hands positioned shoulder-width apart.
2. Hang with your elbows straight, allowing your shoulders to rise up to meet the ears. This is the starting position.
3. Using the muscles around the back and shoulders, pull your shoulders down so that they move away from your ears. You should reach a limit where they cannot move down any further. Hold this position for a few seconds.
4. Now allow your body to drop slowly so that you reach the starting position again. This counts as one repetition.

Teaching Points

If you have never done this type of exercise before, it is tempting to simply bend the elbows to complete the movement. However, this is more akin to a normal pull-up, and the intended target muscles will not be used. Make sure to keep your elbows relaxed and straight, and concentrate on pulling the shoulders down to get them as far away from your ears as possible.

EXERCISE 5.10: SCAPULA PUSH-UP

Primary Target Area: Rotator cuff muscles, muscles around the scapulae
Sets: 3
Reps: 10
Rest: 30–45 seconds

The scapula push-up is one of four scapula-specific strength exercises (the others being the dead hang, scapula dip and scapula pull-up). It is a great introductory exercise for developing the weight-bearing function of the shoulder. The exercise will increase your awareness of how to activate your shoulder muscles before progressing to more advanced body-weight exercises. The intention of the scapula exercises is not to develop the muscles worked in the push-up (such as the pectorals, triceps and deltoids), but rather to develop the muscles supporting the shoulder complex.

1. To perform the scapula push-up, assume a normal push-up position. Your hands should be flat on the floor, shoulder-width apart, and your legs should be straight, with your weight on your toes. Maintain a strong core with a neutral spine position.
2. From here, draw your shoulder blades apart so that your spine begins to rise. Do not bend the elbows. This is the starting position.
3. Allow your spine to lower slowly so that your chest moves towards the floor and your shoulder blades move closer together. Do not bend the elbows, and keep your body as straight as possible.
4. Draw your shoulder blades apart again so that you return to the starting position. This counts as one repetition. Repeat for the required number of repetitions, and then rest.

Teaching Points

The hardest part about the scapula push-up (as with most scapula movements) is controlling the elbow joint. The elbows should remain straight throughout the exercise, in order to place the emphasis on the muscles of the shoulder complex. If you find this difficult at first, try to make the degree of movement smaller, concentrating on drawing the spine up and then down until the controlled ROM increases.

EXERCISE 5.11: BAR SHOULDER DISLOCATE

Primary Target Area: Shoulders
Sets: 1
Reps: 10

When the band shoulder dislocate (Key Exercise 5.4) becomes easy to perform, you can progress to the bar shoulder dislocate. This movement uses a straight, fixed bar instead of a band, which means that the hands have to stay the same width apart at all times. The bar that you use should be light and straight, with little weight to it. Broom handles or exercise class barbells (the light ones) are excellent for this.

1. To perform the bar shoulder dislocate, grab a bar with both hands and hold it in front of your pelvis. Both elbows should be straight and your grip loose but strong. Begin with a wide grip.
2. Start to raise the bar up and over your head, keeping your elbows straight and your arms wide. If you cannot move the bar all the way over your head, move your hands further apart. It will take a little experimentation to find the right width.

3. If you are able, keep going until the bar reaches your lower back. At no point should you bend your elbows.
4. Reverse the movement until you reach the starting position. This counts as one repetition.

Teaching Points

The main sticking point with this exercise is using a grip that is too narrow. Begin with a wide grip and gradually narrow the grip as you progress. The aim is to get the hands as close together as possible while still executing the movement with perfect form.

EXERCISE 5.12: ONE-ARMED DEAD HANG

Target Area: Rotator cuff muscles, muscles around the scapulae
Sets: 5
Duration: as long as possible
Rest: 30–45 seconds

This exercise builds on the dead hang (Exercise 5.8), and is a progression to using just one arm. It will be more difficult, not just because of the extra body weight that your arm will be holding, but also because of the fact that your body will want to twist and rotate. There is also the issue of holding onto the bar with one hand; this will probably be difficult, even for those with good base strength, but practice is the only thing that will improve this strength.

1. To perform the one-armed dead hang, grab the pull-up bar with one arm in an overhand grip.
2. Now hang with a straight arm, keeping the rest of your body relaxed. You may have to bring your free arm across your chest to stop yourself from rotating or swinging. As before, pull your scapula down in the working arm.

3. Pull the shoulder of your working arm down, away from your ear. Do not bend the elbow.
4. Hold this position for as long as possible, and then rest. To ensure the development of both shoulders, you can repeat the exercise on the other arm.

Teaching Points

It is likely that many will find this exercise very difficult, but it is not impossible. The prerequisite is that you should spend a lot of time doing normal two-armed dead hangs before moving on to this version. Depending on your body weight and physical make-up, this movement will be more difficult or less difficult, but even a lighter person will struggle initially. Progress slowly and test yourself regularly, and you will soon be performing one-armed dead hangs.

EXERCISE 5.13: ONE-HANDED SCAPULA PULL-UP

Target Area: Rotator cuff muscles, muscles around the scapulae
Sets: 3
Reps: 5
Rest: 30–45 seconds

Building on the one-armed dead hang (Exercise 5.12), we arrive at the one-handed scapula pull-up. Here, the body is raised up and down, for a given number of repetitions, using the muscles of the shoulder and upper back to engage the scapula and strengthen the area.

1. To perform the one-handed scapula pull-up, grab a pull-up bar with one hand in an overhand grip.
2. Hang with your elbow straight, allowing your shoulder to rise up to meet your ear. This is the starting position.
3. Using the muscles of the shoulder and back pull your shoulder down so that it moves away from your ear. You should reach a limit where you cannot pull yourself up any further. Hold this position for a second.
4. Allow your body to lower slowly so that you reach the starting position again. This counts as one repetition.

Teaching Points

In addition to the difficulty of this exercise, you may find it challenging to stop yourself from spinning when holding onto the bar with a single hand. To remedy this, you can hang a towel or piece of rope from the bar and hold this with your free hand. This will stop you from spinning, but you must make sure to only use the working arm to pull with.

You may also struggle to hold onto the bar for any length of time with only one hand. To rectify this simply spend time hanging from the bar, both with one hand and with two. Over time you will build enough strength to be able to perform this exercise.

■ Goal Exercises for the Shoulder

The exercises given in this chapter so far have been about building ROM, flexibility, stability and strength for injury prevention in the shoulder region and for making this region injury-proof. When performing those exercises, you will have noticed that they are working multiple areas of the body, giving you a fuller workout and a more functional level of conditioning. In this next part, we are going to examine some goal exercises that you should be aiming to perform as a test of both proper function and general strength and fitness. These exercises can be thought of as the 'standards' for each body zone, and are included here to promote your overall physical development.

GOAL EXERCISE 5.14: GERMAN HANG

Target Area: Shoulders
Sets: 3
Duration: Hold for 15 seconds
Rest: 30 seconds

This movement originates from gymnastics and is designed to strengthen and mobilise the shoulder joint; it is great for those looking to injury-proof this area of the body. The German hang can be performed on a pull-up bar or with gymnastic rings. Rings are our preferred method, because pull-up bars are normally situated above head height, and so a fall can be dangerous. Gymnastic rings, on the other hand, can be lowered to waist height, making the movement safer and easier to learn.

1. To perform the German hang, grab the pull-up bar or gymnastic rings with an overhand grip.
2. Keeping your arms straight, tuck your knees into your chest. The closer you can get your knees to your chest the better, as this will make the subsequent rotation easier.
3. Now pull down as hard as you can, aiming to get your legs through the gap in your arms.
4. Keep rotating around until your legs are free of your arms. Next, let your legs straighten and relax so that they point at the ground. You should now be able to see the floor, and your arms should remain straight.
5. Hold this position for as long as you can, aiming for 15–20 seconds. When you get tired or reach the time limit, let go of the bar and land on your feet.

Teaching Points

One of the main sticking points of the German hang is the issue of going upside down. There is both a fear and a physical element to this. The fear element will disappear with time and confidence, but the physical element is different. If you are having trouble rotating all the way around, make sure that your legs are tucked tightly into your chest and that your knees are bent; this will keep your weight centred and rotation will be easier. Be aware that the German hang is a more difficult exercise and is included as a progression of your body-weight training.

GOAL EXERCISE 5.15: PUSH-UP

Target Area: Triceps, deltoids, pectorals
Sets: 3
Reps: 10–20
Rest: 30–45 seconds

The push-up is very well known, and one of the most fundamental body-weight exercises that exists. It is used in the military, in exercise classes, by those who train at home and by anyone who is looking to build strength in their upper body. It is classed as a *pushing exercise*, in that the arms are moving away from the body.

Teaching Points

As with other exercises where the body weight is supported on the hands, making the push-up easier is achieved by placing the hands on a raised platform. The step described in the equipment chapter (Chapter 3) will be perfect for this. The rule here is that the higher the platform, the easier the movement; conversely, the lower the platform, the harder the movement. If you are struggling to perform the exercise, begin with the platform at waist height. As you get stronger, you will be able to gradually reduce the height of this platform until you are strong enough to perform the movement on the floor.

GOAL EXERCISE 5.16: TRICEPS DIP

Target Area: Triceps, deltoids, pectorals
Sets: 3
Reps: 5–10
Rest: 45–60 seconds

1. To perform the push-up, place both hands flat on the ground, shoulder-width apart, and stretch your legs out behind you.
2. Balance on your toes so that a straight line can be drawn through the shoulders, hips and ankles. Maintain a strong core and a neutral spine position.
3. Bend the elbows and start to lower your chest towards the ground. Make sure that your hips do not sag or drop lower than your shoulders. Do not allow the head to protract forwards, and keep the neck neutral and relaxed.
4. Keep lowering until your chest touches the ground. Pause for a second, and then push back up again until your elbows straighten. This counts as one repetition.

The triceps dip is the second pushing exercise in this part, but is more difficult than the push-up; the main reason is that the upper body is supporting the entire body weight. The dip has often been called the upper body equivalent of the squat, and for good reason. It will develop strength throughout the entire upper body, with the chest, triceps and shoulders doing a very large amount of work.

1. To perform the triceps dip, grab a set of dip bars with your palms facing inwards.
2. Push up until your arms are straight, or jump into the air and 'catch' yourself in the top position.
3. Push down and raise your torso so that your ears move away from your shoulders (as in Key Exercise 5.1 – scapula dip). This is the starting position.
4. From here, bend your elbows and start to lower your body towards the ground. Allow your shoulders to move forwards if necessary, and cross your feet and tuck them behind you if they will touch the ground.
5. Keep bending your elbows until you reach the limit of your ROM; this may be at the right-angle position. Pause for a second, and then push back up until you reach the starting position. This counts as one repetition.

Teaching Points

The dip is a difficult exercise for beginners, but there are ways to make it more manageable. One method is to work with the negative phase of the exercise, which is moving with gravity but controlling the rate of descent. Start at the top of the movement, and then lower yourself towards the ground as slowly as possible. Once you reach the limit of your ROM, drop off the bar. This will count as one repetition, and will be much more effective at building strength than doing the exercise with a reduced ROM. As you get stronger, you will be able to start pushing up from the bottom position.

GOAL EXERCISE 5.17: PULL-UP

Target Area: Biceps, latissimus dorsi
Sets: 3
Reps: 5–10
Rest: 30–45 seconds

The pull-up is the king of body-weight exercises, and is still used as a strength marker for many professions that rely on physical fitness, including the military and law enforcement. In the sports world the pull-up is the basis of much upper body training, from gymnasts to football and hockey players. It differs from the negative chin-up in the way the hands grab the bar: in a chin-up the hands are positioned in an underhand grip, which allows a slightly stronger pull. The pull-up, however, is performed with an overhand grip, which allows the hands to be positioned wider, opens up the chest and relies more on the strength of the upper back. As a result, the pull-up is more difficult than the chin-up, but more beneficial in terms of upper body strength building.

1. To perform the pull-up, grab a pull-up bar in an overhand grip. Your hands should be slightly wider than shoulder width, or in whatever position feels the most natural and comfortable.

2. Hang with your legs straight, and allow your shoulders to rise up to meet your ears. This is the starting position.

3. From here, engage your scapula muscles (as in the scapula pull-up – Exercise 5.9), and pull your shoulders down so that they move away from your ears. Do not bend your elbows as you do this.

4. Start to pull with your arms and back. Your elbows will bend as you do this; allow them to flare out to the sides as far as comfort allows.

5. Keep pulling until your chin reaches over the bar, or your chest touches the bar. Pause for a second, and then return under control to the starting position.

Teaching Points

For many people, performing a perfect pull-up eludes them, even after they have been training for many years. There can be a number of reasons why this is the case. First, ensure that you start the pull-up movement with straight arms. Starting with bent arms makes the movement easier, but it does not help to develop strength throughout the whole ROM. The best method is to use the negative phase of the movement: this requires you to start at the top of the movement (with your chin over the bar), and finish at the bottom of the movement. To do this you will need to stand on a platform underneath the pull-up bar. Grab the bar with loose elbows, and then jump into the air. As you do this, pull hard and aim to get your chin over the bar. Once in the top position, slowly lower yourself down towards the ground under control. Once your arms become straight, drop off the bar. This counts as one repetition.

As you get stronger, you will be able to start pulling up from the bottom position, until you can perform the full movement properly.

6

The Elbow

▣ Introduction to the Elbow

Together with the shoulder, the elbow works to manipulate the position of the hand relative to the world around us. Unlike the shoulder, however, which allows a large ROM in multiple directions, the elbow joint is relatively straightforward. The elbow is probably most noteworthy for its muscular double-act – the biceps and triceps muscles. It is also well known for its susceptibility to injuries linked to sporting actions: the nature of golfer's elbow and tennis elbow will be reviewed later in this chapter.

> **KEY POINT:** *The elbow works with the shoulder to position the hand relative to the world around us.*

▣ Functional Anatomy of the Elbow

Passive Structures

Technically speaking, the elbow consists of two joints: 1) a hinge joint, or the 'true' or proper elbow joint, for flexion and extension movements; and 2) a pivot joint, called the *superior (upper) radioulnar joint*, for rotational movements. As the name suggests, the second joint is created by the joining of the two long bones of the forearm – the radius and the ulna. When you turn your palm up and down it is this second elbow joint that allows the forearm bones to rotate relative to one another. The radius and the ulna, along with the humerus, make up the bony anatomy of the elbow, shown in Figure 6.1.

Like all the moveable joints discussed in this book, the elbow joints are surrounded by a weak joint capsule to contain the lubricating joint fluid. The capsule is reinforced

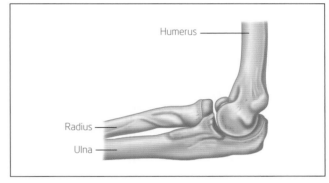

■ **Figure 6.1.** Basic anatomy of the right elbow joint: medial view in 90-degree flexion.

by strong ligaments, some of which might be strained as a result of repetitive throwing stress. This can give rise to a condition in adults that is similar to 'little-league' elbow in children, a condition more common where baseball pitching is a regular sporting movement.

Active Structures

There are, perhaps surprisingly, many muscles either crossing or acting on the elbow joint (Figure 6.2). There are 13 to be exact, but we will concern ourselves with only a few muscles or groups of muscles, specifically:

- Biceps
- Triceps
- Forearm flexors
- Forearm extensors

There are others not mentioned in the list above that contribute to turning the palm up or down, or that assist in flexion and extension of the elbow. The ones selected above have been singled out because they cross more than one joint, and so can be prone to strain injury. These muscles contract and shorten, pulling on their tendons and drawing the anchoring bones closer together. Of the muscles listed above, it is probably the two-headed biceps that has the most demands placed upon it. As we saw in Chapter 5 of this book, the upper tendon of the biceps can be injured as it crosses the shoulder. Then there is the bulk of muscle at the front of the arm that can be subject to tremendous strain. Finally, we have the tendon at the elbow, which flexes the joint and pulls on the radius bone to turn the palm upwards. These different functions have given rise to numerous variations of the biceps curl, as seen in your local gym.

The antagonist of the biceps muscle is the triceps muscle; this three-headed beast pulls on the elbow in the opposite direction, to cause extension. In addition to the biceps and triceps, there are opposing groups of muscles acting from below the elbow.

The muscle groups known as the *forearm flexors and extensors*, as shown in Figure 6.3, originate from the bony bumps on the outer and inner parts of your elbow. These muscles cross both the elbow and the wrist, and so are under dual strain, making them more susceptible to injury. Repeated movements, such as gripping or flicking the wrist, can cause the familiar tennis and golfer's elbow conditions, which are discussed in detail later.

In normal daily movements, the muscles outlined above act on the joints to pull the upper limbs freely through

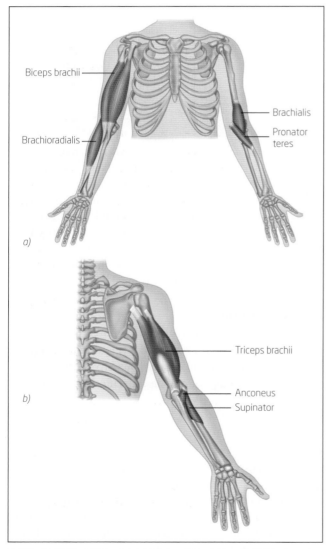

■ **Figure 6.2.** Elbow joint muscles: (a) anterior view; (b) posterior view.

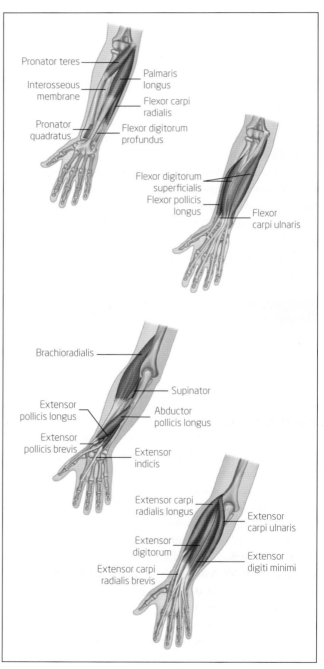

■ **Figure 6.3.** The forearm flexor and extensor muscle groups.

the air (by this we mean that generally the hand is not fixed – think of a biceps curl exercise or handwriting). When you perform body-weight exercises, however, like those described in Chapters 5, 6 and 7 of this book, something different occurs – the hand is generally fixed. This means that the body moves relative to the hand (think of a push-up or pull-up). These movements now create a weight-bearing stability demand on the wrist, elbow and shoulder, and develop the stabilising and control ability of the muscles involved. When the load is progressively increased, these exercises also develop amazing strength, as can be seen in more advanced calisthenics exercises.

> **KEY POINT:** *Whether it is our childhood physical development, or a link to our evolutionary ancestors, humans are no strangers to using the upper limbs for pushing, pulling, hanging, swinging and crawling.*

At first glance, the previous paragraph may seem to contradict the whole ethos of this book: we have so far extolled the benefits of 'functional' exercise and activity. So why on earth would bearing weight through the arms be regarded as functional? If you cast your mind back as far as your early physical development, you may recall that pushing, pulling, hanging, swinging and crawling were all common in your movement repertoire. And it was not too far back in our evolutionary history that the precursors to our species walked intermittently on their upper limbs and climbed trees regularly. While we are not suggesting that we all revert to the behaviour of our evolutionary ancestors, perhaps the 'chimp' or child in all of us needs exercising from time to time!

Before we explore some body-weight exercises to load the upper limbs, let's explore some common elbow problems that would benefit from bulletproofing exercise.

■ Common Elbow Dysfunction

Tennis Elbow

Tennis elbow is the most common elbow complaint and can also be one of the most difficult to manage and resolve (Figure 6.4). It is often regarded as a chronic problem, meaning that it has persisted for more than six weeks; however, it is usually at least three months before some

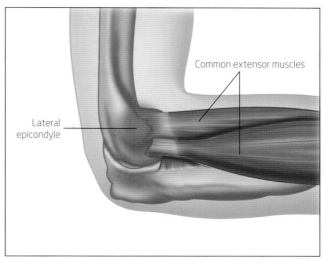

■ **Figure 6.4.** Tennis elbow.

sort of action is taken. Our advice is to start management of this condition early, and this is likely to involve loading exercises. If you are unsure as to how to proceed, we recommend that you seek the advice of a qualified health or medical professional.

The pain of tennis elbow is usually felt on the outer aspect of the elbow, on or just below the bony bump; this is the site of a common tendon attachment for many of the muscles of the forearm. As outlined above, it is the extensor muscle group that attaches on the outer side of the elbow, and so movements involving heavy or repeated gripping can strain this region. Try gripping without cocking your wrist back and you will begin to appreciate the role of the extensor muscle group muscles and their common tendon. If you add more extension stress at the wrist, such as a tennis backhand stroke or the use of a plastering trowel, you may be on your way to developing tennis elbow.

The peak age of onset of tennis elbow is between 35 and 54, and the majority of cases are caused by work-related activities. Rather than being an inflammatory problem, tennis elbow is commonly regarded as a *tendinopathy*, suggesting some degree of tendon breakdown or disruption of its fibres. Management of this problem should therefore involve identifying and modifying aggravating movements; where this is not possible, we recommended developing physical resilience and improved function around the elbow with loaded exercise. Try body-weight Key Exercise 6.1 for starters.

KEY EXERCISE 6.1: INVERTED-WRIST WALL PUSH-UP

Target Area: Elbows, forearms, chest, shoulders
Sets: 3
Reps: 5–20, depending on strength
Rest: 30 seconds

As we have seen, the wrist extensor muscle group operates at both the wrist and the elbow. With the inverted-wrist wall push-up, we can effectively target the muscle during both functions and develop a gradual load on the common tendon. If you have tennis elbow, you may find discomfort when performing this exercise, and so build up slowly. If you are prone to tennis elbow but are currently pain-free, this exercise will improve the chances of staying pain-free.

1. Stand in front of a solid wall, far enough back so that you can lean into the wall with outstretched arms. Now the tricky bit – lean against the wall with the backs of your hands (inverted). Try this with your fingers either pointing downwards or slightly in towards the other hand. Adjust your lean to make the pressure on the wrist and hands more comfortable.

2. Slowly lower your chest towards the wall, allowing your elbows to flex (bend). Take this movement as far as your strength allows. Pause for a second at the end of the movement, and then slowly return to the starting position. Throughout, ensure that you are engaging the wrist extensor muscles to control the back of your hand against the wall.

3. Repeat.

Teaching Points

The degree of difficulty of this exercise can easily be changed by altering your standing position relative to the wall and by reducing the depth of the push-up. To make it harder, the same principles apply. Focus on the wrist and forearm involvement rather than aiming to work the chest. If you do suffer from tennis elbow, you will quite likely need to continue with this exercise for a few months before your body makes the necessary adaptations. Stick with it!

Also recommended: Key Exercise 7.2 (forearm and wrist stretch 2), Key Exercise 7.4 (inverted-wrist push-up support), Exercise 7.8 (kneeling inverted-wrist push-up).

Golfer's Elbow

Golfer's elbow (Figure 6.5) has a very similar cause, process and presentation to tennis elbow as described previously. It is less common than tennis elbow, but when it does occur it can be painful and affect function. With golfer's elbow, the pain will be experienced at the bony bump on the inner part of the elbow. It may be tender to touch but will most often be aggravated by the use of the wrist or elbow. When moving from a resting position, the elbow may feel stiff and painful.

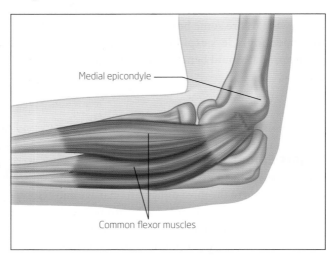

Medial epicondyle

Common flexor muscles

■ **Figure 6.5.** Golfer's elbow.

It is the wrist flexor muscle group that becomes problematic in golfer's elbow; as with tennis elbow, it is the attachment of the common tendon that starts to be troublesome. Unaccustomed use of the flexor muscle group causes breakdown and disruption of the flexor tendon. Once again, we advise a thorough assessment of aggravating movements, with subsequent modification of activity. This should be supplemented with a prolonged period of loading to the tendon and muscles, allowing time for the structures to adapt to the progressive stress. If you are unsure, seek the advice of a health or medical professional. Once you feel able to begin loaded exercise, try the body-weight winner Key Exercise 6.2.

KEY EXERCISE 6.2: PULL-UP/STATIC HANG

Target Area: Elbows, forearms, back muscles
Sets: 3
Reps: 1–20, depending on strength
Rest: 45–60 seconds

The pull-up is a foundation of body-weight exercise, and can be a secret weapon against golfer's elbow. By using an overhand grip of the bar, you automatically engage the wrist flexor muscle group. When pulling on the bar to create the pull-up, the elbow must bend, and it is here that the wrist flexor muscles are subjected to their second loading. The rest of the effort comes from the large muscles of the back. If you cannot complete a pull-up, simply try the initiating movement, or the 'static hold' outlined in the teaching points.

1. Grasp a pull-up bar with an overhand grip. Your hands should be about shoulder-width apart or slightly wider.
2. Hang with the elbows straight – this is a dead hang. It is important for protecting against golfer's elbow that the elbow is able to straighten at the lowest part of the pull-up. It makes the pull-up more difficult, but do not cheat on this.
3. Before you start the pull, shrug your shoulders down first, as demonstrated in Exercise 5.9. Now pull yourself towards the bar, keeping your hips reasonably straight. If able, reach your chest or chin to the bar. Do not be tempted to swing or lift your knees forwards.
4. From the top position, lower yourself down to the starting position, until your elbows straighten again. This is one repetition. Repeat as able.

Teaching Points

If you struggle to perform the pull-up, try a static hold. After grabbing the bar with an overhand grip, assume the pull-up position you wish to hold. If this is the top position, use a step or box to get up to the bar. You can also lower yourself slowly from this position; this is an *eccentric* loading exercise.

Also recommended: Key Exercise 7.1 (forearm and wrist stretch 1), Exercise 7.3 (push-up support), Exercise 7.7 (false-grip hang).

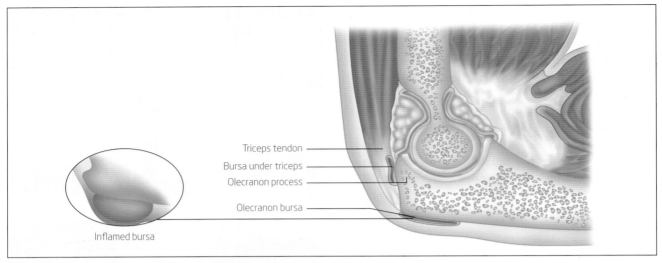

■ **Figure 6.6.** Elbow bursitis.

Bursitis

As mentioned in Chapter 5 (shoulder) and Chapter 9 (knee), a *bursa* (pl. *bursae*) is a fluid-filled sac, which can become swollen or inflamed when subjected to repeated friction or pressure. Bursitis (the swelling of a bursa) can also happen as a result of a direct trauma, but such an injury is not the focus of this book; in this instance, you are directed to seek information on managing acute injuries.

The bursa in question at the elbow is called the *olecranon bursa*; it is so called because it sits alongside the bony olecranon bump at the back of the elbow. This bursa reduces friction between the olecranon bump and the triceps tendon as it pulls to straighten the elbow. Pressure may occur with prolonged or repeated leaning on the back of the elbow (*student's elbow*).

Elbow bursitis (Figure 6.6) may also be the result of repeated straightening of the elbow against load, especially where the pull of the triceps is focused at the elbow because the arm is fixed by the side. One such cause is the gym-based triceps extension exercise: here, the action of the triceps at the shoulder is immobilised and the muscle pull is entirely directed at the elbow through a limited ROM. Once the acute phase of olecranon bursitis has settled, replace your resisted triceps extensions with a body-weight exercise, such as Key Exercise 6.3.

KEY EXERCISE 6.3: LEDGE DIP

Target Area: Elbows, shoulders
Sets: 3
Reps: 10
Rest: 45–60 seconds

The ledge dip is a precursor to the fully-fledged triceps dip, but does not require any specialised equipment to perform. The ledge dip is also easier than the triceps dip, but it will still increase strength and resilience around the elbow joint, without overstressing the olecranon bursa. It will also develop some mobility and flexibility in the shoulder joint as well.

1. To perform the ledge dip, place your hands behind you on an exercise box, bench, step or raised platform, with your fingers facing forwards. You can even use a

windowsill or a kitchen worktop, as long as it is stable and safe. Your hands should be shoulder-width apart. Try a height of around 30–45cm or so for the platform.

2. Stretch your legs out and straighten your knees, balancing on your heels. Keep your back close to your hands.
3. Now bend your elbows and start to descend, until your elbows are bent at a 90-degree angle if possible. You may be limited here by your shoulder flexibility; if this is the case, just descend as far as your mobility allows.
4. Pause for a second, and then push up to return to the starting position. This counts as one repetition. Repeat.

Teaching Points

You may struggle to perform the ledge dip as described, mainly because of a lack of strength or mobility at either the shoulder or the elbow. This is the beauty of body-weight exercise, in that it simultaneously strengthens and mobilises multiple joints; this does, however, make the movements more challenging, but also more rewarding! To reduce the intensity of the movement, you can bend the knees and bring the feet in towards the hands. As you progress, you can straighten the legs out gradually and move on to the full version.

Biceps Tendon Problems

Pain with resisted elbow flexion (bending) or when turning the palm up may be due to a strain of the fleshy bulk of the biceps muscle or of the biceps tendon at its attachment on the radius bone. If the problem came on suddenly with heavy lifting, you may have torn some of the muscle or tendon fibres, or even ruptured the biceps tendon (Figure 6.7); in such cases, we recommend that you get assessed by a health or medical professional. Once you have been cleared to start rehabilitation exercises, you can gradually build up your body-weight exercise routine.

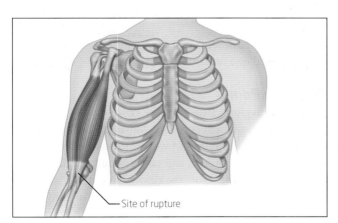

■ **Figure 6.7.** Biceps tendon rupture.

Even if you do not currently have an injury of the biceps, but want to increase your physical resilience here, then Key Exercise 6.4 is a great starting point.

KEY EXERCISE 6.4: NEGATIVE CHIN-UP

Target Area: Elbows, shoulders, forearms
Sets: 3
Reps: 3–10
Rest: 45 seconds

One movement that is great for developing strength in
and around the elbow joint is the negative chin-up. The
negative phase of an exercise (also known as the *eccentric
phase*) is moving with gravity, but without letting gravity
dictate the pace. A negative chin-up therefore starts with
your chin over the bar and finishes in a dead hang.

1. To perform the negative chin-up, stand on a raised box
    or platform underneath a pull-up bar. The box should
    be high enough to allow you to grab the pull-up bar
    with bent elbows.
2. Grasp the bar with an underhand grip, hands slightly
    narrower than your shoulders.
3. Bend your knees and jump as high as you can, pulling with
    your arms so that you finish with your chin over the bar.
4. Hold this position for a second and make sure you
    are comfortable. Then lower yourself down to the
    ground, using your biceps and back muscles to control
    the movement. Throughout the entire movement,
    make sure that your shoulder blades are drawn down,
    engaging the scapula muscles (see Chapter 5).
5. Keep lowering until your elbows are completely
    straight. This counts as one repetition. Repeat for the
    desired number of repetitions then rest.

Teaching Points

The negative chin-up will impart great strength and reduce
the risk of injury around the elbow, precisely because of the
amount of control that must be used to perform the exercise.
It can be very stressful on the ligaments and tendons of the
elbow, so maintain control of the movement. The negative
chin-up uses eccentric loading, which is thought to quickly
increase tendon and muscle strength.

Also recommended: Key Exercise 5.3 (chest stretch).

■ Body-weight Exercises for Improved Elbow Function

EXERCISE 6.5: ARM ROTATION

Target Area: Forearm/elbow muscles
Sets: 3
Reps: 10
Rest: 20 seconds

The arm rotation is a dynamic progression of the forearm
and wrist stretch 1 (Key Exercise 7.1), and develops loading

flexibility in the wrist flexor muscles. It also develops
loading at the shoulder.

1. Crouch down on all fours, with your hands flat on the
    ground, shoulder-width apart.
2. From here, begin to rotate both of your arms inwards,
    while keeping your palms flat on the ground. This will
    require some practice, as it can be difficult to get the
    right muscles to activate.
3. Rotate your arms as far inwards as possible. You may
    feel the strain on the inner elbow. Hold at this point,
    and then reverse the movement, rotating the arms
    outwards (so that the inside of your elbow points
    forwards).
4. When you have returned to the start position, you have
    completed one repetition. Repeat.

Teaching Points

You may struggle to 'switch on' the right muscles and
perform the movement correctly. Most of the activity
comes from the shoulder, but we want you to focus on
keeping the elbow straight and take up the strain in the
forearm muscles that cross the elbow. Do not over-strain
the shoulders with this exercise. Start with a small ROM at
first, and the additional mobility will come with practice.

EXERCISE 6.6: FORKLIFT

Target Area: Elbows
Sets: 3
Reps: 5–10, as you are able
Rest: 30–45 seconds

The forklift is a very unusual exercise that targets the outside of the elbow in an extremely effective manner. It is designed to eliminate the chest and shoulder muscles as much as possible during the pushing movement, and is therefore a lot more difficult than a normal push-up.

1. To perform the forklift, assume a push-up position. Your toes should be in contact with the ground, and your shoulders, hips and knees should form a straight line.
2. Now tuck your elbows into your sides, keeping them pointing towards the rear at all times. Start to bend your elbows and lower yourself towards the floor.
3. Keep moving towards the floor, until your forearms are flat against the ground. Make sure that your elbows point towards the rear. Once your forearms make contact with the ground, pause for a second.

4. From here, push back up to the start again, using mainly the triceps muscles. It is fine if the shoulders and chest do become involved, but try to limit their recruitment.

Teaching Points

This is a tough exercise and has been included here for those wishing to progress towards a complete calisthenics programme. To make the forklift easier, you can move the hands further forward of the shoulders, as if in a Superman position; this allows the shoulders to help out more with the exercise. If it is still too difficult, you can adopt a kneeling position, as if you were doing a kneeling push-up; although this will be much easier than the normal version, it will still allow you to build strength and to progress.

EXERCISE 6.7: PLANCHE LEAN

Target Area: Elbows, shoulders
Sets: 3
Duration: Hold for 10 seconds
Rest: 30–45 seconds

As we have seen in this chapter, sports injuries in the elbow area can be so common that they even have sport-specific names attributed to them: *tennis elbow*, *golfer's elbow* and so on. The planche lean builds additional strength and resilience in the elbow muscles and tendons by requiring the body to apply force with a straight arm. It is not for the faint-hearted!

1. To perform the planche lean, assume a normal push-up position.
2. Point your fingers backwards at an angle of approximately 45 degrees; this will then make the

inside of your elbow point forwards. Make sure that your shoulders are directly over your hands.

3. From here, lean forwards or walk your toes forwards so that your shoulders move past your hands. You should feel pressure on your biceps, forearms and elbow joints.

4. Squeeze your shoulders together and push your spine towards the ceiling. Strive to keep your elbows straight, and 'pull' through the floor to maintain the hold.

5. Aim for a hold of 10 seconds, and then rest. Repeat.

Teaching Points

The planche lean will no doubt be difficult on your first few attempts, but this is expected, since we have included this exercise for those wanting to progress their physical resilience and body-weight strength. Gymnasts use this move in order to build up strength around the elbow joint to prepare them for more advanced movements, such as the planche, handstand and exercises performed on the still rings. Start by only moving the shoulders a short way past the hands, and then gradually increase the distance as you get stronger.

■ Goal Exercises for the Elbow

Goal exercises are usually those that work multiple joints and muscles, but we have included some here that will give the elbow a good workout. As in the other chapters of this book, goal exercises can provide a benchmark test of your current abilities; however, the following exercises can also be used in a routine to develop overall bulletproof strength.

GOAL EXERCISE 6.8: ARCHER PUSH-UP

Target Area: Elbows, shoulders
Sets: 3
Reps: 5–20 each side
Rest: 45–60 seconds

A superb goal exercise for the elbow joint is the archer push-up. This is a little harder than a normal push-up, but the ROM can be adjusted quite dramatically, making it suitable for a wide range of abilities. It can also be performed on the knees, making it easier still.

1. To perform the archer push-up, assume the normal push-up position, but with the working hand positioned at 90 degrees, fingers pointing out to the sides. The hands should be slightly wider than normal.

2. Bend your opposite arm and start to lower your chest to the floor. As you do this, move your upper body over to the side with the bent shoulder. Keep the opposite arm straight.

3. Keep descending towards the ground until your chest touches the floor. At this point. the opposite arm should be completely bent, and the working arm should be very close to the ground, but still straight.

4. From here, push up hard with the bent arm and 'pull' through the floor with the working arm. This will place the demand squarely on the elbow joint of the straight arm.

5. Keep rising until you reach the starting position. This counts as one repetition. Repeat the movement on the opposite side if you need more break between repetitions!

Teaching Points

The archer push-up can be made easier by reducing the ROM; in other words, you do not descend as far on each repetition, and so the working arm will not straighten completely. The exercise as detailed above can also be performed from a kneeling push-up position.

Also recommended: Goal Exercise 5.16 (triceps dip)

7 The Wrist

Introduction to the Wrist

The ability to manipulate the world around us is a major characteristic of humans that sets us apart from the rest of the animal kingdom. It is the wrist joint that couples the dexterous hand with the long levers of the arm. Not only does the wrist play a crucial role in dexterity but it also facilitates phenomenal grip strength through the passage of long tendons to the hand from the more powerful muscles of the forearm. For this reason, many of the exercises in this chapter are intimately linked to the exercises described for the elbow in Chapter 6.

With body-weight exercises, the relationship between the hand and the arm is often reversed, placing a different emphasis on the wrist joint. The hand normally moves freely on a fixed forearm, whereas in many body-weight exercises it is the hand that is fixed so that the arms, or even the entire body, can move; for example, think about the push-up exercise. Accordingly, this chapter will place great emphasis on the stability function of the upper limbs, and will demonstrate strengthening and stretching around the wrist through weight-bearing movements.

> **KEY POINT:** *With body-weight exercise, the wrist functions under load and reverses the relationship between the hand and arm by fixing the hand to create movement of the arm/body.*

Functional Anatomy of the Wrist

Passive Structures
The wrist and hand have many components that, for the most part, function together seamlessly. There are numerous small bones in the hand, and the two long bones of the forearm. The relationship of these passive structures can be seen in Figure 7.1.

As the radius and ulna bones run down towards the wrist joint, you will notice that it is the radius that provides the surface for the first row of carpal bones with which to articulate: this is the wrist joint. Figure 7.1 also shows the scaphoid bone on the inner row of the carpal bones; it is this bone that is commonly injured following a fall onto an outstretched hand. Bridging some of the gap between the lower end of the long ulna bone with the row of carpal bones is a fibrous disc made of cartilage; this structure can also be injured in a fall, or may be subject to wear and tear as the body ages. As with all the joints reviewed in this book, the wrist and hand are bound, supported and restricted by ligaments; there are lots of ligaments between the numerous bones in this region!

The various movements provided by the wrist include some side-to-side 'deviations', while most movement involves flexion (palm to forearm) and extension (back of hand to forearm). Movements to turn the palm of the hand up and down (supination and pronation) do not derive from the wrist, but instead come from the rotation of the radius about the ulna (this action is considered further in Chapter 6 for the elbow). Of course, none of these movements would be possible if it was not for the muscles and tendons pulling on the bones. Before we move on to these all-important active structures, it is worth considering one more passive structure that is unique to the wrist – the carpal tunnel.

The *carpal tunnel*, as depicted in Figure 7.2, is a strong fibrous band running across the wrist joint, below the palm of the hand. As this band runs over the carpal bones,

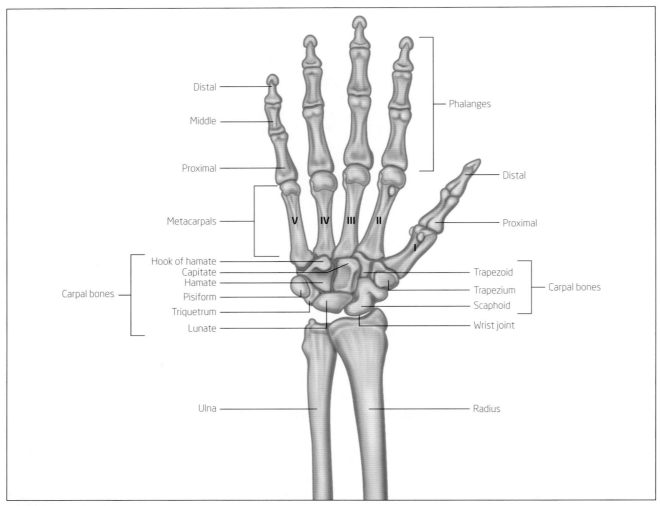

■ **Figure 7.1.**   The bones of the wrist and hand.

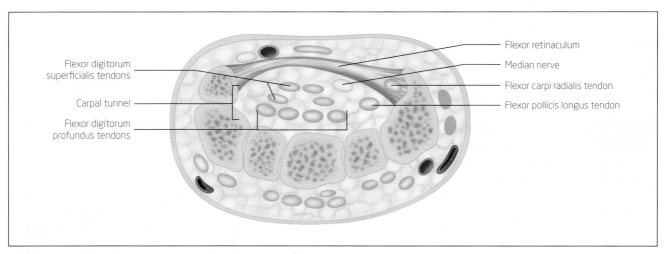

■ **Figure 7.2.**   Here is a cross-section of the carpal tunnel, clearly showing the interrelationship between the muscles and associated structures.

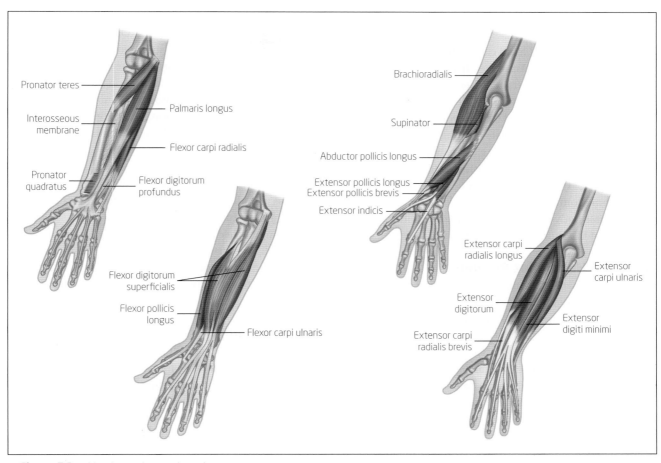

■ **Figure 7.3.** Muscles acting on the wrist.

it creates a tunnel for several structures to run under; these include the tendons we are about to discuss, but also some blood vessels and a nerve. You may already begin to visualise how irritation of the nerve in this tunnel could cause symptoms in the hand. We will examine this further when we get to the section on the common problems affecting the wrist and hand.

Active Structures

The hand houses numerous small muscles that create dexterity by manipulating the thumb and fingers. The muscles mostly responsible for these finer movements start and finish in the hand, and therefore do not cross the wrist joint. The muscles responsible for generating much of the power at the wrist and hand actually begin at the elbow and forearm. Try it for yourself – wiggle your fingers up and down as if typing, and watch what happens to the fleshy part of your forearm just below your outer elbow. The exercises outlined in this chapter may therefore contribute to improved function and reduced pain at the elbow as well as the wrist.

KEY POINT: *The muscles responsible for generating much of the power at the wrist and hand actually begin at the elbow and forearm.*

The larger muscles of the forearm taper into long, thin tendons that cross the wrist on its front and back surfaces. Some of the tendons heading over the back of the wrist and hand actually cross over each other and provide a potential point of friction, as will be explained later in this chapter. On the palm side of the wrist, some of the long tendons will run through the carpal tunnel and may therefore contribute to carpal tunnel syndrome. Figure 7.3 shows some of the muscles on the front and back of the forearm and wrist.

As with all the chapters in this book, you will see that the anatomy produces some very long and complicated names for the various structures. The good news is that we will not need to concentrate on individual named muscles, but instead we will develop complete functional strength and resilience in the forearm, wrist and hand.

■ Common Wrist Dysfunction

Injuries to the wrist and hand can be diverse, from a traumatic fall onto an outstretched hand to an overuse disorder from repetitive strain. Wherever possible, we advocate that prevention of injury is better than cure, but we appreciate that accidental falls or work-related stresses cannot always be avoided. By developing and maintaining a good level of physical resilience in the upper limbs and shoulders, however, it may be possible to limit the effects of such types of trauma should they occur. We will next explore some common wrist-related problems, and identify some suitable body-weight exercises to rehabilitate or injury-proof this vulnerable body area.

Wrist and Hand Joint Problems

Stiffness of the wrist, accompanied by a general restriction of movement, often indicates some sort of arthritis. Osteoarthritis, the wear-and-tear type of arthritis, tends to be less common in the wrist. If you have stiffness in both wrists, we recommend a review by a qualified health or medical professional before starting any new exercise programmes. Osteoarthritis tends to more commonly affect the thumb joint and the finger-end joints. If you do not have the ROM in these joints to comfortably bear weight through the hands, please modify all the exercises included here to allow progressive ROM and weight bearing. Begin with the basic stretch in Key Exercise 7.1 to increase the ability of the wrist to extend backwards under load, but please progress slowly!

KEY EXERCISE 7.1: FOREARM AND WRIST STRETCH 1

Target Area: Wrists, forearms
Sets: 3
Duration: 20 seconds
Rest: 20 seconds

A major part of injury prevention is making sure that the body is not limited in terms of the ROM that it can achieve. Stretching and mobilising the joints and surrounding soft tissues is therefore very important. The forearm and wrist stretch 1, as we have called it, focuses on the wrist flexor muscles and takes the joint into an extended functional position that is crucial for maintaining grip strength. This is the reason why we have included this fundamental movement as a key exercise.

1. To perform forearm stretch 1, crouch down on your knees and place your palms flat on the floor, fingers facing forwards.
2. Keeping the heels of your palms pressed into the ground, lean forwards slowly until you feel the stretch on the underside of your forearms.
3. Hold this position for 20 seconds, and then relax. Repeat.

Teaching Points

Many people are surprised at how much this exercise stretches the muscles of the forearm. You may even feel it pull at the elbow if you have had symptoms suggestive of golfer's elbow (see Chapter 6). If you find that you cannot move forwards very far, keep increasing the stretch little by little during the weeks and months that you train. You will soon see an increase in flexibility and mobility in this area.

Tenosynovitis

Overuse is the most likely culprit of this common type of wrist problem, which involves irritation of the tendon and its surrounding sheath (Figure 7.4). The sheath in which the tendon runs can become thickened, and you may feel a soft-tissue creaking sensation as you work the muscles

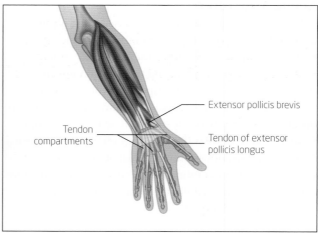

■ **Figure 7.4.** Wrist tenosynovitis.

of the wrist and forearm. Most commonly, this sensation occurs on the radius bone side of the lower forearm as it runs towards the base of the thumb, but may also occur on the ulna side of the wrist as the tendon runs to the base of the little finger. Occasionally, a similar problem can occur higher up in the forearm, about three finger widths above the wrist: this is referred to as *oarsman's wrist*, because of its initial identification in rowers.

Most often, these conditions are part of a work- or leisure-related repetitive strain injury, and so identifying and addressing the cause of the problem should be your first priority. It may be that the 'problem' cannot be addressed, and that you simply have to carry out that work duty or hit that backhand stroke in tennis. In this instance, it may be a case of hardening your body to the stresses imposed on it. By making yourself more physically resilient to stress and strain, you will be well on your way to achieving that bulletproof body. Key exercise 7.2 is a great place to start for a tenosynovitis-type problem.

KEY EXERCISE 7.2: FOREARM AND WRIST STRETCH 2

Target Area: Wrists, forearms
Sets: 3
Duration: 20 seconds
Rest: 20 seconds

Since muscles work in opposing pairs, we must consider both groups when stretching. Forearm and Wrist Stretch 2 targets the wrist extensors, or the muscles that open the hand and wrist. This stretch is important with regard to some of the more difficult exercises in this chapter, like the inverted-wrist push-up, which requires considerable wrist and forearm flexibility.

1. To perform the forearm and wrist stretch 2, crouch down on your knees and place the backs of your hands flat on the floor, fingers facing backwards. Aim to keep your elbows as straight as possible. This may feel slightly awkward at first, but stick with it.
2. Keeping the backs of your hands pressed into the ground, lean backwards slowly until you feel the stretch on the top side of your forearms.
3. Hold this position for 20 seconds. Relax and repeat.

Teaching Points
This stretch is felt more strongly than Key Exercise 7.1 by most people, because the forearm extensors tend to be tighter than the flexors. Go slowly at first and do not overstretch these muscles. Build up the level of stretch over time in a gradual manner.

Wrist Tendon Problems
The site at which a tendon anchors to bone can often be a source of pain and dysfunction. There may be inflammation here, but more often than not it tends to be some degree of degenerative change in the tendon. There is good evidence to support the use of tendon loading as an effective treatment, but this may take weeks or months to work; therefore, stick with these body-weight exercises as long as they do not increase your pain. In such instances, we recommend assessment by a suitably qualified health or medical professional.

The site of dysfunction may be local to the site of tendon attachment, and commonly this will be on either side at the back of the wrist, or on the palm side of the wrist in line with the little finger. Tendon problems, or *tendinopathies*, may be due to repetitive overuse, and so it is worth taking time to see where you can modify your activities. When this is not possible, we recommend developing physical resilience in these tendons. Key Exercise 7.3 is offered as a starting point. If the tendinopathy is affecting the back of your wrist, try Key Exercise 7.4.

KEY EXERCISE 7.3: PUSH-UP SUPPORT

Target Area: Wrists, forearms
Sets: 3
Duration: 20 seconds
Rest: 20 seconds

The most straightforward way to build strength in the hands and wrists is to simply hold a static push-up position. This is very similar in body position to the plank (Key Exercise 11.5), and so will also condition your spine and trunk; however, instead of supporting your body weight on the forearms, the hands take the majority of the load. A demand is placed on the muscles and connective tissues of the wrists and forearms, which in turn builds strength and flexibility in them.

1. To perform the push-up support, kneel on the ground and place your hands in front of you. Your hands should be shoulder-width apart, with the fingers splayed to aid balance.
2. Move your legs backwards and balance on your toes so that a straight line can be drawn through the shoulders, hips and ankles.
3. Hold this position for the required time, and then rest. Repeat.

Teaching Points

If you find this exercise too difficult, it can be made easier by placing the hands on a raised platform. Raising the hands will move more of your body weight onto the lower body. As you progress, you can reduce the height of the platform until you can perform the movement on level ground.

KEY EXERCISE 7.4: INVERTED-WRIST PUSH-UP SUPPORT

Target Area: Wrists, forearms
Sets: 3
Duration: 10–20 seconds, if possible.
Rest: 30–45 seconds
Rest: 20 seconds

Note: *Not recommended when symptoms of carpal tunnel syndrome are present.*

The inverted-wrist push-up support is another great bulletproof movement that is a little unorthodox. Unless you have performed this type of movement before, you are likely to find it very difficult. With gradual practice, this exercise will help to strengthen the wrists in a stressed position, building resilience and helping to fend off injury.

1. To perform the inverted-wrist push-up support, crouch down and place the backs of your hands on the floor, fingers pointing inwards.
2. Stretch your legs out behind you and balance on your toes, as if you are in the top position of a push-up.
3. It is unlikely that you will be able to straighten your elbows, but do not worry about this: it is simply a consequence of anatomy.
4. Hold this position for as long as possible. Rest and repeat.

Teaching Points

It is quite normal not to be able to hold this position for very long; if this applies to you, support yourself for as long as you can and then drop your knees down to the floor. Keep doing this, supporting yourself and then recovering, and over time your strength and ability will increase.

Carpal Tunnel Syndrome

This condition involves some sort of irritation of a nerve as it runs through the carpal tunnel (Figure 7.5). The exact cause is not fully understood and it is likely that there are several contributing factors. Examine your regular movements and positions to identify any obvious causative factors and address them as soon as possible. The symptoms of carpal tunnel syndrome can be varied, but may include a sensation of burning, tingling or numbness in some of the fingertips; these symptoms may wake you up during the night. The hand may also feel clumsy.

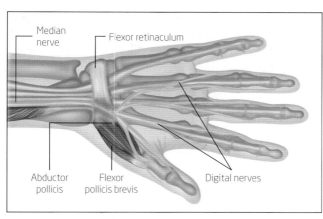

Median nerve
Flexor retinaculum
Abductor pollicis
Flexor pollicis brevis
Digital nerves

■ **Figure 7.5.** Carpal tunnel syndrome.

If you suspect that you may have carpal tunnel syndrome, we strongly recommend that you seek assessment by a qualified health or medical professional. We do not recommend any specific body-weight exercises to address this problem. Once you have been advised on your condition, and are safe to resume exercise, you may build up a generalised routine of body-weight exercise in order to develop your strength and flexibility at the wrist and forearm.

■ **Body-weight Exercises for Improved Wrist Function**

EXERCISE 7.5: FIST PUSH-UP SUPPORT

Target Area: Wrists, forearms
Sets: 3
Duration: 20 seconds
Rest: 30–45 seconds

The fist push-up support is perfect for developing stability and strength in the wrists. It will expose any weakness you might have in wrist stability.

1. To perform the fist push-up support, place your fists on the ground, hands clenched and knuckles flat against the floor.
2. Balance on your toes so that you arrive in a push-up position. Make sure that your hands and forearms form a straight line.
3. Hold this position for the required time, and then rest. Repeat.

Teaching Points

If you are new to this type of exercise, you will no doubt be apprehensive about putting a lot of your body weight onto your wrists. If this is the case, and you are unsure of your ability, you can use a kneeling push-up position: instead of balancing on your toes, balance on your knees. A kneeling position will reduce the amount of body weight on the wrists, and allow you to gradually build up to the full version. Perform the exercise with your fists on towels or padded mats to increase comfort as necessary. Do not be a hero and cause unnecessary injury!

EXERCISE 7.6: FINGERTIP PUSH-UP SUPPORT

Target Area: Wrists, forearms
Sets: 3
Duration: 10–20 seconds
Rest: 30–45 seconds

If you are prepared for a physical challenge, consider the fingertip push-up support position; this is simply a push-up position in which your body weight is supported on the fingertips! This exercise helps hugely in building strength in the hands and forearms, and is a strong foundation for progressing to more complex body-weight exercises.

1. To perform the fingertip push-up support, place your hands on the ground, fingers splayed, with emphasis on the thumbs and index fingers.
2. Stretch your legs out behind you and assume a push-up position. Your shoulders, hips, knees and feet should form a straight line.
3. Hold this position for as long as possible, and then rest. Repeat.

Teaching Points

No doubt this movement will cause some issues if you do not have strong hands, or have weaknesses anywhere in the chain. To remedy this, perform the exercise in exactly the same way, but balance on the knees instead of the toes; this will reduce the amount of body weight being supported by the fingers, and will allow steady progression to the full version.

EXERCISE 7.7: FALSE-GRIP HANG

Target Area: Wrists, forearms
Sets: 3
Duration: 10–20 seconds
Rest: 30–45 seconds

Strengthening the forearms is essential for developing injury resistance and rehabilitation in the wrists and elbows; the

false-grip hang is excellent for doing this in the wrist flexors. The false grip itself is used in gymnastics to impart more control on the bar and on the still rings. Here, we can use it to our advantage in injury prevention and rehabilitation.

1. To perform the false-grip hang, stand on a box under a pull-up bar.
2. Wrap your hands around the bar and flex your hands so that the heels of your palms rest on top of the bar.
3. Keeping this position attempt to hang from the bar, allowing your elbows to straighten. If you have never done this before, you are likely to find it very difficult.
4. Hang for as long as possible, dropping off when your form starts to break down. Rest and repeat.

Teaching Points

The false-grip hang can be very difficult to master, and is included here for those of you wishing to develop higher levels of muscle strength and control. If this is you, then stick with this exercise. To make the movement easier, you can support your body weight with your legs; to do this, hang from the bar but keep your feet on the box or platform. Perform the hang, but support some of your weight with your legs, or with a single leg. As you become stronger, support less of your body weight with your legs.

EXERCISE 7.8 KNEELING INVERTED-WRIST PUSH-UP

Target Area: Wrists
Sets: 3
Reps: 5
Rest: 30–45 seconds

Once you have mastered supporting yourself on your wrists, it will be time to add a pushing element into the movement to make it even more challenging. This exercise will develop the wrist extensor muscles by using the inverted-wrist push-up support (Key Exercise 7.4). These push-ups are quite challenging, so only move on to them when you are ready.

1. To perform the kneeling inverted-wrist push-up, assume a kneeling push-up position but with the backs of your hands flat on the floor, fingers pointing inwards.
2. Keeping the backs of your hands pressed into the ground, start to lower yourself down to the floor by bending your elbows.
3. Keep going until your chest touches the floor (or as far as you can), and then push back up again until you reach the starting position. This counts as one repetition.

Teaching Points

If you find this exercise too difficult, it can be made easier. By bending at the hips, you can reduce the amount of weight put on the upper body, making the movement easier to complete. Another method is to place the hands on a raised platform; this will accomplish the same goal.

◼ Goal Exercises for the Wrist

As with the other areas of the body, and in keeping with the other chapters in this book, we have developed a series of goal exercises that target the wrists, hands and forearms. These are a real test of wrist strength, mobility and flexibility, and will provide you with a benchmark of wrist function and resilience. These exercises can also be built into a full body workout to develop that bulletproof body.

GOAL EXERCISE 7.9: INVERTED-WRIST PUSH-UP

Primary Target Area: Wrists, forearms, shoulders
Sets: 3
Reps: 10
Rest: 30–45 seconds

The inverted-wrist push-up is an advanced exercise and should only be approached once you are familiar with the kneeling version of this exercise (Exercise 7.8). It is best to use an exercise mat here, and preferably one that is thick and offers a lot of cushioning.

1. To perform the inverted-wrist push-up, assume the inverted-wrist push-up support position. Ensure that your body is straight and you are balancing on your toes. Do not worry if you cannot maintain straight elbows.
2. Keeping the backs of your hands pressed into the ground, start to lower yourself down to the floor by bending your elbows. It helps to flex the fingers hard into the ground here, so as to keep the tension in the hands and ensure a solid platform.
3. Keep going until your chest touches the floor (or as far as you can), and then push back up again until you reach the starting position. This counts as one repetition.

Teaching Points

This movement is very unusual for the uninitiated. Many people struggle with the pressure being placed upon the wrist, while others struggle with the flexibility required. Both of these issues can be solved by performing the kneeling version demonstrated previously (Exercise 7.8), and by an overall increase in strength. Proceed slowly and with care and you will develop in time.

If you need to make these easier, you should place your hands on a raised platform; this will take some of the weight off the upper body. As you progress, lower the height of the platform until you can perform these push-ups on level ground.

GOAL EXERCISE 7.10: FALSE-GRIP PULL-UP

Target Area: Wrists, forearms, elbows
Sets: 3
Reps: 3–5
Rest: 45–60 seconds

The false-grip hang (Exercise 7.7) is a great exercise, but we can make it more challenging by performing a pull-up in this position. This will put an extremely large demand on the muscles of the forearm, and help to build a very strong grip and bulletproof wrist flexors.

Once you are able to hang in a false grip for the required number of sets and repetitions, you can move on to the false-grip pull-up. This exercise is exactly what you would expect: the pull-up is performed with your hands in the false-grip position. It is especially difficult, and so do not be alarmed if it takes you some time to perfect it.

1. To perform the false-grip pull-up, assume the false-grip hang position.
2. Start to pull up towards the bar. You should aim to get your chin over the bar or your chest touching the bar.
3. At the top of the movement, hold for a second before lowering down to the starting position. This counts as one repetition.

Teaching Points

As the false-grip pull-up is so tough, it is likely that you will not be able to perform a single repetition at first. To begin, start to pull as far as you can, using a reduced ROM. As you get stronger, the ROM you will be able to use will increase, and you will eventually be able to perform the movement properly.

GOAL EXERCISE 7.11: FIST-SUPPORTED TUCK PLANCHE

Target Area: Wrists, forearms, core muscles
Sets: 3
Reps: 5 seconds
Rest: 30–45 seconds

The planche is a gymnastic movement that is famous for its gravity-defying appearance. We can use a simplified version of it here to really strengthen the wrists. This is a high-level exercise, so only move on to this when ready.

1. To perform the fist-supported tuck planche, crouch down and place your fists on the ground, hands clenched tightly and knuckles against the floor.
2. Lean forwards so that most of your body weight is being supported by your fists.
3. Lift your feet off the ground and tuck them up into your chest, using your core muscles to do so.
4. Balance on your fists for as long as possible. Drop your feet down to the floor quickly if you feel the need or if you lose balance.

Teaching Points

Putting all of your body weight onto your wrists is difficult; if you are struggling with this movement, the best course of action is to raise your feet up for a second or so, and then drop them back down again. Do this to see how the exercise feels and to get an idea of how prepared you are for the movement.

In addition to the difficulty of supporting yourself on your wrists, the tuck planche will put a huge strain on your core and balance skills. It is quite natural for it to take a little time to build up the necessary strength and skill to perform the tuck planche, and so stick at it! Perform the exercise with the fists on a cushioned surface for comfort.

8
The Hip

Introduction to the Hip

Powerful, deep and stable, the hip is one serious joint! It is a crucial weight-bearing structure with more natural mobility and stability than the knee, but without the complexity of the shoulder, which we encountered in Chapter 5. Whether you are moving between sitting and standing, climbing stairs or jumping into the air, it is the hip joint that powerfully levers the upper body over the lower limbs. We will now examine the crucial anatomy behind this mobile force generator, before exploring some common hip problems that could be alleviated with body-weight exercise.

Functional Anatomy of the Hip

Passive Structures

In terms of bony anatomy, things do not come much simpler than the hip joint. The hip is a synovial, or freely mobile, joint that involves the bony hemisphere of the upper thigh bone (femur) sitting in the deep socket offered by the pelvic bones. As with all of the joints we have seen so far, the hip is reinforced with thick ligaments and a joint capsule. The socket of the pelvis is deepened by a fibrous cartilage called the *labrum*, which forms a lip around the edge of the socket. The labrum can be a source of pain and dysfunction, so we will visit this briefly later on. As in the case of the shoulder (Chapter 5), the hip is a ball-and-socket joint, but unlike the shoulder it trades its mobility for weight-bearing ability. Movements available at the hip joint (Figure 8.1) are:

- Flexion
- Extension
- Abduction
- Adduction
- Internal rotation

- External rotation
- Circumduction (a combination of the above)

The final passive structure to mention here is the bursa. Bursae (plural) are fluid-filled sacs that are located around, or between, moving parts to reduce friction. There are two key bursae at the hip: one covers the greater trochanter, and the other is called the *iliopectineal bursa*, which is shown in Figure 8.2 along with the bony anatomy.

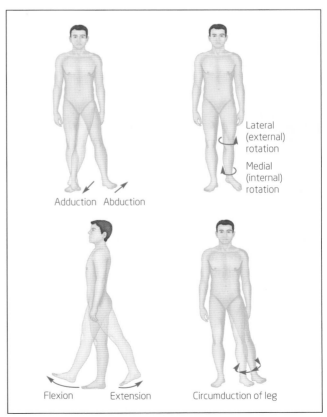

■ **Figure 8.1.** The many movements created by and stabilised through the hip joint.

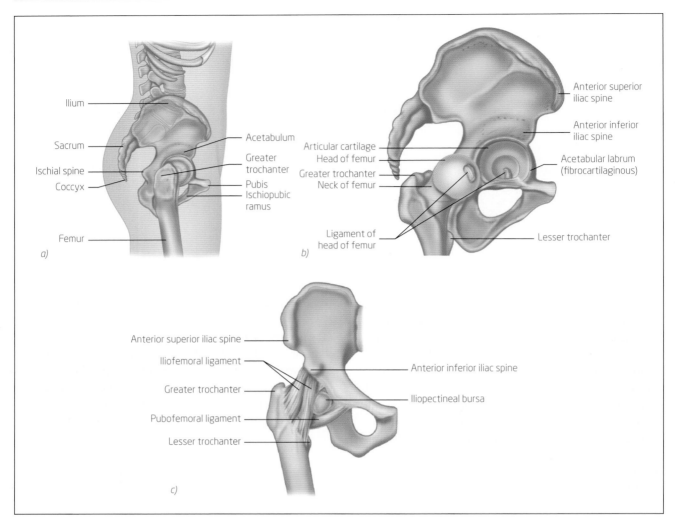

■ **Figure 8.2.** The hip joint: (a) lateral view; (b) lateral view of turned-out hip; (c) ligaments.

KEY POINT: *Unlike the shoulder joint, the hip joint trades mobility for weight-bearing ability.*

Active Structures

As mentioned in previous chapters of this book, active structures are so called because they have a contracting function. This relates to the ability of muscles of the skeleton to shorten and pull on bones via their tendons, and is the basis of maintaining posture against gravity and of human movement.

The hip is an incredibly powerful joint owing to several of the muscles that act upon it. When rising from a chair, or squatting a weighted bar in the gym, it is the force generated by the hip muscles that allows the hip to straighten under load. Some of the many muscles found around the hip joint are shown in Figure 8.3. You will

probably be familiar with many of their names from their common use in everyday language.

Some of the muscles in Figure 8.3 are grouped by their function rather than being named individually. You may be able to link these muscle groups to the movements of the hip discussed earlier in relation to passive structures; for example, *hip abduction* (taking the leg outwards and away from the centre line) is brought about by the contracting action of the *abductor muscles*.

Remember that the brain is thought to work in terms of movements rather than the activation of individual muscles. This is a key part of our message in aiming to promote functional and multi-muscle exercise; it is especially true in the lower limbs, where long muscles can cross two or more joints and act on both simultaneously under load. Look closely again at Figure 8.3 and note how the quadriceps spans the hip and the knee; although

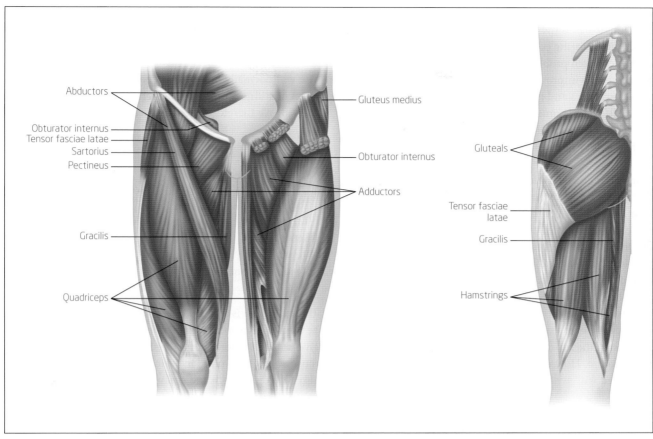

■ **Figure 8.3.** Muscles of the hip.

you may think of working the quadriceps by exercising the knee, you cannot discount the action of the hip in functional muscle training. The same can be said of the hamstrings, which are involved in extending (straightening) the hip and flexing (bending) the knee.

> **KEY POINT:** *Functional exercises will use multiple muscles, often acting over more than one joint.*

Before we leave this discussion of the anatomy of the hip, it is worth pausing for a moment on the iliopsoas muscle. Figure 8.4 shows how this muscle is actually a combination of two muscles, the psoas and iliacus, which merge as they cross the front of the hip. Note how one of the iliopsoas muscles spans the lumbar spine and the front of the hip; now picture how sitting behind your desk or in your car all day could potentially shorten this muscle. Read on for key exercises to help reduce both lower back and hip pain!

■ **Common Hip Dysfunction**

From degenerative osteoarthritis to groin and hamstring strains, there are many reasons for pain in the hip region.

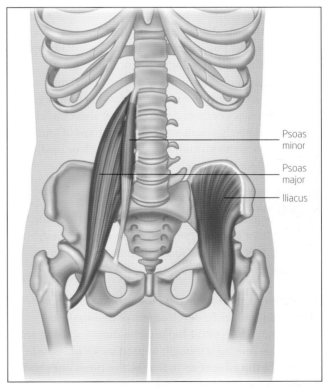

■ **Figure 8.4.** The iliopsoas muscle.

These problems can potentially be alleviated or treated with movement-based therapies that focus on rehabilitating function, restoring pain-free movement and creating resilience. Even problematic bursae can respond positively to exercise by improving the movement around these fluid-filled structures and reducing some of the pressure upon them. Of all the joints discussed in this book, it is probably the hip joint that has the best capacity to improve through body-weight exercise.

One major consideration of hip function is quite simply that in most people the hip is not moved through anywhere near its full ROM. Although you can perhaps say the same of the shoulder, the hip especially lacks use as we become adults. Cast your mind back to your activities as a child: squatting and kneeling to play, running, jumping, climbing and kicking. It is often said by people with hip pain that they do not need therapy exercises for the hip because they are active – they walk everywhere. Walking is a wonderful exercise for general wellbeing and health; for mobilising the hip, however, it is not so good. Get up and walk around. How much range does your hip go through compared with what it could potentially achieve?

We will now explore some common hip problems, before focusing on targeted body-weight exercises.

Hip Joint Dysfunction

Degenerative osteoarthritis is not uncommon in the hip and is mostly seen above the age of 60. It can, however, occur in younger populations, and there are usually many reasons behind such development, including genetic factors, occupational or sporting overuse, previous fracture or trauma, or altered joint mechanics arising from leg length differences or from developmental abnormalities. If you are relatively young and have symptoms of joint arthritis, it is worth visiting a qualified health or medical professional for a thorough assessment.

KEY POINT: *Strong contraction of the hip muscles during walking can produce an increase in load on the hip joint of up to four or five times one's body weight. This increased load might contribute to osteoarthritis at the hip joint.*

It has been suggested that the muscular forces around the hip can lead to the development of osteoarthritis. Strong contraction of the hip muscles during walking and standing on one leg is thought to produce an increase in load on the hip joint of up to four or five times one's body weight. This load increases with fast walking and running

(I did say that walking was not a great exercise for hip pain); moreover, a stumble can create an impact load in excess of eight times the body's weight!

You will normally find that osteoarthritis causes a gradual onset of stiffness in the hip, which eventually becomes painful. We therefore offer Key Exercise 8.1 to mobilise the hip joint.

KEY EXERCISE 8.1: KNEE CIRCLE

Target Area: Hip mobility, shoulder and core strength
Sets: 2
Reps: 10 each leg
Rest: 10 seconds

The knee circle is a great lower body mobility exercise that can be used to develop active hip mobility. The starting position gives a stability workout for the shoulders and core, while the muscle activity involved in performing the knee circles will also develop strength and endurance around the hip.

1. To perform the knee circle, position yourself on your hands and knees.
2. Raise one leg up to the side, taking the knee backwards before circling it forwards as far as you can. As mobility at the hip improves, you may be able to touch your planted arm with your circling knee. Return your knee to the starting position. Repeat on the other leg.

Teaching Point

Aim to draw a large arc with the knee. Use this exercise as a general warm-up exercise once your hip mobility increases. Progress to Exercise 8.8 (mountain climber) and Exercise 8.9 (frog hop).

Although it is not part of the bony structure at the hip, the labrum fibrocartilage sits within the hip joint. Damage to the labrum can be associated with osteoarthritis, or tears in the labrum may be caused by trauma, impingement between the bones of the hip joint, and joint laxity. Often, labrum-related problems cause symptoms including clicking, locking and a feeling of giving way at the hip; there may also be pinching pain when the hip is bent and the knee brought towards the opposite shoulder. In this case, we recommend assessment by a suitably qualified health or medical professional. If you have been cleared to exercise with this type of problem, try Key Exercise 8.2.

performed correctly, the exercise will increase mobility in the hips, knees and ankles. As a youngster, everyone is able to squat low and deep, but as age and sedentary lifestyles take over, this ability is lost. Getting back this ability is one the best things you can do to prevent injury and rehabilitate existing injuries.

1. To perform the deep squat position, place your feet flat on the floor, heels shoulder-width apart and your toes pointing slightly out.
2. Stretch your arms out in front of you and keep your eyes looking forwards, head and neck neutral.
3. Bend your knees, push your hips back and squat down as far as you can. Keep your lower back as straight as possible.
4. The position you are trying to achieve can be seen in the images; if you cannot get down this low, go as low as you can. Hold for 30 seconds, or as long as you are able to.

Teaching Points

Many people will struggle to get into this position at first, but there are a couple of things that can be done to make it more accessible. First, you can place your heels on a raised platform; this platform only needs to be 5cm high at most. Raising the heels in this way reduces the amount of stretch needed in the calves, allowing the knees to move further forwards, and allowing a deeper and lower squat.

Second, you can hold onto something with the hands and then lean back into the deep squat position. Suspension training systems or gymnastic rings are great for this, as you can support most of your weight and lean back; this allows you to get close to the proper position without having the hip mobility or ankle mobility needed to perform the movement without aid.

KEY EXERCISE 8.2: DEEP SQUAT POSITION

Target Area: Hips, knees, ankles
Sets: 3
Duration: 30 seconds
Rest: 20 seconds

Being able to achieve a deep squat position is important in order to maintain a properly functioning lower body; when

Hip Muscle/Tendon Strains

If you have recently had a trauma or strain of the muscles around the hip or thigh, we recommend that you have this assessed before trying any sort of physical exercise, including body-weight exercise. Such acute injuries are not the focus of this book; instead, we are concentrating on those niggles that you have had for some time, perhaps intermittently. These niggles may have started as a sudden strain, or perhaps even resulted from gradual overuse, but for whatever reason have not fully settled and have left you with some area of weakness or physical vulnerability. It is time to give nature some direction and bulletproof these problematic areas with body-weight exercise!

The most common hip and thigh muscle problems tend to include the hamstrings, quadriceps and adductors (inner thigh), although any muscle can be subject to strain or direct trauma. The good news is that we do not need to isolate these muscles. Keep it functional and you should be able to find that weakness and turn it into a strength.

As the hamstrings and quadriceps (rectus femoris) cross both the hip and the knee, there is a greater potential for overuse or sudden strain. Poor posture, poor physical conditioning, inadequate warm-up prior to rapid movements, and muscle fatigue have been described as precipitating factors. Studies have found that muscle imbalances between the hamstrings and quadriceps can increase the risk of hamstring injury by four to five times. Old muscle injuries may have healed after a period of rest, but you could have been left with a tight or short muscle that is vulnerable to re-injury. There is evidence to suggest that graded stretching should be part of your rehabilitation. Thorough functional stretching should also be part of your injury prevention toolkit. Try Key Exercises 8.3 and 8.4 for starters.

1. To perform the hamstring stretch, sit down on the floor with one leg out in front of you. Tuck your other leg into your buttocks and lay it flat on the floor.
2. Reach forwards and bend at the hips, aiming to keep your back straight. You should feel the stretch in the back of the thigh in the straight leg.
3. Move forwards until you feel a good stretch in the hamstrings. Hold for 20 seconds, change legs and repeat.

Teaching Points

Most people do not stretch their hamstrings enough, even if they are following a training programme to increase their flexibility; this is because many people sit for long periods in their daily lives and therefore do not experience a regular functional stretch. The act of sitting shortens and reduces the flexibility of the hamstrings for the simple reason that the sitting position requires the knee joint to be flexed while the pelvis is tilted backwards. If this applies to you, we recommend spending a little more time stretching your hamstrings with the body-weight winner Key Exercise 8.4.

KEY EXERCISE 8.3: HAMSTRING STRETCH

Target Area: Hip mobility, hamstring flexibility
Sets: 3
Duration: 20 seconds each leg
Rest: 20 seconds

The hamstrings can be painful in themselves but can also contribute to the lower back pain discussed in Chapter 11 of this book; the reason for this is that the flexibility of the hamstrings dictates the ability of the lower back, pelvis, hip and knee to move freely. Touching the toes and being able to close the hips is a generally a good indicator of hamstring flexibility, although you may feel the restriction in your lower back.

KEY EXERCISE 8.4: GROIN STRETCH

Target Area: Hips, adductors, hamstrings, lower back
Sets: 3
Duration: 20 seconds
Rest: 20 seconds

In addition to building strength in the hips, it is a very good idea to make sure that they are flexible enough to reduce the risk of strain. The groin stretch presented here is excellent for increasing the flexibility of the adductor muscles, which are the long muscles on the insides of the thighs.

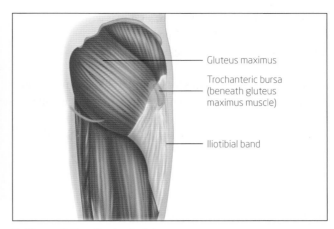

■ **Figure 8.5.** Trochanteric bursa.

1. To perform the groin stretch, sit down with the soles of your feet together. Use your hands to pull your feet as close to your buttocks as possible. If you find that the bony parts on the outer side of each ankle feel uncomfortable, cushion them with a hand towel.

2. Sit up straight and attempt to bring your knees as low to the floor as possible. You can use the muscles on the outsides of your legs to pull your knees down, or you can simply push on them with your arms or hands. Hold this position for 20 seconds.

Teaching Points

To increase the stretch even further, you can lean forwards and try to pull your chest towards your feet; this will also help to stretch some of the gluteal muscles and the lower back. A good practice is to try to get your forearms flat against the floor. This exercise will target multiple muscles in the hip and thigh.

Hip Bursa Dysfunction

Direct trauma to the hip may cause the bursae to swell and become painful, but more often they tend to give pain because of overuse or excessive friction. There are several bursae around the hip, with at least four of them situated between the gluteal muscles. These fluid-filled bags allow moving structures to slide over each other without excessive friction; however, altered joint mechanics, postural stress and muscle imbalances can create so much pressure that the bursae become excessively loaded.

The psoas bursa lies beneath the iliopsoas muscle, which we will discuss below, whereas the trochanteric bursa (Figure 8.5) separates the gluteus maximus muscle from the bony point on the outside of your hip. As mentioned above, the numerous gluteal bursae provide padding for

the gluteal muscles. By correcting muscle imbalances in these areas, you can potentially restore the normal load and functioning of the hip bursae, allowing nature to do its thing and settle any bursal irritation over the following weeks. Key Exercise 8.5 is recommended for stretching the glutes (gluteal or buttock muscles).

KEY EXERCISE 8.5: GLUTE STRETCH

Target Area: Hips, glutes
Sets: 3
Duration: 20 seconds each leg
Rest: 20 seconds

The glutes are the largest and most powerful muscles in the body; it is therefore important to stretch them to maintain performance in running, jumping and other lower body movements. In addition, tightness here can inhibit free movement of the hips, causing other issues further down the line. As with the hamstrings, it is important to keep the glutes functioning correctly, as they power many lower body movements.

1. To perform the glute stretch, sit down with one leg straight and the other leg bent.
2. Now place the foot of the bent leg on the outside of the knee of the straight leg.
3. Push the bent knee towards your straight leg until you feel the stretch in your glute. Keep your hips as square as possible.
4. Hold this position for 20 seconds, change legs and repeat.

Iliopsoas Syndrome/Dysfunction

As discussed above, the iliopsoas muscle has a tendon that crosses the front of the hip, with the psoas bursa sitting between the tendon and the hip joint. In iliopsoas syndrome, there may be increased friction and pressure on the bursa, causing bursitis, or there may be inflammation of the iliopsoas tendon. As a result of modern sedentary postures, there may even be long-term shortening of the iliopsoas muscle, altering the hip joint mechanics and placing stress on the lumbar spine. Hip movements may be restricted and painful, and there may even be a clicking or snapping sensation as the taught tendon moves over surrounding structures. All of these things can cause pain. If you address the primary problem of a shortened/contracted iliopsoas muscle, you will in turn probably restore normal hip and spine movements and offload the tendon and bursa. See how you get on with Key Exercise 8.6.

KEY EXERCISE 8.6: HIP FLEXOR STRETCH

Target Area: Hip flexors, lumbar spine
Sets: 3
Duration: 20 seconds each leg
Rest: 20 seconds

The hip flexor stretch, when done properly and with patience, may well be the best exercise you ever do for hip and lower back pain. The hip flexors include the iliopsoas and the rectus femoris (quadriceps), and so together these muscles span from the lumbar spine to below the knee joint! When you do the stretch, remember this fact and maintain a good posture of your trunk. Modern sedentary lifestyles make this area prone to poor function; keeping the hip flexor muscles flexible can therefore be key to reducing injury risk at the hip and lower back.

1. To perform the hip flexor stretch, assume a kneeling position with one leg in front of you. Keep your torso upright.
2. Lean forwards, aiming to push the hips forwards and down. Rest your arms on your front leg to aid balance.
3. You should feel a stretch at the top of your rear leg, at the front of the straight hip, and possibly deep in your back. If you do not, gently contract your glute muscles to push the hip forwards and increase the stretch. Hold this position for 20 seconds, change sides and repeat.

Teaching Points

The hip flexor stretch is one that should progress fairly rapidly, but some readers may still need to make it a little easier to manage. If you wish to make the exercise easier, move the knee and the foot closer together.

If you are looking to increase the stretch, you can drive the hip further forwards, or you can grab your rear foot and pull it up to your buttocks to stretch the quadriceps (rectus femoris). For an increased stretch of the iliopsoas, take the arm on the side being stretched and reach it over your head, flexing your trunk away from the stretch.

■ Body-weight Exercises for Improved Hip Function

EXERCISE 8.7: PIRIFORMIS FOAM ROLL AND STRETCH

Target Area: Hips
Sets: 3
Duration: 20–30 seconds each leg
Rest: 30 seconds

Incorporating squatting and lunging movements into your training can increase the tightness and irritation of the piriformis, a muscle deep in the buttock. If the

piriformis muscle becomes tight, it can manifest itself with sciatica-like symptoms in the affected area. To take care of this problem, we can foam roll the piriformis; this can be performed with either a foam roller or a tennis ball. Beware – this exercise can be uncomfortable, so go slowly at first!

1. To foam roll and stretch your piriformis, sit down and place your right foot on the left knee, as if you were going to cross your legs.
2. Now sit directly on the foam roller with the piriformis. You will know if you are on the right spot, as it should feel tender. It may even feel knotted deep in the buttock.
3. Roll over the tight spot slowly for 20–30 seconds, and then change legs and repeat.
4. Once you have foam rolled both sides, you should perform a static stretch. To do this, sit on a chair with one foot flat on the floor and your knee at 90 degrees.
5. Place your free foot on the knee of the working leg, and push down on the knee of the free foot. You will feel the stretch in the piriformis/deep buttock. Keep the torso upright and breathe deeply. Hold the stretch for 20 seconds, and then change sides and repeat.

Teaching Points

Piriformis foam rolling can be a sore process. This is expected, but it is best to start with a soft foam roller; then, as you become more experienced, move to firmer foam rollers. You can also use a tennis ball (progressing to a baseball or a cricket ball) to really get into the muscle; this is recommended for experienced exercisers only, as the pain can be quite intense.

EXERCISE 8.8: MOUNTAIN CLIMBER

Target Area: Hips
Sets: 3
Reps: 10 each leg
Rest: 30 seconds

Climb every mountain! The mountain climber is a superb all-round exercise that is normally performed as a cardiovascular exercise in boot camps or group exercise classes. With some alterations, however, it can be very good for increasing strength and mobility in the hips. The exercise is a little more vigorous than the stretches in this chapter, so approach it with care if you are new to physical training.

1. To perform the mountain climber, assume a push-up position. Stretch one leg out behind you and place the other leg as close to the outside of your hand as possible.
2. Keeping your arms straight. jump both feet into the air and change them over so that the rear foot comes to the front and the front foot goes to the rear.
3. Repeat for 10 repetitions each leg, i.e. 20 repetitions in total, with each individual jump counting as a single repetition.

Teaching Points

The aim of this exercise is to increase strength and mobility in the hips; therefore, do not worry about trying to do the repetitions as fast as possible. Slow, controlled movement is the best course of action here. It may take you some time to build up the mobility in your hips to be able to achieve the ROM shown in the images. In this case, you could step the bent leg back along the straight leg, and then step the other leg in towards the arms. Keep at it and the flexibility will come!

Teaching Points

To make the frog hop easier, you can place your hands on a platform or step of some sort. Raising the hands in this way will allow you to develop the hip flexibility and mobility gradually, which is especially useful if you have problems or an injury in this area. Over time, you can move the hands closer to the ground.

EXERCISE 8.9: FROG HOP

Target Area: Hips
Sets: 3
Reps: 10
Rest: 30 seconds

The frog hop can be a progression from the mountain climber if you want to add an aerobic emphasis, but it can also be done in a controlled way to focus on hip mobility and strength. The frog hop is included here as a dynamic movement, which differs from the static stretches and foam rolling seen previously.

1. To perform the frog hop, assume a push-up position. Your hands should be flat on the floor, shoulder-width apart.
2. From here, jump both feet forwards. You should be aiming to get them to land on the outside of your hands. If you do not have the mobility to do this, go as far forward as you can.
3. Pause for a second, and then jump your feet backwards so that you arrive back in the push-up position. This counts as one repetition.

Progression/Variation

To progress the frog hop to become more of an all-over conditioning exercise, and to get more dynamic mobility at the hips and lower back, try travelling from the frog position by leading with your arms and hopping forwards in a straight line. Each time you jump to your arms, place them out in front of you again and repeat the process of hopping into your arms. This variation can also be performed backwards by pushing through the arms and then hopping the legs backwards, before bringing the arms back to meet the legs and repeating.

KEY POINT: *The frog hop is a personal favourite of ours and has given good results with chronic hip and lower back stiffness and pain. Build up slowly, though!*

■ Goal Exercises for the Hips

As with the other chapters of this book, we present some goal exercises; these will build hip strength and mobility and also act as a test of your physical condition. The movements actually build on the movements discussed previously, and include a greater ROM and a greater use of strength.

GOAL EXERCISE 8.10: BODY-WEIGHT SQUAT

Target Area: Hips, knees, ankles
Sets: 3
Reps: 10–20
Rest: 30–45 seconds

The body-weight squat is perhaps the most useful lower body exercise with regard to strength and mobility; this is because it is a compound movement. A *compound movement* is one which involves many joints and muscle groups all working in unison, which is what contributes to the potential strength gains and increases in usable mobility. This is the essence of developing a bulletproof body.

1. To perform the body-weight squat, stand with your feet shoulder-width apart, toes pointing out at a slight angle.
2. Push your hips back and bend the knees, beginning the squat. Allow your arms to reach forwards to aid balance.
3. Keep descending, forcing the knees out so that they follow the line made by your toes.
4. Keep the lower back straight and tight, and the head and eyes neutral and looking forwards.
5. Descend as far as your strength and mobility allow: this is the bottom part of the squat. Ideally, you should be aiming to reach the depth shown in the images.
6. Pause for a second, and then return to a standing position. This counts as one repetition.

Teaching Points

The body-weight squat looks simple but can take a while to perform perfectly. In addition to the strength required, mobility is the aspect that will cause issues for most people. The deep squat position (Key Exercise 8.2) will help with this, as will the various lower body stretches in this chapter.

You may be restricted by mobility of the ankle joint. To solve this problem, your heels can be placed on a very small platform, 2.5cm or so in height; you can use anything sturdy and solid for this, as long as the object does not move. This method raises the heels and requires less ankle flexibility, which will allow you to drop lower into the squat while still maintaining proper form. As you progress, simply take away the platform under the heels, and transition to the full movement.

GOAL EXERCISE 8.11: DUCK WALK

Target Area: Hips
Sets: 3
Reps: 10–20 steps
Rest: 30–45 seconds

The duck walk is a great exercise for testing the mobility and strength of the hips; it can be thought of as a natural progression of the deep squat position (Key Exercise 8.2). The duck walk is exactly what it sounds like: a moving exercise in which the aim is to keep the buttocks as low to the ground as possible, while moving the hips through a large ROM. In other words, it involves walking like a duck!

1. To perform the duck walk, assume a deep squat position. Place the arms wherever they feel comfortable, and in a position where they can aid balance.
2. Without rising up too much, take a step forwards. The distance will need to be small in order to avoid raising the hips into the air.
3. As you place the front foot down, allow the rear heel to rise. Once you are settled on the front foot, take a step forwards with the other foot. You may have to rotate the hips slightly to do this.
4. Keep going for the required number of steps, rest and repeat.

Teaching Points

If you cannot perform the duck walk as outlined, simply squat down as low as your mobility allows and then walk in this position. As your strength and mobility increase, you should be able to drop the hips lower and lower until you can perform the movement as demonstrated. You can also spend more time practising the deep squat position to build up the flexibility in your hips.

9

The Knee

■ Introduction to the Knee

Unlike the deep-fitting hip joint, the knee joint lacks bony stability. In the knee, the bulbous lower end of the thighbone sits on a flat bony shelf offered by the upper end of the shinbone. When you stand from a seated position, the moving thighbone rolls forwards over the upper shinbone while also sliding backwards. With no bony limit to the amount of sliding, it is down to the numerous ligaments in the knee to stop one bone sliding free of the other. When you kick a football, the reverse action occurs, with the shinbone rolling and sliding forwards on the thighbone. Once again, the ligaments of the knee ensure that the lower leg does not follow the ball as it flies through the air.

The knee joint is truly a structure that is greater than the sum of its parts. It is much more than a collection of bones and ligaments: in this chapter, we outline the other numerous structures that make the knee unique, but also susceptible to injury.

■ Functional Anatomy of the Knee

Passive Structures
The knee allows the transmission of weight from the thigh to the lower leg, while facilitating movement during functions such as walking, running and jumping. Most of this movement occurs at a specific joint in the knee, where the femur (thigh bone) meets the tibia (shin bone). There is also another very important joint at the knee, created where the femur joins the patella (knee cap). The relationship of these joints and their bones can be seen in Figure 9.1. You will also see that the thinner fibula bone creates a third, less mobile, joint with the tibia.

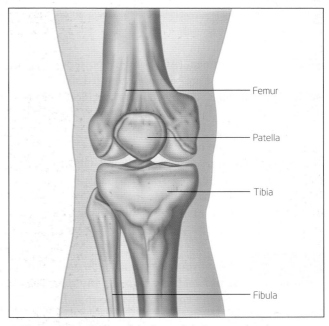

■ **Figure 9.1.** Bones of the knee, right leg, anterior view.

The patellofemoral joint allows the patella to ride over the lower femur as the knee flexes and extends, and also plays a role in distributing the powerful forces created by the muscles at the front of the knee. The 'true' knee joint, between the tibia and the femur, is where the more familiar functions of the knee are permitted. As a hinge joint, it facilitates flexion and extension, allowing you to squat, sit, stand and more. The limitation to these movements comes not from the bony shape of the knee joint, but from the ligaments that bind the bones and restrain further range. Figure 9.2(a) identifies the main ligaments of the knee.

The ligaments of the knee include the lateral collateral ligament (LCL) and medial collateral ligament (MCL), as well as the more familiar cruciate ligaments – the

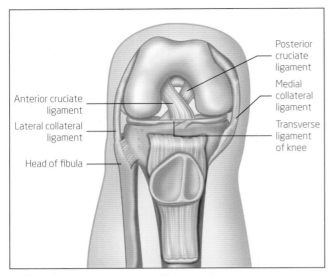

■ **Figure 9.2a.** Ligaments of the knee (right leg, anterior view, with knee bent at 90 degrees).

anterior cruciate ligament (ACL) and the posterior cruciate ligament (PCL). These are commonly injured structures in the knee and will be discussed more specifically later in this chapter.

The otherwise flat top of the tibia is deepened by two ring-like cartilage structures that provide some stability and cushioning to the knee joint. These cartilages are known as the *menisci* (plural), illustrated in Figure 9.2(b), and these too can be susceptible to injury, as we shall see later in this chapter.

> **KEY POINT:** *The moveable knee is made up of two main joints: one between the shin and the thighbone, and one between the kneecap and the thighbone.*

The knee is reported to have between 11 and 14 bursae. These fluid-filled sacs can be an extension of the joint capsule and its lubricating fluid; they are located around the mobile structures of the knee joint to prevent friction between the joint's moving parts. The bursae can, however, be subjected to excessive friction and pressure and consequently become problematic, as we shall see later in this chapter.

Active Structures

The knee is crossed by tendons or tendon-like structures on all four sides, which further act to stabilise the lower femur on the flat upper tibia. No fewer than 12 muscles provide support to the knee, and when they contract they will contribute to the movement available here. Figure 9.3 shows several of these muscles. You may recognise some of the names of the muscles that make up the muscle groups of the hamstrings and quadriceps. As a general rule, those muscles passing the front of the knee will extend the joint when they contract, while those passing behind the centre line of the joint will cause it to flex.

It is not just the knee joint being acted upon by some of the muscles in Figure 9.3. As we have seen in the upper limbs elsewhere in this book, several long muscles span two or more joints, and those crossing the knee are no exception. Some of these begin above the hip joint and pass to just below the knee. Others, such as the gastrocnemius and plantaris, originate just above the knee and descend to below the ankle (see Chapter 10). Two-joint muscles have a dual role to play at any given time; they can therefore be more susceptible to injury in terms of strains or chronic stress. These muscles may be stabilising one joint while moving the other, stabilising

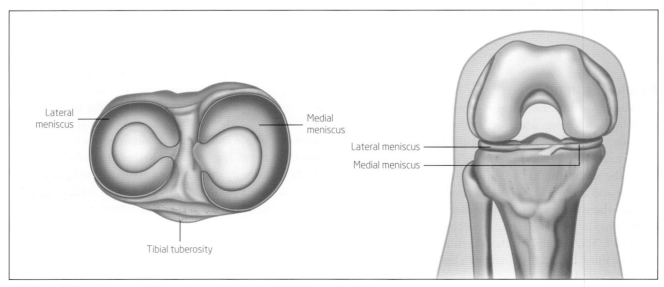

■ **Figure 9.2b.** The menisci (right leg, anterior view) with bird's eye view inset.

both joints simultaneously against another force, or moving both joints at the same time. Body-weight exercises are therefore ideal for injury-proofing the muscles crossing the knee by developing multi-joint activity and stability.

> **KEY POINT:** *As a general rule, those muscles passing the front of the knee will extend the joint, while those passing behind the centre line of the joint will cause it to flex.*

The muscles of the knee merge into tendons before anchoring at their bony destination. There are several tendons crossing the knee: these include the three long tendons of the hamstring group, and the single patellar tendon of the quadriceps group. In addition to these more familiar tendons, we will also consider the iliotibial band (ITB) on the outer aspect of the knee, and the three-pronged ('goose-foot') tendon structure on the inner aspect of the knee. These are all points of potential injury or weakness, and will therefore be reviewed in relation to specific knee problems.

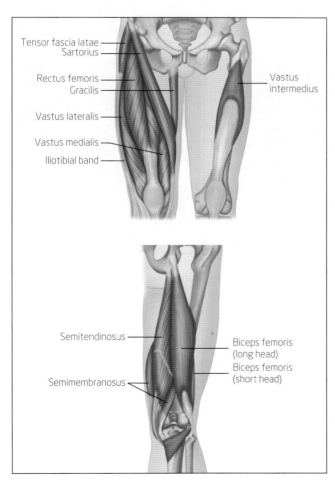

Tensor fascia latae
Sartorius
Rectus femoris
Gracilis
Vastus lateralis
Vastus medialis
Iliotibial band
Vastus intermedius

Semitendinosus
Biceps femoris (long head)
Biceps femoris (short head)
Semimembranosus

■ **Figure 9.3.** Muscles of the knee.

■ Common Knee Dysfunction

During childhood, it would have been commonplace for your knees to fully flex and extend regularly throughout the day. As we become adults, however, the knee tends to be subjected to less ROM, which means that some parts of the joint become less loaded, stretched and lubricated over time. There may now be valid reasons why you are no longer able to squat, kneel or sit cross-legged, but it may also be that these movements are no longer accessible to you because you have not 'trained' for them in a while. In this way, you become trapped in a cycle of stiffness and pain that can lock you into a world of reduced function.

> **KEY POINT:** *During childhood, it would have been commonplace for your knees to fully flex and extend throughout the day, receiving increased load, more movement and better lubrication.*

We will explore how body-weight exercises might be used to break the cycle of knee pain and reduced function, allowing you to live a fuller and freer life of movement.

Knee Joint Arthritis

The knee is the most common site in the body for osteoarthritis: it is estimated that, at the time of writing, about 18% of the population of England aged 45 and over have osteoarthritis of the knee. Not all knee osteoarthritis, however, is painful or restrictive. In the USA, around 12% of adults aged 65 or over have problematic knee osteoarthritis. Unless the arthritis is advanced or severe (relatively few cases in people under 65 years of age), there is a wonder treatment to help manage the pain, stiffness and reduced function in the knee. It is a treatment that has support from the research literature, and is emphasised in clinical guidelines in the UK and elsewhere in the world. It is a treatment known as 'exercise'! That's right, *exercise*. When tailored to your own needs, it can help reduce and manage some of the problems associated with knee arthritis. Before we go on to look at some suitable body-weight exercises for an arthritic knee, let us first consider briefly the nature of osteoarthritis.

> **KEY POINT:** *There exists a wonder treatment for managing knee osteoarthritis that is well supported by research evidence. It is called 'exercise'!*

Osteoarthritis is very different from rheumatoid arthritis, and the management of the two conditions will differ accordingly. If you are unsure which condition you are experiencing, we suggest you are reviewed by a medical or health professional. Osteoarthritis is a condition that affects your joints; through mostly 'wear-and-tear' damage, the smooth cartilage on the ends of the bones becomes patchy, thin and roughened. The damaged cartilage can irritate the joint from time to time, causing it to swell. The joint may also become thickened, or lose its original shape over time as the body compensates with new bone growth. Osteoarthritis tends to flare and settle in the joints intermittently. Seek medical or health care reassurance for the flare-ups; otherwise, we recommend managing the settled osteoarthritic knee with tailored exercise. Body-weight exercise can form part of this management plan, and we recommend Key Exercise 9.1.

KEY EXERCISE 9.1: SQUAT

Target Area: Knees, hips
Sets: 3
Reps: 5–20
Rest: 45 seconds

The squat is a fundamental lower body exercise requiring nothing more than good form and your body weight to get real results. Using a hip drive technique, the knees and hips are brought into extension from deep flexion using the muscles we have discussed previously. This exercise is included here because it will promote knee flexion, which is often first affected in knee osteoarthritis, and will develop the muscles around the knee that can become wasted.

1. To perform the squat, stand with heels shoulder-width apart and hands folded across your chest or out in front of you. Keep your toes pointed forwards or out-turned by about 30 degrees, whichever is most comfortable for you.
2. Bend at the knees, keeping your back straight and your head up with your eyes looking forwards. Push your hips back and downwards at the same time. As you descend, allow your knees to fall outwards slightly so that the hips can fall between them. Do not allow your knees to move forward of your toes. Keep your feet flat.
3. Squat down as low as your mobility and ability allow. As you progress with ROM and strength, your hips may sit lower than your knees. It takes time, though, so persevere.

4. From this bottom position, drive your hips up and forwards and gradually extend your knee to develop the inner quadriceps muscle bulk.

Teaching Points
This is a complex movement with lots going on. Good form is essential here, so pay attention to your body position and do not overstress your knees too soon. As strength and mobility improve, you can make the squat deeper.

Also recommended: Key Exercise 8.2 (deep squat position).

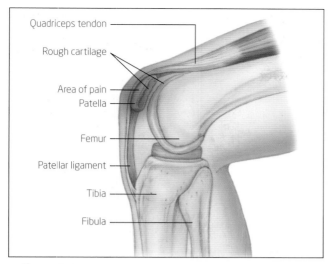

Quadriceps tendon
Rough cartilage
Area of pain
Patella
Femur
Patellar ligament
Tibia
Fibula

■ **Figure 9.4.** Patellofemoral pain syndrome.

Patellofemoral Pain Syndrome

Patellofemoral pain syndrome (or PFPS for short) is a condition characterised by pain around the front of the knee (Figure 9.4). The pain may be felt under the kneecap, but can often be a vague ache around the knee. The problem mostly originates from the area where the back of the patella (knee cap) makes contact with the lower end of the femur (thigh bone). The diagnosis is usually made when other more specific problems have been ruled out. If you are unsure, see a medical or health or professional.

The cause of PFPS is usually some form of increased or excessive pressure on the patellofemoral joint of the knee. This abnormal pressure may be due to muscle imbalances, tight soft-tissue structures, unaccustomed physical activity, or biomechanical pressures from changes to lower-limb posture.

First-line treatment involves relative rest from the initial cause, followed by exercise therapy to include stretching and strengthening exercises for the legs and hips/buttocks. Key Exercise 9.2 should definitely be in your routine, along with a few other essential exercises that we also recommend.

KEY EXERCISE 9.2: QUADRICEPS STRETCH

Target Area: Knees, quadriceps muscles
Sets: 3
Duration: 20–30 seconds each leg
Rest: 20 seconds

It is important to maintain mobility and muscular flexibility around the knee to relieve some pressure on the patellofemoral joint. The quadriceps stretch maintains and increases flexibility in the front of the thigh.

1. To perform the quadriceps stretch, lie face down. Position one forearm on the ground so that your chest and shoulders are slightly raised.
2. Keep one leg straight and bring the heel of the other leg up to your buttocks. Grab the bent leg with your free hand.
3. Pull your foot to your buttocks, making sure to keep your leg square onto your hips. Pull your foot until you feel a stretch in your quadriceps at the front of your thigh. This should be a mildly uncomfortable position, but never painful.
4. Hold this position for 20–30 seconds, and then change legs and repeat.

Teaching Points

If you do have flexibility issues around the front of the knee, this stretch is a must. Work within your limits, and then increase the ROM over time.

Also recommended: Key Exercise 8.3 (hamstring stretch), Key Exercise 8.4 (groin stretch), Key Exercise 8.6 (hip flexor stretch).

Knee Ligament Injury

As we outlined earlier in this chapter, there are four main ligaments that bind the knee and help prevent excessive movement at this joint: these are the ACL, PCL, MCL and LCL (Figure 9.5). The cruciates sit inside the knee joint and roughly cross each other from the front to the back (cruciate = cross-shaped).

Crudely speaking, the ACL and PCL prevent excessive forwards-backwards movement of the shinbone under

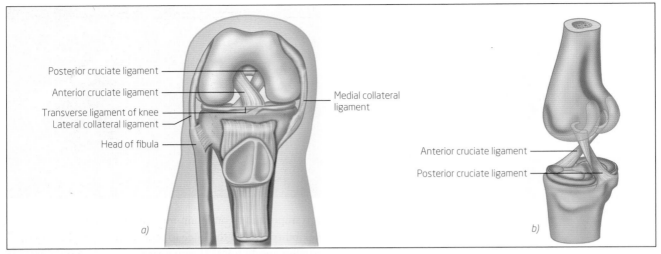

■ **Figure 9.5.** The four main knee ligaments. (a) right leg, anterior view; (b) right leg, posterior view.

the thighbone. These two ligaments also offer some rotational support, so any injury involving rotation or hyperextension (over-straightening) of the knee may traumatise them. Because of the mechanism of injury common to the knee, it is most likely to be the ACL that is damaged. If you are experiencing an acute injury, we recommend that a health or medical professional assesses you. If you have an ongoing degree of instability in the knee and have been told that you do not require surgical repair, add Key Exercise 9.3 to your routine. If you do not have a history of ACL injury but instead want to injury-proof this ligament, you should definitely work on this exercise.

KEY EXERCISE 9.3: GYM BALL HAMSTRING CURL

Target Area: Knees, hamstrings
Sets: 3
Reps: 10
Rest: 20 seconds

This exercise requires a gym (Swiss) ball, but can also be done (but with more difficulty) using a soccer ball or basketball. The gym ball hamstring curl develops the ability of the hamstring muscles to lengthen under load and control the extension of the knee. It also develops active stability in the knee by creating a less stable base.

1. Lie on your back with straight legs and place your heels up onto a gym ball. Use your glutes and hamstrings to raise your buttocks off the floor. Some of your weight

will now be resting onto the back of the shoulders. Do not strain your head or neck. Work on controlling stability here, as the ball will want to move side to side in the starting position. Place your hands and arms flat on the floor either side of you for increased stability.

2. Keeping shoulders and arms firmly in contact with the floor, begin to roll the ball towards your buttocks by 'curling' your hamstrings. Work hard on maintaining

stability and balance as you draw the ball under your bent knees.

3. Slowly roll the ball back to the starting position, feeling the hamstrings lengthen under the strain. As you approach the starting position again, do not allow your knees to snap into extension. This should be a controlled return movement. Repeat.

Teaching Points

Play around with different-size gym balls to change the stability aspect. As suggested, you can even use a basketball or similar. Vary the speed of the movement to develop a more dynamic extension of the knee. If you want a real challenge, work towards performing the exercise one leg at a time!

Also recommended: Exercise 11.14 (bridge).

The collateral ligaments sit along either side of the joint and contribute to stability on the inner and outer aspects of the joint. The LCL is shorter and thicker, and sits slightly away from the joint; the MCL is thinner and flatter, sits close to the side of the joint and has a common mechanism of injury, making it prone to trauma. If you have a chronic instability at the MCL, or want to make this ligament resilient to future injury, try Key Exercise 9.4.

KEY EXERCISE 9.4: V-UP WITH BALL SQUEEZE

Target Area: Core and adductor muscles
Sets: 3
Reps: 5–10
Rest: 30 seconds

The V-up is a combination of a sit-up and a leg extension, but when you add a ball to the mix it takes on a different challenge. With the use of a football or similar, the aim here is to apply a gentle squeeze on the ball by the feet; this puts a slight stress on the inner knee to activate the adductor muscles. As the knee then moves through flexion and extension, this activation is maintained to develop support around the MCL.

1. Lie on your back with a ball held between both feet.
2. Brace your core and raise your upper back off the floor. Keeps your arms by your sides to reduce the lever strain on your trunk.
3. Raise your torso further by using your abdominal muscles. Simultaneously bend your knees and raise them towards your chest. Keep hold of the ball between your feet!
4. Once your chest and knees have almost met in the middle, hold this position momentarily before slowly returning to the starting position. Remember, the aim is to maintain the squeeze on the ball as the knees move through the range. Repeat.

Teaching Points

If the core aspect of this exercise is too difficult, keep your back flat on the floor and simply extend and return your feet while keeping hold of the ball. For more of a challenge, use a weighted ball and balls of different sizes.

Also recommended: Exercise 11.10 (side plank).

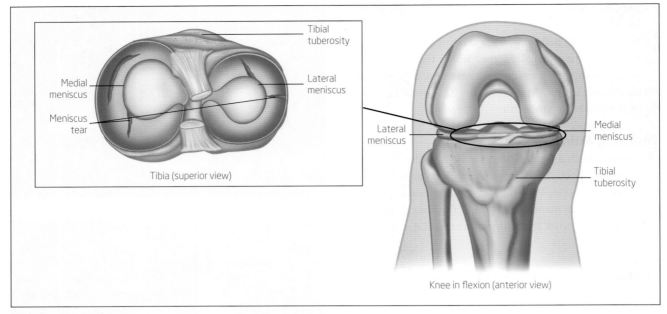

■ **Figure 9.6.** Meniscus tear.

Knee Cartilage Dysfunction

There are two types of cartilage found in the knee joint:
1) smooth 'articular' cartilage, which covers the joining
surfaces of bones and reduces the friction of joint
movement; and 2) fibrous cartilage, which makes up the
crescent-shaped ('sickle-moon') menisci. Each meniscus
sits on top of the shinbone and cushions the impact of the
lower thighbone. The cartilaginous menisci can degenerate
and fray with time and use, leading to niggles in later
life. In younger life, they may be subject to outright tears,
usually resulting from excessive rotational movements
(Figure 9.6). As the medial (inner) meniscus bears more
load and has less rotational freedom it is most likely to
be injured.

If you have been advised by a health professional to
exercise the knee to deal with this problem, or you want
to reduce your injury risk here, give Key Exercise 9.5 a go.

KEY EXERCISE 9.5: SINGLE-LEG SQUAT

Target Area: Knees, quadriceps, glutes
Sets: 3
Reps: 2–5 each leg
Rest: 30 seconds

The single-leg squat is a great exercise for strengthening
the knee, but its major benefits here are improved control
and stability of this joint; the exercise can also improve or
maintain the knee ROM. It can be a challenging exercise

for beginners, but we recommend starting with a shallow
single-leg squat and focusing on balance and control at
the knee; this will help protect and preserve the meniscus
cartilages. In time, the increased squatting range will come,
and with it, increased strength at the knee.

1. To perform the single-leg squat, stand on one foot with
   the other outstretched in front of you. Reach your arms
   forwards to aid with balance.
2. Bend your stance knee and start to squat down, keeping
   your stance foot flat on the floor. Aim to 'sit back' into
   the squat, ensuring that the knee does not pass forward
   of the toes.
3. As you descend, move your free foot forwards,
   straightening your knee as you do so.
4. Keep descending until you reach your current limit
   of ability; you may be able to descend so far that your
   posterior thigh touches your calf. This will be your
   end-point.
5. Pause for a second, and then use the quadriceps and
   glutes to push through the stance hip and knee until
   you are back at the starting position. This counts as one
   repetition. Repeat. Change legs.

Teaching Points

The single-leg squat can be very challenging. Start with
a shallow squat, and if necessary use external support to
help with control. We would recommend, however, trying
to work without external support in order to develop your
stability and control, and instead sacrificing the depth of
the squat initially.

under load (think of running and cycling), there is steady rubbing of the ITB over the lateral bony bump of the lower femur (Figure 9.7). This irritation leads to inflammation and pain, which can be experienced when moving off from rest.

ITB syndrome can be a particularly resistant and debilitating problem to have. As its other name suggests, this condition is common in runners, with whom it is the leading cause of lateral (outer) knee pain. The condition can also be experienced, however, with cycling, squatting and non-sporting populations.

Prevention is better than cure in this situation. Develop strong knees that are capable of moving regularly through a full range – Key Exercise 9.6 will help you get there! Avoid excessive load and repetitive knee movements until you have developed a strong base of strength and control. If you are currently experiencing ITB syndrome, manage the symptoms first before starting rehabilitation exercises. See a health or medical professional if you are stuck in the acute stage of runner's knee.

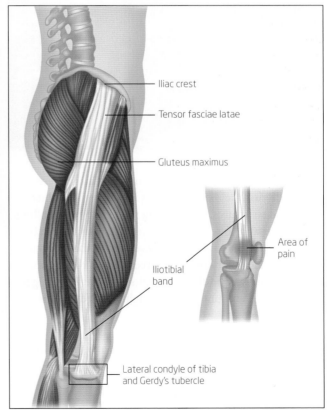

■ **Figure 9.7.** Iliotibial band syndrome.

ITB Syndrome (Runner's Knee)

The ITB is a thick band of connective tissue called *fascia*; it runs from the outer upper thigh, travels down the outer thigh to cross the knee, and anchors into the outer upper shin (tibia). This fascial band has a crucial role in stabilising and supporting the knee during movement, but also provides a surface for attachment for some large muscles in the buttock, hip and thigh. With any repeated bending and straightening of the knee joint, especially

KEY EXERCISE 9.6: ITB FOAM ROLL

Target Area: ITB
Sets: 3
Duration: 30 seconds each leg
Rest: 30 seconds

The idea of stretching the ITB is controversial, so here we will discuss the mobility of this fibrous band and its associated structures. By exposing the ITB to foam rolling, you may be able to restore or improve its mobility relative to the structures around it. In consequence, the ITB may move over the outer knee more freely. Foam rolling can feel particularly painful in this region; we therefore suggest modifying the amount of body weight applied as your comfort dictates.

1. To perform the ITB foam roll, lie down on one side with the foam roller underneath your lower outer-thigh, at 90 degrees to your body.
2. Support your body weight with your hands, and then start to roll up and down the foam roller.
3. Keep your legs together and tense/brace them if it helps with stability. If there are any sore areas, spend more time

and attention on these parts. You can also place the upper leg on the floor to support some of your body weight.
4. Roll for the required time, and then change legs and repeat.

Teaching Points

As with the other foam-rolling exercises, if you find that your legs are too sore to perform the movement properly, try using a softer foam roller. You can move on to a harder foam roller as your tolerance allows.

Also recommended: Key Exercise 8.5 (glute stretch), Exercise 9.10 (ITB mobilisation).

Bursitis

As we saw earlier in this chapter, there can be between 11 and 14 bursae in the average knee! Some are more susceptible to injury than others and this usually involves an excessive amount of friction or pressure at the site; the bursae will become swollen and painful in response. Bursae may also be injured through direct trauma, but that is not the focus of this book.

Commonly injured knee bursae include the prepatellar bursa, the infrapatellar bursa and the pes anserine ('goose-foot') bursa. Prepatellar bursitis is more commonly known as *housemaid's knee*, while infrapatellar bursitis is often named *clergyman's knee*; other causative professions have included *floor-layer's knee* and *plumber's knee*. Be careful, it is a dangerous world out there! We recommend avoiding the causative factors and using padding for kneeling activities. See a health or medical professional for advice on managing the acute symptoms of a knee bursitis. There are no specific body-weight exercises advised for this condition.

> **KEY POINT:** *Prevention is better than cure for most injuries, including those to the knees. Develop strong knees that are capable of moving regularly through a full range.*

Knee Muscle and Tendon Problems

Niggling hamstring problems are the blight of many athletic individuals. These issues can prevent you from kicking a football, striding out during a run, or completing some lower-limb gym exercises. They can even niggle during day-to-day activities, such as bending forwards to pick something up or tying shoelaces. As a two-joint muscle, the hamstrings are susceptible to injury, and this is usually caused by a sudden stretch or rapid contraction. Over time, this injury may not settle fully and you can be left with a chronic hamstring strain. Subsequently, there will nearly always be muscle imbalances, with tightening and shortening of the hamstrings. Rehabilitate this fully, or better still prevent this type of injury, with Key Exercise 9.7.

KEY EXERCISE 9.7: ROLLOVER INTO STRADDLE SIT

Target Area: Hamstrings, lower back, glutes, adductors
Sets: 3
Reps: 10
Rest: 30 seconds

The rollover develops mobility and flexibility in the lower back, glutes and groin. The exercise is included here for its dynamic ability to stretch the hamstrings in two positions – first when the legs are overhead, and second when in the straddle sit (which can itself be done as a stand-alone exercise). Only take this movement as far as you are comfortable, and avoid excessive stress on the neck and head.

1. To perform the rollover into straddle sit, assume a seated position on the ground with your legs stretched out in front of you.
2. Now roll backwards onto your upper back and allow your straight legs to lower over your head. Place your hands by the sides of your head for increased support and stability.
3. Using a pushing action from your arms and also some work from your trunk, bring yourself forwards and upright to a seated position, but this time spread your legs into a wide straddle position. Once in this position, reach forwards between your legs until you feel the stretch in the lower back and hamstrings. Hold this position for a second before repeating the exercise.

Teaching Points
The rollover part of this exercise requires trunk control and strength, making it an excellent bulletproof-body exercise by developing overall conditioning. If, however, you find this difficult, or you have a problem with your neck that precludes the rollover, just do the straddle sit stretch. This stretch will target the hamstrings, lower back and the adductor muscles (which also have a hamstring function!).

Also recommended: Key Exercise 8.3 (hamstring stretch), Exercise 9.8 (negative hamstring curl).

Following a history of overuse, the tendons of the hamstring muscles may become painful. Discomfort is usually experienced at the back of the knee and will be felt most when the knee flexes with resistance. The pain will be towards the outer or inner aspect of the posterior knee, and this will localise the problematic hamstring tendon. As we have seen in Chapters 5 and 6 of this book, tendon problems now tend to be regarded as *tendinopathies*, which means that rather than inflamed tendons they often show cellular signs of tendon breakdown. There is a sound body of evidence now to suggest that exercise therapy is a key part of rehabilitation for this problem. Progressive, loaded body-weight exercises may also defend against the development of tendinopathy. We offer Key Exercise 9.8 for this problem.

KEY EXERCISE 9.8: NEGATIVE HAMSTRING CURL

Target Area: Hamstrings, spinal extensor muscles
Sets: 3
Reps: 2–5
Rest: 30 seconds

Although performing hamstring curls on a machine is a great movement, the exercise can be modified to be even more effective with a bodyweight variation. The exercise presented here is in line with a well-evidenced rehabilitation programme for hamstring problems, and will help you develop bulletproof thighs. The machine version of the hamstring curl is reversed by fixing the ankle and moving the body relative to the lower leg; this allows a body-weight exercise that activates the hips and trunk, which is an all-round win. There are many variations of this exercise, but we will focus on the negative version in order to develop the eccentric loading of the hamstring tendons and muscles. Note that it can be very difficult to find the specific piece of equipment required to perform the negative hamstring curl. If this is the case, you can perform the exercise with the aid of a partner, getting them to hold your ankles securely while you lower your torso towards the ground.

1. To perform the negative hamstring curl, start in the upright kneeling position. Secure your ankles and pad the underside of your knees.
2. Keeping the torso straight, begin to extend your knees and lower yourself towards the floor. Aim to make this movement slow and controlled. Keep your hands out in front of you to guard against descending rapidly towards the floor.
3. Lower yourself as far as you feel able to. If this is not very far at first, do not worry – this will improve as your strength increases.
4. Return to the starting position. You can come out of the curl position by pushing yourself up with your arms (great for upper body strength), or by using your hamstrings to draw yourself back up.
5. Repeat.

Teaching Points
Variations on this exercise include the assisted and full hamstring curl (with eccentric and concentric phases).

In the assisted version, you can use a stick/pole in your hands to push against the floor and support some of your upper body weight.

Also recommended: Key Exercise 8.3 (hamstring stretch), Key Exercise 9.7 (rollover to straddle sit).

Perhaps the most common tendon problem at the knee is patellar tendinopathy; again, this is not usually an inflamed tendon problem but a degenerative-type issue. The cause is usually excessive or unaccustomed load-bearing activity, which may be sports related (jumper's knee), but could equally be associated with an occupational activity. This type of problem can affect the tendon above or below the kneecap (patella), but most commonly affects the lower part of the tendon. A similar problem can affect the connective tissue 'expansions' on either side of the patella. Tendon failure and degeneration around the knee can lead to a gradual onset of pain around the front of the knee, and this may be worse with resisted knee extension. Tendinopathy problems appear to respond well to gradually loaded exercise, in which body-weight exercises have a crucial role. Add Key Exercise 9.9 to your resilience or rehabilitation programme, but be prepared to stick with it, since tendinopathies may take several weeks to respond to the load at a cellular level. If your pain worsens, we suggest you see a health or medical professional for tailored advice.

KEY EXERCISE 9.9: LUNGE

Target Area: Knees, quadriceps, patellar tendon
Sets: 3
Reps: 10 each leg
Rest: 30 seconds

The lunge is a great exercise for the knee, as each is loaded individually; this develops the added elements of stability and control. The exercise also imparts an eccentric (lengthening) load to the individual quadriceps and patellar tendon. You can also vary the difficulty, making it suitable for widely varying fitness and ability levels.

1. To perform the lunge, stand with your feet shoulder-width apart, arms by your sides in a relaxed posture.
2. Take a large step forwards with one leg, planting the foot firmly on the ground.
3. Bend the front knee and allow your rear knee to move towards the floor; this creates an eccentric load on the quadriceps and patellar tendon of the front knee.

4. Keep going until your front knee is bent at 90 degrees, and your rear knee is almost touching the ground. Now push up on the front leg to return to the starting position. Change legs and repeat.

Teaching Points

If this exercise is too difficult, you can reduce the ROM to make it a lot easier. To do this, bend your knees by a smaller amount and only descend part way towards the ground. As you get stronger and more confident, you can keep descending all the way down to the floor.

■ Body-weight Exercises for Improved Knee Function

EXERCISE 9.10: ITB MOBILISATION

Target Area: ITB, glutes, lateral quadriceps
Sets: 3
Duration: 20–30 seconds
Rest: 20 seconds

The ITB provides a connective tissue anchor for some of the large muscles of the hip and thigh, and also stabilises the knee joint. Whether the ITB can be stretched is controversial, but the muscles that attach to it certainly can. The ITB 'mobilisation' suggested here is intended to improve mobility of the ITB in order to reduce the pressure where it crosses the outer knee.

1. To perform the ITB mobilisation, crouch down with your hands and feet on the floor.
2. Move one leg sideways, making sure that it goes behind the leg that stays planted on the ground. Use your hands to support your body weight when you do this.
3. Keep stretching your leg out sideways, and rest this leg on the outside of your other foot. You should feel a strain in the outside of your leg, running from your hip down to your outer knee.
4. Hold this position for the required time, and then change legs and repeat.

Teaching Points

The ITB mobilisation should help to alleviate any stress at the outer knee. If the injury is acute and the area is sore and inflamed, we recommend assessment and advice from a health or medical professional in the first instance.

EXERCISE 9.11: ADDUCTOR FOAM ROLL

Target Area: Adductor muscles of the thigh
Sets: 3
Duration: 30 seconds each leg
Rest: 20 seconds

On the opposite side to the abductor muscles and the ITB are the adductor muscles. These muscles act to bring the leg in towards the centre line of the body, and also help in stabilisation of the hip and knee during running, jumping, squatting and other lower body movements. Foam rolling this area can help to improve any soft-tissue restrictions.

1. To perform the adductor foam roll, position your foam roller parallel to your torso, and crouch down on top of it.
2. Keep one leg straight and bend the other at the knee, placing the inside of your thigh on top of the foam roller.
3. Support yourself on your hands, and start to roll backwards and forwards over the roller. Work all the way up to the groin area, and then down to the top of the knee.
4. Keep rolling for 30 seconds, and then change legs and repeat.

Teaching Points

As with the other foam-rolling exercises, you will want to start with a softer foam roller or reduce your body-weight pressure against the roller.

■ Goal Exercises for the Knee

Goal exercises have been presented in other chapters of this book both to serve as a measure of your general body-weight strength and fitness, and to provide you with developmental exercises that can be incorporated in a bulletproof-body exercise routine. The knee joint is no exception – a few exercises for developing lower-limb strength and injury resistance are given below. Combine these with the goal exercises in Chapters 8 and 10 for a fuller workout.

GOAL EXERCISE 9.12: ICE SKATER

Target Area: Knees, quadriceps
Sets: 3
Reps: 10 (5 each leg)
Rest: 30 seconds

this exercise, begin by making small jumps, gradually moving up in difficulty as your strength and mobility progress.

Target Area: Knees, quadriceps, glutes, calves
Sets: 3
Reps: 15 (or 20 seconds duration)
Rest: 45 seconds

The ice skater will test the strength of the lower body as well as promote good stability in the knees. This exercise requires adequate jumping ability; therefore, if you have knee or lower body joint problems, seek advice from your medical professional beforehand. The ice skater can be thought of as a natural progression from the lunge (Exercise 9.10). Ideally, wear shoes with good grip and use a non-slip floor surface.

1. To perform the ice skater, stand in a neutral position and keep the arms relaxed.
2. From here, move your weight onto one foot and jump forwards at an angle, aiming to land with the opposite foot.
3. As you land on one foot, bend the knee to absorb the shock.
4. Jump forwards again at an angle, but this time to the other side, and land on the opposite foot. Keep doing this for the required repetitions (or distance if preferred), and then rest.

Teaching Points

The multidirectional and dynamic stress of this exercise contribute to improved knee stability. The further you jump both forwards and laterally, the greater the stress put on the knees. If you are just starting out with

In this exercise we introduce an explosive component to the mix. The squat is great for the hips and knees in general, but the jump squat adds an element of instability to the movement, especially on the landing phase. The forces applied to the knees are also higher because of the deceleration required to counteract the downward movement. Before attempting this exercise, make sure that you are fully versed and experienced in the normal body-weight squat (Key Exercise 9.1) and the deep squat position (Key Exercise 8.2).

1. To perform the jump squat, stand with your feet shoulder-width apart, toes pointing out slightly, and your arms loose by your sides.
2. Squat down, bending the knees, pushing the hips back and down, and moving the arms forwards to aid balance.
3. Keep descending until your thighs are parallel to the ground. If you really want to push the boundaries, continue until you reach the deep squat position.
4. Push up hard, extending your hips, knees and ankles as forcefully as possible. Jump into the air, keeping your eyes looking forwards to stay balanced.
5. Land under control, immediately bending the knees, descending into the squat position once again. Continue for the desired number of reps, or for a set period of time.

Teaching Points

As with any explosive or plyometric exercise, care must be taken not to subject the target area to excessive force. If you are working with the jump squat for the first time, or have had some time away from training and are returning to it, start small and build up. Do this by only descending until your thighs are horizontal and only jumping into the air a few centimetres. As time progresses and you become stronger and more confident, you can descend lower and jump higher.

GOAL EXERCISE 9.14: JUMP LUNGE

Target Area: Knees, quadriceps
Sets: 3
Reps: 10 (or 20 seconds duration)
Rest: 45 seconds

In addition to the jump squat there is the jump lunge. This is the same type of progression from the lunge as the jump squat from the body-weight squat. The instability and coordination required in the jump lunge, however, is higher than in both squat variations. Each knee will be tested vigorously, and each repetition will require the positions of the feet to be swapped in mid-air; this introduces a coordination requirement that may come easily (or not), depending on your training experience. We recommend only attempting this when you are comfortable with the jump squat.

1. To perform the jump lunge, stand in a stretched-out lunge position, with both knees nearly straight. Let your arms hang loosely by your sides, ready to help with balance.
2. From here, descend to the floor, bending both knees by an equal amount so that your torso stays vertical. Stop just short of your rear knee touching the ground.
3. Push up hard, extending your hips, knees and ankles and jumping into the air.
4. Once you are in the air, move your front leg backwards and your rear leg forwards. You should be aiming to land with your feet the same distance apart as when you started.

5. Land under control, bending both knees to absorb the shock. Descend to the bottom position immediately, to prepare for the next repetition.

Teaching Points

The jump lunge is a demanding exercise, but it can be made easier by simply reducing the ROM and the intensity of the movement. You can accomplish this by not dropping as low when descending towards the floor, and by not jumping as high when leaving the ground. As you get stronger and more confident, you can start to descend all the way and jump as high into the air as possible.

The Lower Leg, Ankle and Foot

◼ Introduction to the Lower Leg, Ankle and Foot

Humans have been walking on two legs for about two million years, with evidence of bipedal locomotion (walking on two legs) in primates extending back four million years. Over this period of time, the foot and ankle have evolved, with the development of enlarged heels for weight bearing, smaller toes for supporting rather than grasping, and arched rather than flat feet. The result is a platform to support the entire weight of the body, and a mechanism for transferring that weight in an energy-efficient way. Despite the fact that human walking is 75% more efficient than human running, we have managed amazing feats of athletic ability, from running the marathon in 2 hours 3 minutes to sprinting 100m in 9.58 seconds.

As babies, we must learn this most fundamental of human skills, which can take on average 12–15 months to master. Along the way, there are trips and falls as our ability to maintain balance over two feet is constantly challenged. In this chapter we look at some of the key locomotive structures of the lower leg, ankle and foot that keep us up and running. We will also explore some common injuries and dysfunction of this region, and finish with a range of body-weight exercises to keep you on your toes!

◼ Functional Anatomy of the Lower Leg, Ankle and Foot

Passive Structures

As we saw in Chapter 9, the tibia is a large weight-bearing bone of the lower limb and forms part of the knee joint.

The tibia transmits the weight of the upper body and thigh and transfers it to the talus bone in the ankle joint. Alongside the heavy-duty tibia sits the more slender fibula bone. The distance between these two bones is spanned along their length by a fibrous membrane, creating a firm union between the bones but allowing a certain degree of flexing when weight bearing; this flexing ability of the fibula and the joining membrane is put to the test when landing on the feet from a height. The end of the fibula is slightly lower than the tibia, with both of these long bones having endings that create a mortise for the talus bone to sit in. The bony structure of the lower leg and ankle is shown in Figure 10.1.

The talus bone of the ankle sits on the heel bone (calcaneus) and transfers the body weight to the ground through the heel and the rest of the foot. The foot is made up of 26 bones that form a total of 33 intricate joints. All of these joints, including those of the ankle, are supported by ligaments that bind the bones together and prevent unwanted movements. The ligaments on the outer side of

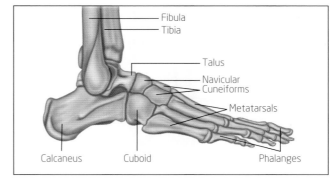

◼ **Figure 10.1.** The bony structures of the foot and ankle joint, lateral view.

the ankle can be stressed during an ankle sprain, as we shall see later in this chapter. The bones of the foot form a natural arch, and this contributes to the spring in our step; this bony architecture can be seen in Figure 10.1. In addition to the numerous ligaments of the foot and ankle, the load-bearing ability of the foot is increased by a connective tissue structure called the *plantar fascia*: this tough fibrous band sits under the length of the foot and supports the arch.

Active Structures

The lower leg houses the powerful calf muscle known as the *gastrocnemius*: this muscle is capable of pulling on the heel bone (calcaneus) via the strong Achilles tendon to raise you up on tip-toes, allowing you to walk and run. Several other muscles can be found in the lower leg; these contribute to postural stability and control, keeping you upright against gravity for up to several hours at a time when standing. The numerous tendons of these muscles, shown in Figure 10.2, cross the ankle joint and contribute to the dynamic stability and movement of this joint.

The muscles at the front of the shin cross the ankle and contract to draw your foot and toes towards your shin in a movement called *dorsiflexion*. A key muscle here is the tibialis anterior, which is hard at work when you walk on your heels. The fibularis brevis and longus muscles run down the outside of the lower leg and ankle, and pull on the foot when you turn the soles of your feet outwards. This muscle activity contributes to maintaining and supporting the arches of the foot, and is also important in protecting the outer ankle from 'inversion' ankle sprains.

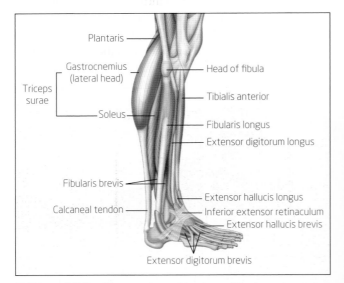

■ **Figure 10.2.** The muscles and tendons of the lower leg and ankle, lateral view.

> **KEY POINT:** *Muscles in the lower leg provide powerful propulsive forces, have incredible endurance in maintaining balance during standing, support the arches of the feet, and contribute to the stability of the ankle joint.*

■ Common Lower Leg, Ankle and Foot Dysfunction

Calf Strain

Excessive or sudden loading of the calf muscles can lead to tearing of some of the fibres in the muscles at the back of the lower leg. If only a few fibres are affected, you may notice little impact on your daily or sporting activities other than some muscle soreness. The greater the number of disrupted fibres, the more pronounced the pain and limitation. If the calf injury is acute and you are uncertain about the degree of damage, we recommend that you seek assessment by a qualified health or medical professional.

Tennis leg is a type of calf strain that can affect the plantaris (a deep muscle of the calf) or commonly the powerful gastrocnemius muscle. Gastrocnemius has two sections or 'heads' to it; the inner (medial) head is the one more prone to tear or partially rupture. If you have been advised to exercise for rehabilitation of a calf strain, or have a recurrent injury in this region, add Key Exercise 10.1 to your training programme to build resilience in this muscle group.

KEY EXERCISE 10.1: DOWNWARD DOG

Target Area: Ankle joints, calf muscles, sciatic nerve, wrists, shoulders, spine
Sets: 3
Duration: Hold for 20–30 seconds
Rest: 30 seconds

Yoga fans will be no strangers to this exercise and will quickly tell you about its benefits. If you have never done yoga before, we recommend that you try this exercise over any other. The downward dog uses multiple joints and muscles simultaneously, and is the ultimate definition of a body-weight exercise. We include it here for its benefits in developing length under tension at the calf, but also for mobilising the ankle, mobilising the sciatic nerve and stretching the hamstrings. Dysfunction in any of these areas can contribute to ongoing calf problems.

1. To perform the downward dog, assume a push-up position and walk your feet towards your hands while keeping your knees straight. Walk in as far as you can until you have taken up the strain across the back of the legs, the lower back and the shoulders.
2. Keep your feet facing forwards and try to place your heels flat on the ground. Ensure that you have safely loaded your arms and shoulders by spreading the fingers wide, with the middle finger facing forwards and the palms shoulder-width apart.
3. Use straight elbows to support your weight, but do not lock them out. Push backwards through the arms to adjust the strain in the calf muscles.
4. With the feet hip-width apart, press the heels into the floor to create a stretch in the back of the legs. Try a slight bend in the knees if you need to focus the stretch on the calves.
5. Keep the back flat and relax the neck. Hold the position for 20 seconds.

Teaching Points

This is a true bulletproof-body exercise that develops strength, stamina and suppleness in multiple body areas. If you have weakness or pain in any other region of your body while doing this exercise, we recommend that you address those issues first by consulting other chapters of this book. Do not perform this exercise if you have uncontrolled high blood pressure.

Ankle Sprain

Sprains of the outer ankle ligaments are the most common ankle injury and usually involve an 'inversion' injury, whereby you roll over the outside of your ankle (Figure 10.3). Lateral ankle sprains are graded according to severity, from a mild overstretch (grade 1) to a complete rupture (grade 3). Most people, however, will experience a partial ligament tear (grade 2), but if you are unsure, first seek the attention of a health or medical professional. A *chronic lateral ankle sprain* is one that has a history of spraining and never fully settles, or keeps recurring. There may be instability, pain or ongoing swelling/inflammation.

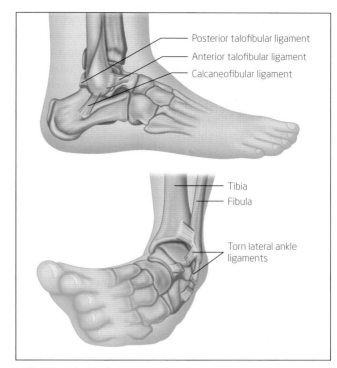

Posterior talofibular ligament
Anterior talofibular ligament
Calcaneofibular ligament

Tibia
Fibula

Torn lateral ankle ligaments

■ **Figure 10.3.** Ankle sprain.

Functional rehabilitation of the ankle is the goal here, and this should include proprioceptive retraining (see below), and the development of muscular stability and control at the ankle joint. Rehabilitation should be continued for anything up to several months to fully regain lost function at the ankle. Key Exercise 10.2 is an essential part of an ankle sprain rehabilitation programme.

KEY EXERCISE 10.2: SINGLE-LEG BALANCE

Target Area: Ankles
Sets: 3
Duration: Hold for 20–60 seconds
Rest: 30 seconds

You might think that body-weight exercises do not come any simpler than this, but they also do not come any more effective in terms of regaining ankle function. *Proprioception* is the body's internal sense of the relative position of body parts and their efforts during movement. Put more simply, it is the ability of a joint (here, your ankle) to respond quickly and subconsciously to stresses placed on it. This straightforward exercise helps retrain this function and creates a base for developing more complex exercises.

1. To perform the single-leg balance, assume a standing position on a firm, non-slip surface. Slowly place increasing body weight onto the affected ankle until you are standing on one leg. The aim is to challenge balance, so where possible do not hold onto anything, but have a stable support close by should you lose balance.
2. You may begin to wobble slightly during the exercise, but do not worry, as this is the point. If you occasionally need to touch down with the other foot, that is allowable too.
3. Hold for the required time and really focus on maintaining your balance, even if you sway a lot. Change legs to compare the ability of each side.

Teaching Points

If this exercise is too easy, you can progress it in several ways. Try standing on a more challenging surface, try with your eyes closed, have someone throw a ball to you to catch, or juggle a ball while standing on the one leg. All of these will further challenge your balance ability. As you make progress, add sport-specific movements or plyometric jumps and maintain your balance on landing.

Achilles Tendon Dysfunction

The Achilles tendon is the longest tendon in the body and is thought to have a tensile strength capable of withstanding forces of up to 12 times body weight. It is a common site for injury and is susceptible to tears and even complete rupture. More likely, though, is the development of a *tendinopathy*, a degenerative change within the tendon that leads to pain, tendon thickening and stiffness. The onset of this problem is usually gradual, and the pain can persist for many months. Excessive or unaccustomed forces through the Achilles tendon are the likely cause of tendinopathy; the problem is commonly seen in athletic populations of all levels, and generally between the mid-thirties and the early fifties. To determine whether your Achilles pain is due to tendinopathy or a tear, we

recommend you seek assessment from a qualified health or medical professional.

Management of Achilles tendon pain caused by degenerative change should include a modification of the causative factor. Return to sport may take up to three months as the tendon adapts to a progressive load. This load can be applied through body-weight exercise very effectively, and the use of eccentric loading in the calf muscles has gained popularity as an effective treatment. Key Exercise 10.3 shows you how to apply an eccentric load through the Achilles tendon.

KEY EXERCISE 10.3: NEGATIVE CALF RAISE

Target Area: Ankle joints, calf muscles
Sets: 3
Reps: 10–20
Rest: 30 seconds

The muscles of the calf are responsible for much of the strength necessary for ankle plantar flexion, an essential requirement for walking, running and jumping activities. Make yourself more resilient to calf injury, and possibly increase athletic performance, by working on this exercise. The negative calf raise uses body weight effectively to build strength and also to develop ankle mobility.

1. To perform the negative calf raise, stand on a step or platform with your toes on the edge. Hold onto something to aid your balance.
2. Use your calf muscles to raise your heels as high as possible. Think about pointing your toes to make this happen. This is the starting position.
3. Allow your heels to lower slowly to create an eccentric (lengthening) contraction of the calf muscles. Keep lowering until you feel a stretch in the these muscles. Hold this position for a second, before quickly contracting the calf muscles to return to the starting position. This counts as one repetition.
4. Repeat.

Teaching Points

If you find that just using your own body weight is not enough resistance, you can add weight to this movement. The easiest way to do this is to perform the exercise while standing on one leg. Once you have done the required number of repetitions, change legs. Alternatively, hold a dumbbell in each hand; start with a light weight, and build up from there.

Plantar Fasciitis

The plantar fascia is a strong connective tissue structure that runs under the length of the foot and contributes to the load-bearing function of the foot by supporting the arches. The plantar fascia anchors to the underside of the heel bone (calcaneus), and this is a potential site of injury and pain. Pain in the heel may be due to plantar fasciitis, usually resulting from small tears in the fascia through microtrauma or traction stress. Whether heel spurs are relevant in this pain condition is debatable, since these calcium deposits have been found in people not experiencing heel pain.

Whether the plantar fascia can be stretched is questionable, although it is acknowledged there is probably some 'give' in the structure when under load. Despite this uncertainty, there exists some research to suggest that stretching the plantar fascia may be an effective treatment. If you have this condition, you could also consider reviewing your choice of footwear, modifying any aggravating activity, and developing the small muscles of the feet through exercise and load bearing. Key Exercise 10.4 is a good place to start.

Target Area: Ankle joints, plantar fasciae
Sets: 3
Duration: Hold for 10–20 seconds, once in position
Rest: 30 seconds

The modified frog stance is a variation of the frog stance (Key Exercise 5.2) – a gold-standard body-weight exercise seen in Chapter 5. This is a testament to body-weight exercises that incorporate multiple joints and soft tissues – you get an all-over workout in one go!

In this modification the key is to focus on the ankle and toe positions, aiming to flex (dorsiflex) the foot and toes simultaneously. Use the support of the arms to control the stretch through the foot and therefore the plantar fascia.

1. To perform the modified frog stance, place your hands on the floor in front of you, with your fingers facing forwards or slightly outwards and your hands shoulder-width apart.
2. Position your knees on the outsides of your elbows, as far forwards as you can manage. If flexibility at the hips is an issue, refer to Chapter 8 of this book, but just do what you can for now.
3. Lean forwards onto your hands and onto the balls of your feet. In this position your ankles and toes will be flexed and this should be felt as a stretch through the plantar fascia. If you need to take some of this load off the plantar fascia, continue to lean forwards and place more load onto the arms. Leaning forwards can also be used to add further stretch by further flexing the toes; however, do not lean so far forwards that your feet leave the ground (unless you want to add a shoulder and hip workout at the same time!).

Teaching Points

Use the arms to add or reduce loading on the plantar fascia. You may find that the initial starting position is sufficient. When you are comfortable in this position you can slowly roll backwards and forwards on the balls of your feet to mobilise the plantar fascia.

Osteoarthritis of the Ankle

The ankle is not a common site for osteoarthritis, but you may have a history of ankle injury, fracture or excessive occupational or sporting use. *Osteoarthritis* is a degenerative condition of the cartilage on the surfaces of joining bones, and is associated with risk factors including obesity, being over 40 years of age, and biomechanical changes to the joint (resulting from, for example, flat feet or unsuitable footwear).

If you have a degree of osteoarthritis in the ankle joint, you may find that you have slightly more limitation when pointing your toes away from you (plantar flexion) than when drawing your toes towards you (dorsiflexion). Work gradually into Key Exercise 10.5 to restore some of this movement and ease any joint stiffness.

KEY EXERCISE 10.5: HEEL SIT

Target Area: Ankle joints, muscles at the front of the shins
Sets: 3
Duration: Hold for 10–20 seconds
Rest: 30 seconds

The heel sit exercise uses body weight to stretch the front of the ankle joints while also flexing the knees. Do not hold

this position for too long, as you may place excessive strain on the knees and ankles. Use the time while in this position to do some breathing exercises, and even practise some relaxation or mindfulness. Just remember to cushion your knees first on a comfortable surface.

1. To perform the heel sit, take up a kneeling position on a comfortable surface. Place your feet behind you with the ankles in a plantar-flexed position.
2. Sit back onto your heels and take up as much strain on the fronts of the ankles as is comfortable. Use your body weight to add load. Hold for the required time.
3. Come slowly out of the stretch into a high kneeling position. Rest for a moment in this position, before sitting back onto the heels and repeating the stretch.

Teaching Points

This simple exercise can improve joint mobility and function of the ankles. It is also a great stretch for the muscles at the front of the shins and may be used where there is compartment syndrome present.

■ Body-weight Exercises for Improved Lower Leg, Ankle and Foot Function

EXERCISE 10.6: UNLOADED DORSIFLEXION

Target Area: Ankle joints, calf muscles
Sets: 3
Reps: 10 each leg
Rest: 20 seconds

As the ankles can be elevated relatively easily, we can use this position to perform unloaded (without weight)

ankle mobility exercises. There are four of these exercises, corresponding to the four movements that occur naturally around the ankle.

The first of these exercises, unloaded ankle dorsiflexion, can be used to increase or maintain ROM, to gently load recovering soft-tissue after injury or to aide circulation.

1. To perform unloaded dorsiflexion, sit or lie down, making sure that the ankle is supported but free to move.
2. From here, use your lower leg muscles to pull your foot towards your shin. Curl your toes up as well, to help increase the ROM.
3. Hold this position for a second or so, and then relax your ankle. Perform the required number of repetitions. Change legs and repeat.

EXERCISE 10.7: UNLOADED PLANTAR FLEXION

Target Area: Ankle joints, anterior tibial muscles
Sets: 3
Reps: 10 each leg
Rest: 20 seconds

The unloaded ankle plantar-flexion exercise increases mobility at the ankle joint, but also primes the calf muscles for more vigorous body-weight exercise. It is also good for maintaining circulation in the leg if you are immobilised for any reason. *Plantar flexion* describes the downward movement of the foot or, more simply, pointing of the toes. Focus on this position when performing this exercise.

1. To perform unloaded plantar flexion, sit or lie down, making sure that the ankle is supported but free to move.
2. Use your lower leg muscles to point your toes. Scrunch your toes towards the sole of your foot to help increase the ROM.
3. Hold this position for a second or so, and then relax your ankle. Perform the required number of repetitions. Change legs and repeat.

EXERCISE 10.8: UNLOADED INVERSION

Target Area: Ankle joints, lateral ankle ligaments
Sets: 3
Reps: 10 each leg
Rest: 20 seconds

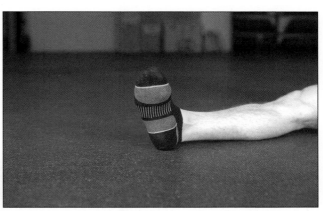

The unloaded ankle inversion exercise is very useful for mobilising the ankle joint, but also for developing a therapeutic stress on the outer ankle ligaments after an ankle sprain. Performing this exercise in an unloaded position reduces the risk of further injury in the early stages of rehabilitation.

1. To perform unloaded inversion, sit or lie down, making sure that the ankle is supported but free to move.
2. Use your lower leg muscles to pull your foot inwards so that the sole of your foot points towards your other foot. For comparison purposes, do the exercise on both ankles simultaneously.
3. Hold this position for a second or so, and then relax your ankle. Perform the required number of repetitions. Change legs if doing the exercise one ankle at a time, and repeat.

EXERCISE 10.9: UNLOADED EVERSION

Target Area: Ankle joints, fibularis muscles
Sets: 3
Reps: 10 each leg
Rest: 20 seconds

1. To perform unloaded eversion, sit or lie down, making sure that the ankle is supported but free to move.
2. From here, use your lower leg muscles to pull your foot outwards so that the sole of your foot points away from your other foot.
3. Hold for a second or so, and then relax your ankle. Perform the required number of repetitions. Change legs and repeat.

EXERCISE 10.10: ANTERIOR TIBIAL MUSCLE STRETCH

Target Area: Quadriceps, anterior tibial muscles
Sets: 3
Duration: 20–30 seconds
Rest: 20 seconds

The muscles in front of the shin, including the tibialis anterior, can come under strain with repeated running, cycling and jumping activities. Pain can start after an activity level or type not previously done, and also when running in footwear that is too tight or too loose, or otherwise does not fit properly. The painful condition experienced may be a type of 'shin splints'. Try this stretch along with Key Exercise 10.5 to help keep this area flexible and functioning properly.

1. To perform the anterior tibial muscle stretch, stand up straight, with one foot flat on the ground and the other supported on the toes.
2. Pull the heel towards your buttocks by bending at the knee and holding the foot in a plantar-flexed position as shown in the image, so that you feel the stretch in the front of the shin. Keep the thighs parallel and push forwards at the hip to increase the stretch.
3. To add mobility at the ankle, you may want to rotate your ankle around slowly. Hold this position for 20–30 seconds. Change legs and repeat.

EXERCISE 10.11: CALF STRETCH

Primary Target Area: Ankle and calf muscles
Sets: 3
Duration: Hold for 20–30 seconds
Rest: 20 seconds

Stretching the calves is good practice for maintaining full ROM at the ankle and the knee, as the gastrocnemius muscle crosses both of these joints. The calf stretch also maintains the tone and length of the calf muscles and regularly loads the Achilles tendon. There are many ways to perform the stretch, but we have found that the following method is a practical approach to achieving the above aims, and can be adjusted to suit varying levels of flexibility.

1. To perform the calf stretch, stand facing a wall. Position the toes of one foot against the wall and the other foot approximately 60cm (24″) behind you. The feet should be pointing forwards.
2. Keeping the heel of your rear foot against the ground, lean forwards into the wall, supporting your weight with your arms. You should feel a stretch in the bottom of your rear leg; if not, move your rear foot further away from the wall.
3. Hold this position for 20–30 seconds, and then switch legs and repeat.

Teaching Points

If you find that the method outlined above does not provide sufficient stretch, you can perform it in the following way. Stand on the edge of a step or stair, with the toes of both feet just in contact with the platform. From this position, allow your heels to drop towards the ground. Keep lowering the heels until you reach the limit of your stretch, hold for the required amount of time and then rest.

■ Goal Exercises for the Lower Leg, Ankle and Foot

Goal exercises are suggested here for further developing the rehabilitation and resilience of the lower leg and ankle. These particular exercises can be added to your training programme to build strength and mobility, and also act as a test of your physical condition.

GOAL EXERCISE 10.12: SKIPPING

Target Area: Calf muscles, ankles, cardiovascular fitness
Sets: 3
Duration: 30–60 seconds
Rest: 45–60 seconds

There is no better exercise for working your calves and keeping you on your toes than skipping with a rope. If you take this exercise up for this first time, be warned that you will feel it in the calf muscles, so go easy at first. It is a classic exercise for boxers to get them bouncing on their toes and also to develop cardiovascular fitness.

1. With or without a skipping rope, start gently by bouncing on the balls of your feet, either transferring your weight from one foot to the other or distributing your weight evenly on both feet at the same time.
2. Once the calf muscles are warm, increase the depth of the bounce, again shifting your weight or maintaining equal load on the feet.
3. Now add in a few high jumps, tucking your knees towards your chest. Settle back into a bounce while you get your breath back. Repeat the high jumps when ready.

Teaching Points

When you get fitter and more confident, you can mix things up with single-leg skipping, doubling up the jumps per rope swing, or even crossing the rope. You will have calves like Rocky Balboa in no time with this body-weight winner!

(11)

The Spine

■ Introduction to the Spine

In this chapter we will explore the wondrous structure that is the spine. Although the spine is one continuous integral structure (Figure 11.1), it can be broken down from a movement and support perspective into three main sections:

- Cervical spine (neck)
- Thoracic spine (upper back)
- Lumbar spine (lower back)

When considering the global effects and benefits of body-weight exercise, it is difficult to say very much about the impact on neck problems, other than the benefits that come from improved neck and shoulder posture. Improving thoracic spine and shoulder posture can translate into significant reductions in general neck pain. This pain reduction occurs because the thoracic spine is the base on which the cervical spine sits, and having a slumped chest, ribcage and shoulders will lead to poor neck posture. Postural changes in the neck place the muscles, ligaments, joints and discs of the cervical spine under additional loads, thus leading to pain and dysfunction. Accordingly, the cervical spine section below will give a brief overview of the need-to-know anatomy of the neck to help you understand and appreciate the role of good posture. A key exercise to aid in addressing postural dysfunction of the neck will also be offered in due course.

Should your neck pain persist, or if you develop arm pain or symptoms such as pins and needles, reduced arm power or changes in sensation, you are advised to seek qualified and experienced assessment. You may find in this instance that strenuous activity of any type aggravates your neck pain, and so it would be unwise to persist with body-weight exercises in general.

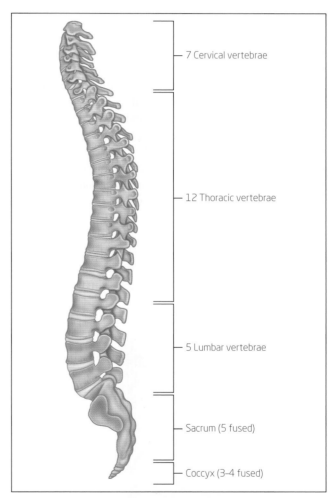

- 7 Cervical vertebrae

- 12 Thoracic vertebrae

- 5 Lumbar vertebrae

- Sacrum (5 fused)

- Coccyx (3–4 fused)

■ **Figure 11.1.** The spine (vertebral column), lateral view.

The thoracic and lumbar spines can be a common source of pain that can limit daily function; this could include problems such as twisting to reach for a seatbelt, bending to put on shoes and socks, and of course limitation of sport and exercise pursuits. These two spinal regions will also be given consideration here and will be outlined in relation to body-weight exercises to condition and rehabilitate this most crucial of body structures.

■ Functional Anatomy of the Spine

Cervical Spine

The neck is formed by the cervical spine, a critical structure that supports and moves the head. It houses the blood vessels and nervous tissue that connect the brain with the rest of the body, and is thus a vulnerable region. We would therefore not recommend loaded body-weight exercises here unless they are performed under the direction of a suitably qualified health or fitness professional.

Seven vertebral bones make up the cervical spine, with discs cushioning the spaces between them from the second to the seventh vertebrae and beyond. The cervical spine is built for mobility, with much of this movement coming from small facet joints on either side of adjacent vertebrae. In addition to the discs and the vertebral bones and their joints, the neck has multiple ligaments that reinforce the structures and their movements. The relationship of adjacent vertebrae and all of their shared structures is commonly referred to as a *motion segment*. An outline of the cervical spine structure can be seen in Figure 11.2.

The underlying shape of the vertebral bones and the discs gives the neck a natural forward curvature; this is termed a *lordosis*. The degree of postural lordosis differs in all of

us; however, given the modern lifestyles that many of us have, the cervical lordosis is likely to be an exaggerated one. Poor sitting postures and prolonged use of electronic screens, such as smartphones and laptops, can contribute to this. If you look at the motion segment illustrated in Figure 11.2, you may begin to appreciate the load that this increased postural lordosis places on the discs, facet joints and ligaments. To offload the stress of postural neck pain, we offer a key exercise in the common spinal dysfunction section below; this exercise will also stretch the short and tight muscles at the back of the neck, which may be giving you neck and head pain.

Each motion segment of the spine is acted upon by multiple muscles to create a complex pattern of movements. The movement of rotation mostly comes from the upper part of the neck, between the first and second cervical vertebrae (C1 and C2), while the movements of flexion, extension and side flexion come from the lower cervical section (C3 to C7). Some examples of the muscles acting on the neck are outlined in Figure 11.3.

As can be seen in Figure 11.3, there are many muscles in the neck region, and most of them have tricky names! There are also other muscles to be aware of, such as the trapezius muscles, but the great news is that you do not need to know about individual muscles. It is believed that the brain works in terms of movement patterns, not individual muscle recruitment; good-quality movements will therefore condition the muscles of the neck for normal functioning.

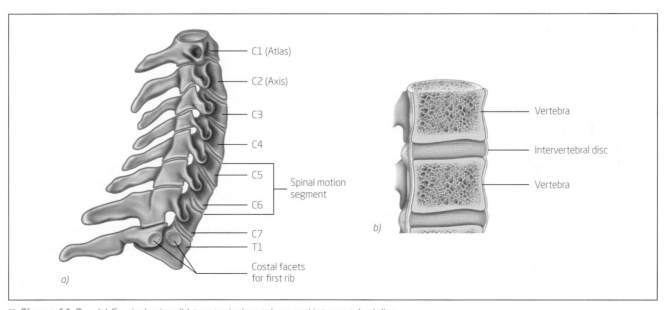

■ **Figure 11.2.** (a) Cervical spine; (b) two typical vertebrae and intervertebral disc.

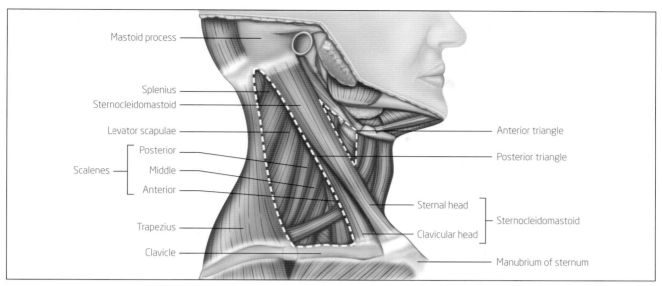

■ **Figure 11.3.** Muscles of the neck, lateral view.

KEY POINT: *The brain works in movement patterns, not individual muscle recruitment. Good-quality movements will condition the muscles of the neck for normal functioning.*

A final comment on neck anatomy should include a consideration of the nerve roots. These neural structures emerge at each level of the spine from above the first cervical vertebra (C1) to beyond the lowest level of the lumbar spine (L5), as we shall see later. There are eight nerve roots leaving either side of the cervical spine, as can be seen in Figure 11.4, and irritation or impingement of these structures can give you symptoms in the head, neck, shoulder, arm or hand. A suitably qualified health or medical professional should assess such symptoms before you start any physical activity, including body-weight exercise. You may find, however, that simple ROM exercises (for example, Key Exercise 11.2) may ease some of your symptoms. Our advice would be to maintain these movements within your pain-free range.

Thoracic Spine

Compared with the spinal regions lying above and below it, the thoracic spine is a relatively stiff area. The ribcage contributes to this immobility by fixing most of the thoracic spine to the breast bone (sternum) at the front of the chest. The major benefit of this is that the internal organs of the heart and lungs are protected in a bony cage. There is, however, a certain amount flexing in this spinal region, as you will notice when you breathe in and out. It is this small degree of movement, and the

structures that facilitate it, that can come under strain and generate pain.

The basic structure of the thoracic spine (Figure 11.5) follows the same blueprint that gave us the cervical spine outlined earlier. Twelve thicker vertebral bones are all cushioned by discs that transmit an increasing load from structures above; the discs also act to stabilise this

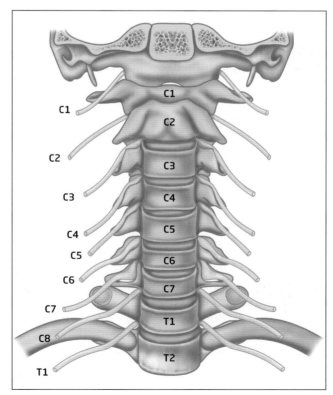

■ **Figure 11.4.** Cervical spine nerve roots.

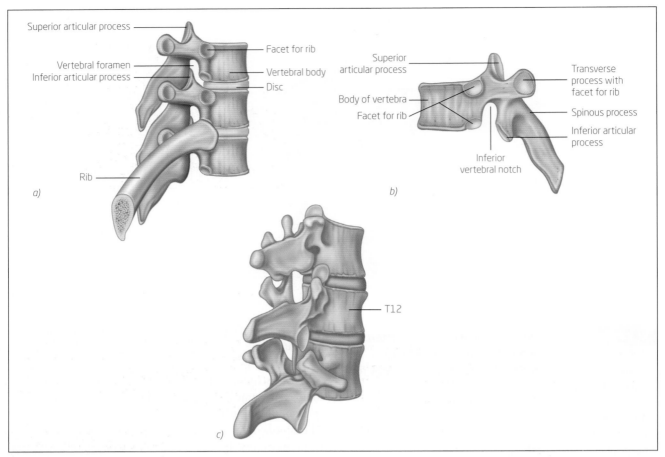

Superior articular process

Facet for rib

Vertebral foramen

Vertebral body

Inferior articular process

Disc

Rib

a)

Superior articular process

Transverse process with facet for rib

Body of vertebra

Facet for rib

Spinous process

Inferior articular process

Inferior vertebral notch

b)

T12

c)

■ **Figure 11.5.**   (a) Thoracic spine; b) typical thoracic vertebra [T6]; (c) the change in angle between the facet joints lends itself to the movements that are possible at each section of vertebrae.

section of the spine. The combination of these structures, along with the ligaments and rib attachments, means that the thoracic spine has limited movement. That said, the facet joints of the thoracic spine are angled to allow greater rotation than the lumbar spine, while still allowing some forward flexion, side flexion and extension. In the space created in front of the thoracic facet joints, the pairs of nerve roots leave at each level from below T1 to T12. Symptoms from these structures are thought to be relatively rare.

Unlike the cervical and lumbar spines, the thoracic spine creates a natural backward curvature called a *kyphosis*. This completes a springy 'S' shape, which gives the spine its load-bearing capabilities. It is therefore a perfectly natural curve that varies between individuals; however, as discussed in the case of the cervical spine, the lumbar curve can be exaggerated with poor posture. The effects of increased postural loads will be explained in more detail in the section on common spinal problems.

Lumbar Spine

The lumbar spine forms the lowest part of the mobile spine regions and sits on the sacral bones. Its natural forward curvature, known as the *lumbar lordosis*, is a secondary curve that forms in humans once we begin to walk. Comprising five vertebral bones and intervening intervertebral discs, the chunky lumbar spine reflects its load-bearing role, as can be seen in Figure 11.6.

The facet joints in this spinal region are oriented in such a way as to limit rotation, which was more freely available in the thoracic spine. The lumbar spine, however, has at its disposal a good range of flexion and extension movements, which are ultimately restrained by the discs and ligaments. Sustained extremes of lumbar spine flexion due to postural strain will stress the lumbar discs and ligaments, causing them to *creep*. This is a term commonly used in material sciences to describe the tendency for solid structures to deform under prolonged stress. The results of this phenomenon will be explored further when we discuss common lower back problems.

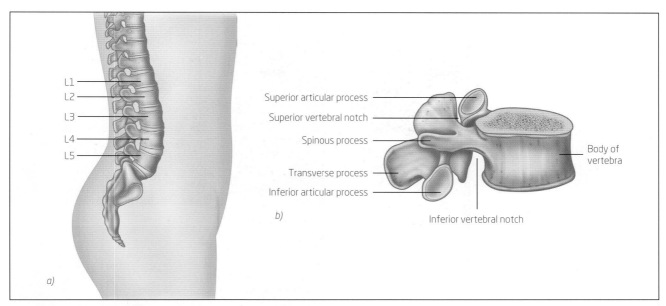

■ **Figure 11.6.** (a) Lumbar spine; (b) typical lumbar vertebra (L3).

> **KEY POINT:** *Lumbar spinal discs and ligaments can slowly deform under sustained loads, such as poor posture. Prevention is better than cure, so work on good posture and avoid prolonged postures.*

There are five pairs of spinal nerves in the lumbar spine, which exit at their corresponding levels on either side of the bony spinal column. These nerve roots can supply various sections of the buttocks and legs, down to the feet and toes. The nerves can be susceptible to mechanical irritation as they travel within the bony spinal column or as they exit it. If you have symptoms of pain, changes in sensation, or weakness of the legs, we strongly recommend that you seek qualified health or medical advice before commencing any corrective exercise, including body-weight exercise.

In the absence of these symptoms, some common causes of spinal pain and dysfunction will now be examined, along with some body-weight exercises to condition and rehabilitate the spine.

■ Common Spinal Dysfunction

Postural Dysfunction of the Neck

We have already discussed several functions of the spinal column, from providing support and movement, to protecting the internal organs of the chest. The spinal column also houses the spinal cord, which connects the body with the brain. The neck, however, has one crucial function that we should not overlook – it must position the head in such a way that our senses can operate effectively.

Take a moment to think about how you position your head in order to hear a faint sound or to adjust your visual field. And what about the inner ear, which maintains your balance? A poorly positioned head means major disruption to this delicate balance system.

> **KEY POINT:** *The neck must position itself in such a way that it sustains the ability of the head to operate the senses of vision and hearing, and also to maintain balance, effectively.*

When the rest of your spine is slumped in a poor posture, the neck must then make up the difference in order for the head to maintain its position. This is often the basis of cervical spine postural dysfunction. It is a relatively common condition, causing pain in the neck when there is no significant trauma or tissue damage.

Adopting poor spinal postures over a prolonged period of time is the main cause of this condition. This can be any position, but more often than not it involves the modern-day curses of sitting, watching television, driving a car or using a computer. Increasingly sedentary lifestyles or working patterns can therefore lead to muscle weakness and lengthening, while other muscles at the neck and shoulders become tight and overactive.

An example of how these muscle imbalances can develop is given in Figure 11.7, which shows a posture that increases the load of the head by more than three times its normal weight. This load can be as much as 20kg, or 45lb! Just imagine this extra stress on your neck structures every day!

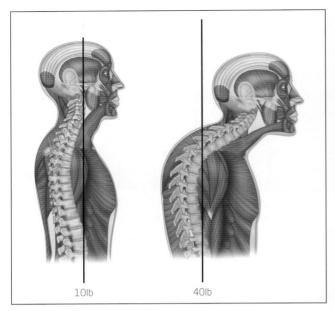

■ **Figure 11.7.** Cervical postural dysfunction.

KEY EXERCISE 11.1: NECK RETRACTION

Target Area: Cervical spine
Sets: 2
Reps: 10
Rest: 20 seconds

The neck retraction is great for addressing the problem of a pronounced postural lordosis in the neck.

1. To perform the neck retraction, stand up in a relaxed position.
2. Allow the neck and head to settle into a neutral position. Draw your shoulders gently away from your ears and imagine your neck lengthening.
3. Now move your chin directly backwards in a horizontal plane. You should feel your neck muscles below your jaw tense gently in effort. Feel the stretch at the base of your skull and at the back of the neck.
4. Hold this position for a few seconds, and then return your head to the starting position. This counts as one repetition.

Teaching Points

The main issue with the neck retraction exercise is not moving the head directly backwards, but rather tilting or pivoting it in order to lower the chin. To resolve this issue, it can help to film yourself performing the exercise, or get a friend or training partner to watch you.

Postural Dysfunction of the Thoracic Spine

Postural dysfunction, or postural syndrome, can also affect the upper back (thoracic spine) and is a relatively common cause of pain in this region of the spine in the absence of any trauma. If you are experiencing pain from postural syndrome, this will mainly occur while doing activities that place prolonged stress on your otherwise normal spinal structures.

Postural syndrome in the upper back occurs in a similar fashion to the cervical spine, through sitting or standing in poor positions for prolonged periods of time. This may even include sports such as cycling or hockey.

With prolonged sitting or standing, the thoracic spine can begin to slouch under the effects of gravity. The thoracic kyphosis increases, and as the ribcage slumps, the shoulder blades slide forwards, causing the shoulders to round. The neck must now increase its lordosis posture to compensate for the thoracic spine, because otherwise your line of sight would angle towards the floor. Try it for yourself and see what happens when you do not adapt the posture at the neck. Before too long, you will begin to realise why upper back, neck and shoulder pain and dysfunction occur. We have not even started on the lower back yet!

KEY POINT: *As the thoracic kyphosis increases with postural stress, the shoulders slump forwards and become rounded and the neck lordosis must increase in order to compensate.*

KEY EXERCISE 11.2: UPPER SPINE FOAM ROLL

Target Area: Thoracic spine
Sets: 3
Duration: 30 seconds
Rest: 30 seconds

Foam rolling is great for working knotted and sore areas of the targeted muscles. Your body weight is used to massage the sore areas. By the very nature of the body position, this exercise will reduce the thoracic kyphosis and unload that postural strain!

1. To perform the upper spine foam roll, sit down on the ground with the foam roller behind you.
2. Lie back onto the roller so that it is positioned across the lower parts of your shoulder blades. Raise your hips off the ground. Plant your feet with bent knees.
3. Wrap your arms around you so that your back is rounded. This will make it easier to target the middle spine and ribs.
4. Roll backwards and forwards slowly, starting from the top of your back and moving down to just above the lower back. If there are any sore areas, pay particular attention to these parts. Roll for 30 seconds and then rest. While resting, you may find that you get a beneficial stretch by allowing the middle spine to arch over the foam roller.

Teaching Points

When first starting to foam roll, you will need to use a soft foam roller, as this will be the least painful. As you progress, you can move on to harder rollers, which will support the spine more and apply firmer pressure to the soft tissues.

Rib Joint Dysfunction (Thoracic Spine)

Rib joint dysfunction has been regarded as a potentially common problem that involves poor joint stability where the ribs meet the thoracic spine. The joints here are relatively shallow, making them susceptible to mechanical over-stressing. Pain is often sudden, sometimes after working in a rotated-spine position. Deep breathing, stretching the spine backwards and performing rotational spinal movements may worsen the pain. Such a problem can be a result of underlying poor postural habits, as explained above. Symptoms often settle after a few days. To reduce the chance of recurrence, and to ease the pain associated with this condition, we offer Key Exercise 11.3.

KEY EXERCISE 11.3: UPPER BACK STRETCH

Target Area: Thoracic and cervical spines
Sets: 3
Duration: 20 seconds each side
Rest: 30 seconds

Stretching the muscles of the upper back is important in view of modern-day postures. In addition to stretching the muscles of the back, this exercise will also provide some gentle traction to the middle spine and the ribs.

The stretching exercise for the upper back is simple and effective, and can be performed almost anywhere.

1. To perform the upper back stretch, hold onto a solid object. If you are in a gym, a bar or frame of some sort will be perfect, provided it cannot move. If you are at home, a doorframe or any other solid object will suffice.
2. Keep the working arm straight, and wrap your free arm around yourself.
3. Now lean back, keeping your feet flat on the ground and dropping your hips if necessary. You may need to twist your body slightly in order to transfer the stretch to all areas of the muscle.
4. Hold the stretch for 20 seconds, and then switch sides and repeat.

Teaching Points

If you experience any natural popping or clicking of the spine with this exercise, please be reassured that this is quite normal. Do not force your spine to make these noises, though; if they occur naturally during a stretch, then that is fine.

Try this exercise along with Key Exercise 11.2 for a more effective approach to this problem.

Thoracic Disc Dysfunction

Thoracic disc dysfunction is a less common condition and will therefore be covered only briefly here. Some reports in the literature suggest a rate of one in a thousand, while others have proposed one in a million. When the condition is minor and uncomplicated, intermittent thoracic pain may be experienced, usually in the lower region, and is worse with sitting, rotating or side-bending. There may even be some pain around the chest or from the back to the front. In these situations, we suggest trying Key Exercise 11.4.

If there are signs of changes in control and sensation of the legs, bladder or bowel, we recommend urgent medical attention.

KEY EXERCISE 11.4: COBRA STRETCH

Target Area: Thoracic and lumbar spines
Sets: 3
Duration: 10–20 seconds
Rest: 30 seconds

The cobra stretch is designed to target the lower abdominal muscles, and to stretch through the thoracic and lumbar spines. It is a good stretch to perform if you have a low level of spinal flexibility, and also if you have been doing some demanding core exercise.

1. To perform the cobra stretch, lie face down with your hands flat on the floor. Stretch your legs out behind you.
2. Push up with your arms, keeping your hips in contact with the ground. Curl your spine and look up at the ceiling until you feel the stretch in your back or abdominal muscles.
3. Try to extend your elbows to maximise the stretch. If you are able, you can breathe out as you arch backwards in order to increase the stretch a little at a time. Hold this position for 10–20 seconds, and then release slowly and rest.

Teaching Points

If you are not strong enough to support yourself with your arms, you can perform this stretch by supporting yourself on your forearms.

Lower Back Pain

Most lower back pain is non-serious in nature and is likely to improve over time, with the possibility of intermittent pain flare-ups. Some research suggests that up to 35% of the UK adult population will suffer back pain at any one time, with up to 80% of the same population experiencing some back pain over their lifetime. It is therefore reasonable to say that back pain is a common occurrence in the human life span. Some might even suggest that it is 'normal' for it to occur at some point within the human lifetime according to the statistics. That said, there are some causes of back pain that are more serious; if you are in any doubt, you should see a qualified health or medical professional.

The following sections will deal with non-serious and common causes of lower back pain that have the potential to respond very well to physical activity. Accordingly, we will suggest some appropriate body-weight exercises for you to consider.

Nonspecific Lower Back Pain

Nonspecific lower back pain or *simple lower back pain* are common terms for lower back pain that is non-serious and has no clear single cause with regard to the pain and dysfunction being experienced. The majority of cases of this type of back pain improve within four months, although it is acknowledged that pain can persist in some for up to a year. What we hope has become clear so far in this book is that the human musculoskeletal system is incredibly complex, and the spine is probably the best example of this with all of its intricate structures. From reading other parts of this book, you will also have noticed that we have avoided the use of specific diagnostic titles in many areas; you will have seen that we have justified this position from a perspective of increased knowledge of human pain. You may need to read that last sentence again – we know more about pain now than we have ever done in the past, yet we use less specific diagnostic terminology for many musculoskeletal problems. Nonspecific back pain is a prime example of this, and we will now explain why in relation to the pain you may be experiencing.

Any structure in the lumbar spine that is supplied by nerves (which is most of it) can cause symptoms of lower back pain and even referred pain to the buttocks, legs or feet. This long list of potential pain-causing structures has already been highlighted in the spine anatomy and briefly includes the muscles, ligaments, nerve roots, facet joints, discs, vertebral bones and even the connective tissue that wraps around nearly everything else in the spine.

At this point you are probably thinking, 'Yes, but wouldn't a scan of my spine show which of these structures is causing my pain?' Unless there is a single serious cause of your back pain, which is less common, the answer is, 'No, it wouldn't.' For example, evidence of a herniated disc has been observed with medical imaging, such as CT and MRI scans, in 20% to 75% of people with no sciatic pain. This means that some people with disc problems will have back pain, while others with similar-looking disc problems on the medical imaging pictures will have no symptoms.

If you have nonspecific or simple lower back pain and you have been checked by a medical or health professional, you may benefit from 'nonspecific' body-weight exercises that stretch and strengthen your spine and other body areas. Over time, these exercises will condition you to move better and to withstand the physical stresses and strains of modern living. We recommend Key Exercises 11.4 and 11.5, but if you currently have little or no lower back pain, try the body-weight winner Key Exercise 11.5.

KEY EXERCISE 11.5: PLANK

Target Area: Thoracic and lumbar spines
Sets: 3
Duration: 10–60 seconds, depending on ability
Rest: 30 seconds

Perhaps the simplest and most effective exercise for the core, and therefore the spine, is the plank. The plank consists of holding the body horizontally, with support on the forearms and toes. The main areas worked by this exercise are the muscles supporting the thoracic and lumbar spine. It is a great introductory exercise that can be expanded in many ways.

1. To perform the plank, place your forearms on the ground. Stretch your legs out behind you and balance on your toes.
2. Make sure that your upper arms are vertical, and then raise your hips up until they are level with your shoulders. Your back should be as straight as possible, with no sagging of the lower back.
3. If you feel a pinching or straining sensation in the lower back, try to tuck your tailbone under in order to reduce the pressure here and to maintain a stronger and more neutral spine position.

Teaching Points

If this version of the plank is too difficult, you can make it easier by resting on your knees instead of your toes; this will reduce the amount of body weight being supported by the core. You can also rest your arms on a raised platform to move more of your body weight onto the lower body.

Lumbar Disc and Joint Degenerative Changes

Generally speaking, this is a problem more likely to be seen in the older age group, and is a gradual change in the mobility of the facet joints of the spine and the movement available due to the intervertebral discs (Figure 11.8). If you start to develop a stiff spine suddenly or at a relatively young age, we suggest that you have an assessment by a suitably qualified health or medical professional.

You may have noticed that your spinal movements have gradually stiffened and eventually given rise to lower back pain with no recent injury. If you find that bending forwards is relatively easy, but straightening your spine or flexing to the sides is more difficult or uncomfortable, then you could be suffering from degenerative changes to the spinal column. This may or may not show on x-rays of the spine; moreover, studies have found degenerative changes on spinal x-rays in the absence of lower back pain. If you have been advised by a qualified health or medical professional to exercise and mobilise your spine, we recommend Key Exercise 11.6.

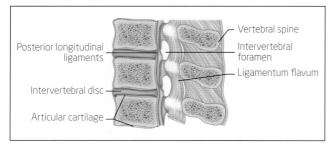

■ **Figure 11.8.** Anatomy of the lumbar spine and the intervertebral disc.

KEY EXERCISE 11.6: STANDING SIDE STRETCH

Target Area: Thoracic and lumbar spines
Sets: 3 each side
Duration: 20 seconds each side
Rest: 30 seconds

The standing side stretch is designed to increase the mobility in both the thoracic and the lumbar spine. You will feel a stretch in the oblique muscles and possibly around the spine itself. The oblique muscles at the sides of the core aid in bending and twisting motions, and may have tightened because of a stiff spine.

1. To perform the standing side stretch, stand with your feet shoulder-width apart and your arms by your sides.
2. Bend at the waist and start to slide one hand down your side. You should feel the stretch in the extended side of your core.
3. Keep going until you reach the limit of your mobility. Hold the stretch for 20 seconds, change sides and repeat.

Teaching Points

If you find that this method does not give you a sufficiently satisfying stretch, you can raise one arm and reach over to the side of your torso. Reaching with the arm in this way will also help maintain or develop shoulder mobility.

■ Body-weight Exercises for Improved Spine Function

The following exercises have been put together to assist you in further alleviating back and neck pain, or to help develop a resilient and injury-resistant spine.

EXERCISE 11.7: LOWER SPINE FOAM ROLL

Target Area: Lumbar spine
Sets: 3
Duration: 10–30 seconds, depending on tolerance
Rest: 30 seconds

Continuing our look at spinal foam rolling, we arrive at the lumbar spine. Many factors can contribute to lower back pain, some of which may be muscular in origin. Foam rolling is a great way to 'iron out' some of that muscular tension.

1. To perform the lower spine foam roll, sit down on the ground with the foam roller behind you.
2. Lie back onto the roller so that it is positioned across your lower back. In order to create the pressure against the low back, you may need to slightly raise your hips off the ground. Plant your feet with bent knees.
3. Place your arms on the ground behind you, supporting your weight.
4. Roll backwards and forwards slowly, concentrating on the bottom of your back. After you have rolled for around 20 seconds, pause at the bottom of your spine and allow your back to curl over the foam roller. Hold this position for 10–30 seconds.

Teaching Points

As before, if you are just starting to foam roll, you will want to begin with a soft foam roller. This will be less uncomfortable and will allow you to build up to harder rollers.

EXERCISE 11.8: CAT STRETCH

Target Area: Thoracic, cervical and lumbar spines
Sets: 3
Duration: 30 seconds
Rest: 30 seconds

For anybody who has mobility or flexibility issues with the thoracic area of the spine, the cat stretch is a good starting point. It is a stretch that is often seen in yoga and other flexibility programmes, and is an essential exercise in our bulletproof programme.

1. To perform the cat stretch, get down onto your hands and knees. Your arms and thighs should be vertical. Your neck should be relaxed and your eyes looking down.
2. From here, push your spine up towards the ceiling. Think about separating your shoulder blades and tucking your tailbone under.
3. Push up as far as you can, and then hold for 30 seconds.

Teaching Points

Moving the spine in this way can be difficult, especially if you are struggling to know what muscles to use to make the movement happen. To help with this, try arching your back and sticking your buttocks out first, and then push your spine up towards the ceiling. You will find that this helps to activate the opposing muscle groups, and you will be able to feel which muscles to use. You will also develop better awareness of your spinal posture.

EXERCISE 11.9: SKYDIVER

Target Area: Thoracic and lumbar spines
Sets: 3
Duration: 20 seconds
Rest: 30 seconds

The skydiver exercise works the extensor muscles of the lower back and develops active extension of the lumbar spine. Many people might struggle with this movement, because the muscles running down the spine (the erector spinae group) are weak in many of us. It is very important to strengthen these muscles to support proper spinal function.

1. To perform the skydiver, lie face down with your arms out in front of you, elbows bent at 90 degrees.
2. Now use the muscles of your back to raise your legs and your upper body off the ground. The muscles of the upper and middle back will work to hold the upper body off the floor, while the lumbar muscles of the lower back will work to hold the legs off the floor.
3. Raise your upper and lower body off the ground as far as you can, and then hold this position for 20 seconds.

Teaching Points
When performing the skydiver, think about squeezing all of the muscles of the back, including the buttocks; this will ensure that you get the maximum benefit out of the movement. In addition, try not to bounce, and stay as still as possible once in the skydiver position. Try also not to strain the hamstrings at the backs of your thighs.

EXERCISE 11.10: SIDE PLANK

Target Area: Thoracic and lumbar spines
Sets: 2
Duration: 10–60 seconds each side
Rest: 30 seconds

Although the plank works the core very well, the demand on the muscles in the sides of the core (the obliques) is much less. To target these muscles more effectively, we can perform the side plank; this uses the same principle as the plank, in that the body is held rigid, using gravity as the resistance. The key here is to hold a good 'neutral' spinal posture against the force of gravity.

1. To perform the side plank, lie on your side with your lower forearm flat on the floor, at 90 degrees to your body.
2. Place both legs together with one foot on top of the other.
3. From here, raise your hips into the air, until a straight line can be drawn through your shoulders, hips, knees and ankles. Place your free arm by your side, in the air, or touching the ground to help with balance.
4. Keeping your head and neck neutral, hold this position for the required time, and then rest and repeat on the opposite side.

Teaching Points

The side plank should be manageable for short lengths of time, even for those who have not trained before. If you do find it difficult to perform, you can adapt it in the same way as the normal plank, by resting on the knees instead of the feet; this reduces the proportion of weight supported by the core, and therefore makes the exercise easier.

EXERCISE 11.11: SIDE LEAN

Target Area: Thoracic and lumbar spines
Sets: 3
Reps: 10 (5 each side)
Rest: 20 seconds

The side lean helps to strengthen the lumbar and thoracic spines, and aids in working on any poor side-leaning postures you may have developed. The exercise will help to increase the flexibility of your spine as well. For this exercise, you will need a light bar, such as a broom handle or exercise barbell.

1. To perform the side lean, grasp the bar with a wide grip and hold it above your head. Stand with your feet wide apart so that your entire body forms a large 'X' shape.
2. From here, bend over to one side at the waist, controlling the movement using the muscles in the sides of your core. Keep your arms straight at all times, and do not allow your shoulders to move towards your head; the movement must come just from your waist.
3. Once you have leant as far as you can, return to the upright position and repeat on the other side. This counts as one repetition.

Teaching Points

The main area that requires attention in this exercise is ensuring that the arms stay straight and relatively static in relation to the head. It is tempting to allow the arms to move independently of the spine, but this is not correct form. Maintaining proper form will make the movement much more effective.

EXERCISE 11.12: REAR SUPPORT

Target Area: Thoracic and lumbar spines, shoulders
Sets: 3
Duration: 10–30 seconds
Rest: 30 seconds

The rear support is another static move that targets most of the muscles of the back, in addition to the shoulders and other muscles of the upper body. All in all, it is a great example of using body-weight exercise to become injury-proof. As an exercise, it is the polar opposite of the plank, and works the opposing muscles groups. It is harder than the plank, mainly because the position is not one that the human body is placed in very often.

1. To perform the rear support, sit on the ground with your hands flat on the floor, fingers pointing backwards, and your legs straight out in front of you.
2. From here push your hips into the air, keeping your arms straight.
3. Keep pushing your hips up into the air until a straight line can be drawn through your shoulders, hips, knees and ankles. Balance on your heels.
4. Keep your head neutral and neck straight. Hold this position for the required time, and then rest.

Teaching Points

You may find that at first you do not have either the strength to perform the movement, or the shoulder flexibility to allow the position. The bar shoulder dislocate (Chapter 5, Exercise 5.11) will help here, as will the other shoulder stretching exercises. In addition, the exercise can also be performed with the hands resting on a raised platform so that they are higher than the feet. This will make the movement easier to perform, allowing the hands to be moved closer to the ground over time.

EXERCISE 11.13: DISH

Target Area: Thoracic spine, core muscles
Sets: 3
Duration: 20–30 seconds
Rest: 30 seconds

If the strength of the core is increased, the resilience of the spine to injury is also increased. Developing muscle around the torso, and making the muscles that reside there as resilient as possible, constitute a good course of action for injury prevention. The dish exercise will take your strength to the next level.

1. To perform the dish, lie on your back with your legs straight and your arms by your sides.
2. From here curl your shoulders off the ground and lift your feet and arms about 5cm (2″) into the air at the same time.
3. Keep your pelvis pressed into the ground, while allowing your upper back to rise. To help with this movement, think of trying to curl your body around a large ball.
4. Hold this position for the required time, and then rest.

Teaching Points

Although it looks like it might be easy, the dish is a tough exercise and much trickier to perform properly than the plank. To make it easier, you can bend your knees to bring the weight of your legs closer to your centre of gravity; if you do this, make sure that your feet stay close to the ground, with only your knees bending. As you progress, extend your legs until they are straight.

EXERCISE 11.14: BRIDGE

Target Area: Spine, buttocks, hips
Sets: 3
Duration: 10–20 seconds
Rest: 30 seconds

One of the best movements for spinal health is the bridge, or 'back bend'; this type of movement is used in gymnastics, calisthenics and even yoga. Another bulletproof classic, the bridge is more difficult to perform than many movements in this book, but the benefits cannot be overstated. As this exercise is so tough, not just strengthwise but also in terms of mobility and flexibility, take your time with it.

1. To perform the bridge, lie down on your back and bend your knees so that your feet are flat on the floor. Make sure that your feet are not too far away from your buttocks, but not too close either.
2. Lift your arms into the air and place your palms on the ground, fingers pointing towards your feet. This position will require good shoulder and wrist flexibility; if this is lacking, you should spend time on the relevant exercises in Chapters 5 and 7 of this book.

EXERCISE 11.15: EXTENDED PLANK

Target Area: Thoracic and lumbar spines, core muscles
Sets: 3
Duration: 5–15 seconds
Rest: 30 seconds

3. Making sure that your hands and feet are firmly planted, try to push your torso into the air. Use all of the muscles of your back to do this, while straightening your arms and legs as much as possible.
4. Once you have pushed your torso up as high as possible, hold the position for the required amount of time, and then rest.

Teaching Points

There is no doubt that the bridge is one of the most difficult exercises in this chapter; for this reason, make sure that you only attempt it when you are ready. In terms of making the movement easier, this can be achieved by moving the hands and feet further apart. As your flexibility and strength increase, you can move your hands and feet closer together, which will place more demand on the flexibility and mobility of the spine and shoulders.

If you have mastered the plank and want to take your strength to the next level, you can try the extended plank. This is a variable exercise, in that it can be made more or less difficult depending on your strength. In terms of equipment, make sure that the floor you perform this movement on is as non-slip as possible.

1. To perform the extended plank, assume a standard push-up position. Your hands should be shoulder-width apart and your arms vertical, and you should be balancing on your toes.
2. Now walk your hands forwards slowly until you feel the muscles in your core working to hold the position.
3. Keep your neck and head neutral and arms straight, and hold the position for as long as you can, aiming for 15 seconds.

Teaching Points

The extended plank is an exercise with great scope. If you need to make this exercise easier, move your hands and feet closer together; if you need to make it more difficult, move them further apart. The end goal of this movement is to hold the position with the chest and torso very close to, but not touching, the ground; this will stress the spine and the core, building high levels of strength and injury resistance.

■ Goal Exercises for the Spine

As in the case of other body parts, the spine and core have their own goal exercises; these are designed to test and build overall strength and mobility, and will give you a clear picture of how your core strength and spinal mobility are progressing. The movements can also be used as exercises in their own right, as part of a larger routine, or once you need a greater challenge in your workouts.

GOAL EXERCISE 11.16: KNEELING ROLL-OUT

Target Area: Thoracic and lumbar spines
Sets: 3
Reps: 5–10
Rest: 45 seconds

The kneeling roll-out is an extremely tough but useful exercise, but is nowhere near as popular or well known as it ought to be. The reason for both the difficulty and the benefits of this exercise is that the core is forced to keep the spine in a stable position while exerting tremendous amounts of force. This means that the kneeling roll-out differs from movements such as sit-ups and crunches, which *shorten* the length of the torso. This exercise, which requires an abdominal wheel, will develop strength and injury resistance while working with the spine as a long lever.

1. To perform the kneeling roll-out, get down onto your knees and hold the abdominal wheel with both hands.
2. Ensure that your elbows are straight, your spine is horizontal and your thighs are vertical. This is the starting and finishing position.
3. Begin to roll the wheel forwards, keeping your arms and legs at the same relative angle throughout the movement.
4. Keep the head and neck position neutral, and roll forwards until your chest touches the ground. Pause for a second, and then reverse the movement until you arrive back in the starting position. This counts as one repetition.

Teaching Points

As the kneeling roll-out is such a tough exercise, most people will have to make the movement easier in order to progress with it. Rolling the abdominal wheel into a wall or other solid object can help here. To use this method, assume the starting position, with the abdominal wheel a small distance away from the base of the wall or a solid, stationary object. Roll forwards until the wheel stops against the wall, and then use your core muscles to roll back again. Begin with the wheel close to the wall and move steadily further away until you can perform the kneeling roll-out with no assistance.

GOAL EXERCISE 11.17: HANGING LEG RAISE

Target Area: Thoracic spine
Sets: 3
Reps: 5–10
Rest: 45 seconds

The hanging leg raise is an excellent test of core strength, while also encouraging spinal mobility in the same exercise. It is a standard movement in gymnastic circles, and uses the weight of the lower body as the resistance. You will need a pull-up bar or gymnastic rings.

1. Grab onto a pull-up bar with an overhand grip; the hands should be shoulder-width apart or slightly wider.
2. Hang with a straight body and straight legs, with the scapulae engaged and the shoulders pulled down.
3. Contract your core muscles and begin to raise your legs into the air, bending at the waist. Pull down hard with your upper body to stop any momentum.
4. Keep raising your legs until they are at least horizontal. You may even strive to reach a higher position, to touch your hands with your toes!
5. Pause for a second, and then return your legs to the starting position, always under control.

Teaching Points

If the full version of the hanging leg raise is too difficult for you, it can be made easier by doing a hanging knee raise; this is performed in exactly the same way, except that the knees are bent and brought up to the chest, instead of the legs being kept straight. With your knees bent, more of your body weight is kept closer to your centre of gravity, and so the resistance that the core muscles are working against will feel much less. As your core strength increases, you can progress to straightening your legs a little at a time.

Another issue that can affect one's ability to perform the leg raise is a lack of flexibility in the hamstrings. To remedy this, spend time on increasing flexibility in this area, most notably with the hamstring stretch (Key Exercise 8.3).

GOAL EXERCISE 11.18: ARCH-UP

Target Area: Thoracic and lumbar spines
Sets: 3
Reps: 10
Rest: 30 seconds

One goal exercise that concentrates on the lumbar spine is the arch-up. This is an extension of the skydiver exercise, and requires the arms and legs to be stretched out from your centre of gravity.

1. To perform the arch-up, lie face down with your arms stretched out in front of you and your legs straight behind you. This is the starting position.

2. From here, raise your arms and legs into the air at the same time, contracting the muscles in your back.
3. Keep raising your arms and legs as far as possible, aiming to get them well into the air.
4. Pause for a second, and then return your arms and legs to the starting position. This counts as one repetition.

Teaching Points

For many people, the arch-up should not pose too much of a problem; the real challenge is in developing enough strength and mobility to raise the upper body and legs high into the air. This is something that will develop with time. Stick with it!

12
Upper Body Training Programmes

Note: *It is worth reiterating that the training programmes outlined over the next few chapters are guides only, and not every part of every programme will be applicable to every reader. For example, if you have a particular shoulder injury, you may be able to perform the shoulder exercises only at the beginner level, but the lower body and spinal exercises at the advanced level. This is normal and should be expected in these situations.*

Now that you have an idea of the anatomy of each joint, and are familiar with the injuries that can occur and the exercises that will help to build injury prevention in each area, it is time to look at various training programmes. These guides will consolidate all of this knowledge in a structured way that you can follow in your training sessions and workouts.

■ Upper Body: Beginner Programme

The upper body programme actually consists of three separate programmes, divided into beginner, intermediate and advanced levels of ability. The beginner programme can be seen in Table 12.1. Notice that the name of the exercise, the number of sets, the number of repetitions or the duration, and the amount of rest time is included for ease of use.

As you can see, in this beginner programme there are exercises for the wrist, elbow and shoulder. Ideally you will follow the programme from top to bottom, performing each exercise for the required number of sets and repetitions before moving on to the next exercise, progressing all the way down the table until you finish. A programme like this will be extremely beneficial if you introduce it into your routine. As it will not take a huge

■ **Table 12.1.** Upper body: beginner programme.

	Sets	Reps/duration	Rest
Wrist exercises			
Forearm and wrist stretch 1	3	20 seconds	20 seconds
Forearm and wrist stretch 2	3	20 seconds	20 seconds
Push-up support	3	20 seconds	20 seconds
Elbow exercises			
Inverted-wrist wall push-up	3	5–20, depending on strength	30 seconds
Ledge dip	3	10	45 seconds
Arm rotation	3	10	20 seconds
Shoulder exercises			
Chest stretch	3	15 seconds	10 seconds
Shoulder stretch	3	15 seconds	10 seconds
Rotator cuff stretch	3	10 seconds	10 seconds
Scapula foam roll	3	10 seconds	30–45 seconds

amount of time, it is possible to perform this programme three to five times a week without it impacting on your life too much.

In your weekly training schedule, you will need some rest days, and so a week in which you train three times might be as follows:

Monday:	Train
Tuesday:	Rest
Wednesday:	Train
Thursday:	Rest
Friday:	Train
Saturday:	Rest
Sunday:	Rest

This method can be followed for the other programmes set out in Chapters 12, 13, 14 and 15.

■ Upper Body: Intermediate Programme

Once you have some experience with the beginner programme, or when the exercises in it do not present much of a challenge, you can move on to the intermediate programme (Table 12.2), which is suitable for those with intermediate ability. These exercises will still work the same joints and muscles, though in slightly different ways, but the benefits will nevertheless be felt. Again, as there are a limited number of exercises specified, this entire programme can be performed three to five times a week comfortably, with rest days inserted in between your training days.

■ **Table 12.2.** Upper body: intermediate programme.

	Sets	Reps/duration	Rest
Wrist exercises			
Fist push-up support	3	20 seconds	30 seconds
Fingertip push-up support	3	10–20 seconds	30 seconds
Elbow exercises			
Forklift	3	5–10, depending on strength	30 seconds
Planche lean	3	10 seconds	30 seconds
Shoulder exercises			
Dead hang	3	20 seconds	30 seconds
Scapula push-up	3	10	30 seconds
Band shoulder dislocate	3	10	20 seconds

■ Upper Body: Advanced Programme

Once the exercises in the intermediate programme become too easy, or if you are looking for more variation and a greater challenge, you can move on to the advanced programme (Table 12.3), which contains exercises suitable for advanced exercisers. The same method should be followed here: perform all of the exercises (if possible), for the required number of sets, number of repetitions or duration, and rest times, until you have worked your way through the table and completed all of the exercises. Again, as there are only eight exercises here, performing the programme three to five times a week is possible, and recommended.

■ **Table 12.3.** Upper body: advanced programme.

	Sets	Reps/duration	Rest
Wrist exercises			
Inverted-wrist push-up support	3	10–20 seconds	45 seconds
False-grip hang	3	10–20 seconds	45 seconds
Kneeling inverted-wrist push-up	3	5	45 seconds
Elbow exercises			
Pull-up/static hang	3	1–20, depending on strength	45 seconds
Negative chin-up	3	3–10	45 seconds
Shoulder exercises			
Scapula dip	3	10	30 seconds
Frog stance	3	10 seconds	30 seconds
Scapula pull-up	3	10	30 seconds

13

Lower Body Training Programmes

The lower body is home to many potential injuries, from sprains and strains of the ankle, to ligament issues in the knee and dysfunctions of the hip. The programmes we have devised here will help in all aspects of injury prevention and rehabilitation of the lower body, regardless of your level of ability or your current injury status.

Monday:	Train
Tuesday:	Rest
Wednesday:	Train
Thursday:	Rest
Friday:	Train
Saturday:	Rest
Sunday:	Rest

■ Lower Body: Beginner Programme

The beginner programme for the lower body (Table 13.1) is designed to get you moving again after a long time away from physical training, or when you are too injured to perform many of the strength-building movements. Accordingly, the exercises in this programme revolve around mobility and flexibility, with the chief aim being to restore movement in preparation for more demanding exercises.

As with the programmes for the other parts of the body, this programme should ideally be followed and performed from start to finish, beginning at the top of the table and working your way down until all of the exercises are completed. If for any reason you cannot perform any of the exercises, leave them out and only do the ones you can. As your injury gets better, or your strength or mobility increases, you can then introduce the other exercises.

As regards training frequency, again this programme can be performed three to five times a week with very little disruption to your daily life. In your weekly training schedule, you will need some rest days, and so a week in which you train three times might be as follows:

■ **Table 13.1.** Lower body: beginner programme.

	Sets	Reps/duration	Rest
Hip exercises			
Knee circle	3	10 each leg	10 seconds
Hamstring stretch	3	20 seconds each leg	20 seconds
Hip flexor stretch	3	20 seconds each leg	20 seconds
Knee exercises			
ITB mobilisation	3	20–30 seconds	20 seconds
Adductor foam roll	3	30 seconds each leg	20 seconds
Quadriceps stretch	3	30 seconds each leg	20 seconds
Gym ball hamstring curl	3	10	20 seconds
Ankle exercises			
Unloaded dorsiflexion	3	10 each leg	20 seconds
Unloaded plantar flexion	3	10 each leg	20 seconds
Unloaded inversion	3	10 each leg	20 seconds
Unloaded eversion	3	10 each leg	20 seconds
Calf stretch	3	20 seconds	20 seconds

■ Lower Body: Intermediate Programme

Once the beginner programme becomes too easy, or you need to inject some strength movements into your routine, this intermediate programme will be where to start (Table 13.2). Some of the movements in this programme are stretching and mobility based (e.g. the groin stretch and ITB foam roll) and some are strength based (e.g. the squat and the lunge).

As before, the idea is to run through the table of exercises, performing each for the required number of sets and repetitions (or specified duration) until they are finished. If you unable to perform any of the exercises for any reason, leave them out until you are capable of doing so. Regarding frequency, three to five times a week will give great returns.

■ **Table 13.2.**   Lower body: intermediate programme.

	Sets	Reps/duration	Rest
Hip exercises			
Deep squat position	3	30 seconds	20 seconds
Groin stretch	3	20 seconds	20 seconds
Glute stretch	3	20 seconds each leg	20 seconds
Knee exercises			
V-up with ball squeeze	3	5–10	30 seconds
Squat	3	15–20	45 seconds
ITB foam roll	3	30 seconds each leg	30 seconds
Lunge	3	10 each leg	30 seconds
Ankle exercises			
Anterior tibial muscle stretch	3	30 seconds	20 seconds
Downward dog	3	30 seconds	30 seconds
Single-leg balance	3	20–60 seconds	30 seconds

■ Lower Body: Advanced Programme

When the intermediate programme becomes too easy, or the exercises are not serving to increase strength and protect against injury, it will be time to move on to the advanced programme (Table 13.3). This contains exercises that will really test your strength (e.g the single-leg squat) and your mobility (e.g. the frog hop). Accordingly, we advise only moving on to this programme when you are ready. If you feel like attempting some of the movements beforehand, then go ahead: this is a great way to gauge your progress and see if you are ready for the next step.

As before, the number of exercises here is not excessive and will allow you to perform the programme three to five times a week, and to also add in other programmes from the upper body and the spine.

■ **Table 13.3.**   Lower body: advanced programme.

	Sets	Reps/duration	Rest
Hip exercises			
Piriformis foam roll and stretch	3	20–30 seconds each leg	30 seconds
Mountain climber	3	10 each leg	30 seconds
Frog hop	3	10	30 seconds
Knee exercises			
Single-leg squat	3	2–5 each leg	30 seconds
Rollover into straddle sit	3	10	30 seconds
Negative hamstring curl	3	2–5	30 seconds
Ankle exercises			
Negative calf raise	3	10–20	30 seconds
Modified frog stance	3	10–20 seconds	30 seconds
Heel sit	3	10–20 seconds	30 seconds

14

Spine Training Programmes

The spine and core are very important areas to train, as Chapter 11 hopefully convinced you. Many injuries can occur in the spine and its associated muscles, and so making this area as strong and resilient as possible is a no-brainer. The spine is considered holistically here, and so exercises for each spinal region are presented.

As with the upper body, we have split the exercises for the spine into three distinct programmes, namely beginner, intermediate and advanced. These programmes will be examined next.

Spine: Beginner Programme

The beginner programme for the spine (Table 14.1) consists of five exercises, which have been chosen to increase mobility and flexibility in the spine, and to get the muscles in the core working. This programme is ideal for those who have not trained in a long time (or never), and for those who are coming back from injury and cannot exert much force with their core muscles.

■ **Table 14.1.** Spine: beginner programme.

	Sets	Reps/duration	Rest
Spine exercises			
Upper spine foam roll	3	30 seconds	30 seconds
Upper back stretch	3	20 seconds each side	30 seconds
Cobra stretch	3	20 seconds	30 seconds
Standing side stretch	3	20 seconds each side	30 seconds
Lower spine foam roll	3	30 seconds	30 seconds
Cat stretch	3	30 seconds	30 seconds

As there are only five exercises, it is recommended to perform the entire programme as written here, three to five times a week. In addition, it can be combined with the upper body and lower body programmes (using the programme that is suitable for your ability) in order to create a more rounded routine.

Spine: Intermediate Programme

Once the beginner programme becomes too easy, or if you are looking for more variation, you can move on to the intermediate programme (Table 14.2). This contains some strength-building movements, unlike the beginner programme, which is more about stretching and increasing mobility in the spine and core.

Spine: Advanced Programme

The advanced programme (Table 14.3) is what you should move on to after the intermediate programme becomes too easy. The exercises in this programme can in fact be used as a workout in their own right. The dish, for example, is used in gymnastic programmes all over the world, and the extended plank can be made very difficult and used to develop great strength.

■ **Table 14.2.** Spine: intermediate programme.

	Sets	Reps/duration	Rest
Spine exercises			
Skydiver	3	20 seconds	30 seconds
Plank	3	20 seconds	30 seconds
Side lean	3	10 (5 each side)	20 seconds
Side plank	3	20 seconds each side	30 seconds
Neck retraction	2	10	20 seconds

■ **Table 14.3.** Spine: advanced programme.

	Sets	Reps/duration	Rest
Spine exercises			
Rear support	3	20 seconds or more	30 seconds
Dish	3	20–30 seconds	30 seconds
Bridge	3	10–20 seconds	30 seconds
Extended plank	3	5–15 seconds	30 seconds

Full Body Training Programmes

Although the body-part-specific training programmes are great for those looking to concentrate on a particular body part or injury, it is likely that many people will perform movements for the whole body; indeed, this is something that we highly recommend. If you have an injury just in your shoulder or upper body, it is very good practice to train the spine and the lower body as well; this will both protect against injury in those parts of the body, and avoid any potential imbalances that may result from training only one body part.

▪ Full Body: Beginner Programme

The full body programme for beginners (Table 15.1) is ideal for those who need a rounded routine to start their injury prevention or rehabilitation journey. The exercises here are the same as those in the beginner programmes for the specific parts of the body, but now linked together. The idea is that you perform all of the movements for the required sets and repetitions, thus completing the workout. This entire programme should not take more than an hour, and can be performed three to five times a week.

▪ **Table 15.1.** Full body: beginner programme.

	Sets	Reps/duration	Rest
Wrist exercises			
Forearm stretch 1	3	20 seconds	20 seconds
Forearm stretch 2	3	20 seconds	20 seconds
Push-up support	3	20 seconds	20 seconds
Elbow exercises			
Inverted-wrist wall push-up	3	5–20, depending on strength	30 seconds
Ledge dip	3	10	45 seconds
Arm rotation	3	10	20 seconds
Shoulder exercises			
Chest stretch	3	15 seconds	10 seconds
Shoulder stretch	3	15 seconds	10 seconds
Rotator cuff stretch	3	10 seconds	10 seconds
Scapula foam roll	3	10 seconds	30–45 seconds
Spine exercises			
Upper back stretch	3	20 seconds each side	30 seconds
Upper spine foam roll	3	30 seconds	30 seconds
Cobra stretch	3	20 seconds	30 seconds
Standing side stretch	3	20 seconds	30 seconds

	Sets	Reps/duration	Rest
Lower spine foam roll	3	30 seconds	30 seconds
Cat stretch	3	30 seconds	30 seconds
Hip exercises			
Knee circle	3	10 each leg	10 seconds
Hamstring stretch	3	20 seconds each leg	20 seconds
Hip flexor stretch	3	20 seconds each leg	20 seconds
Knee exercises			
ITB mobilisation	3	20–30 seconds	20 seconds
Adductor foam roll	3	30 seconds each leg	20 seconds
Quadriceps stretch	3	30 seconds each leg	20 seconds
Gym ball hamstring curl	3	10	20 seconds
Ankle exercises			
Unloaded dorsiflexion	3	10 each leg	20 seconds
Unloaded plantar flexion	3	10 each leg	20 seconds
Unloaded inversion	3	10 each leg	20 seconds
Unloaded eversion	3	10 each leg	20 seconds
Calf stretch	3	20 seconds	20 seconds

Full Body: Intermediate Programme

The intermediate programme for the full body (Table 15.2) contains more advanced exercises than the beginner programme, and it is here that we see more strength-based exercises rather than just stretching and mobility ones. Accordingly, it is important that you take your time with the newer exercises. If some prove too difficult, feel free to insert exercises from the beginner programme; this is completely normal and expected, especially if you are recovering from injury or returning after a period of deconditioning.

Full Body: Advanced Programme

The advanced programme for the full body (Table 15.3) contains the most demanding exercises with regard to injury prevention and rehabilitation. As with the other programmes in this chapter, the advanced programme should be performed three to five times a week in order to get a training effect, with dedicated rest days in between. If you cannot perform some of the movements, feel free to substitute some of the exercises from the intermediate or beginner programmes where necessary.

■ **Table 15.2.** Full body: intermediate programme.

	Sets	Reps/duration	Rest
Wrist exercises			
Fist push-up support	3	20 seconds	30 seconds
Fingertip push-up support	3	10–20 seconds	30 seconds
Elbow exercises			
Forklift	3	5–10, depending on strength	30 seconds
Planche lean	3	10 seconds	30 seconds
Shoulder exercises			
Dead hang	3	20 seconds	30 seconds
Scapula push-up	3	10	30 seconds
Band shoulder dislocate	3	10	20 seconds
Spine exercises			
Skydiver	3	20 seconds	30 seconds
Plank	3	20 seconds	30 seconds
Side lean	3	10 (5 each side)	20 seconds
Side plank	3	20 seconds each side	30 seconds
Neck retraction	2	10	20 seconds
Hip exercises			
Deep squat position	3	30 seconds	20 seconds
Groin stretch	3	20 seconds	20 seconds
Glute stretch	3	20 seconds each leg	20 seconds
Knee exercises			
V-up with ball squeeze	3	5–10	30 seconds
Squat	3	15–20	45 seconds
ITB foam roll	3	30 seconds each leg	30 seconds
Lunge	3	10 each leg	30 seconds
Ankle exercises			
Anterior tibial muscle stretch	3	30 seconds	20 seconds
Downward dog	3	30 seconds	30 seconds
Single-leg balance	3	20–60 seconds	30 seconds

■ **Table 15.3.** Full body: advanced programme.

	Sets	Reps/duration	Rest
Wrist exercises			
Inverted-wrist push-up support	3	10–20 seconds	45 seconds
False-grip hang	3	10–20 seconds	45 seconds
Kneeling inverted-wrist push-up	3	5	45 seconds
Elbow exercises			
Pull-up/static hang	3	1–20, depending on strength	45 seconds
Negative chin-up	3	3–10	45 seconds
Shoulder exercises			
Scapula dip	3	10	30 seconds
Frog stance	3	10 seconds	30 seconds
Scapula pull-up	3	10	30 seconds
Spine exercises			
Rear support	3	20 seconds or more	30 seconds
Dish	3	20–30 seconds	30 seconds
Bridge	3	10–20 seconds	30 seconds
Extended plank	3	5–15 seconds	30 seconds
Hip exercises			
Piriformis foam roll and stretch	3	20–30 seconds each leg	30 seconds
Mountain climber	3	10 each leg	30 seconds
Frog hop	3	10	30 seconds
Knee exercises			
Single-leg squat	3	2–5 each leg	30 seconds
Rollover into straddle sit	3	10	30 seconds
Negative hamstring curl	3	2–5	30 seconds
Ankle exercises			
Negative calf raise	3	10–20	30 seconds
Modified frog stance	3	10–20 seconds	30 seconds
Heel sit	3	10–20 seconds	30 seconds

16
Goal Training Programme

By now it should be clear that there are broadly two categories of exercise in this book. The first category consists of the injury prevention and rehabilitation exercises, which cover the major joints of the body, while the second comprises the goal exercises, which are found at the end of each chapter. As we have said before, the goal exercises are there to help you gauge how you are progressing, and also to act as developmental exercises in their own right. They can also be grouped together to create a more advanced training programme. This type of programme will contribute further to both preventing and rehabilitating injury, and to increasing your strength, mobility, flexibility and overall physical capacity. In other words, it can be used as a normal workout routine that you can perform for many months, or even years, and also as a precursor to more demanding body-weight exercises, such as those found in the book by Kalym on calisthenics, available from Lotus Publishing.*

The exercises, sets, repetitions/duration and rest times of the goal programme are listed in Table 16.1 for convenience.

All of the movements listed in the goal programme will give your body a complete workout, using most muscle groups. As these are body-weight exercises, they will work many muscles simultaneously, to either move the body or support it.

Ideally you should perform all of the exercises here three to five times a week, with rest days interspersed between your training days. As this is the hardest programme in the book, do not be disheartened if you cannot perform all of the movements at first. Progress will come, and with time you will notice your body getting stronger and more mobile.

■ **Table 16.1.** Goal programme.

	Sets	Reps/duration	Rest
Wrist exercises			
Inverted-wrist push-up	3	10	30 seconds
False-grip pull-up	3	3-5	45 seconds
Fist-supported tuck planche	3	5–20 seconds	45 seconds
Elbow exercises			
Triceps dip	3	5-10	45 seconds
Archer push-up	3	5-10 each side	45 seconds
Shoulder exercises			
Pull-up	3	5-10	45 seconds
German hang	3	15 seconds	30 seconds
Spine exercises			
Kneeling roll-out	3	5-10	45 seconds
Hanging leg raise	3	5-10	45 seconds
Arch-up	3	10	30 seconds
Hip exercises			
Body-weight squat	3	20	45 seconds
Duck walk	3	10-20 steps	45 seconds
Knee exercises			
Ice skater	3	10 (5 each leg)	30 seconds
Jump squat	3	10-15	45 seconds
Jump lunge	3	10-15	45 seconds
Ankle exercises			
Skipping	3	30-60 seconds	45 seconds

---

*Kalym, A. 2014, *Complete Calisthenics – The Ultimate Guide to Bodyweight Exercise*, Chichester, UK: Lotus Publishing.

Creating Your Own Programmes

In this part of the book, we are going to look at designing your own programmes. The ideas presented will help you to create a bespoke series of exercises to target your injuries or physical weaknesses. Injuries vary from person to person, so rehabilitation should focus on individual needs. All of us have niggles and injuries that are unique (to us) in terms of their locations, intensities and combinations. Note that this chapter has been written with the understanding that not everyone reading it will be highly experienced in either exercise or programme writing. In other words, we want this chapter to be usable by even the most inexperienced reader.

First, it is essential that you know which area of your body you want (or need) to injury-proof. For example, if your primary physical activity or pastime is running and you find you are developing knee problems, you will most likely want to injury-proof the knees, in addition to the other lower body joints, such as the hips and ankles. There would of course be some benefit in performing the upper body movements, but since running impacts the joints of the lower body more, it would make sense that the exercises picked in this case are the lower body ones.

Second, your experience and ability will dictate which of the exercises you can include in your programme. If

we take the runner in the above example, they would be unwise to include the single-leg squat if they do not have the leg strength to perform it. If you are unsure of your ability level, simply start with the easiest movements and progress when you are ready. You will know it is time to move on when the exercises you are performing become too easy, or when the programme no longer proves challenging.

Third, try to follow the recommended number of sets, number of repetitions or duration, and rest times listed in the programmes, and adapt them if you need to. For example, if you find that three sets of push-ups are too much, drop to two sets and see how that suits. If you need 60 seconds of rest instead of 45 seconds, feel free to change this guide as well.

To finish, we have included some blank tables for you to copy and use for designing your own programmes. There is space to write the name of the programme and the type of upper body, spine and lower body exercise, as well as the number of sets, the number of repetitions or the duration, and the amount of rest time between sets.

Programme Name:	Sets	Reps/duration	Rest
Wrist exercises			
Elbow exercises			
Shoulder exercises			
Spine exercises			
Hip exercises			
Knee exercises			
Ankle exercises			

Programme Name:		Sets	Reps/duration	Rest
Wrist exercises				
Elbow exercises				
Shoulder exercises				
Spine exercises				
Hip exercises				
Knee exercises				
Ankle exercises				

Programme Name:	Sets	Reps/duration	Rest
Wrist exercises			
Elbow exercises			
Shoulder exercises			
Spine exercises			
Hip exercises			
Knee exercises			
Ankle exercises			

18
Frequently Asked Questions

In this chapter we answer some common questions that many people have concerning body-weight exercise and injury prevention/rehabilitation. If you have a specific query not addressed here, please email us at: bulletproofbodies@email.com.

Q1. I have never been injured. Why should I bother training to prevent injury?

A. You should think of training to prevent injury in the same way as taking out insurance on your house: you hope you do not need home insurance, but it is unwise not to purchase it. Training to prevent injury takes little time, but will do a number of things: apart from helping to prevent injury, it will build strength in areas of the body that traditional training might not develop, and it will allow improved physical function and performance in many areas of your daily life.

We have developed the exercises and training programmes in this book to be performed as a warm-up to a more extensive workout, or as simple daily routines to carry out regardless of whether a more extensive workout is planned. This way, you will be insured against injury.

Q2. Is it OK for me to only do exercises for a specific joint or area?

A. This is fine, but we would also recommend overall conditioning for other areas of the body. Imbalances can and do occur, and these situations often require more training to correct. If you only have time to train a specific body part in your training session, include the relevant exercises from this book in that session, and aim to perform the exercises for the rest of the body parts on other relevant training days. Take, for example, a training strategy where you run on Monday, train arms on Wednesday and do core on Friday; you could then do injury prevention for the lower body on Monday, injury prevention for the upper body on Wednesday and spinal injury prevention on Friday. The exercises themselves do not take a huge amount of time, and can be easily built into a daily routine, once you know the exercises that give you most benefit.

Q3. I already have a warm-up routine. Can I simply replace my old routine with a programme from this book?

A. Yes, this can be done, but only if the warm-up routine you are currently following does not help to prevent injury. If your current warm-up is simply jogging on the treadmill for five minutes and then doing a few quick stretches, it is unlikely that your routine will target troublesome areas; it may even be contributing to your injuries. Always warm up the body prior to strength or flexibility work.

Q4. I am retired and not as mobile or strong as I used to be. Are the exercises in this book suitable for me?

A. The exercises in this book are suitable for every reader, regardless of age. We have graded the movements so that you know which ones are easier and which are more challenging. Furthermore, the order in which the exercises appear is also an indication of their difficulty. The exercises in this book are designed to help with loss of strength and mobility, and there is good evidence to suggest that these physical functions provide a greater quality of life in older age.

Q5. I already have a physiotherapist/physical therapist, and the exercises in this book differ from the ones they have given me. How do I know which exercises are going to work and which are not?

A. All registered physiotherapists/physical therapists will be qualified, and will have sufficient knowledge to assess injuries and rehabilitate them. They may not be familiar with body-weight exercise, either from personal experience or from their therapy training. This book therefore offers an alternative or adjunct to your standard physical therapy.

We approach injury prevention and rehabilitation from the perspective of making the body as strong, mobile and injury resistant as possible. The exercises in this book will encourage you to identify and work on any physical deficits you may be suffering from. If the programme you are following does not have a global aim to maximise your physical function, it may be a good idea to supplement your current rehabilitation with the exercises in this book. We do not advocate discontinuing any prescribed exercise advice unless you feel it is the right thing to do.

Q6. I am pregnant. Are the exercises in this book safe for me?

A. The answer to this question is complicated: some of the exercises may be less safe than others. For example, some of the simpler stretches are obviously safer than the German hang, which requires you to support your own body weight from a bar while hanging upside down. In addition, some of the other exercises that require strong muscular contractions may raise blood pressure excessively. In preparation for childbirth, pregnancy can make ligaments much more lax than they would normally be, which could lead to injury with strenuous exercise. If you were to do any exercises from this book, we would advise only the low-level core stability exercises and stretches that do not position your body in such a way as to create unnecessary physical stress. If you are unsure, please ask your doctor or health professional whether it is safe for you to do any of these exercises. They will have knowledge of your unique situation and be able to advise accordingly.

Q7. I don't really have time to work out properly. Can I just do the injury prevention and rehabilitation routines from this book instead?

A. If you do not have enough time to train in a proper way, then yes, the routines and exercises in this book can be used on their own to maintain or improve your physical capabilities. Even though the actual injury prevention and rehabilitation exercises are great for building strength and mobility, the goal exercises for each chapter can be used very effectively as a proper workout routine on their own. For example, the shoulder chapter has the push-up, the triceps dip and the pull-up as goal exercises; these three movements are very good for building and maintaining a base of strength and fitness, and require very little time or equipment to perform. The same applies to all of the other muscle groups, and you can build a full routine out of the goal exercises.

Q8. I have had physical therapy/personal training before, and am comfortable using machines and other equipment for exercises. What makes body-weight exercise so special?

A. While machines and other similar equipment can be used fairly effectively, they take away a very important aspect of human movement – stabilisation and control. Movement in the real world takes place in three dimensions; this means that the joints are free to move in practically any direction, and it is down to the muscles and other connective structures to control this movement. With exercise machines, however, the movement is almost always two-dimensional; in other words, the machine guides the direction and limits the movement.

Imagine a chest press machine as an example. This machine consists of handles that can be pushed forwards against a resistance. There is only one path that the handles can take, and so the muscles and joints do not have to worry about controlling the weight, balance or anything that resembles a natural human movement. This exercise would develop chest strength that involves only pushing forwards, but this would not necessarily replicate any other movement in the real world.

If we compare the chest press to a push-up, it is immediately apparent that the push-up is a three-dimensional movement, since the shoulders are free to move forwards, backwards and sideways – in fact, any direction they choose. Consequently, the push-up requires much more control than a pushing exercise on a machine. Moreover, consider the core strength needed to maintain the push-up position, and the control and stability required of the hips and legs. All this would give you an all-round workout in the same time that you could have worked only the chest on a press machine.

These facts are not hugely important if we are just talking about general training, but we are trying to prevent and rehabilitate injuries here. As this is the case, then three-dimensional exercises are exactly the kinds of movement that we should be carrying out, in order to strengthen and improve the control of the body as a whole. Body-weight exercise is especially good for this, because every movement that is performed by the body is three-dimensional. In addition, body-weight exercise can be scaled up and down and very easily.

Q9. I have a child who is injured. Are these exercises safe for them to perform?

A. This another complicated question: it depends on the child, their age and their current training background, and on the skill of the adult in supervising and guiding the child. In theory, many of the exercises would be suitable for teenagers to perform, but be aware that excessive or heavy exercise at a young age can lead to problems with the muscles and skeleton. Seek advice from a medical or health professional.

Q10. The exercises for the cervical spine are not that advanced. Are there more advanced cervical exercises out there, to develop a strong neck area?

A. It is true that the exercises for the cervical spine in this book are not very advanced. This is intentional for a very good reason: since we are not present when you are performing the movements, we cannot be certain that you are doing them correctly. This is not too much of an issue with the vast majority of the movements discussed; however, as the cervical spine area is very vulnerable and serious injury could result, we have decided to leave out many advanced cervical neck exercises. If you are interested in some advanced techniques, the best places to go are martial arts gymnasiums, and other gyms (or coaches) that specialise in contact sports; these will have both the equipment and the knowledge to be able to oversee your neck training in a safe environment. Many of the common neck problems actually require adjustments to posture in the chest and lower spinal regions, and so addressing these will avoid the need for intensive neck exercises.

Index of Exercises

(† = key exercise; * = goal exercise)